JOURNAL FOR THE STUDY OF THE NEW TESTAMENT
SUPPLEMENT SERIES
21

Executive Editor, Supplement Series
David Hill

Publishing Editor
David E Orton

JSOT Press
Sheffield

THE DEPARTURE
OF JESUS
IN LUKE–ACTS

The Ascension Narratives in Context

Mikeal C. Parsons

Journal for the Study of the New Testament
Supplement Series 21

To Jeanne
For her Faith, Hope, and Love

BT
500
,P370
1987

Published by JSOT Press
JSOT Press is an imprint of
Sheffield Academic Press Ltd
The University of Sheffield
343 Fulwood Road
Sheffield S10 3BP
England

Typeset by Sheffield Academic Press
and
printed in Great Britain
by Billing & Sons Ltd
Worcester

British Library Cataloguing in Publication Data

Parsons, Mikeal C.
     The departure of Jesus in Luke-Acts : the
     Ascension narratives in context.—
     (Journal for the study of the New Testament,
     supplement series, ISSN 0143-5108; 21).
     1. Jesus Christ—Ascension 2. Bible.
     N.T.—Criticism, interpretation, etc.
     I. Title   II. Series
     232.9'7   BT1500

     ISBN 1-85075-077-7
     ISBN 1-85075-076-9 Pbk

CONTENTS

PREFACE

This volume was originally presented as a doctoral dissertation to the Faculty of The Southern Baptist Theological Seminary in Louisville, Kentucky. Extensive revisions of the original document have, I hope, improved the overall quality of the work. Earlier drafts of material from Chapters 2 and 3 were presented to regional and national professional meetings of the Society of Biblical Literature. Grateful acknowledgment is made to the Society of Biblical Literature for permission to use in this book material from my articles, 'A Christological Tendency in P75', *JBL* 105 (1986), pp. 463-79, and 'Narrative Closure and Openness in the Plot of the Third Gospel: The Sense of an Ending in Luke 24:50-53', *1986 SBL Seminar Papers* (Atlanta: Scholars Press, 1986), pp. 201-23. Gratitude is also expressed to the Catholic Biblical Association for permission to use material from my essay, 'The Text of Acts 1.2 Reconsidered', *CBQ* (forthcoming).

The contributions of several persons to this project are noteworthy. John Polhill, Roger Omanson, and Harold Songer proved to be able guides through the pertinent literature during the dissertation stages of this manuscript. I am most thankful. I would also like to register a debt of gratitude to Charles Talbert and Robert Tannehill, who read the manuscript in its entirety and made many helpful suggestions.

A special word of gratitude is offered to R. Alan Culpepper, whose enthusiasm and encouragement helped bring this manuscript to publication. He has extended the careful and gracious consideration to my work that has endeared him to all those who have had opportunity to work with him. My colleagues in the Religion Department at Baylor University supplied much-needed support in the final stages of publication, and my graduate assistants, Marvin Hudson and Sharon Moore, also gave timely assistance. President Herbert Reynolds of Baylor University provided the financial resources for the final revisions which turned a doctoral dissertation into this book. The publishers and editorial staff at Sheffield Academic Press, especially David Hill and David Orton, improved both the form and content of this work. The flaws that remain can only be my responsibility. To all of these persons I offer my heartfelt thanks.

Most of all, I thank my family. Jeanne has been my *sine qua non* companion and fellow sojourner from the beginning. Both she and Lauren have so patiently endured while I spent 'one more night' on the book.

Mikeal C. Parsons
Waco, Texas

ABBREVIATIONS

AB	Anchor Bible
AbrN	*Abr-Nahrain*
AnBib	Analecta Biblica
AJT	*American Journal of Theology*
ASV	American Standard Version
ATR	*Anglican Theological Review*
AUSS	*Andrews University Seminary Studies*
BBC	*Bulletin of the Bezan Club*
Bib	*Biblica*
BibWorld	*Biblical World*
BR	*Biblical Research*
BSac	*Bibliotheca Sacra*
BTB	*Biblical Theology Bulletin*
CBQ	*Catholic Biblical Quarterly*
ClassBul	*Classical Bulletin*
ClassRev	*Classical Review*
ClassWorld	*Classical World*
CTM	*Concordia Theological Monthly*
ETL	*Ephemerides theologicae lovanienses*
EvT	*Evangelische Theologie*
Expos	*Expositor*
ExpTim	*Expository Times*
GNB	Good News Bible
GR	*Greece and Rome*
HTR	*Harvard Theological Review*
ICC	International Critical Commentary
Int	*Interpretation*
JAAR	*Journal of the American Academy of Religion*
JBL	*Journal of Biblical Literature*
JTS	*Journal of Theological Studies*
JR	*Journal of Religion*
JSNT	*Journal for the Study of the New Testament*
NEB	New English Bible
NIV	New International Version
NTS	*New Testament Studies*
NovT	*Novum Testamentum*

NIGTC	New International Greek Testament Commentary
PersRelSt	*Perspectives in Religious Studies*
RB	*Revue biblique*
R&E	*Review and Expositor*
RHPR	*Revue d'histoire et de philosophie religieuses*
RSV	Revised Standard Version
RSV–RVCE	Revised Standard Version–Revised Version Catholic Edition
SD	Studies and Documents
SE	*Studia Evangelica*
StBibTh	*Studies in Biblical Theology*
TRu	*Theologische Rundschau*
TS	*Theological Studies*
TSK	*Theologische Studien und Kritiken*
VD	*Verbum domini*
W&D	*Wort und Dienst*
ZNW	*Zeitschrift für die neutestamentliche Wissenschaft*

INTRODUCTION

Chapter 1

THE ASCENSION NARRATIVES IN
INTERPRETIVE CONTEXT:
RETROSPECT AND PROSPECT

Ascension Day has never held any eminent place in the Church
Calendar. Falling forty days after Easter, Ascensiontide has never
had the good fortune of being celebrated on a Sunday. To be sure,
certain individuals in the Church have acclaimed the importance of
the ascension. Jerome wrote that 'the Lord's Day is . . . also called
the Lord's Day because on it the Lord ascended as a victor to the
Father'.[1]

The ancient creeds of the Church also affirmed faith in the
ascension. The Apostles' Creed stated: 'The third day he rose again
from the dead. He ascended into heaven, and is seated at the right
hand of God the Father almighty; from there he shall come to judge
the living and the dead'.[2] And in the Nicene Creed one reads: 'On the
third day he rose again in fulfillment of the Scriptures; he ascended
into heaven and is seated at the right hand of the Father. He will
come again in glory to judge the living and the dead'.[3]

Such assessments, however, made little impact on the liturgical
observance of the ascension. In fact, the Ascension Festival was not
certainly celebrated as a separate Holy Day until the fourth century
and the *Pax Constantina*. Before that time, observance of Ascensiontide, if it were celebrated at all, was collapsed into the
commemoration of Pentecost.[4]

The apparent neglect of the ascension by the early church may be
justified by its sparse and sporadic treatment by the New Testament
writers. While passages which assume the heavenly session of Christ
without mention of an ascension are quite numerous (e.g., Rom.
8.34, 10.6; Eph. 1.20-21; Col. 3.1) and others refer to the ascension as
a theological reality without reference to its temporal or corporeal
aspects (e.g., John 6.62; 20.17; Eph. 4.8-10; 1 Tim. 3.16), only Luke

narrates the ascension as an observable, historical, verifiable transfer from earth to heaven (Luke 24.50-53; Acts 1.9-11).[5] Nowhere else in the NT is the ascension of Jesus related in narrative form.[6]

Despite such a meagre harvest of at most seven verses from the entire New Testament, the fact that these verses were penned by the same author, and that they occupy such important places in the narratives of Luke–Acts (at the conclusion of one document and the beginning of the other), suggests that an intensive examination of these passages might prove to be a worthy enterprise. The value of such a study would not lie in enhancing the significance of Ascensiontide in ecclesiastical liturgy, but rather in facilitating the reader's understanding of the ascension stories in their historical and narrative contexts.

Retrospect: Previous Studies

In the preface to his study on the doctrine of the ascension, J.G. Davies remarked: 'Of all the articles in the Creed there is none that has been so neglected in the present century as that which affirms our Lord's ascension into heaven'.[7] As a perusal of the bibliography will demonstrate, the topic of the ascension has not been altogether neglected since 1958. In fact, it has received significant attention in doctrinal surveys, studies in the resurrection narratives, and monographs.[8] Below are mentioned several of the more significant works, followed by a brief critique of each approach. The intent is not to be exhaustive, but to show that there is room for yet another work on the ascension narratives!

Doctrinal Studies

A few studies, like J.G. Davies' *He Ascended Into Heaven*, have attempted to deal with all the New Testament references to the ascension as well as the creedal and patristic evidence in a comprehensive history of doctrine. Davies' systematic analysis, though a helpful historical survey, was not sensitive to the distinction between references to the ascension which attempt to describe Christ's exaltation and narratives of the ascension which attempt to describe the event itself. Nor did Davies' work take seriously the nature of the various documents, whether narrative or epistle, which contain references to the ascension.

Some other older studies are also flawed in that they attempt to present an apology for the historicity of the ascension.[9] This concern to recover the historical details of the event itself often overrides the particular emphases which the narrative develops. Too often the question 'How did the event happen?' grinds discussion to a halt, so that the larger question 'How does the narrative function?' remains untouched. Such misguided inquiries into the temporal and spatial aspects of the ascension often result in misplaced conclusions. These concerns have distorted not only the understanding of the ascension by older scholars, but many contemporary scholars as well. Bruce Metzger, noted text critic, has claimed:

> What is being suggested, therefore, is that though Jesus did not need to ascend in order to return to that sphere which we call heaven, yet in fact he did ascend a certain distance into the sky, until a cloud took him out of sight. By such a miraculous sign he impressed upon his followers the conviction that this was now the last time he would appear to them, and that henceforth they should not expect another manifestation, but should realize that the transitional period had ended.[10]

Preoccupation with historical questions, coupled with disregard for the literary context of the passage, may easily lead to a distortion of the significance of the pericope for understanding the larger story of Jesus and his followers in Luke–Acts.

Studies in the Resurrection Narratives
When Reginald Fuller wrote his first edition of *The Formation of the Resurrection Narratives* in 1969-70, he was able to assert with confidence: 'Such a work has not been undertaken in the English-speaking world for over a generation'.[11] By the time of the second edition a decade later, Fuller admitted:

> Since 1970, however, the situation has radically changed, and in fact the appearance of my book coincided with the beginning of a spate of books on the Easter accounts, in English (both British and American) as well as in French and German.[12]

These studies have employed the basic tools of historical criticism and have either emphasized the historicity of the narratives (source criticism) or the theology of the evangelist (redaction criticism).[13] While the efforts of these scholars are to be applauded and though their conclusions are not to be considered insignificant, the interpretation of the ascension narratives has suffered considerably from this particular approach of historical criticism.[14]

First, the Lukan ascension narrative is very much the orphan child of the resurrection narratives. The missiological significance of Matt. 28.16-20, the notorious text-critical problem at the ending of Mark, the liturgical import of the Lukan Emmaus story in 24.13-35, and the source questions of John 20 and 21 have so intrigued most New Testament scholars that investigation of the Lukan ascension usually involved determining what type of appearance story it resembled[15] or solving the chronological difference of forty days between Luke 24 and Acts 1.[16] In addition, historical and redactional interest in the empty tomb and post-resurrection appearance stories (common to all four Gospels) leaves little space to devote to examining the uniquely Lukan ascension narrative.[17]

A deeper concern involves the use of the historical method itself. Most studies in source and redaction criticism are based on K. Lachmann's two-document hypothesis or B.H. Streeter's modified two-source theory. In this theory, of course, Mark and the hypothetical 'Q' document serve as sources for Matthew and Luke, along with special 'M' or 'L' sources (which were not necessarily written).[18] Others, especially William R. Farmer, have proposed reviving J.J. Griesbach's hypothesis that Luke used Matthew, and Mark abbreviated Matthew and Luke.[19] Adherents of these two views have been adamant in their positions.[20]

It is not my intention to argue the merits of either of these theories. Rather, this ferment in New Testament studies vitiates attempts to argue for the theology or intentionality of the evangelists. The situation is made more complex by the growing number of scholars, especially in the American context, who are becoming more dissatisfied with the two-source hypothesis and who find the alternative Griesbach hypothesis even less compelling.[21] Typical is the response of Charles H. Talbert. In 1972, Talbert published an article co-written with Edgar McKnight in which they examined the Griesbach hypothesis and found it less convincing than some other alternatives.[22] Just four years later, Talbert would write:

> Employing Mark as a control today is about as compelling as using Colossians and Second Thessalonians, to describe Paul's theology. It may very well be legitimate to do so, but so many have problems with the procedure that such an assumption narrows considerably the circles with whom one can converse.[23]

The conclusions one draws from such a debated method are immediately suspect to a growing number of scholars. Joseph Tyson has suggested:

If one takes seriously the various challenges to the two–document hypothesis and the proposed alternatives to it, it then becomes necessary to raise questions about the relationship between redaction criticism and any particular solution to the synoptic problem, as well as questions about the usefulness of results that depend upon source theories.[24]

Since most of these studies in the resurrection narratives not only emphasize elements other than the ascension, but also employ the redactional tools based on a disputed source theory, one would conclude that the ascension narratives have not received the attention they deserve in these special studies.[25]

Monographs on Luke 24 and the Ascension in Luke–Acts
While a spate of studies have been overly preoccupied with historical or redactional concerns, there still have been numerous investigations which treat the Lukan ascension narratives with sensitivity. By far the most significant treatment of the ascension is the study by Gerhard Lohfink, *Die Himmelfahrt Jesu*. Originally written under the supervision of Rudolf Schnackenburg and presented as the author's dissertation to the faculty of the University of Würzburg, the thesis was published in 1971. Lohfink began by surveying the ascension in the world of the New Testament (Greek, Roman, the Old Testament, and Judaism) and then examined the structure of the Lukan ascension from a history-of-religions perspective. In chapter 2, Lohfink compares the ascension of Jesus in Luke–Acts with the New Testament writings and the patristic literature. Chapter 3 is devoted to a form analysis of the two passages, perhaps Lohfink's most valuable contribution. On Luke 24.50-53, Lohfink concluded:

> Innerhalb der neutestamentlichen Literatur ist also diese Art, eine Erscheinung abzuschliessen, typisch lukanisch. Man wird deshalb mit noch viel grösserer Sicherheit sagen dürfen, dass die Abschiedsszene Lk 24, 50-53 ursprünglich nicht zu der Erscheinung Jesus vor allen Jüngern gehört hat, sondern erst von Lukas angefügt wurde. Wie Lukas bei der Erzählung von Engeler-scheinungen das Bedürfnis empfand, die Rückkehr der Engel in den Himmel eigens zu vermerken, so hielt er es offensichtlich auch für notwendig, den Abschied des Auferstandenen zu erzählen und nicht einfach mit dessen letzten Worten zu schliessen.[26]

Chapter 4 is a brief *Motivanalyse* of the two passages, while chapter 5 examines the remaining references to the ascension and

exaltation of Jesus in Luke–Acts. Chapter 6 is a ten-page reconstruction of the history of tradition, and the concluding chapter is a
brief examination of the theological design of the ascension narrative.
Here Lohfink considers the ascension as the end of the earthly works
of Jesus, as the expectation (*Ausblick*) of the Parousia, as the
continuation between Jesus and the Church, and as a translation
story (*Erhöhung*). The importance of this work for understanding the
significance of heavenly-assumption stories in antiquity cannot be
overestimated.[27]

One other significant study should be mentioned in passing.
Richard J. Dillon's dissertation, *From Eye-witnesses to Ministers of the
Word* (1978) is a study of tradition and composition in Luke 24.
While helpful in understanding the structure and content of the
entire Lukan resurrection narrative, less than twenty pages are
devoted to the ascension narrative and most of that is mere
acceptance or slight modification of Lohfink.[28]

Prospect: A Proposed Methodology

Generations of Old and New Testament scholars have employed the
tools of the traditional historical-critical method to analyze biblical
texts. Textual criticism helps establish the best text. Form, source,
and redaction (or composition) analyses have been used to examine
the various stages through which the biblical traditions have passed
until reaching their final canonical form. The basic premise of
historical criticism is that the meaning of a text may be derived by
tracing the historical progression of the traditions. Viewing the text
as 'windows' on the historical events, scholars assumed that the
meaning of the texts was to be found in the history which they
record.[29] Recently, some scholarly circles are labeling such efforts as
diachronic analysis, which is 'a methodological approach characterized
by its treatment of a phenomenon in terms of temporal process or
historical development'.[30]

In the past decade, many scholars, while recognizing the value of
the historical-critical method, have also detected serious limitations
with that approach in understanding and interpreting the biblical
narratives.[31] As a result, a number of new methodologies have
emerged, forged by scholars who believe 'the meaning of a narrative
lies not in what it is about or in the author's intention but in the text
itself'.[32] The text is not a window through which one views meaning;
rather, it is a mirror which reflects meaning created in the act of

reading.[33] Terence Keegan has suggested that such methodologies as structuralism, narrative criticism, and canonical criticism are *synchronic* analyses which are 'primarily concerned with enabling the text itself to yield the depth and richness of its meaning'.[34]

While Keegan has described the older *diachronic* approach of historical criticism and the newer *synchronic* method as 'two radically opposed interpretive methods',[35] it is my assumption that both are of value in interpreting the departure of Jesus in Luke–Acts. In fact, to eschew completely the results of nearly a century of biblical criticism would be both helplessly naive and recklessly arrogant.[36] Perhaps it is also wrong to assume that historical criticism is important, but *merely* preliminary to a synchronic analysis. To be sure, the bulk of this study is devoted to the synchronic analysis of the texts because so little attention has been given to this approach to Luke 24 and Acts 1. Both diachronic and synchronic analyses, however, are preliminary to a theological reading of the text as canonical scripture.

Diachronic Analysis
Textual, form and source analyses are the three diachronic approaches employed in this study.[37] In some respects, this work will build upon and modify the work of other textual, source, and form critics. By re-examining the material through diachronic lenses, however, it may be possible to focus more sharply on the intersection with the synchronic analysis.

Textual Criticism. Several objections could be raised against labeling textual criticism as a form of *diachronic* analysis. First, unlike the other two, textual criticism does not seek to probe behind the text to the underlying traditions (source criticism) or to the pristine oral forms of those pre-existing sources (form criticism). Textual criticism does, however, seek to establish the original text or at least the pre-existing text behind the final, canonical form of the text. In that sense, textual criticism is *diachronic* 'through time'. Brevard Childs has also noted the similarity in task of textual criticism and historical-critical investigation:

> Clearly there is an important parallel between tradition-historical developments of the canonical literature of the New Testament and the tradition-historical development of the canonical text. Indeed the line between them is quite fluid at times. Both processes involve the reception of normative tradition which includes an

interpretation of the material along with the activity of its transmission.[38]

A second objection, however, might be lodged by Childs himself against the goal of textual criticism accepted in this study. In Childs' canonical program, 'theoretically, the goal of text criticism, which is commensurate with its canonical role, is to recover that New Testament text which best reflects the true apostolic witness found in the church's scripture'.[39] According to Childs, his new canonical proposal for New Testament textual criticism would have several methodological repercussions.

The first, that the *Textus Receptus* provide the initial context for textual analysis, seems only to restrict the textual critic from posing conjectural emendations. In fact, with the wealth of manuscript evidence available for New Testament study, conjectural emendation has never carried the same weight as emendation to the Old Testament text. In the second place, Childs makes the point that the quest is for the 'best received, that is, canonical text'.[40] In other words, the text critic is not choosing between a neutral or interpreted text; rather, the judgment is 'between the *qualities* of received or interpreted texts' (emphasis mine).[41] The problem it seems is in determining what constitutes the text which best reflects the 'true apostolic witness'. Childs admits the difficulty in answering his own question:

> Is there any means of locating a text which is by definition different from the original author's autograph and at the same time is not to be identified with an uncritical text represented by the last stages of a stabilized *koine* text? No one should be deceived as to the difficulties involved in escaping the horns of this dilemma.[42]

The problem of recapturing the earliest form of the canonical text is no less difficult than the quest for the 'original text'. To say that there were 'a variety of traditions, written and oral, which competed for recognition in the ensuing period',[43] is to reflect on the problem of finding the text which enjoyed the canonical authority conferred upon it by the early church. I find it equally plausible that there was also a written narrative which came from the hand of the author(s) of Luke–Acts. The most that could be said for the textual analysis of this study is that its goal is to recover the text which best reflects the original text. Less ambitiously, at least this study establishes a text which from the early centuries held a prominent place in the church's canon.

Form Analysis. Luke 24.50-53 has been variously compared with the *Gattung* of Old Testament theophany stories, commissioning scenes of the Hebrew Bible, the priestly blessing of Simon in Ben Sira 50.20-21, and farewell addresses of the Greek Old Testament. Along with assessing these proposals, the form analysis in this study will also attempt to determine the affinities with other forms of departure stories (with or without farewell addresses) in writings of antiquity. Acts 1.1-11 will be examined in light of ancient heavenly assumption stories, with the assistance of Gerhard Lohfink's careful and insightful work.

Source Analysis. Since the ascension narratives are uniquely Lukan material, it will be possible to examine the composition of the texts with no recourse to any particular source theory. In other words, the primary question to be addressed by a source analysis of the ascension stories in Luke-Acts is: Do the ascension narratives reflect an underlying tradition which Luke has modified or are they the product of the writer's creativity? Of course, different answers may be given to the same question based on the divergent data found in the two quite distinct pericopae.

The reference to the 'Historical Context' in the subtitle of those chapters dealing with the diachronic analyses needs a word of explanation. I am speaking here of the historical context of the primitive traditions (if any) which lie behind the text, not the historical event (if any) which underlies the traditions. The traditional tools of form and source analyses (not to mention textual criticism) were not designed to describe the details of historical events. To do so is to press the outer limits of the historical-critical method and to ask it to bear more weight than it was designed to do. Though I have a deep interest in the historical nature of the biblical texts, I will be satisfied to trace the history of the tradition in these sections until more reliable tools are developed for historical investigation.

Synchronic Analysis
Because of the strategic placement of the departure of Jesus at the end of one story and the beginning of the other, narrative criticism is the formal method of synchronic analysis employed in this study. Narrative analysis is a relatively new field of research in New Testament studies.[44] Historical and theological concerns have at times obscured the story which the evangelist is trying to tell. Source

theories often confuse rather than clarify. Joseph Tyson has called on Lukan scholars to give the text a hearing independent of any source theory:

> Luke has not heretofore been seriously treated independently of the other Synoptic Gospels. In both of the two leading source hypotheses, Luke is regarded as dependent on another gospel—on Mark according to the two-document hypothesis; on Matthew according to the Griesbach hypothesis. A treatment of Luke without assuming its dependence on another gospel is, at least, a new approach.[45]

Narrative analysis is that new approach which attempts to understand how stories are told. Interest, then, remains at the level of the text and does not seek to go behind the text in search of sources, historicity, or even the intentionality of the evangelist. Narrative criticism seeks to loosen the grip of the historian and the redaction critic from around the neck of the story-teller, at least long enough for him to whisper his tale. In a sense, narrative investigations absolutize the text; but if the critic or scholar is willing to live within those limitations, there is much to be learned from that text.[46]

Several criticisms could and have been lodged against this approach to biblical studies.[47] Most serious, I think, is the one which questions the application of a model honed on nineteenth- and twentieth-century texts to first-century texts. Surely it is anachronistic to apply these inductive methods to texts whose authors knew nothing about the latest literary theory. The next generation of scholars will think the methodology employed in this study, drawn as it is from modern literary criticism, is awkward and clumsy. A literary theory based on an inductive study of other ancient literature would be preferable in applying literary theory to the Gospels. But even that approach is problematic.

A poetics of ancient literature would in fact bring the critic no closer than modern poetics. The problem involves the genre of the Gospels. To which body of ancient literature do the Gospels belong? That question has been given a wide array of responses: Luke–Acts has been variously understood as belonging to the genres of history, biography, and the romance novel—the three major forms of writing in Greek antiquity.

Traditionally, Luke–Acts (especially Acts) has been understood as belonging to the genre of ancient history. W.C. van Unnik has argued most cogently for the similarities in vocabulary and procedure between Luke–Acts and ancient historians like Sallust, Plutarch, and Tacitus.[48] Charles Talbert, on the other hand, has argued extensively that the Gospels belong to the genre of ancient biography. He claimed: '. . . when the early Christians told their story of Jesus, on some occasions they followed the conventions of self-expression that clustered together in what we regard as ancient biography'.[49] Most recently, Luke and Acts have been read as belonging to the genre of the ancient novel. In an unpublished Harvard dissertation, Richard I. Pervo argued that Acts should be classified as a popular historical novel.[50] Like the ancient novel, the purpose of Acts, according to Pervo, is entertainment.[51] More recently, Susan Praeder has argued that 'Luke–Acts with its message of salvation for all people came to expression in that one of the three ancient prose narrative genres most intended for all people, the ancient novel'.[52] However, she still rejected Pervo's notion that either Luke or Acts was written for pure entertainment.

It is not my purpose to adjudicate the question of the genre of Luke–Acts. The fact that evidence can be found to support all three views should serve as a caveat to those who remain obdurate in their opinion. As Robert Karris has suggested:

> It seems to me that one of the chief problems so far encountered in the young life of a literary-critical approach to Luke–Acts is that we scholars have been playing the game of all-or-nothing. Luke–Acts is either biography or history or story, but not all three together.[53]

Because Gospels exhibit characteristics of all three ancient genres, Karris has labeled the genre of Luke–Acts a *genus mixtum*.[54] For Karris, the challenge is this: 'If we view Luke–Acts as a *genus mixtum*, then we New Testament literary critics have our work cut out for us. How do we weigh the contributions the various genera make to the *genus mixtum* we call Luke–Acts?'[55]

Until the problem of genre in Gospel studies is solved, to suggest that one must apply a literary theory developed from the study of ancient literature is to argue a moot point.[56] What is really needed is a poetics of the Gospels to which other ancient literature of various types could be compared. Until then, studies like this one can only hope to contribute to the process. Culpepper's purpose in *Anatomy of the Fourth Gospel* is a modest, yet noble, goal toward which all biblical scholars in their initial soundings in narrative criticism should strive:

> It would be preferable if we could utilize literary categories which
> are peculiarly suitable for the study of the gospels rather than those
> which have been developed from the study of other literary genres,
> but perhaps some progress toward that ability can be made by a
> study such as the present one.[57]

Another criticism could be leveled against the methodology of this
study. Both redaction and literary critics alike agree that any study of
Luke must involve Acts and vice versa. Typical is this statement
about the unity of Luke–Acts by Robert Smith:

> That hyphenated label may seem inelegant or even barbarous, yet
> it is useful in the extreme; for it handily summarizes a hard-won
> position that is (or should be) a presupposition for all investigation
> of the Third Gospel and the Book of Acts: the entire work from
> Luke 1.1 to Acts 28.31 is a unified whole. The Gospel and Acts are
> not just two books chancing to derive from the same pen. They are
> part one and part two of a single book, and neither should be
> studied in isolation from the other.[58]

I am in whole-hearted agreement with the position that Luke–Acts
must be taken as a unified whole. That the two works have the same
real author is axiomatic; however, that the implied author or
narrator of both works is the same has been seriously questioned.[59]
For this study, it is more important to note that certain themes and
plot lines are developed throughout Luke–Acts; but the plot
strategies, literary techniques, and narrative patterns vary between
the two works. Therefore, I would like to loosen the hyphen a bit and
examine the ascension narrative in Luke for the ways in which it
brings proper closure to the Gospel and the ascension narrative in
Acts for the ways in which it functions as a narrative beginning,
anticipating major plot developments in the story of Acts. Attention
is given to the verbal and thematic linkage between the two texts, but
primarily the study shows that the ascension narrative in Luke
functions differently from that in Acts.

Conclusion

The purpose of this study is to place the ascension narratives of
Luke–Acts in context. By means of the diachronic methodologies of
textual, form and source analyses the ascension narratives will be
positioned in historical context, establishing the text to be read and
determining affinities with antecedent or contemporary traditions

(oral or written). By means of the synchronic analysis of narrative criticism, it will be possible to determine the function of the two pericopae in their narrative contexts. Finally, by comparing the two texts to one another, the departure of Jesus will be located in its canonical context.

The work is divided into two major parts. Part I, 'The Departure of Jesus in Luke', is comprised of two chapters which deal with the diachronic analysis (Chapter 2) and narrative analysis (Chapter 3) of Luke 24.50-53. Part II, 'The Departure of Jesus in Acts', follows a common methodological path: Chapter 4 provides the diachronic analysis and Chapter 5 probes the literary function of Acts 1.1-11. The Conclusion (Chapter 6) examines the similarities and variations between the two narratives in canonical context, reflecting on the significance of Jesus' departure in Luke and Acts. By holding these two 'radically opposed' methods of diachronic and synchronic analyses in tension, it is hoped that due consideration may be given to Luke–Acts both as first-century writings and as timeless literary structures.

PART I
THE DEPARTURE OF JESUS IN LUKE

Chapter 2

LUKE 24.50-53 IN HISTORICAL CONTEXT:
A DIACHRONIC ANALYSIS

The historical-critical method is essentially diachronic as it seeks to press behind the final, canonical form of the text in search of an older text tradition, underlying sources, and more pristine oral forms. In this chapter we will explore the historical context of the departure of Jesus in Luke through textual, source, and form analyses in order to give Luke serious treatment as an ancient writing.

Text-Critical Analysis:
Establishing the Text of Luke 24.50-53

The Lukan resurrection narrative is riddled with textual problems. Seven passages in particular raise serious problems for the student or scholar seeking to interpret the Lukan resurrection narrative in general, and the ascension narrative in particular. In attempting to understand and explain these passages, popularly known as *Western non-interpolations*, the historical development in modern scholarship since Westcott and Hort will be traced, including a summary and critique of the reasons usually cited as evidence for the longer and shorter readings. Then, an alternative methodology will be offered as a possible way of establishing the text. The text which will serve as the foundation for the diachronic and synchronic analyses of the Lukan ascension story will be translated, followed by form and source analyses of the pericope.

History of Scholarship
In 1881, after twenty-eight years of collaboration, B.F. Westcott and F.J.A. Hort issued a two-volume work entitled, *The New Testament in the Original Greek*. The modest task undertaken, as evinced by the

title, was 'to present exactly the original words of the New Testament, so far as they can now be determined from surviving documents'.[1] Though criticized from all sides of scholarship, Westcott and Hort were largely successful in at least one purpose: their endeavor stood as the crowning work in an attempt to replace the *Textus Receptus* 'with a portable Gk. Test., which shall not be disfigured with Byzantine corruptions'.[2]

In the companion volume to the text, Westcott and Hort (WH) developed the principles and procedures of textual criticism by which they established their text. Four criteria were identified by WH as indispensable in deciding the correct reading: (1) internal evidence of readings; (2) internal evidence of documents; (3) genealogical evidence; and (4) internal evidence of groups. In this last category, WH identified four text-types: Syrian, Alexandrian, Western, and Neutral. It is obvious from the question-begging name *Neutral*, that WH regarded this text as containing the 'apparently more original text'.[3] WH saw the concordant testimony of Codex Sinaiticus (א) and Codex Vaticanus (B), the major representatives of the Neutral text, as equivalent to the testimony of a manuscript older than either of them by at least 200 years. They worked unashamedly with these two presuppositions:

> (1) that readings of א B should be accepted as the true readings until strong internal evidence is found to the contrary and (2) that no readings of א B can safely be rejected absolutely, though it is sometimes right to place them on an alternative footing, especially where they receive no support from Versions or Fathers.[4]

While acknowledging the primacy of the Neutral text in general, WH did recognize a few Western readings as genuine. Though the Western text is generally considered to be an expansionist text, WH identified nine omissions in particular as 'exceptional instances of the preservation of the original text in exclusively Western readings'.[5] With the exception of Matt. 27.29 and Luke 22.19b-20, the omissions are to be found in the last chapter of Luke (24.3, 6, 12, 36, 40, 51, 52). Unable to bring themselves to identify these textual problems as *Neutral interpolations*, they instead preferred the clumsy nomenclature *Western non-interpolations*.[6] These nine passages are marked in WH's Greek text with double brackets (see Table 1).

WH exerted a great deal of influence on subsequent English translations, commentaries, and critical editions of the Greek New Testament.[7] With particular reference to the Western non-interpolations in Luke 24, the RSV (1946, 1962) and the NEB (1961) have either adopted WH's method of double-bracketing the problem passages or have relegated them to a marginal note in the text. The ERV (1881) and the ASV (1901) read the non-interpolations in the text and place a note in the margin which reads: 'Some ancient authorities omit . . . '. Although WH served on the translation committee for the ERV and exerted a great deal of influence on the printed text, they did not persuade the committee to print the shorter text. The ERV was published just five days after WH's work was released.[8] Table 1 below compares the way eight English translations have treated the non-interpolations.

Table 1

Treatment of Non-Interpolations in
Modern English Translations

Verse	ERV	ASV	RSV 1962	RSV 1971	RSV CE	NEB	GNB	NIV
24.3	+*	+*	-*	-*	-*	-	+	-
24.6	+*	+*	-*	-*	+*	-*	+	+
24.12	+*	+*	-*	-*	+*	-*	+*	+
24.36	+*	+*	-*	-*	+*	-*	+*	+
24.40	+*	+*	-*	-*	+*	-*	+*	+
24.51	+*	+*	-*	+*	+*	-*	+*	+
24.52	+*	+*	-*	-*	+*	-*	+	+

-    indicates the passage is omitted from the text with no accompanying note.
+   indicates the passage is included in the text with no accompanying note.
-*   indicates the passage is omitted from the text but included in a footnote.
+*   indicates the passage is included in the text but accompanied by a footnote which explains the passage is omitted by some ancient authorities.

Nearly all the scholarly commentaries on Luke before *circa* 1965 agreed with WH's evaluation of the Western non-interpolations in Luke. Plummer (1896),[9] Balmforth (1930),[10] Manson (1930),[11] Creed (1950),[12] Geldenhuys (1951),[13] and Gilmour (1952),[14] agreed with most, if not all, of WH's text-critical judgments on the authenticity of the shorter Western readings.[15]

By far the most important influence exerted by WH has been in the area of the critical editions of the Greek New Testament between 1900 and 1965. By no means have all critical editions followed WH, particularly in their judgment on the textual problems in Luke 24,[16] but the impact of WH on von Soden (1913), Vogels (1922), Kilpatrick (1958), Tasker (1964), N-A[25] (1963), and UBS[1] (1966), is clearly evident. These editions differed in their particular treatment of the non-interpolations, but Table 2 demonstrates that all of them in some way, through brackets or footnotes, reflect their preference for WH in most of the passages.

Table 2

Treatment of the Non-Interpolations in the Critical
Editions of the Greek NT

Verse	von Soden	Vogels	Kil-patrick	Tasker	N-A[25]	UBS[1]	UBS[2]	UBS[3] N-A[26]
24.3	+*	SB	SB	−*	SB	SB	SB	+*
24.6	+*	SB	SB	−*	DB	SB	+*	+*
24.12	+*	DB	−*	−*	−*	SB	+*	+*
24.36	SB	SB	−*	−*	−*	SB	+*	+*
24.40	SB	SB	−*	−*	−*	SB	+*	+*
24.51	SB	DB	+	−*	−*	SB	+*	+*
24.52	SB	DB	−*	−*	−*	SB	+*	+*

−   indicates the passage is included in the text with no accompanying note.

−*   indicates the passage is omitted from the text but included in the critical apparatus or an accompanying footnote.

+*   indicates the passage is included in the text accompanied by pertinent information in the critical apparatus.

SB   indicates the passage is included in the text but is demarcated by single brackets

DB   indicates the passage is included in the text but is demarcated by double brackets.

Unchallenged in pre-eminence, WH's text became the standard text for most translations, commentaries, and Greek editions of the

New Testament, and WH's principles of textual criticism were accepted almost without question. In effect, WH's Greek text not only succeeded in dethroning the *Textus Receptus*, it also managed to replace it as reigning monarch for nearly eighty years!

In recent years, however, there has been a significant shift away from WH's judgments concerning the authenticity of the Western non-interpolations. This shift may be best understood after a perusal of contemporary English translations, recent commentaries, and current critical editions of the Greek New Testament. Among the contemporary English translations, the Jerusalem Bible (1966), the Good News Bible (1976), and the New International Version (1974), have shown a preference for the longer text in Luke 24. With the exception of Luke 24.3, the Catholic Edition of the RSV (1965) has reversed its predecessor by reading the longer text in six of the problem texts (see Table 1).

Perhaps the best recent commentaries on the Gospel of Luke are those of I. Howard Marshall (1978),[17] Joseph A. Fitzmyer (1981),[18] and C.H. Talbert (1983).[19] In every instance of a textual problem involving a Western non-interpolation, Marshall opted for the longer reading.[20] Fitzmyer has given a cursory treatment of the problem in the section of his Introduction entitled 'The Gospel Text'.[21] Fitzmyer claimed 'even though our translation has been based on the 25th edition of Nestle and Aland, these [longer] readings are considered part of the original text'.[22] In his discussion of each individual passage, Fitzmyer appealed to external evidence to justify his inclusion of the longer texts.[23] Talbert in his discussion of 24.12 argued 'the trend of recent research is to accept this verse as integral to the gospel'.[24] Talbert has assumed the longer text throughout his analysis of chapter 24. In his classic treatment of the Acts of the Apostles, E. Haenchen argued that the longer text of Luke 24 'is no scholarly construction, but rather a text which was not, or at any rate only a little, affected by the adaptation to contemporary taste which set in in the second century or by the arbitrary procedure of the scribes'.[25] In addition, E. Schweizer (1984) and E. Earle Ellis (1981) preferred the longer text supported by the Alexandrian (Neutral) witnesses.[26]

The most significant changes are to be found in some of the current Greek editions of the New Testament. The first noticeable shift was made between the first (1966) and the second (1968) editions of the UBS text. In the first edition, all seven non-interpolations were placed within single brackets in the text and were regarded as having dubious textual validity.[27] In the second edition, with the exception of 24.3 (still in brackets), all the passages were placed in the text without any markings whatsoever. By the time the third edition was published, all seven longer readings stood within the printed text with no markings at all[28] (see Table 2).

This brief survey of scholarship indicates a change in scholarly opinion concerning the authenticity of the Western non-interpolations. How does one account for this seemingly sudden shift in which significant translations, commentaries, and critical texts have raised an almost harmonious voice in acceptance of the Western non-interpolations? A comprehensive survey of all the contributing factors cannot be attempted here; instead, two influential reasons for the shift will be presented.[29]

The first is an example of the ability of a single scholar to alter views. In the first edition of *Das Abendmahlsworte Jesu*, Joachim Jeremias accepted the shorter text of the Lord's Supper in Luke 22.14-20.[30] In subsequent editions, he argued for the longer texts. Not satisfied with considering only Luke 22.19-20, Jeremias surveyed all the major lacunae of Codex Bezae in Luke, with the curious exception of 24.3. He concluded that the evidence is overwhelmingly in favor of the longer text in every instance, though he was somewhat uncertain at 24.36, 40.[31] Marshall relied heavily on the conclusions of Jeremias, making reference to his work at each of the seven problem passages, except 24.6.[32]

More important than Jeremias has been the discovery and publication of Bodmer Papyrus XIV, known simply as p[75].[33] Dated between 175 and 225 CE, p[75] is the earliest witness, by some 200 years, to the longer readings in Luke 24. From its discovery p[75] has been widely acclaimed from all corners. Victor Martin and Rudolphe Kasser, editors of the published text, opened their preface with these bold words:

> Le papyrus publié ci-après ne le cède en rien au P. Bodmer II sous le rapport de l'âge et de l'importance. . . . Il prend place ainsi à côté du précédent et du P. Chester Beatty I, et peut être compté au nombre des représentants les plus proches des origines des Evangiles canoniques.[34]

Kurt Aland has claimed: 'With p[75] new ground has been opened to us'.[35] He also insisted that with the discovery of p[75] 'WH's so-called "Western non-interpolations" have been, so to speak, stripped of their original nimbus and . . . although interesting, they are no longer regarded, or should no longer be regarded, as authoritative'.[36] Elsewhere, Aland has argued for the authenticity of the longer Alexandrian readings in Luke 24, primarily based on the evidence of p[75].[37] Bruce Metzger, while slightly more cautious than Aland, assured his readers that 'although the full significance of this remarkable papyrus still remains to be assessed . . . it is obvious that the textual critic must be exceedingly grateful for acquisition of such an early witness'.[38] Carlo Martini has also been impressed by the antiquity and quality of p[75]. Martini has written: 'In particulae relate ad 'Western non-interpolations' (v.g. Lc 24.1-53) eorum praesentia in textu saeculo II existente nunc extra omne dubium ponitur'.[39]

These three scholars, Aland, Metzger, and Martini, were not chosen at random. All three men were members of the United Bible Society Committee responsible for the UBSGNT[3] and Nestle-Aland[26] critical editions of the Greek New Testament. There is little wonder that a majority of the committee decided that the external evidence, particularly p[75], weighed heavily in favor of the longer readings in Luke 24. The transition from WH's acceptance of the shorter readings to a preference, on the part of most scholars, for the longer readings is seemingly completed in the UBSGNT[3] and Nestle-Aland[26] critical editions.[40]

Consideration of the Texts
A number of reasons, based on internal evidence, have been suggested for the Western and Alexandrian texts in Luke 24. Below, in summary fashion, are listed major arguments for and against the shorter and longer texts.

Luke 24.3. τοῦ κυρίου Ἰησοῦ. Arguments for the shorter text include: (1) the combination κύριος Ἰησοῦς is not found in the genuine text of the Gospels;[41] (2) there is evidence of scribal expansion for identification of the body.[42] Arguments for the longer text include: (1) it is a double expression which serves in the Lukan narrative as an indispensable link between Jesus' public life and the time after the resurrection;[43] (2) the phrase was omitted by scribal error due either to an assimilation to Matt. 27.58 or Mark 15.43;[44] the excision or a seemingly superfluous description;[45] or the influence of 24.23 on the scribe.[46]

Luke 24.6. οὐκ ἔστιν ὧδε, ἀλλὰ ἠγέρθη. Arguments for the shorter text include: (1) the longer text represents scribal harmonization to Matt. 28.6 or Mark 16.6;[47] (2) the inclusion of the words disturbs the author's intention for the passage.[48] Arguments for the longer text include: (1) the presence of ἀλλά indicates an independent Lukan formulation from that of Matthew and Mark;[49] (2) the phrase was omitted because the statement is superfluous and seems out of place.[50]

Luke 24.12. Ὁ δὲ Πέτρος ἀναστὰς ἔδραμεν ἐπὶ τὸ μνημεῖον καὶ παρακύψας βλέπει τὰ ὀθόνια μόνα, καὶ ἀπῆλθεν πρὸς ἑαυτὸν θαυμάζων τὸ γεγονός. Arguments for the shorter text include: (1) the verse is a condensed and simplified summary of John 20.3-10;[51] (2) the verse was appended to Luke by a redactor only to be omitted later by Western scribes;[52] (3) the historic present is rare in Luke, but common in John;[53] (4) the Lukan idiom may be explained as an attempt on the part of the redactor to imitate Luke's style;[54] (5) some scribe was concerned to preserve a specific, valuable tradition which was otherwise known only to the Gospel of John;[55] (6) the verse serves to place apostolic confirmation upon the fact of the empty tomb.[56] Arguments for the longer text include: (1) the verbal similarities between Luke and John, however striking, are not without parallels elsewhere in Luke;[57] (2) despite similarities, Peter alone approaches the tomb in Luke, while John speaks of two disciples;[58] (3) the verse exhibits Lukan idiom;[59] (4) the similarity between Luke and John may be explained by assuming either a common source, written or oral,[60] or John's knowledge and redactional editing of the synoptic Gospels (here Luke);[61] (5) there seems to be a flashback to 24.12 in 24.23.[62]

Luke 24.36. καὶ λέγει αὐτοῖς Εἰρήνη ὑμῖν. Arguments for the shorter text are: (1) the verse represents a harmonization of Luke with John;[63] (2) the use of the historic present λέγει is not Lukan;[64] (3) the text seems to be more important to the Fourth Gospel than to Luke.[65] Arguments for the longer text are: (1) John depended on a Lukan source;[66] (2) the greeting may be an essential element of the Christophany;[67] (3) the omission is an attempt to diminish the extreme reaction of the disciples.[68]

Luke 24.40. καὶ τοῦτο εἰπὼν ἔδειξεν αὐτοῖς τὰς χεῖρας καὶ τοὺς πόδας. Arguments for the shorter text are: (1) there is harmonization of Luke with John;[69] (2) the use of δείκνυμι and εἰπών is uncharacteristic of Luke.[70] Arguments for the longer text are: (1) a gloss would have left some trace of origin by retaining πλευράν in place of πόδας;[71] (2) the phrase would have been offensive or at least superfluous to a copyist.[72]

Luke 24.51. καὶ ἀνεφέρετο εἰς τὸν οὐρανόν. Arguments for the shorter text include: (1) the addition represents an attempt to give the Gospel its proper ascension story;[73] (2) the addition represents a careless attempt to harmonize Luke 24 with Acts 1.[74] Arguments for the longer text include: (1) the omission is due to harmonization with Acts 1.1-12;[75] (2) if this were a copyist's addition, a form of ἀναλαμβάνω would be expected;[76] (3) the omission may be explained as a scribal error due to haplography.[77]

Luke 24.52. προσκυνήσαντες αὐτόν. One argument has been given for the shorter text: the addition represents an attempt to portray the response appropriate for those who have been in the presence of the risen Lord.[78] Arguments for the longer text are: (1) the omission is due to haplography;[79] (2) the reading is a deliberate omission to accord better with the shorter text in 24.51.[80]

Evaluation of the Arguments
These arguments do not exhaust the list of explanations given for either the longer or shorter texts, but they do serve as a basis for the following assertion: to date, arguments offered by textual critics and commentators regarding the text of Luke 24 have been largely inadequate. While space, time, and prudence prohibit a detailed analysis of the reasons given for the shorter or longer texts, a few general comments are in order.

First, as has already been shown, scholarly opinion tends to divide along chronological lines. The older scholars, particularly before 1960, tended to support WH's preference for the shorter text, while more recent scholars have followed the lead of Aland, Metzger, and Martini. Most modern scholars base their arguments on the weight of p^{75}, but this argument is considerably damaged when one recalls the warning of E.C. Colwell:

> Hort did not possess p^{75}, but he imagined it. He insisted that there was a very early ancestor of his Neutral text, that the common ancestor of Vaticanus and Sinaiticus was a remote ancestor, not a close ancestor. p^{75} does not add a new argument for or against that theory.[81]

Robert Mahoney is right when he claims that the value of p^{75} in the non-interpolations debate is neither to be found in the fact that the papyrus manuscript contains the longer reading—the majority does as well, nor does it consist in the manuscript's age—the Western text is commonly agreed to derive from an archetype of the late second or early third century. Rather, according to Mahoney:

> The manuscript's chief value for our problem at hand is actually

> not the direct evidence it supplies for the contested non-inter-
> polations, but the indirect evidence it delivers by presenting such a
> good example at an early date of the *kind* of text that includes these
> contested passages.[82]

In other words, the discovery of p[75] has laid to rest the mistaken
theory of an Alexandrian recension in the fourth century.[83] The
results are an enhancement of the Alexandrian text-type, and
conversely, a further denigration of the Western text.[84] Eldon Epp
has claimed: 'The discovery of p[75], so extraordinarily significant in
several respects, does not, as many seem to think, solve this puzzle of
Neutral versus Western, nor does it in this respect carry us beyond
Westcott-Hort'.[85]

The problem, in short, is that there is a conflict of accepted New
Testament canons in these passages. On the one hand, based on the
overall character of the manuscripts, the Alexandrian is generally
preferred over the Western as a more reliable text-type. Therefore,
Alexandrian readings are *usually* preferred on the grounds of external
evidence. On the other hand, one of the more important canons for
New Testament textual criticism is *Lectio brevior, potior*, that is, a
shorter reading is to be preferred over a longer one; this argument is
based on internal evidence. The mere presence of p[75], however, does
not invalidate Hort's text-critical judgments in Luke 24, as many
believe.

Second, there appears to be a tendency on the part of scholars
either to accept or to reject the readings *en masse* (with the possible
exception of 24.51, 52). Despite the multiplicity and intricacy of
arguments and solutions presented above, these solutions do not
adequately address the phenomenon of so many significant variants
of such remarkable similarity clustered in so narrow a context. That
there is the possibility of some sort of unifying purpose for the
omission or addition must not be dismissed too quickly. The
tendency of scholars to treat the texts together, the sheer number of
variants within such a limited space, and the contextual evidence of
the problem texts, all point to the conclusion that there is a unifying
element that distinguishes these seven passages from other Western
omissions, if not from most textual variants.

Two crucial questions remain unanswered. If the passages are
additions to the original text, why did the scribe(s) expand the text?
Or if the longer text is closer to the original, why would a scribe
excise certain portions? These questions assume that the common

element in these verses is the result of deliberate scribal activity. This scribal redaction is obscured by many modern scholars who either argue that the mistakes are purely accidental,[86] or ignore the distinction made by WH between non-interpolations and that intermediate class of passages which *may* involve Western non-interpolations.[87]

The problem may be explained as a theological *Tendenz* on the part of p[75] or Codex D. Such a suggestion is not novel. Metzger and others have alluded to both possibilities.[88] In one instance Metzger claimed: 'scholars have begun to give renewed attention to the possibility that special theological interests on the part of the scribes may account for the deletion of certain passages in Western witnesses'.[89] Unfortunately, he fails to mention which scholars and which passages he had in mind.

On the other hand, the minority of the committee, arguing for the shorter readings, claimed: 'There is discernible in these passages a Christological-theological motivation that accounts for their having been added, while there is no clear reason that accounts for their having been omitted'.[90] Again, there is an unhappy paucity of information. Who constituted the minority and why did he not write a note defending his position?[91] Such is assumed to be the practice of the committee. In the Introduction to the *Commentary*, Metzger wrote:

> In special cases, when a member holding a minority opinion had strong feelings that the majority had gone astray, opportunity was given for him to express his own point of view. Such occasional comments, identified by the writer's initials and enclosed within square brackets, are appended to the main discussion of the textual problem in question.[92]

While no published 'minority report' has yet been found, the surfacing of such a theological tendency may provide the only outlet to the present impasse.[93]

Theological Tendencies and Text-Critical Methodology
In order to test the hypothesis that a theological tendency stands behind, and even motivates, the alterations in the text, the following methodology is suggested. First, Codex Bezae Cantabrigiensis (D)[94] and the Bodmer papyrus XIV (p[75]) should be employed because they are the main extant representatives of the Western and Alexandrian text-types in Luke.[95] It is safer and sounder, methodologically

speaking, to deal with real texts which are accessible in facsimile and published form, than to deal with a hypothetical and somewhat contrived category known as *text-type*. Both manuscripts should be examined to determine whether or not there is a distinguishable tendency which would support or deny the presence of deliberate scribal activity in Luke 24. In the case of Codex D, one might first suspect scribal inclinations to lower or diminish the picture of Christ in Luke. Or, for p[75], an inductive study would be used to support or deny a possible scribal tendency to heighten Luke's christology which highlights both the glorified and corporeal—divine and human—nature of Jesus.

The scribal tendency to make editorial change on the basis of theological bias may not be demonstrated by reference to unintentional changes, spelling habits, and the like. Rather, following the methodology proposed recently by Larry Hurtado, the assumption is made: 'when a variant cannot be attributed to the common scribal mistakes in copying, and especially when the variant can be attributed to a reasonable editorial intention, it is very likely that the variant is an intentional change'.[96] In this regard, singular readings which are found in only one Greek manuscript are most useful. Because of the early date of p[75], fewer true singular readings may be expected. Singular readings constitute only a provisional category at best, since new manuscript discoveries could remove the singularity of any reading (cf. p[75] and B). Of secondary importance, but important nonetheless, are all other variants, subsingular and insignificant, which should be examined in light of the broader theological context.[97] In addition, harmonizations with passages in the other Gospels, vocabulary preferences, changes toward concise expression, additions for clarification, significant sense changes, and changes in word order, all contribute to the understanding of scribal purposes and theological tendencies.[98] Such a methodology is certainly a step beyond what most perceive to be the task of the text-critic, scrutinizing and collating manuscripts.[99]

If a theological tendency is thought to be detected, then the caution of E.C. Colwell must be heeded: 'We can be sure of theological motivation for a variant reading only when the history of theology in that manuscript's time and place is already well known'.[100] Thus, it would be necessary to research the background of either Codex D or p[75] to determine whether or not the larger historical and theological context would allow for such a theological tendency to be probable on the part of a scribe. At this point, some might argue that the editorial changes are not the work of the copyist of the manuscript under consideration, but represent the work of earlier scribes. Hurtado's comments on Codex W are *apropos* here:

> If the changes . . . are not the work of the scribe of W, they are still evidence that deliberate and independent changes were made in the textual tradition of Mark represented by Codex W. That is, whether the copyist made the changes, they were still intentional changes apparently created with clear editorial purposes in view. The conclusions that such deliberate changes were probably made by other scribes and that agreements in such readings are coincidental would stand whether the particular scribe of Codex W or an earlier copyist made the changes here offered as evidence.[101]

For this study such a claim would only mean that a larger historical and theological context—one which would include the hypothetical archetype of the manuscript—would need to be examined in order to show that the theological climate was conducive to such alterations, whether by the scribes of D or p[75], or their predecessors.

Below is a textual analysis based on the methodological principles stated above. K.W. Clark demonstrated the significance and validity of such an approach:

> The recognition that a textual critic must be also historian and theologian has obvious corollaries. There must be co-ordination between all three: the investigation of textual data, the study of theological history, and research in ecclesiastical history. This threefold alliance is advantageous, even essential, to each field of research, as it serves to extend and to inform each specialization with greater comprehension and refinement. Collaboration of the three fields would make more comprehensive the scholarship of each.[102]

Codex Bezae Cantabrigiensis

Following the lead of E.J. Epp,[103] G.E. Rice has recently argued in an unpublished dissertation that five distinct biases emerge from the D variants in Luke.[104] One of the biases is of particular interest here: 'Jesus is exalted beyond his portrayal in the "normal" text of Luke'.[105] Though it is impossible to discuss all of Rice's evidence for this statement, several examples will be cited and discussed.[106]

Luke 3.22ff. An intriguing variant unit, involving two variants, is applied by Rice to his arguments. According to D, after Jesus emerges from the baptismal waters, a voice from heaven says, 'You are my son, today I have begotten you'. This verse, a direct quotation

from the LXX version of Psalm 2.7, has been understood in many
different ways. Many interpret the variant to be an adoptionist
reading, whether original or from the hand of a scribe.[107] Rice,
however, claimed that the intention of D cannot be understood until
the variants in 3.23ff. are considered. Here D sets aside Luke's
genealogy and incorporates Matthew's kingly line with some
corrections.[108] Since D has quoted from a royal Psalm of David, it is
appropriate now for D to supply Jesus with the royal line borrowed
from Matthew. Rice's conclusion is worth quoting here in full:

> Because of the royal significance of Psalm 2, and because the
> Church saw in this Psalm a prophecy of the Messiah, D quite
> naturally applied it to Jesus. Because this variant appears in
> connection with the baptism of Jesus, D views this baptism as the
> anointing of Jesus as the Messianic King.[109]

Luke 9.11. Rice also attempted to demonstrate D's heightening of
the exaltation of Christ through variation in the miracle stories. In
9.11, D adds 'his' to 'healing', implying that those present could not
be healed through normal medical practices, but rather were in need
of Jesus' miraculous healing (cf. 8.42-48). By adding 'all', D glorifies
Jesus as the divine healer who turned away none, regardless of their
affliction.[110]

Luke 24.49. This variation is found within the resurrection
narrative. Codex B reads: 'And behold I send the promise of *my
Father* upon you', while D reads: 'And I send *my* promise upon you'.
The omission of 'Father' tends to elevate Jesus to the point that he no
longer must rely on the Father. Jesus is able to dispense his own
blessing on his disciples.[111]

To these texts considered by Rice may be added the following.

Luke 6.5. Here the textual evidence is quite complicated. D omits
verse 5, only to restore it after verse 10. In its place, D includes: 'On
the same day, seeing a certain man working on the Sabbath, he said
to him, "Man, if you know what you are doing, you are blessed; if
you do not know, you are cursed and a transgressor of the law"'.
Codex D has expanded the pericope from one to three Sabbath
stories, including the healing of the man with withered hand (6.6-10).
The pronouncement about the son of man being lord over the
Sabbath is, in effect, tripled in significance.

Luke 23.53, 24.1. D adds to 23.53 these words: 'and when he was
interred a stone was placed upon the tomb which twenty could
hardly roll'. And at 24.1 D includes: 'and they began to reason among

themselves, "Who will roll the stone away?"' (cf. Mark 16.3). The combination of these two variants seems to accentuate the miracle of the stone rolled away.

These passages are sufficient to show that there seems to be within D the tendency to heighten, not diminish, the Lukan christology. Returning to the resurrection account, this analysis casts serious doubt on the view that the Western scribes are working to lower the christology in Luke. It is very unlikely a reversal of tendency could occur so quickly. Although this does not discredit other theological motives on the scribe's agenda, it does eliminate the most obvious one.

In a recent article, 'Western Non-Interpolations: A Defense of the Apostolate', Rice has argued for a theological tendency in Codex D which explains the textual problems in Luke 24.[112] Rice suggested that the scribe of D has attempted to offer an apology for the apostolate by omitting or changing passages which cast the apostles in a bad light. Rice claimed:

> There are seven non-interpolations in Luke 24 identified by Westcott and Hort. Five of the seven lend themselves to this motif. They are all set in the context of the empty tomb and the post-resurrection appearances and include vv. 3, 6, 12, 36, and 40. The two remaining non-interpolations, v. 51 and 52, are set in the context of the ascension.[113]

Rice's methodology is similar to the one outlined here, though not nearly so rigorous. Several critical comments on Rice's work are in order at this point.

First, on a positive note, Rice is to be commended for attempting to discover a theological tendency which would explain the text of Luke 24. Second, Rice has limited himself to a much too narrow scope. His study involves only the end of Luke 23 and all of chapter 24, excluding the ascension narrative! Rice gave no reason for not considering the ascension narrative, other than the fact that those two non-interpolations did not fit into his pattern of a defense for the apostolate. It is puzzling to understand why a scribe so concerned to write an apology for the disciples would remove one of the nicest things said about them in 24.52 'and they worshipped him'. In order to be convincing, Rice would need to examine not only the rest of Luke, but at least the entirety of Codex D in Matthew and Mark. Otherwise, he would be forced to explain why the same scribe, or community of scribes, would redact Luke 24 with an eye to defending the apostles and not remove the much more offensive passages, for example, in Mark.[114] Finally, Rice has given no attention to the historical and theological context which would give rise to such an apologetic interest on the part of the scribes of D. To date, therefore, no adequate explanation of the problem passages as omissions has been presented.

Bodmer Papyrus XIV

That the interpolations are in fact additions used by the scribe of p[75] to heighten Luke's christology, especially emphasizing the corporeal reality of the resurrection, is the major contention of the remainder of this chapter. When dealing with the scribe of p[75], several peculiarities should be observed. First, while p[75] is one of the most extensive papyri, it is still extant only at Luke 3–24 and John 1–15. Therefore, comparison of scribal activity in Luke is limited to John.

Second, E.C. Colwell has demonstrated that 'the text that is produced can be explained in all its variants as the result of a single force, namely the disciplined scribe who writes with the intention of being careful and accurate'.[115] Third, though careful, the scribe of p[75] is not immune to careless errors. Most of these errors involve the omission or addition of a single letter.[116] There are places, however, where the variants are more substantial.[117] Due to the nature of the text and scribal habits, fewer variants may be expected. But where variants are significant, either in substance or meaning, one may inquire why they are there and what weight should be attached to them in order to understand the theological program of p[75]. Below are some examples of the types of variants which have been discovered in p[75].[118]

Luke 17.14. After the ten lepers cry out to Jesus: 'Have mercy on us', p[75] has the variant: 'I will. Be cleansed, and immediately they were cleansed'. K.W. Clark argued that this variant shows a theological interest on the part of the scribe: 'At this point the scribe of p[75] borrows from Matt. 8.3 the reply of Jesus'.[119] The variant appears to elevate the miraculous powers of Jesus. A close examination of the facsimile, however, shows that this passage is obviously from a corrector's hand. This phenomenon is correctly noted by Fee,[120] and the critical apparatus of Nestle-Aland[26]. This variant is useful for reconstructing the textual history and transmission of the manuscript, but will be of secondary significance in the attempt to discover theological tendencies on the part of p[75] since the date and background of the corrector are unknown.[121]

Luke 16.30, 31. The parable of the rich man and Lazarus has within it several interesting variants. The singular reading of p[75] has the word ἐγέρθη in place of πορεύθη in verse 30. Likewise, at verse 31, p[75] and a few other later manuscripts read ἐγέρθη instead of ἀναστῇ. The significance is manifold. First, the story of Lazarus and the rich man is given an explicit reference to the resurrection. The reader can hardly miss the implication in 16.30-31 that the τις is none other than Jesus who was raised from the dead, nor does one miss the indictment that the ones who did not hear Moses and the prophets will not be persuaded by the one raised from the dead. Second, this interpretation is strengthened by the fact that the word ἠγέρθη recurs at 24.6, one of the problem passages in Luke 24. It is not too fanciful to argue that the scribe has indeed introduced the familiar term for the resurrection here and in Luke 24 out of theological, or more properly christological, concerns.[122]

Luke 9.34. The omission of αὐτούς may suggest that only Jesus entered the cloud at the transfiguration. This variant reading would then serve to heighten the mystery and exaltation of the transfiguration narrative in Luke where Jesus *and* the inner circle of disciples enter into the cloud.

Luke 9.48; 11.31; 23.3. There are several places in Luke where the scribe of p[75] appears to have harmonized Luke with parallel passages found in Matthew. While these harmonizations are not significant, usually only involving a change in word order or tense or the omission or addition of a single word, the fact that the scribe might well have had a copy of Matthew, or at least was very familiar with Matthew's Gospel, could be crucial in our consideration of Luke 24.6. In 9.48, the word order of τὸ τοῦτο παιδίον has been changed to conform to Matt. 18.4. The pronoun αὐτούς has been changed in 11.31 to αὐτήν, harmonizing the logion with Matt. 12.42. The word αὐτῷ in 23.3 was dropped in p[75], conforming the phrase to Matt. 27.11. Here p[75] agrees with Matthew against Mark 15.2. A similar phenomenon occurs at 8.21 where p[75] changes αὐτούς to αὐτόν, agreeing, in sense, with Matt. 12.48. The singular is demanded in Matthew by the context, but it is certainly out of place in Luke where the passive ἀπηγγέλη makes no indication as to number. Returning to Luke 24.6, it would be entirely possible to argue that the scribe of p[75] has borrowed the phrase 'He is not here, but he is risen' from an available copy of Matthew.

Luke 16.19. Within the same pericope is another interesting variant. The only Greek manuscript to agree with the Sahidic versions in giving the rich man in the parable a name is p[75]. While this variant has no direct bearing on any theological tendencies on the scribe's part, it is noteworthy for another reason: the inclusion of a name for an otherwise anonymous character. The addition shows that p[75] would not be averse to interpolating a name to give explicit identification to an unknown or ambiguous figure. This observation could have some significance for the variant at 24.3, where the words τοῦ κυρίου ᾿Ιησοῦ may be added for much the same reasons as Νευῆς at 16.19.

Luke 22.47. Here p[75] changes 'Judas, one of the twelve, was leading them', to 'Judas one of the twelve, was approaching them'. While the tendency of the scribe to copy letter by letter would argue for a careless error, the fact that the variant does not produce a nonsense reading would point to a deliberate change. There is a qualitative difference in the meaning of these two words. Bauer defined προήρχετο in 22.47 as meaning 'to go before as a forerunner or leader'.[123] Thus, the meaning in context here would be that Judas was the ringleader of the group coming out against Jesus. On the other hand, προσήρχετο means, in one sense, to come to or approach a deity and the parallel phrase 'and he approached Jesus' would serve to identify explicitly who the divine one was—Jesus. This alteration leaves a grammatical problem, however. The αὐτούς naturally refers to the crowd as its antecedent and not to Jesus and the disciples.[125]

Luke 24.26. Here the word βασιλείαν has replaced δόξαν. The word δόξαν, however, was written in the margin just above βασιλείαν. Unlike 17.14, this correction seems to have come from the hand of the scribe and not a later corrector. If so, there may be several explanations. The *Vorlage* of the scribe may have read 'kingdom', but the scribe may have remembered 'glory', from another tradition. Or the scribe may have felt that the word 'glory' fits the context better than 'kingdom'. This word, glory, may serve as a theologically 'loaded' term for the scribe and may represent in a succinct way the mood of the resurrection narrative. It is difficult to move beyond the point of conjecture, but the possibilities of this variant are multifarious.

Luke 24.27. The word order in p[75] has shifted. τὰ περί ἑαυτοῦ is placed before ἐν πάσαις ταῖς γραφαῖς. The scribe may be intent on placing Christ before the scriptures in order to elevate the place of Christ in the early church. On the other hand, by placing the phrase, 'in all the scriptures' at the end of the sentence, the scribe may be, as

Marchant King has suggested, 'giving them [the scriptures] considerably greater emphasis and suggesting how deeply impressed was this scribe or some earlier one by the fullness of the Old Testament testimony to Christ'.[126]

To these singular and sub-singular readings of p^{75} in Luke may be added the following examples from John.

John 6.19. Here p^{75} has changed the case ending of θάλασσα from genitive to accusative. The variant seems to be the result of scribal activity which attempted to assert that Jesus was walking *on* the sea, and not *beside* it. Such a correction could only be assumed after a detailed study of the use of prepositions and case endings by the scribe. We can, at this stage, affirm that the scribe of p^{75} was interested in the force of prepositions and their accompanying objects.[127]

John 8.57. The question asked by the Jews, 'Have you seen Abraham?' has been changed in p^{75} to 'Has Abraham seen you?' The result is an ironical statement which serves to heighten the status of Jesus in the mind of the reader. The variant makes more explicit Jesus' affirmation, 'Before Abraham was, I am'.

John 11.12. Again in John 11.12, p^{75} is the only Greek manuscript to read ἐγερθήσεται instead of σωθήσεται. The disciples, speaking of Lazarus, said, 'Lord, if he is asleep, then he will be raised'. Here is another example of the scribe's preoccupation with the resurrection. The variant cannot be dismissed as harmonization to the context, since the word used in this context for resurrection is ἀνάστασις (John 11.23, 24, 25).

While the evidence will not bear the weight of hard and fast conclusions, there does seem to be the strong possibility of a theological *Tendenz* in p^{75}. Assuming the possibility of theological interests, the question would still remain concerning a broader theological and historical context appropriate to such christological interests.

Circumstantial evidence is intriguing at this point. Third-century Egypt, particularly Alexandria, was a melting pot for various religious, social, and cultural factions. In a fascinating study soon to be published, J.M. Robinson has recounted the discovery of the Bodmer Papyri.[128] Robinson claims that the Dishna papers are to be identified with the Bodmer Papyri.[129] If Robinson is correct—and he seems to have made the connection most cogently and clearly—then the site of the discovery, Abu Mana, is little more than twelve miles upstream from the place where the Nag Hammadi codices were found.[130] While such close proximity may be due to nothing more than Egypt's arid climate (ideal for the preservation of old manuscripts),[131] these archaeological discoveries *may* provide the link needed to establish the historical context necessary to argue that p^{75}'s scribes have employed Luke to refute the heretical tendencies of gnosticism. At the very least, the historical milieu does not discredit such a theory.

Several documents, including *Treatise on Resurrection* and the *Gospel of Philip*, deal specifically with the topic of the resurrection of Jesus.[132] For example, the *Gospel of Philip*, logion 21, reverses the canonical order of the death and resurrection of Jesus: 'Those who say that the Lord died first and (then) arose are in error. For he arose and then he died'.[133] No attempt is being made here to establish a direct literary relationship between p^{75} and the *Gospel of Philip* or any other document for that matter. And while the view that gnosticism reached back into the New Testament period is much disputed, there can be no doubt that it was present by the second century CE in Egypt. To claim that the scribe of p^{75} was concerned with the problem of Christian gnosticism in general, and with gnostic views regarding the resurrection in particular, is not too far-fetched.[134]

One explanation for the additions of p^{75} to the Lukan resurrection narrative would be that the scribe was using the document for polemical purposes. By including the longer texts, the scribe of p^{75} was able: (1) to specify whose body was gone (24.3); (2) to supply a glorious and unmistakable reference to the resurrection at the empty tomb (24.6); (3) to provide apostolic confirmation of the empty tomb (24.12); (4) to furnish a greeting of peace from the risen Lord (24.36); (5) to stress the continuity between the crucified Christ and the risen Lord (24.40); (6) to emphasize both the corporeal nature and exalted state of the body of the risen Lord by making explicit reference to Christ's ascension into heaven (24.51); (7) to record the appropriate attitude of worship of the bodily ascended Christ by the disciples (24.52). All the elements mentioned above would have been devices employed by the scribe of p^{75} to accent an already exalted christology.[135]

Luke and John, with their emphasis on the materiality of the risen Lord, would be well-suited for such a purpose. If the Johannine resurrection narrative were extant in p^{75} many of the questions might be settled. Yet the fact that p^{75} is extant only in Luke and John makes one conclude that either the rest of the manuscript has been lost accidentally to posterity or that p[75] existed only in Luke and John. The above evidence does suggest that the theological and historical context necessary for a scribal tendency to elevate the continuity between and corporeality of the crucified Christ and risen Lord was, at least, possible. The argument is further strengthened by the observation of K.W. Clark in the conclusion to his study of the text of John in third-century Egypt: 'The testimony of p[66] and p[75] is adequate evidence that their variant readings were known and used in third-century Egyptian Christianity'.[136]

Conclusions

If the suggestion of a theological tendency in p[75] is accepted, how would such a theological interest on the part of p[75] explain the rest of the evidence? While maintaining an overall unifying element found in the special interests of p[75] to combat gnosticism, the passages would need to be divided into subunits to explain the textual phenomena. Luke 24.3, 6 assume a basic knowledge of at least one of the other synoptics. As has already been suggested, p[75] seems to have had access to at least parts of the Gospel of Matthew. The references to the *nomen sacrum* in 24.3 are drawn from the account of the *angeli interpres* in Matthew (or Mark). The intent of 24.6 is to urge the reader to recall the statements made in 16.31 (in p[75]) about resurrection and to emphasize the fact of the empty tomb and resurrection.

Luke 24.12, 36 and 40 form the second subunit. Here the common denominator is a dependence on John. While the relationship between John and the synoptic Gospels cannot be decided by these texts alone,[137] it is much simpler to understand the similarity as scribal harmonization for doctrinal reasons. Otherwise, one is forced to posit some hypothetical written or oral source, or else explain the resemblance as direct dependence of John on Luke or vice versa. Again, the answer to the question 'Why?' is obvious. The scribe of p[75] borrowed from John to give an apostolic witness to the empty tomb, a glorious greeting of the risen Lord, and an expression of the continuity between the crucified Christ and the risen Lord.

Luke 24.51, 52 form the third subunit. The problem here is more complicated because of possible harmonization with Acts 1. The word ἀναφέρω appears only here in Luke–Acts, and is normally associated with the sacrificial cult.[138] It may be that along with christological concerns, the scribe was interested in couching the ascension narrative in liturgical language to be used in an early

Christian worship service.[139] The word προσκυνέω would certainly favor this view. The explicit reference to the ascension, in addition to the subsequent worship which followed, would only serve to heighten the exaltation of the risen Christ.

Despite these arguments, it may well be that here is a case distinct from the others. A scribe could have omitted the reference to the ascension in order to smooth over the difficulties between the ascension stories in Luke and Acts. A solution is problematic nonetheless. Few scholars recognize that the same manuscript, Codex D, which omits the reference to the ascension in Luke includes the ascension in the longer ending of Mark (16.19). Even Eldon Epp, who has recently argued that the Western text may have deliberately tried to diminish or remove any references to a narrated ascension, has admitted that the presence of the ascension in D at Mark 16.19 militates against his argument.[140]

The question might legitimately be raised: if the scribe were intent to heighten Luke's christology, why not more radical changes? In other words, why not redact the text thoroughly in order to gain the desired effects? The answer to this important question may lie in G. Fee and E.C. Colwell's description of p[75]'s scribal habits.[141] The scribe of p[75] was careful and meticulous; this fact is commonly agreed upon. It may be argued coherently that the scribe here felt compelled to change the text to reflect certain christological concerns. At the same time, however, the scribe's redactional activity was restrained by the following control: all the additions in Luke 24 were borrowed from the other canonical Gospels. The result of these two scribal tendencies, to produce carefully and faithfully the archetype and to heighten Lukan christology, was the papyrus manuscript p[75].

Being a *rational* eclectic, I acknowledge the difficulty of establishing the Western text as the original text, particularly since only one Greek manuscript attests to the shorter reading.[142] Fee must be right when he says 'singular readings by their very nature are suspect, which means that there must be *decisive internal evidence* in favor of such a reading before it is considered as original'.[143] Fee's statement must be counterbalanced with the following observation by Eldon Epp:

> Yet, the obvious importance of Codex Bezae in tracking the early history of the New Testament text and the early and widespread nature of the 'Western' text in general should caution against any procedure that would rule out of court, almost without a hearing, a

large body of early, interesting, and unmistakably important evidence: this indeed would be the fate of a great many of D's readings if singularity is to be defined with reference solely to the Greek manuscript tradition, for these numerous singular readings of D... then could play no role in questions of the original text... when in reality the greater number of the 'unique' D-readings have support—sometimes broad support—from manuscripts of one, two, or more of the most ancient versions of the New Testament.[144]

Based on the evidence cited above, the shorter text of the ascension narrative is assumed to be closer to the original and will serve as the basis for the analyses of the Lukan narrative.[145] Below is my translation of the text of Luke 24.50-53 utilized in this study:[146]

> [50]He led them out around the neighborhood of Bethany, and after he had raised his hands, he blessed them. [51]And it happened while he was blessing them, he departed from them. [52]And they returned into Jerusalem with great joy, [53]and they were blessing God continually in the temple.

In one respect, this textual analysis is a return to the conclusions of WH reached over 100 years ago. Aland's warning is well known: '*None* of us would entrust himself to a ship of the year 1881 in order to cross the Atlantic, even if the ship were renovated or he was promised danger money. Why then do we still do so in NT textual criticism?'[147]

The paradox here is that Aland and others have 'out-Horted' Hort. Even Hort, whose affinity for the Alexandrian text led him to coin such biased terms as *Neutral text* and *non-interpolations*, was willing to suspend his affection for the Old Uncials long enough to allow puzzling internal evidence to have a voice. As a result, Hort accepted a cluster of Western readings in Luke 24 as reflecting the original text of the resurrection narrative. Aland, Metzger, Martini, and others, however, have been less than open-minded.

This effort is not an attempt to revive Hort (certainly some of the methodology employed here would be completely unacceptable to him); it is, however, an attempt to re-open what has been considered to be a shut and closed case for the past twenty years. In the words of Fee, 'more likely the point of wonder is not that we still follow Westcott and Hort, but that they, without our discoveries and advances revealed such remarkable judgments'.[148] Such seems to be

the case with the Western non-interpolations in the Lukan resurrection narrative.

Form Analysis:
Establishing the Shape of Luke 24.50-53

Because of the obvious, characteristic Lukan constructions and
vocabulary and the highly compressed nature of the narrative of
Luke 24.50-53,[149] conclusions about the formal elements of this
passage are difficult to draw.[150] At least four sources have been
suggested as possible antecedents for the form of Luke 24.50-53: OT
theophany stories; commissioning scenes in the Hebrew Bible; Ben
Sira 50; and farewell scenes in the Greek OT and intertestamental
literature.[151]

Old Testament Theophany Stories
John Alsup has argued that the post-resurrection appearance stories
of the Gospel tradition are based on Old Testament anthropomorphic
theophanies.[152] Alsup's evaluation of Luke 24.50-53 as the culmination
of the Lukan appearance story is ambiguous. In his 'Text-Synopsis'
Alsup included Luke 24.50-53 as the conclusion of Luke 24.36-49
and he has argued that the OT *Gattung* 'culminates with a
disappearance or a departure of some sort'.[153]

The conclusions of the major Old Testament theophanies which
Alsup examines, however, reveal few consistent formal elements: in
Gen. 18, both the Lord and Abraham depart; in Exod. 3, 'Moses
went back to Jethro'; in Judg. 6, the angel of the Lord vanishes; in
Judg. 13, the angel of the Lord ascended in the flame of the altar; in
1 Sam. 3, 'Samuel lay until morning'; and in Tob. 12, Tobit and Tobias
'stood up' and saw the angel no more. Alsup admits an 'overall
variety on this point in the theophanies'.[154] Since these theophanies
have no fixed way of ending, it is improbable that Luke 24.50-53
drew its formal characteristics from the OT theophany story.

Primitive Apostolic Commissioning Scene
In a thorough exegetical study of Matt. 28.16-20, B.J. Hubbard
attempted to demonstrate that Matthew's commissioning scene is
patterned after the *Gattung* of commissions in the Hebrew Bible.[155]
After a detailed analysis of the commissionings in the Law, the
Prophets, and the Writings,[156] Hubbard concluded that the following
formal elements comprised the *Gattung* of the commissioning in the

Hebrew Bible: 1. Introduction; 2. Confrontation; 3. Reaction; 4. Commission; 5. Protest;[157] 6. Reassurance; 7. Conclusion.[158] Hubbard detects many of the elements of this seven-part *Gattung* in the commissioning scenes found in Matt. 28.16-20, Pseudo-Mark 16.14-20, Luke 24.36-53, and John 20.19-23. In this schematization, only Luke contains as many as six parts of the commissioning scene form; only the protest is missing.

Germane to our subject is Hubbard's treatment of the last of these elements, the Conclusion, for it is here obviously that he included Luke 24.50-53. Hubbard argued: 'The commission usually concludes in a more or less formal way, most often with a statement that the one commissioned starts to carry out his work'.[159] In fact, of the three canonical commissioning scenes, only Luke has the concluding element.[160] Yet, in Luke, the disciples do not immediately assume the task for which they have been commissioned—the characteristic behavior of the commissionees in the OT narratives. This activity must wait until Pentecost. For these reasons, Hubbard concluded with regard to the commissioning scene in the canonical Gospels: 'We think, therefore, that it is impossible to tell if there was a CONC [conclusion] in the proto-commissioning'.[161]

More recently, Hubbard has focused his attention on the commissioning accounts in Luke–Acts in light of commissioning stories in the LXX and other ancient Near Eastern texts.[162] While it may be unclear whether the proto-commissioning tradition inherited by the Gospel writers has a typical concluding element, it is obvious from Hubbard's study that Luke almost always provides a conclusion to each of these commissioning stories.[163] In fact, according to Hubbard's statistics, 92% of the commissioning scenes in Luke–Acts contain a concluding element.[164] Luke's christophany to the disciples in Luke 24.36-49 is concluded by the departure of Jesus in 24.50-53.[165] A closer examination of the concluding elements in Luke–Acts, however, fails to demonstrate any schematized way which Luke used to conclude the commissioning stories.[166]

Two inferences may be drawn from this data. First, it is unclear, perhaps unlikely, that Luke's proto-commissioning story included a concluding element.[167] Second, though Luke habitually provides a conclusion for his commissioning pericopae, there is no evidence that this conclusion follows any type of consistent pattern which Luke may have borrowed from OT commissioning stories. From the evidence—or lack of it—I am inclined to think that the proto-commissioning scene employed by the Evangelists did not contain a concluding element like those of the commissioning accounts in the Hebrew Bible,[168] and that Luke was forced to look elsewhere for the type-scene with which to end his Gospel.

Wisdom of Ben Sira

The similarity between the departure scene in Luke 24 and the liturgy of Simon the highpriest, with which Ben Sira ends his catena of heroes of Israel (Sir. 50.20-22, cf. Sir. 44ff.) has been frequently noted.[169] To be sure, the formal parallelism between these two passages is quite remarkable (see Table 3 below).

Table 3

Comparison of Sir. 50.20-22 and Luke 24.50-53

Sir. 50.20-22	Luke 24.50-53
τότε καταβὰς ἐπῆρεν χεῖρας αὐτοῦ	καὶ ἐπάρας τὰς χεῖρας αὐτοῦ
ἐπὶ πᾶσαν ἐκκλησίαν υἱῶν ' Ισραὴλ	
δοῦναι εὐλογίαν κυρίου ἐκ χειλέων	εὐλόγησεν αὐτούς...
αὐτοῦ	
καὶ ἐν ὀνόματι αὐτοῦ καυχήσασθαι	
καὶ ἐδευτέρωσαν ἐν προσκυνήσει	[καὶ αὐτοὶ προσκυνήσαντες]
ἐπιδέξασθαι τὴν εὐλογίαν	
παρὰ ὑψίστου.	
καὶ νῦν εὐλογήσατε τὸν θεὸν πάντων	εὐλογοῦντες τὸν θεόν

Similar formal elements include: the raising of hands in a levitical gesture (cf. also Lev. 9.22), the blessing, and the respondents' praise of God.[170] P.A. van Stempvoort suggested that Ben Sira's description of the liturgy of Simon the high priest served as 'the literary background of Luke's description of the last Christophany'.[171] Of particular interest is the twofold use of εὐλογέω in both passages: the first describes the blessing of the people by the 'priest' (Sir. 50.21; Luke 24.50b); the second describes human praise of God (Sir. 50.22; Luke 24.53). R.J. Dillon has argued: 'The parallel εὐλογίαι in 24.50b and 53 involve a combination of two senses of εὐλογεῖν that is perhaps the surest sign of our author's literary dependency upon Ben Sira'.[172]

In fact, Dillon has pressed for the judgment that 'a conjunction of elements unites the two passages and seems to require more than a merely formal parallelism between them'.[173] Such close resemblance between these two passages has led Dillon to find not only a shared form but a shared function as well: 'the scenes have the same function of a solemn, impressive conclusion in each instance; and not just a literary conclusion at that, since each brings *sacred history's course to a climax* affecting the author and his readers in the present'.[174]

To argue, however, that there is significant literary parallelism between Luke and Ben Sira is one thing; to argue that Luke consciously used Ben Sira as the conceptual background for the conclusion to the Gospel is quite another. The kind of literary dependence where Ben Sira is fixed as the conceptual (as well as formal) framework which Luke utilizes to end the Gospel seems to be drawing conclusions which the evidence cannot sustain. To seek Luke's motives by probing the intent of Sir. 44-50 does not seem to be the most profitable way of understanding the force of this passage. Therefore, the judgments of van Stempvoort and Lohfink who simply note the formal characteristics shared between Ben Sira and Luke appear more reasonable. Furthermore, the significance of the passage for Luke will be sought by understanding how the passage functions in its narrative context, not simply by measuring the degree to which it is possibly patterned on another source.

Death and Departure Scenes

A significant pattern of common elements in the departure scenes which follow OT farewell addresses may be detected also in Luke 24.50-53. Johannes Munck in a short essay, 'Discours d'adieu dans le Nouveau Testament et dans la littérature biblique', attempted to show that several NT passages, including Luke 24.36-53, were based on the farewell addresses of the OT narratives.[175] He suggested:

> On peut dire que la littérature du judaïsme tardif . . . du salaire et de la punition, alors que les discours d'adieu du N.T., qui ont quelques parallèles dans l'A.T. et dans le judaïsme, rappellent la vie de celui qui s'en va et les circonstances que les survivants ont vécues avec lui. Sa conduite demeure un exemple, qu'il s'agisse de Jésus ou de ses apôtres.[176]

Munck's work is of limited value to us. First, he is chiefly interested in the *content* of the farewell speeches, i.e. the monologue/dialogue of the dying or departing hero, not the narration which follows the last testament. Second, Munck's position has been criticized, particularly in reference to the last testament character of the post-resurrection appearance story in Luke.[177] More helpful, perhaps, is the recent work of William Kurz.[178] Kurz's thesis is that 'Luke 22.14-38 imitates biblical farewell speeches for readers in a Hellenistic culture'.[179] After a convincing presentation of the connections between the form of Jesus' last supper discourse in Luke and the farewell addresses of biblical heroes, Kurz makes the following comment:

> Luke had deferred from chap. 22 the usual blessing at the end of a farewell speech (e.g. 1 Macc. 2.69) and notice of death and mourning (e.g. 1 Macc. 2.70). The blessing comes before the risen Jesus departs at the end of the Gospel (Luke 24.50-51). Luke's is the only Gospel to mention the people mourning after Jesus' death (Luke 23.48). This is not to claim Luke is imitating 1 Macc. 2.69-70 in Luke 24.50-51 and 23.48. But one can suggest that similar elements of farewell addresses have influenced both the Lucan and Maccabean passages.[180]

A more detailed analysis of the narrative conclusions of these farewell addresses strengthens Kurz's suggestion. Upon closer examination several common elements shared by most of these stories emerged: (1) A summary statement following the farewell address proper in which the narrator reaffirms the *act* of blessing or commissioning, rather than the *content* of the blessing (BLESS); (2) The farewell scene in which the hero either departs or dies (DPT); (3) The response of the witnesses, usually of grief and mourning (RESP); (4) An act of obedience or piety, usually fulfilling a death wish by the departing hero (most usually, but not always, involving burial) (OBED). What follows in Table 4 is an examination of these formal elements in the conclusions to a number of farewell scenes found in the Old Testament and Jewish intertestamental literature, as well as one NT pericope.

Robert Alter has noted that one of the most common biblical type-scenes is that of the dying hero's last testament.[181] Several elements in this final departure scene are shared in common with Luke 24.50-53. It contains the blessing (24.50-51), the departure (24.51), the response of the witnesses (24.52b), and the act of obedience (24.52a; cf. 24.49). Luke clothes this final departure scene in liturgical vestments by framing it with language reminiscent of Sir. 50.20-22 in the 'raising of the hands' and the blessing of God by the disciples.[182]

Table 4

Text	BLESS	DPT	RESP	OBED
Genesis 49–50	X (49.28)	X (49.33)	X (50.1)	X (50.7)
Deuteronomy 33–34	X (33.1)	X (34.5)	X (34.8)	X (34.9)
Joshua 24	X (24.25)	X (24.29)		X (24.30)
1 Macc. 2.69–3.1	X (2.69a)	X (2.69b)	X (2.70b)	X (3.1)
Tobit 14.3-12	X (14.11b)	X (14.11c)		X (14.12bc)
Jubilees 22.11–23.7	X (22.25)	X (23.1)	X (23.5)	X (23.7)
Jubilees 45.14-15	X (45.14)	X (45.15a)		X (45.15b)
T. *Joseph*[a] 20	X (20.4a)	X (20.4b)	X (20.5)	X (20.6)
Ps-Philo *Bib. Ant.* 33	X (33.4)	X (33.6a)	X (33.6c)	X (33.6b)
Acts 20.36–21.1	X (20.36)	X (21.1)	X (20.37)	X (20.38b)

[a]One should note here that in *The Testament of the Twelve Patriarchs*, all twelve narratives contain the blessing, departure and act of obedience (except T. Issachar), but only the Testament of Joseph contains the response of mourning. This act of reverence on the part of all of Egypt and Israel is reserved for the most famous and important of the twelve patriarchs. This is true despite the fact that the death of Joseph in the biblical account does not record any response—mourning or otherwise—on the part of those present (Gen. 50.26). That mourning over death was a true sign of greatness may be seen in Philo's comment in *De Vita Mosis*, II, 291, where he extols the life of Moses as king, lawgiver, high priest, and prophet by showing the marks of greatness, one of which was that 'all the nation wept and mourned for him a whole month and made open display, private and public, of their sorrow, in memory of his vast benevolence and watchful care for each one of them and for all'.

These common elements would cause the readers familiar with other farewell scenes to prepare for the departure of Jesus.

One could go a step further and suggest that Luke has taken the response element of the last blessing type-scene and given it a surprising twist. The reader who is familiar with the farewell scenes of Jewish literature expects the disciples to react to Jesus' departure with remorse and grief, or at least with a healthy dose of fear mixed with wonder (cf. 24.37). Instead, the disciples return immediately and obediently to Jerusalem 'with great joy'! This message arrests the reader who expects the conventional response of grief, only to find that sorrow turned to joy.[183] As Alter has noted:

> Instead of relegating every perceived recurrence in the text to the limbo of duplicate sources or fixed folkloric archetypes, we may begin to see that the resurgence of certain pronounced patterns at certain narrative junctures was conventionally anticipated, even counted on, and that against that ground of anticipation the biblical authors sent words, motifs, themes, personages, and actions into an elaborate dance of significant innovation.[184]

While such a proposal that Luke 24.50-53 is 'an elaborate dance of significant innovation' of a common biblical type-scene is highly suggestive, it might also be criticized for being highly imaginative. The most obvious difference in the farewell scenes and Luke 24.50-53 is that Jesus does not die, he simply departs. That this exception is possible for Luke is evidenced by the attention that Acts 20.17-38 has drawn as a farewell address, even though Paul also departs and does not die.[185]

Since neither of the two most likely candidates for the *Gattung* of Luke 24.50-53, the OT theophany and the commissioning story, had a fixed pattern of conclusion, Luke was forced to look elsewhere to bring his final story to a proper dénouement. Having already used the form of the biblical farewell address in Luke 22, it is most natural that he return there at the end of his Gospel. By delaying the concluding elements to this point in the narrative, Luke is able to tie the entire passion, resurrection, and departure of Jesus into an *inclusio* introduced by the farewell address of Luke 22 and concluded by the departure of Jesus in the pattern of a departing hero in Luke 24.[186]

Source Analysis:
Establishing the Origins of Luke 24.50-53

The traditional elements of the recognition scene (Luke 24.36-43) and the commission to the disciples (Luke 24.44-49) have been clearly demonstrated by a number of different scholars.[187] The bifurcated schema of recognition and commission is well established in the resurrection tradition, being found in Matt. 28.16-20, John 20.19-23 (the main parallels to Luke 24.36-49), as well as Matt. 28.9-10, John 21.1-23, and John 20.14-18. Whether or not Luke 24.50-53 is a pre-Lukan tradition reworked by the Evangelist or the purely compositional creation of Luke, however, is a question which may never be fully resolved. Dillon has clearly articulated the source-critical problem of Luke 24.50-53: 'The bipartite schema [of recognition and commissioning] is clearly well established in the tradition, quite independently of Luke. On the other hand, in none of the [other] accounts ... is the disappearance or departure of the Lord recorded'.[188]

Lohfink has concluded that 'die Abschiedsszene Lk 24, 50-53 ursprünglich nicht zu der Erscheinung Jesu vor allen Jüngern gehört hat, sondern erst von Lukas angefügt wurde'.[189] While Lohfink based much of his discussion on the longer ascension text, most of his argument is pertinent regardless of which text is selected. The commonality of Luke 24.44-49 with the other commissioning scenes (Matt. 28.9-10, 16-20; John 20.14-18, 19-23, 26-29; 21.1-23) has already been discussed. Lohfink has noted that all these passages end with the words of the Resurrected One. Unlike Luke, there is no interest on the part of other evangelists in recording the departure of the Lord. This phenomenon is also true where other heavenly beings appear. Matt. 1.20f., 2.13f., 28.2-7, Mark 16.5-7, John 20.12f., all fail to record the departure of the heavenly apparition.[190]

Luke, according to Lohfink, consistently records the departure or disappearance of angels or heavenly personages. Luke 1.38, 2.15, 9.33, 24.31; Acts. 10.7, 12.10 all record the leave-taking of heavenly visitor(s) (see Table 5 overleaf).[191]

Such evidence led Lohfink to conclude that attaching departures to apparitions is a Lukan habit. He maintained: 'Innerhalb der neutestamentlichen Literatur ist also diese Art, eine Erscheinung abzuschliessen, typisch lukanisch'.[192]

Lohfink's incisive evaluation has drawn widespread support. Several minor objections, however, could be lodged against his

Table 5

Departure of Heavenly Personages in Luke

Luke	1.38	'and the angel departed from her'.
Luke	2.15	'as the angels went away from them into heaven . . .'
Luke	9.33	'while they were departing from him . . .'
Luke	24.31	'and he became invisible from them'.
Acts	10.7	'when the angel who had spoken to him had departed . . .'
Acts	12.10	'and immediately the angel departed from him'.

evidence and the conclusions he has drawn from it. First, the Lukan habit of describing the withdrawal of heavenly apparitions is not nearly so consistent as Lohfink seems to suggest. In several instances, those which Luke ostensibly intended to be understood as heavenly or supernatural characters do not depart.

The first such example may be found in the first appearance of a heavenly messenger in Luke 1.11. Here an angel of the Lord appears to Zechariah while he is burning incense in the temple. After an exchange between the two, Zechariah emerges from the holy place, with no mention of the angel (Luke 1.22). Similar scenes of divine beings and their 'failure' to depart may be found in Acts 5.19, 8.26, and 12.23.

Another example may be found in the resurrection narrative at Luke 24.7. According to the analysis presented by Lohfink, one would expect the two men in dazzling apparel to depart after proclaiming the kerygma to the women. But, in fact, they do not disappear. Likewise in Acts 1.11, the two men in white apparel do not leave after their encounter with the disciples. In both these instances, the witnesses—in Luke the women who see the empty tomb and in Acts the disciples who observe the ascension—depart, leaving the heavenly messengers to fade into the background.[193] Thus, these examples at least demonstrate that Luke was not as consistent in exiting his heavenly characters from the stage as Lohfink thought.[194]

It is possible that Luke has not included the departure of the two men because their exit is not necessary to the movement of the story. In both instances, the earthly witnesses take the initiative to leave. The exit of the women back to the disciples (Luke 24.9) and the disciples back to the upper room (Acts 1.12) may serve as sufficient transition. While this might be true, one would then be hard-pressed to explain why Luke found it necessary to record the departure of Jesus in Luke 24.31 and Luke 24.51, the first of which is followed by the movement of Cleopas and his nameless companion and the second by the retreat of the disciples into Jerusalem.

A second minor argument may be registered against Lohfink. Heavenly beings are not the only characters who typically, though as we have seen, not consistently, end a scene with their departure. In fact, such departures, whether by angelic figures, disciples, minor characters, or Jesus himself, appear to be a convenient way for Luke to change from one scene to another. Several words are used to describe the Lukan characters: ἀπέρχομαι, ἀφίστημι, and—χωρίζω. Zechariah goes home (Luke 1.23); Jesus withdraws to pray (5.16); the messengers of John withdraw (7.24); the robbers in the Parable of the Good Samaritan depart, leaving the traveler half dead (10.30); Ananias departs (Acts 9.17); the Jews depart (28.29).[195]

Such criticisms are marshalled, not to disprove Luke's interest in the final destination of his heavenly personages, but simply to warn against pressing the evidence too far. Lohfink is surely correct when he asserts that the placement of a departure of Jesus scene after the appearance to the disciples is a redactional seam created by the author.[196] To move from arguing that the linking of the appearance story with the departure scene is redactional to claiming, as Lohfink seems to do, that the departure scene itself is a Lukan composition is moving beyond what the evidence can sustain. Lohfink's conclusion, in large measure, is based on the departure stories of other Lukan heavenly personages, which we have seen are not nearly so consistent in the Gospel as Lohfink suggests. Here I agree with Dillon's conclusion that Lohfink's arguments

> which are effective as far as they go, do not settle the issue of tradition vs. redaction in the final scene itself, vv. 50-53. At most they show that any quest for a pre-Lucan foundation of the scene should concentrate on the passage itself, since one cannot assume it originated of a pre-Lucan christophany account comprised of recognition and mission.[197]

Source analysis of Luke 24.50-53 has generally resulted in several distinct conclusions. There are those who argue that Luke inherited an ascension tradition and certain traditional elements are still recoverable.[198] *Bethany* (Luke 24.50) is often identified as evidence of a pre-Lukan traditional element,[199] yet even here there may be literary and theological reasons for mentioning Bethany as the site of Jesus' departure.[200] Then, of course, there is the suggestion by Lohfink that the passage was a literary conclusion with a literary origin.[201]

Perhaps the most satisfactory assessment of Luke 24.50-53 is the conclusion of Bultmann: 'Jesus' Farewell is also a literary creation, which Luke may have had on hand'.[202] I take this to mean that Luke may have known of a departure or ascension tradition but the redactional hand is so heavy in Luke 24.50-53 that whatever the traditional elements, they are beyond recovery. As Dillon has noted:

> the case for pre-Lucan tradition here is too meagre to argue successfully ... if Luke had any predecessor in narrating the Lord's visible ascension ... we should rather explore Acts 1, 9-11 for traces of such an antecedent account, rather than posit them here in the gospel's finale.[203]

Taking Dillon's suggestion one step further, I conclude that Luke 24.50-53, while not an independent witness of an ascension tradition (on either text- or source-critical grounds), may best be explained as the result of an ascension scene which was transmitted through the tradition and compressed in the Gospel to construct a leave-taking scene along the lines of a biblical farewell account, and expanded in Acts by formal elements of heavenly assumption stories. The evidence and arguments for this conclusion are given in the source analysis of Acts 1.1-11 in Chapter 4.

Conclusion

This diachronic analysis of Luke 24.50-53 has enabled us to place the pericope in several different contexts. First, through text-critical analysis, the attempt was made to establish the text which best reflects the original text and which will serve as the foundation for the remaining investigations of this study. Through form-critical analysis, the conclusion was reached that the departure of Jesus in Luke was shaped along the contours of a biblical farewell scene. Source-critical probes, while yielding no definitive results, seem to suggest that Luke is the first to join a departure scene with a post-resurrection appearance narrative. The origins of the departure scene itself, however, are less clear. While certainly not a convincing witness to a primitive ascension narrative, the farewell scene of Jesus in Luke has too easily been dismissed as purely the compositional creation of the author. It is plausible, at least, that for literary and theological reasons, Luke shaped an ascension story inherited from primitive tradition into a final departure scene in Luke 24.50-53 and a heavenly-assumption story, complete with apocalyptic stage-props, in Acts 1.[204] At any rate, whatever pristine tradition may have existed prior to Luke is irrecoverable from the heavily redacted passage in Luke 24.50-53.

Chapter 3

LUKE 24.50-53 IN NARRATIVE CONTEXT:
A SYNCHRONIC ANALYSIS

In the now oft quoted words of B.H. Streeter, the author of Luke–
Acts was 'a consummate literary artist'.[1] The majestic artistry of
Luke was recognized as early as the eighth century when the Third
Evangelist was credited with being a patron of the painters' guild,
and a painter himself.[2] More recent efforts to understand the literary
genius of Luke have been admirably chronicled by C.H. Talbert.[3]
What follows is a summary of scholarship on Luke–Acts since
Talbert's work was published in 1974.[4]

History of Scholarship

Talbert has shown that probes into the sources behind the Third
Gospel,[5] critical analyses of the redactional activity of the Evangelist,[6]
and apologetics regarding the historical reliability of Luke–Acts,[7]
overshadowed the work of those like Henry J. Cadbury who were
sensitive to the literary achievements of Luke–Acts.[8] The distance
which redaction criticism in particular had led New Testament
scholars away from the literary concerns of style, vocabulary, and
parallels may be seen by noting that Hans Conzelmann's seminal
work, *Die Mitte der Zeit*, contained only one passing reference to
Cadbury's *The Making of Luke–Acts*.

Renewed Interest in Luke as a Literary Artist
In the last decade, a new wave of interest in Luke the *littérateur* has
broken on the Luke–Acts scene. Talbert himself, in a sense
representing the older 'New Criticism', spearheaded this renewed
concern for the Gospel as literature. He employed what he termed
architecture analysis to 'detect the formal patterns, rhythms,

architectonic designs, or architecture of a writing'.[9]

The degree to which Talbert has finally eschewed traditional redactional studies may be seen from the fact that in *Reading Luke*, he made no references whatsoever to *The Theology of St. Luke* and mentioned Conzelmann only once.[10] While his literary method is older than the one espoused here, Talbert's sensitivity to the literary quality of Luke-Acts is much appreciated. More recent works based on the fruits of secular literary theory, however, have proven to be more immediately helpful.

Narrative Criticism
Most recently, an increasing number of New Testament scholars are employing the insights and methodologies of secular literary theory to the Gospel texts. This new narrative criticism has shown much promise for the understanding of the text and the ways in which the text shapes its readers. Recent books by David Rhoads and Donald Michie, *Mark as Story*, and R. Alan Culpepper, *The Anatomy of the Fourth Gospel*, have attempted to apply this literary theory in a rigorous and consistent way to the narratives of Mark and John respectively. Numerous articles and a spate of dissertations are being rushed to publishers and printers. A journal, *Semeia*, was established to 'serve as a vehicle for innovative work in progress and for communication among workers in all aspects of language running from literary criticism to linguistics'.[11] In Lukan studies, one might mention Luke Johnson's *The Literary Function of Possessions in Luke-Acts* and the recent work by Robert J. Karris, *Luke: Artist and Theologian: Luke's Passion Account as Literature*.[12] Even more recent are Joseph Tyson's *The Death of Jesus in Luke-Acts* and Robert Tannehill's *The Narrative Unity of Luke-Acts*.[13]

There is no need to explore this recent development in biblical research. The concern here is to apply the appropriate methods of literary theory to the ascension narrative in a way which might illuminate its function as an ending to the Gospel, and its relation to the resolution of the plot of the Third Gospel.

Literary Theory and Closure in Fiction
Aristotle once defined an artistic whole simply as 'that which has a beginning, a middle, and an end'.[14] The ending has always been a requisite element in the composition of a narrative. The way stories end has always intrigued readers, listeners, and viewers. Who has not

had their experience of watching a film ruined by one who has already seen the movie and 'gives away' the ending? Begin to tell a story to an ordinary hearer and the plea not to reveal the outcome or 'punchline' is predictable. Reading a good book most often entails resisting the temptation to turn to the conclusion and see how it turns out.

Works prior to 1967

In 1884, the novelist Henry James lamented that novels were considered to be 'good' only if they had a 'happy ending' which was nothing more than 'a distribution at the last of prizes, pensions, husbands, wives, babies, millions, appended paragraphs, and cheerful remarks'.[15] According to E.M. Forster, a story's only merit is 'that of making the audience want to know what happened next'[16]—a curiosity which must only be resolved by the ending.

Despite these passing references to the significance of endings, it has been only recently that literary critics have turned their attention toward the task of developing a methodology which allows critical examination of the significance of endings of narratives. Réné Girard published *Mensonge romantique et vérité romanesque* in 1961. The work appeared in English translation, *Deceit, Desire, and the Novel*, in 1965.[17] Girard went so far as to claim that all narrative endings could be reduced to two fundamental categories: 'those conclusions which portray a solitary hero who rejoins other men and those which portray a "gregarious" hero gaining solitude'.[19] In his attempt to regulate literary conclusions, Girard maintained that any differences between novelistic conclusions are 'less a question of opposition than of a shift of accent'.[20]

Girard's conclusions are badly flawed for two reasons. First, his concern to synthesize and categorize 'novelistic conclusions' forced him to overlook significant differences in the way narratives end.[21] Second, Girard is guilty of a converse fallacy of accident; that is, he has drawn general conclusions from too few specific examples. Only selected novels by Stendahl, Dostoyevsky, and Proust are used to bolster his argument; yet he has summarized the nature of all narrative closure.

Alan Friedman published *The Turn of the Novel* in 1966. The turn of the novel, for Friedman, occurred when the closed endings of nineteenth-century novels yielded to the 'open-ended' nature of their twentieth-century counterparts. Friedman stated: 'My theme and argument in this book is the existence in the novel of a gradual historical shift from a closed form to an open form'.[22] Friedman's work, while helpful in many respects, is colored by his polemical attempts to justify 'open-ended' twentieth-century novels as possessing 'truer endings' which are 'either an ever-widening disorder or a finally open "order" which embraces all the opposed directions on whatever ethical compass it has brought along for the trip'.[23] When we come to the Gospel of Luke, insights gleaned from Friedman on narrative closure will be employed, but with a certain amount of caution because of the particular concerns which shape his arguments.

Works after 1967
Frank Kermode maade significant contribution to the study of closure in his 1965 Mary Flexner Lectures delivered at Bryn Mawr College.[24] According to one scholar, 'Much discussion of the subject [closure] was spurred by the publication of Frank Kermode's lectures on *The Sense of an Ending* in 1967, which explored endings posited by literature and myth'.[25]

Kermode's work, while important, is more concerned with describing humanity's need to provide closure in socio-cultural terms. Close analysis of literary texts, with the exception of Sartre's *La Nausée*, is missing. Therefore, *The Sense of an Ending* is less than helpful in our attempts to describe the specific closural techniques of the Third Gospel.[26]

Barbara Herrnstein Smith published *Poetic Closure* in 1968, in which she argued that closure in poetry has 'the sense of finality, stability, and integrity' and 'has an effect that depends primarily upon the reader's experience of the structure of the entire poem'.[27] While Smith's work focused almost exclusively on poetry, she does include a brief section on narrative fiction.[28] She has attempted to provide a non-polemical terminology and methodology for studying closure in poetry. In fact, much of the vocabulary she employs in her discussion of poetry has found its way into the terminology of those concerned with closure in fiction.[29]

David Richter's *Fable's End: Completeness and Closure in Rhetorical Fiction*, published in 1974, was the next major work dealing with closure in fiction. Richter's study dealt with rhetorical fictions (fables and apologues) which he considered to be a significant subgenre of the contemporary novel. His stated purpose was to examine 'the architectonic principles of coherence, completeness, and closure in a group of novels whose structure is generated not by plot but by doctrines, themes, attitudes, or theses'.[30] Richter has drawn heavily from Smith, particularly from her definition of closure. Unlike Girard and Friedman, who examined the problem of openness, Richter was concerned to explore the significance of closure, which he understood as 'the sense of recounting a completed process of change, either in external circumstances or in internal consciousness, taking place in the protagonists'.[31] Richter's examination of the techniques in rhetorical fiction whereby the reader is given the sense of completeness is helpful to us in the search for the literary devices which Luke employs to bring closure to his Gospel.

In 1978, the University of California Press published a special issue on 'Narrative Endings' in the journal *Nineteenth-Century Fiction*, which was later reprinted as a book.[32] The first and last articles are the most significant. The first, 'The Problematic of Ending in Narrative', by J. Hillis Miller suggested that 'the notion of ending in narrative is inherently "undecidable"'.[33] Miller stated the futility of the problem in this way:

> Attempts to characterize the fiction of a given period by its commitment to closure or to open-endedness are blocked from the beginning by the impossibility of ever demonstrating whether a given narrative is closed or open. Analysis of endings leads always, if carried far enough, to the paralysis of this inability to decide.[34]

Fortunately, Frank Kermode, at the end of these essays, is able to write in response to Miller: 'Clearly this matter is not at an end when pronounced undecidable, for we have here a strong and constructive group of essays, and may move towards decision, even if we don't get there'.[35]

The Closural Model of Marianna Torgovnick

Commenting on these articles, Marianna Torgovnick has claimed that the issue, *Narrative Endings*, 'indicates a continuing preoccupation with endings; at the same time, it reveals the lack of any consistent framework within which to describe narrative endings, and even the lack of any shared sense of what an ending is'.[36] Torgovnick has attempted to resolve these problems in vocabulary, definition, and methodology by proposing 'flexible, non-polemical ways to describe endings and strategies of closure'.[37] She has noted the importance of endings for studies in narrative fiction:

> In any narrative, 'what happens next' ceases to be a pertinent

question only at the conclusion, and the word 'end' in a novel
consequently carries with it not just the notion of the turnable last
page, but also that of the 'goal' of reading, the finish-line toward
which our bookmarks aim. In long works of fiction, endings are
important for another commonplace but true reason: it is difficult
to recall all of a work after a completed reading, but climactic
moments, dramatic scenes, and beginnings and endings remain in
the memory and decisively shape our sense of a novel as a
whole.[38]

Torgovnick is interested in the shape of fictions, that is, the 'formal
relationship of ending to beginning and middle'.[39] Such examination
requires the study of novelistic closure as well as novelistic endings.
For Torgovnick, closure 'designates the process by which a novel
reaches an adequate and appropriate conclusion ... a sense that
nothing necessary has been omitted from a work'.[40]

To facilitate such study, Torgovnick has created a vocabulary to
delineate four categories which describe the significant relationships
influencing closure. These terms describe: (1) 'the relationship of
ending to beginning and middle, to the shape of the fiction';[41] (2) 'the
author's and the reader's viewpoint on the novel's characters and
major action at the novel's end';[42] (3) 'the relationship between
author and reader during closure';[43] (4) 'the author's relationship to
his own ideas during closure, to indicate the degree of his self-
awareness and of his control over the closural process'.[44]

The last set of terms requires consideration of extratextual
information (biographical, autobiographical, or otherwise) and
statements of intention. Since the author of Luke–Acts has left no
such literary remains, this category will receive little consideration in
the following analysis. The other three sets of terms correspond to
what literary theorists have typically labeled (1) plot, (2) point of
view and focalization, and (3) reader response. Torgovnick's model,
coupled with salient discussion by other literary critics, will provide
the needed vocabulary, techniques, and framework to discuss Luke
24.50-53 in its narrative context.[45]

Two terms are employed by Torgovnick to describe successful
closural strategies: circularity and parallelism. *Circularity* is the
controlling closural strategy when 'the ending of a novel clearly
recalls the beginning in language, in situation, in the grouping of
characters, or in several of these ways'.[46] *Parallelism* as a closural
device occurs 'when language, situation, or the grouping of characters
refers not just to the beginning of the work but to a series of points in
the text'.[47]

Two other terms are used to describe closural strategies which produce ambiguity or openness. *Linkage* is the term employed by Torgovnick to describe the ending which 'links the novel not to its own beginning and middle, but to the body of another, often as yet unwritten, novel'.[48] *Incompletion* 'omits one or more crucial elements necessary for full circularity or parallelism'.[49] Following a brief discussion of the definition of plot in literary theory, Luke 24.50-53 will be examined in light of strategies of closure and openness, using Torgovnick's categories of circularity and parallelism in discussing closure, and incompleteness and linkage in describing openness.

Below is an attempt to understand the closing pericope of Luke's Gospel in the context of the whole narrative. Torgovnick's model of closure will be employed with the following words of caution in mind: 'A theoretical framework for the discussion of closure can help us define particular contents and effects, but cannot, in itself, substitute for practical critical analyses, and for the kinds of fine distinctions called for by a given text'.[50] Following a brief discussion of the theoretical underpinnings, then, a close reading of Luke 24.50-53 in light of Torgovnick's framework will be undertaken.

Closure and Plot Development in Literary Theory

In order to analyze closure, Torgovnick proposed that 'we first need a set of terms to describe the relationship of ending to beginning and middle, to the shape of the fiction'.[51] This relationship of the ending to the shape of the fiction is generally couched in literary theorists' discussion of plot. Though the term *plot* is as old as Aristotle,[52] consensus regarding definition of the term is sorely lacking. E.M. Forster proposed one of the first and simplest definitions of plot when he related plot to causality: '"The king died and then the queen died"' is a story. "The king died, and then the queen died of grief", is a plot. The time-sequence is preserved, but the sense of causality overshadows it'.[53]

Shlomith Rimmon-Kenan objected to Forster's definition: 'there is nothing to prevent a causally-minded reader from supplementing Forster's first example with the causal link that would make it into an implicit plot'.[54] This sense of causality, while important, is hardly a sufficient explanation of plot. R.S. Crane, likewise resisting Forster's one-dimensional definition of plot, has suggested that there are *plots of action* in which the situation of the protagonist changes gradually or suddenly, *plots of character* in which the moral character of the protagonist experiences change, and *plots of thought* in which the change occurs in the thought or feelings of the protagonist.[55]

Frank Kermode compared plot to the tick-tock of a clock, though he willingly admitted: 'Tick is a humble genesis, tock a feeble apocalypse; and tick-tock is in any case not much of a plot'.[56] In a stimulating article, Kieran Egan likened the relationship of plot-to-story to that of syntax-to-sentence. He claimed: 'Put briefly, it seems that plots do not simply organize events, they *determine* them; that is, plotting involves determining the nature of the units that shall compose any particular story'.[57] M.H. Abrams has succinctly defined the plot of a narrative as 'the structure of its actions, as these are ordered and rendered toward achieving particular emotional and artistic effects'.[58] And finally Culpepper has sought to understand plot in terms of the narrative's sequence, casuality, unity, and affective power.[59]

In the face of such divergent opinion and lack of any universal definition, one might be inclined to share Rimmon-Kenan's recalcitrance in employing the term: 'If I use "plot" at all—and I am rather wary of a term which has become too vague in ordinary critical usage—I take it to designate one type of story (the type which emphasizes causality) rather than a narrative form opposed to the story'.[60] Culpepper has rightly suggested that a Gospel does indeed have a plot, though it is best to discover the contours of that plot by walking the landscape for oneself.[61] To try to impose categories *a priori* on the Gospels would rob each of its full-orbed plot and story-line. Accepting in this essay the rather minimalist definition that plot is shaped by the sequence, causality, and unity of events, it is still best to heed Philip Stevick's caution:

> Plot can be a useful category only when the word enters the critical vocabulary neutral of values ... so that the word designates something of the total work, in all of its uniqueness, complexity and power.[62]

Closure and Plot Development in Luke

The crucial importance of a work's conclusion for its plotting or story-line is well-known. According to Rimmon-Kenan, 'causality and closure (i.e. a sense of completion) may be the most interesting features of stories, and the features on which their quality as stories is most often judged'.[63] Kermode has suggested that any plot 'presupposes and requires that an end will bestow upon the whole duration and meaning'.[64] Similarly, Edgar Allan Poe remarked:

> It is only with the denouement constantly in view that we can give a plot its indispensable air of consequence, of causation, by making the incidents, and especially the tone at all points, tend to the development of the intention.[65]

Unfortunately at times this high regard for the place of closure or conclusions in a narrative led to overstatement and distortion. Noted literary critic, Réné Girard has written:

> Truth is active throughout the great novel but its primary location is in the conclusion. The conclusion is the temple of that truth. The conclusion is the site of the presence of truth, and therefore a place avoided by error.[66]

Before accepting the 'indispensable' significance of the ending as the 'temple of truth', however, one should hear the caveat of D.A. Miller who suggested 'closure never has the totalizing powers of organization that these critics claim for it . . . My real argument, of course, is not that novels do not "build" toward closure, but that they are never fully or finally governed by it'.[67] Miller provides a helpful admonishment which prevents finding closural techniques too easily without at least acknowledging that the Gospel narrative may not conclude so neatly.[68] In examining the ending of Luke's Gospel, then, the various narrative strategies of closure and openness in some of the major plot lines will be exposed; however, the strong sense of closure will not obscure the fact that there are a number of narrative strands that remain ungathered even at the end of the story.

Circularity
Circularity, that is, the recalling at the end of a story of characters, settings, or situations which have not recurred since the beginning, is 'one of the most common of closural patterns'.[69] Indeed, circularity plays an important role in closure of the Third Gospel. The continuity between Luke 1–2 and the rest of the Gospel has been firmly established. Paul Minear and Raymond E. Brown, among others, have labored successfully to dismiss the interpolation theory popularized by Conzelmann and others.[70] Although similarities between the beginning and the end of the Gospel have been noted, there has been no systematic attempt to examine the relationship between the two—certainly not from the perspective of providing closure to the Gospel.

It is important to establish parameters for investigation at the outset. Torgovnick claimed the word *ending* 'straightforwardly designates the last definable unit of work—section, scene, chapter, page, paragraph, sentence—whichever seems most appropriate for a given text'.[71] For present purposes, Luke 24.50-53 will be given priority as the ending of the Gospel. It must be recognized, however, that our pericope is closely associated with the last appearance to the eleven (Luke 24.36-49), which is ultimately an integral part of the resurrection narrative (Luke 24.1-53).

On the other hand, the beginning of the Gospel is obviously the preface (1.1-4). That section is really an attempt to introduce the reader to the story world of Luke and is, in fact, outside the narrative time of the story; the narrative proper does not begin until 1.5 with the story of Zechariah and Elizabeth. Nonetheless, just as Luke 24.50-53 is interwoven into the resurrection narrative, so Luke 1.5-23 is inextricably linked to the remainder of the infancy narrative (chs. 1–2). Therefore, when comparing ending to beginning, first circularity between 24.50-53 and 1.5-23 will be sought. Next the relationship between 24.36-53 and Luke 1–2 will be considered; and finally, similarities in language, situation, and grouping of characters between the infancy and resurrection narratives will be noted. In this way, the specific means by which Luke 24.50-53 brings closure to the Gospel may be delineated; at the same time, sensitivity to the fact that the entire resurrection narrative was designed to give closure to Luke's story of Jesus is not ignored.

Priestly Blessings. In the first episode of the Gospel, Zechariah is incapable of discharging his duties as priest; he is unable to bless the people who patiently await his service. He returns home, unable to speak, task unfinished (1.23). At the end of the Gospel Jesus raises his hands in levitical fashion and blesses his disciples who also are waiting. In effect, Jesus completes what Zechariah could not do: he blesses the people of God. Then, in a sense, Jesus too returns to 'his own home'. Eduard Schweizer commented on Luke 24.51: 'The book ends with Jesus doing what the priest could not do in 1.22: he blesses'.[72] Or as Herman Hendrickx has put it: 'Luke concludes his gospel with the great high priest blessing his community. The blessing means assurance of God's favour and support'.[73]

This completion by Jesus of Zechariah's unfinished priestly rite fits neatly into Torgovnick's understanding of the effect of circularity. Circularity 'may return to the novel's initial themes in order to resolve them . . ., to repeat them . . ., or to reaffirm an ambivalence developed throughout the novel'.[74] Here, of course, the narrator returns to the theme of priestly blessing in order to resolve it.

This understanding of Jesus' gesture in Luke 24.50 does address the major criticism of identifying Jesus' action with that of Zechariah's inaction. Dillon has criticized this position precisely because the motif of Jesus as priest is totally missing from the rest of the Gospel narrative.[75] Fitzmyer may be correct in suggesting that Luke's 'theology is not concerned with Jesus as priest (this is the sole reference to it and it is implicit, rather than explicit)'.[76] If, however, the use of the priestly motif is a literary device of the narrator designed to assist in bringing closure to the narrative, then this particular criticism is empty.[77] In addition, as Fitzmyer rightly observed, the blessing of Jesus is 'a token of his leave-taking', reinforcing the finality of this departure scene.

Returning to Jerusalem. In Luke 24.52 the disciples 'returned to Jerusalem'. While the word *return* (ὑποστρέφω) is common in Luke,[78] the phrase 'returned to Jerusalem' occurs only in the resurrection narrative (24.33, 52) and in the infancy narrative (2.45).[79] In the second chapter, Mary and Joseph, realizing that Jesus is not in the company of the pilgrims homeward bound after the Passover, 'returned to Jerusalem, seeking him'. Both the parents and the travelers on the road to Emmaus return to Jerusalem to be met by a questioning Jesus: 'How is it that you sought me? Did you not know that I must be in my Father's house?' (2.49) and 'Why are you troubled, and why do questionings rise in your hearts? . . . Have you anything to eat?' (24.38, 41). The disciples in Luke 24.52, on the other hand, return to Jerusalem after being with him. The significance of Jerusalem will be discussed below. Suffice it to say that the return to Jerusalem in the first case (24.33) repeats the initial theme in 2.45—finding Jesus in Jerusalem; the second (24.52) moves the reader beyond that point—disciples return to Jerusalem not to seek Jesus, but in obedience to him.[80]

Heavenly Beings. Angels who appear in the infancy narrative (1.11, 26; 2.13) vanish from the narrative, only to reappear in the context of the resurrection narrative.[81] Angels are certainly mentioned in dialogue material in other parts of Luke, mostly eschatological discourse (4.10; 9.26; 12.8, 9; 15.10; 16.22); but they only appear as characters who populate the story in the opening and closing scenes.[82] This phenomenon is interesting when one considers the comparative frequency with which angels appear in Acts (Acts 5.19; 8.26; 10.3, 7; 12.7, 8, 9, 10, 23; 27.23).[83] So angels, in Luke, are heralds proclaiming the coming and going of Jesus and interpreting the significance of those events for the characters and readers. The angels in Luke 24 provide a sense of circularity, and thus complement the closural effect of the Gospel.

The Pious People of God. The opening chapters of the narrative establish the qualities of the people of God. From the people standing outside the temple praying, to the songs of Simeon and Anna inside the temple, to the obedience of Jesus' parents in fulfilling the law, the narrator is establishing what it means to be the people of God. By the end, the disciples have replaced the pious persons of Israel found in the early chapters of the Gospel. The disciples are the ones who are obediently (24.49), joyously (24.52), and continually (24.53) in the temple blessing God. Apart from 1.64, 2.28, and 24.53, the verb εὐλογέω is not used in Luke–Acts with God as object. This circular pattern of closure seems, in Torgovnick's words, 'to reaffirm an ambivalence developed throughout the novel'.[84] To be sure, as the plot develops—particularly through the temple and synagogue conflict scenes—one begins to wonder if Israel, the people of God who have certain privileges with God, is in fact going to lose that privileged status.[85]

The Temple and Jerusalem. Strictly speaking, some references in Luke to the temple fall outside the parameters of the infancy and resurrection narratives.[86] Nonetheless, Luke's two terms for temple are clustered at the beginning and the end (ναός 1.9, 21, 22; 23.45; ἱερόν 2.27, 37, 46; 4.9; 19.45, 47; 20.1; 21.5, 37, 38; 22.52, 53; 24.53). Only one direct reference to the temple occurs in the central section of Luke at 18.10.

Likewise, Jerusalem is the context for the opening scene of the Gospel. It is the city of destiny—the goal of Jesus' journey. There Jesus is arrested and crucified; it is also the place of the post-resurrection appearances of Jesus (contra Matt. 28, John 20, and Mark 16 by implication). Jerusalem is also the place to which the disciples returned to await the promise of the Father (24.49). Culpepper has noted, 'Luke begins within the chrysalis of Judaism and traces the life of Jesus to Jerusalem, the point at which the disciples are ready to begin the work of the church'.[87] Both Jerusalem and the temple are effective circular closural devices.

The narrative ends where it began—with the pious people of God blessing Him in His house. As Henry James has expressed it: 'Really, universally, relations stop nowhere, and the exquisite problem of the artist is eternally but to draw, by a geometry of his own, the circle with which they shall happily *appear* to do so'.[88] Or as T.S. Eliot wrote in *Four Quartets*:

> We shall not cease from exploration
> And the end of all our exploring
> Will be to arrive where we started
> And know the place for the first time.

Certainly the painting evangelist of the Third Gospel has effectively related the end of his story to the beginning, and in so doing has drawn his own circle on the Gospel canvas. The narrator ends the narrative where it started and the readers, already familiar with the Gospel, are able to know the place and the story perhaps for the first time.[89]

Parallelism

Torgovnick utilized the term *parallelism* to describe the relationship between the ending and the middle of a narrative work.[90] She also suggested that such parallel closural patterns may often be detected upon retrospective analysis. Below is an attempt to analyze Luke 24.50-53 in relationship to the middle or body of the Gospel, paying particularly close attention to the way the major story lines are resolved in the ascension narrative and to some extent in the larger resurrection narrative.

Movement in the plot is facilitated by several plot devices. A plot device, according to the Russian formalist Victor Shlovsky, organizes the indiscriminate materials of the story-stuff into a dynamically coherent structure.[91] While there are a number of these plot devices at work in the narrative of Luke, at least three major plot devices or strategies are resolved by the conclusion of Luke. First, the plot is developed by the repeated occurrences of conflict: conflict at table between Jesus and Pharisees, conflict between God's messengers and his people in the context of temple and synagogues, and conflict between Jesus and his disciples. Second, the plot device of prophecy and fulfillment helps sustain interest in the story, as well as reinforcing the idea that God is one who keeps His promises. Third, the well-known journey motif is employed by the narrator as a way to demonstrate God's fidelity to His son. The presence of these three plot strategies in the text has been generally acknowledged by Lukan scholarship, though scholars have not agreed regarding the shape or extent of each, much less adopted the nomenclature 'plot device'. What follows below is an attempt to justify the inclusion of these three plot strategies as crucial to the development of Luke's Gospel and to show how the ending of the Gospel provides closure to these movements.

Conflict Scenes. Conflict is, indeed, a common device in plot development.[92] Conflict between Jesus and various groups of characters is crucial to Luke.[93] The ending of Luke is shaped, in large measure, by the resolution of these conflicts. Especially significant are the confrontations between Jesus and the religious authorities and the misunderstandings between Jesus and his disciples.

In the analysis of the disputes between Jesus and the religious authorities in Luke, a distinction has been made between those conflicts which occur in the midst of table fellowship in a house (often of a Pharisee) and those confrontations between Jesus and the authorities in the temple/synagogue. Here I am attempting to be sensitive to the *setting* of the conflict, recognizing that the 'where' is as important as the 'who' (characters), the 'what' (plot or conflict), and the 'when' (sequence in the narrative).[94] The contrast between the meal-time conflicts and the temple/synagogue confrontation scenes is striking. The house is a private setting; the synagogue/temple is a public setting.[95] The house is a residential setting; the temple/synagogue is a religious setting.[96] The house is a profane setting; the temple/synagogue is a sacred setting.[97] Therefore, it seems best to examine the meal-time conflicts between Jesus and the religious authorities which occur in the private, residential, profane setting of a house apart from those temple/synagogue scenes which are presented in a public, religious, and sacred setting.[98]

Not only is Jesus found in conflict with religious authorities, he also has confrontations with his followers at various points in the narrative. Only the temple/synagogue confrontation scenes actually find resolution in the departure scene of Luke 24.50-53. However, to omit discussion of the other two, meal-time conflicts and misunderstandings with the disciples—which do find resolution in the larger narrative of Luke 24—would be to define the story-line too narrowly. Therefore, I will deal with these three types of conflict in the order in which they are resolved in the narrative: meal-time conflicts, misunderstandings with disciples, and temple/synagogue confrontation scenes.

1. Meal-time Conflicts. There is an impressive series of meal conflicts which occur in the house of a Pharisee (7.36-50; 11.37-54; 14.1-24). One may also include the meal conflict in Luke 5.29-32 which, though set in the house of Levi the tax-collector, is the site of

conflict between Jesus and the Pharisees, and the commentary in 15.1-2 where the Pharisees repeat their grumbling that Jesus eats with sinners (5.30; 15.2).[99] In each of these passages, the religious authorities are critical of Jesus' action (or inaction as the case may be). In Luke 5, the religious leaders rebuke Jesus' disciples for eating and drinking with tax collectors and sinners. In Luke 7, Simon the Pharisee criticizes Jesus for allowing a sinful woman to touch him. The Pharisee who invites Jesus to dine with him in ch. 11 is astonished that Jesus does not wash before the meal. And in ch. 14, in the house of a Pharisee, the religious leaders watch Jesus (παρατηρέω cf. 20.20) to see if he would heal on the Sabbath.[100]

A 'last' supper scene of ch. 22 occurs in the house of an anonymous benefactor (22.10-13). Again, Jesus sits at table (cf. 5.29; 7.36; 11.37; 14.15), this time only with the apostles (22.14). The absence of the religious authorities from this meal might suggest some sense of resolution to the table conflict were it not for the fact that the hand hired by those same religious authorities to betray Jesus was at the table with him (22.3-6, 21).

The 'last supper' in Luke 22 is not, in fact, the last meal Jesus eats with his followers. Jesus dines in the home of two travelers from Emmaus. There are several similarities with the other meal scenes. Jesus reclines at table (ἀναπίπτω; cf. 11.37). He takes bread, blesses it, breaks it and gives it to those with him (cf. 9.16, though there εὐλογέω is found rather than εὐχαριστέω).[101] What is different is that for the first time Jesus is able to sit down to a meal in peace! Though there had been misunderstanding on the road between Jesus and these two travelers (24.17-27), there is no conflict at table in the travelers' home, even though these two had spoken to Jesus about the evil deeds of '*our* chief priests and rulers' (24.20).

If there is not resolution of conflict at least there is the absence of conflict at the table. The meal-time confrontations were caused by the religious authorities' inability to recognize who Jesus was because they were so busy watching him (14.1)! Now the table, so often the place of mistaken identity and misunderstood purpose for Luke, becomes the site of self-disclosure, revelation, and recognition (24.30-31). As Dillon has observed: 'although the travelers' hearts were "burning" during the Stranger's Scripture exposition "on the road" (v. 32), it was properly ἐν τῇ κλάσει τοῦ ἄρτου that the recognition of the risen One occurred (v. 31)'.[102] The meal-time conflicts with the religious authorities are implicitly resolved; the table now becomes the site of christological revelation.[103] This resolution, or at least the absence of conflict, contributes to the sense of closure at the end of Luke's Gospel.[104]

2. Misunderstandings by the Disciples. In Luke 9 the relationship between Jesus and his followers becomes strained. The disciples demonstrate in a variety of ways that they are not prepared for their impending mission. These failures hinge on a basic misunderstanding of Jesus' vocation. The disciples simply do not understand that Jesus must suffer and die. This fundamental failure on the part of the disciples is emphasized by a threefold repetition in 9.45 (cf. also 18.34) and is highlighted throughout the passion narrative.

Luke 24 is not simply the story of the risen Christ's appearances. It is the story of how the disciples finally come to understand that 'it was necessary that the Christ suffer and enter into his glory' (24.26). Thus Luke 24 constitutes an extensive recognition scene, a point of illumination for characters who previously were blind. The crucial importance of the enlightenment of the disciples is shown by the fact that the three episodes of the empty tomb, the walk to Emmaus, and the appearance in Jerusalem are united by the repeated insistence that Jesus' passion prophecies and scripture have been fulfilled through Jesus' death and resurrection (24.6-8, 26-27, 44-46). Even at this point in the story the new insight does not come easily; the chapter is more than half over before eyes are opened. This awareness requires something more than just seeing the risen Christ. The disciples must understand that the events of the passion were 'necessary', that is, they were essential to the fulfillment of God's purpose witnessed to in scripture.

A major tension in the plot is resolved when the disciples finally understand this through the teaching of the risen Christ. The turning point comes when Jesus announces their mission in 24.47-49.[105] Even when he appears to them and invites them to touch him, some disbelieve (cf. 24.11), even if for joy (24.41).[106] But now they are prepared for this mission and with Jesus' blessing (24.51) they return obediently and joyfully to Jerusalem to wait for 'power from on high'. The resolution of this misunderstanding between Jesus and his followers is a major contributing factor to the sense of closure in Luke 24.[107]

3. Temple and Synagogue Confrontation Scenes. If the disciples had simply returned to Jerusalem to wait for the gift of 'power from on high', we might surmise that the concluding paragraph provided closure only to the conflict between Jesus and his disciples. In fact, the narrator is very careful to locate the disciples both spatially and

temporally: 'they were constantly in the temple blessing God' (24.53). This location in the temple is by no means insignificant. While Jesus is in conflict with various persons in sundry places in Luke, the encounters of Jesus with Jewish leaders in the synagogues and the temple in the Gospel and the confrontation between the disciples and Paul with Jewish leaders in Jewish sanctuaries in Acts are peculiarly significant in the plot development of Luke–Acts. As Norman Petersen has noted:

> both the sequential and parallel aspects of Luke's composition, the rejection of God's agents by God's people in connection with God's sanctuaries (synagogues and temple), represent the plot device by which the movement of the narrative as a whole is motivated.[108]

While Petersen identified only six confrontation incidents in all of Luke–Acts, the list here has been extended to include six in Luke alone.[109]

The opening scene in the Gospel (Luke 1.5-23) establishes the conflict between the people of God and his agents. Tyson has noted: 'The literary function of the infancy narratives appears to be to alert the reader to the significance of the events to follow'.[110] Zechariah, who the narrator tells us, was 'righteous before God, walking in all the commandments of the Lord, blameless' (1.5-6), is one of God's people. While in God's sanctuary (the temple, v. 9), God's agent, an angel of the Lord (vv. 11, 19), appears to him. The conflict begins in 1.18 when Zechariah doubts the angel's prophecy that he and Elizabeth will have a son. The angel rebukes Zechariah, revealing to him that he is none other than Gabriel who 'was sent to speak to you' (1.19).[111] The conflict is resolved when Gabriel strikes Zechariah speechless. Zechariah then returns home. This initial episode provides the type-scene of the other synagogue/temple encounters. The tension seems to intensify with each subsequent conflict. The other conflict incidents between God's agents with God's people in God's house may be diagrammed as in Table 6 (overleaf).

The sequence and repetition of these conflicts are aided in affective power by references to God's agent (Jesus) in direct conflict with God's adversary (Satan) on the pinnacle of God's house, the temple, in the temptation narrative 4.9-12.[112] According to Tyson, this passage is 'a narrative that intensifies conflict and sets it in a cosmic dimension'.[113] Likewise at 4.31-37, Jesus is again functioning as God's agent, 'the Holy One of God' (4.34), in conflict with a man 'who had the spirit of an unclean demon', God's adversary, in the

Table 6

Temple and Synagogue Confrontation Scenes in Luke

Text	God's Sanctuary	God's People	God's Agent	Conflict
1.5-23	temple	Zechariah	Gabriel	1.18-20
2.41-51	temple	Jesus' parents	Jesus	1.48-50
4.16-30	synagogue	all	Jesus	4.23-30
6.6-11	synagogue	scribes/ Pharisees	Jesus	6.8-11
13.10-17	synagogue	ruler/synagogue	Jesus	13.14-17
19.45-48	temple	chief priests/ scribes	Jesus	19.47

synagogue at Capernaum. These two parallel stories, while they do not record the tension between God's people and his agent, do in fact heighten the controversies. The reader realizes that what at first appeared to be a skirmish between a pious person of Israel (Zechariah, Jesus' parents) and God's guide for his people (Gabriel, Jesus), has now turned into a full-fledged war between God's messengers and 'the power of darkness' (22.53).

Petersen may be correct in identifying only the confrontation incidents in 4.16-30 and 19.45-47 as the crucial conflicts in Luke. Certainly the conflict is much more serious in these two episodes; in both cases, the antagonists seek to destroy Jesus. The last conflict, in 19.45-47, provides the climax, and the tension is almost unbearable.

How does the narrative resolve these conflicts in the Gospel?[114] God's faithfulness is revealed in the resurrection narrative. His messenger is put to death by adversaries; but in the end, God vindicates him. This reversal begins even on the cross where Jesus' last words are not 'My God, My God, why has thou forsaken me?' but rather the expressive utterance of Jesus, who is obedient to his vocation, 'Father, into thy hands I commit my spirit'.

Resolution continues through the empty tomb and post-resurrection appearance stories and culminates in the very last phrase of the Gospel. There we find the disciples 'continually in the temple blessing God'. The Gospel ends, then, with God's agents (now the disciples) in God's house (a cleansed temple) blessing God.[115] Where the disciples are and what they are doing are of equal significance. They are in the temple, the institution which was itself 'a major issue in the debates between Jesus and the chief priests';[116] they are there now unchallenged. They are blessing God, not worshiping Jesus (see Matt. 28.17).[117] Blessing a God who is faithful to vindicate his messengers and restore them to his sanctuaries is the only fitting response.[118] This parallel pattern of closure between Luke 24.53 and the conflict stories in the Gospel is often obscured by those who take notice of the similarity between the opening and closing scenes, both of which take place in the temple.[119] The final line of the narrative, then, with its concordances between the end and the body of the Gospel, provides an effective parallel closure to one of the major plot strategies.[120]

Promise and Fulfillment. In 1957, Paul Schubert published an article entitled 'The Structure and Significance of Luke 24', in which he argued that the last chapter of the Third Gospel is organized around the motif of 'proof from prophecy' and that this theme of prophecy-fulfillment is central to Luke–Acts.[121] Other scholars, particularly Minear, Dahl, Johnson, and Karris, have adopted Schubert's basic proposal with some modifications.[122]

In a brief article, Talbert has recently described the basic tenets of the 'proof-from-prophecy' school and offered a telling critique.[123] Shared between these proponents is their understanding of proof-from-prophecy as (1) meaning 'essentially fulfillment of the Old Testament promises'; and (2) 'functioning to establish historical continuity between the church and Israel'; and (3) 'a guarantee of future fulfillment of as yet unrealized promises'.[124]

In his thoughtful critique, Talbert raised two questions for the proof-from-prophecy school. The first concerned the data to be considered when speaking about proof-from-prophecy theology in Luke–Acts. Talbert convincingly demonstrated: 'The data are broader than the fulfillment of the Old Testament and not all Lucan uses of the Jewish scriptures fit into a promise-fulfillment pattern'.[125] Talbert butressed his first argument—that the proof-from-prophecy pattern is broader than the theme of fulfillment of Old Testament promises—by showing that the theme includes not only (1) fulfillment of specific Old Testament prophecy; but also (2) fulfillment of a prophecy given by a heavenly being (whether an angel or the risen Christ); and (3) fulfillment of a prediction by a living prophet (whether Jewish, Jesus, or Christian).[126]

Talbert's second argument that 'not all references and allusions to the Old Testament in Luke–Acts fall into the promise-fulfillment schema'[127] is supported by the fact that in several places (Luke 2.23-24; 7.11-17; 9.52-56) Old Testament scripture is being used to express a hermeneutical, typological, or ethical concern.[128] In particular, Talbert argued that 'the fulfillment of the divine *dei* in Luke–Acts means fulfillment both of the prophetic promise and of the ethical demand. The latter, however, is not a promise-fulfillment schema'.[129]

Despite Talbert's caveat against understanding 'proof-from-prophecy' as the major theme to which all others must acquiesce and his much needed corrective to the indiscriminate references to prophecy and fulfillment in Luke–Acts, 'there can be no doubt that the theme of prophecy-fulfillment is a major one in Luke–Acts', even though 'it is certainly not the only one'.[130] To understand the significance of promise and fulfillment in Luke–Acts not as a theme but as a plot device which helps structure the story-line, the various ways in which the narrator employs this particular technique must first be delineated. Talbert's categories of scripture, heavenly beings, and living prophets provide a springboard, but must be expanded by adding a fourth category: those passages where the promise is narrated by the narrator himself.[131] While these instances are few, they are especially crucial. In addition, categories of what literary theorists call 'narrative time' will be helpful in distinguishing those passages which emphasize the promise aspect over the fulfillment or vice versa.[132]

At this point it is necessary to introduce some technical terminology along with definitions. Order and frequency of narrative time and the ways in which sequence can effect and affect the dramatic quality of the narrative are of particular interest here. Luke obviously does not narrate his story of Jesus in chronological order.[133] As early as 1.13, reference is made to a prayer by Zechariah which had not been mentioned previously, but obviously had occurred prior to the meeting of Zechariah and Gabriel. Genette defined 'any evocation after the fact of an event that took place earlier than the point in the story where we are at any given moment' as an *analepsis*.[134] Conversely, a *prolepsis* is 'any narrative maneuver that consists of narrating or evoking in advance an event that will take place later'.[135]

Internal and *external* refer to whether or not the event described lies within or outside the story time. Therefore, it is possible to have internal or external analepses or internal or external prolepses. In addition, *mixed analepses* begin prior to the story time and continue into it, while *mixed prolepses* refer to events which begin within the story time but continue beyond it.

A special problem surfaces here in Luke–Acts. Some events will be external prolepses to the Gospel, but internal to the whole of Luke–Acts (for example, the promise of the Father and the ensuing provision of power from on high in Luke 24.49 is fulfilled externally to the time of the Gospel narrative, but internally to the time of the Acts narrative—Acts 2). Or events which are external analepses to the story time of Acts may be internal to the whole of Luke–Acts (for example, most of the references to Jesus in Peter's Pentecost sermon are external to the time of Acts, while they are internal to the Luke–Acts narrative as a whole).

In the Tables below, the passages will be cited as *analepsis* or *prolepsis* according to the relationship which they have to the narrative in which they are found. Those events, however, which fall outside their respective narrative, but within the whole two-volume work, will be marked by 'I' enclosed in brackets.[136] Below then are the prophecies and predictions of Luke–Acts, identified by means of *who* (or what, in the case of scripture) is doing the prophesying, *where* in the narrative the prophecy is fulfilled (in the case of prolepses), as well as the *type* of order of narrative time.

Table 7

Fulfillment of Scripture

Promise	Fulfillment	Type of Reference
Luke 3.4-6		Mixed Prolepsis
Luke 4.18-19	(4.21)	Analepsis and Prolepsis
Luke 18.31	(22–24)	Mixed Prolepsis
Luke 21.22		External Prolepsis
Luke 22.37	(22.47-53; 23.33)	Internal Prolepsis
Luke 24.26		Internal Analepsis
Luke 24.44		Internal Analepsis
Luke 24.46		Internal Analepsis
Luke 24.47	(Acts 2)	External Prolepsis (I)

Acts 3.18	External Analepsis (I)
Acts 10.43	External Analepsis
Acts 13.22-23	External Analepsis (M)
Acts 13.29-31	External Analepsis (I)
Acts 15.15-18	Mixed Analepsis
Acts 26.23	Mixed Analepsis

It is interesting to note that while most of the scripture references in Acts point back to the time of the Gospel or even before it, a significant number of the references in the Gospel function as prolepses pointing the reader ahead to a particular point in the narrative. Cosgrove has noted about the use of scripture in Luke:

> An element, however, which has not, to my knowledge, received sufficient attention is the way in which prophecy functions as a divine mandate in Luke–Acts. Luke has added something to the familiar New Testament 'Scripture-proof'. Whereas in Matthew or Paul, for example, an Old Testament text is construed as prophetic ex post facto as a stamp of divine endorsement, Luke introduces Scripture prophecy not only after its fulfillment (as a proof) but also narratively before.[137]

In Luke 3.4-6, Isaiah 40 is quoted. Here is a mixed prolepsis in which the first part of the quotation is fulfilled in story time, but the latter part of the prophecy that 'all flesh shall see the salvation of God' (v. 6) does not find fulfillment either in Luke or Acts (or in fact by the time of the composition of the Gospel). The next appeal to scripture is found in Luke 4, which many consider to be the 'Frontispiece' to the Gospel. The categories at this particular point may not be helpful. The scripture is read and then immediately Jesus says, 'Today this scripture has been fulfilled in your hearing'. The other appeals to fulfillment of scripture in Luke are clearly prolepses.

Both Luke 4.18-21 and 22.37 (as well as 3.4-6) explicitly quote specific Old Testament passages (both from Isaiah). Often the narrator uses broad categories like 'all the things written by the prophets' (Luke 18.31; cf. Acts 3.18; 13.27), 'all things that are written' (Luke 21.22), 'the scriptures' or 'all the scriptures' (Luke 24.27, 32, 45), and the Old Testament is divided into the law, prophets, and the psalms (Luke 24.44).[138] Such evidence has led Maddox to remark:

It is mainly in this broad sense that Luke thinks of fulfilment. The whole Christian story—the story of Jesus and of the church—is the fulfilment of the whole purpose of God as set forth in the whole of the Old Testament.[139]

This prophecy-fulfillment schema provides another parallel pattern of closure in Luke. First, the rather simplistic observation may be made that before Luke 24, all of the scripture references which fall into the prophecy-fulfillment schema are predictive—that is, they represent prolepses which suggest resolution will occur later in the story. In chapter 24, however, all of the scripture references except one are analepses which refer to earlier events in the story.[140]

Interesting also is the fact that, with few exceptions, the references to the fulfillment of scripture are to the high points of the Gospel plot. Again, Maddox's comments are on target:

Unlike Matthew and John, who frequently identify details of the life of Jesus (sometimes even quite trivial ones) as the fulfilment of particular OT texts, Luke usually relates 'promise' and 'fulfilment' in a much more sweeping way. The only specific events seen as fulfilment are the high points of the story: Jesus' mission, death, resurrection and ascension, the gift of the holy spirit, the Gentile mission and the destruction of Jerusalem.[141]

This phenomenon suggests that scripture holds a very prominent place as a source of authority in the Gospel text. And unlike the other Gospels, which may speak of trivial details like the division of Jesus' garments as the fulfillment of scripture (see John 19.24; Matt. 27.35), the narrator of Luke reserves references to scripture fulfillment for the development of the main plot lines in the Gospel of Luke. This strategy of employing scripture in a predictive manner in order to maintain interest in the story-line finds closure in the last chapter of the Gospel where prolepses become fulfilled analepses. In this way prophecy and fulfillment serve to bring the story of Jesus in Luke to closure.

Obviously, all the prophecies credited to heavenly beings (whether angels or the risen Christ) are internal or external prolepses except one. That exception, Luke 24.5-7, is significant and functions in a similar way to the use of scripture in Luke 24. Angels stand at the beginning and end of the story bearing witness to the ways in which God filled a womb and emptied a tomb. The difference is that, at the beginning, all the prophecies pointed forward to sustain suspense; while at the empty tomb, they point back to an earlier moment in the

Table 8

Prophecy of a Heavenly Being

Prophecy	Fulfillment	Type of Reference
1.13-17	(1.41, 44-45, 57-63; 3.3-17)	Internal Prolepsis
1.26-27, 31	(2.7, 21)	Internal Prolepsis
1.32a	(8.28)	Internal Prolepsis
1.33	(cf. Acts 2.30)	External Prolepsis
1.35	(3.22, 4.41, 8.35, Acts 9.20)	Internal Prolepsis
2.8-12	(2.15-16)	Internal Prolepsis
24.5-7		Internal Analepsis
24.47-49	(Acts 2.1; *passim*)	External Prolepsis (I)
Acts 1.4-5	(Acts 2.1ff.)	Internal Prolepsis
Acts 1.8	narratives of Acts	Internal Prolepsis
Acts 18.9-10	(Acts 18.12-17)	Internal Prolepsis

narrative (9.22) when the women are reminded: 'Remember how he spoke to you while he was still in Galilee, saying, "The Son of man must be delivered into the hands of sinful people and crucified and on the third day rise"' (Luke 24.7-8).[142] Turning the story inward in this manner serves to resolve the tensions created by the textual markers before this point.

Again, all the prophecies assigned to living prophets (pious Jews, Jesus, and Christians) are prolepses, and in most cases internal prolepses—at least internal to the whole of Luke-Acts. These predictions which find their fulfillment throughout the course of the narrative serve a particularly important function. The repeated fulfillment of predictions lends credibility to the speaker, in most cases, Jesus. The reader becomes more and more confident that what Jesus says will in fact come to pass. This is especially true of those external prolepses of Jesus, too numerous to list below, which may either be historical references which the reader knows to have

3. *Luke 24.50-53 in Narrative Context*

Table 9

Prophecy of a Living Prophet

Prophecy	Fulfillment	Type of Reference
Luke 1.69-79	narrative of Luke	Mixed Prolepsis
Luke 2.29-32	narrative of Acts (2.32 is unfulfilled)	External Prolepsis (I)
Luke 9.22, 44	(chs. 22–44)	Internal Prolepsis
Luke 11.13	(Acts 2.1)	External Prolepsis (I)
Luke 13.35b	unfulfilled	External Prolepsis
Luke 19.29-31	(19.32-34)	Internal Prolepsis
Luke 21.12	(Acts 8.3, 12.4)	External Prolepsis (I)
Luke 21.15	(Acts 6.10)	External Prolepsis (I)
Luke 22.10-12	(22.13)	Internal Prolepsis
Luke 22.34	(22.54-61)	Internal Prolepsis
Acts 11.27-28a	(Acts 11.28b)	Internal Prolepsis
Acts 21.10-11	(Acts 21.30-36)	Internal Prolepsis
Acts 27.22, 34	(Acts 27.44)	Internal Prolepsis

happened (persecution of Christians—Luke 12.11-12; destruction of the temple—13.35a, 21.6; capture of Jerusalem by Gentiles—19.43-44; 21.20-24; 23.28-31) or eschatological sayings which the reader is coaxed into believing will happen in the way Jesus foretells (see 21.25-36; 22.30).[143]

Since there are no references to what might be called 'living prophets' in the resurrection narrative (here the risen Christ is considered to be a heavenly being), it may be concluded that predictions by prophets serve functions other than providing textual closure to the Gospel, that is, to establish reliability on the part of the chief protagonist and the narrator. In a larger sense, however, these eschatological prolepses may very well serve existentially to provide assurance of an appropriate ending to people who live 'in the middest'.[144] Since this analysis examines specifically textual closure, such concerns, even though legitimate, lie outside the boundaries of this present study.

Only two significant internal prolepses are found in the commentary of the narrator to the narratee. The first, Luke 9.31, occurs in the transfiguration scene where Moses and Elijah speak to Jesus about his departure (ἔξοδος). The narrator goes on to add 'which he was to accomplish at Jerusalem'. The other reference may be found at 9.51, which reads: 'It happened that the days of his being taken up were being fulfilled and he himself set his face to journey into Jerusalem'. While these references to Jesus' exodus and journey to Jerusalem will be discussed in much greater detail below, a word does need to be said about the relationship between these two motifs and the fulfillment schema of Luke–Acts.[145]

In his critique of Schubert, Talbert claimed, 'the proof-from-prophecy theme is not the unifying element in *all* of Luke 24. Luke 24.50-53 has no promise-fulfillment component'.[146] While Talbert is correct in suggesting that no Old Testament prophecy is fulfilled in Luke 24.50-53, the argument that the passage 'has no promise-fulfillment component' is certainly overstated. The exodus and journey motifs, which are closely related to the crucifixion-resurrection-exaltation events of Jerusalem and which are couched from the outset in fulfillment language (Luke 9.31, 51), are not completed (hence not fulfilled) until the final paragraph of the Gospel. Jesus leads them out (ἐξάγω) and departs from them, and the days of his journey and exodus are fulfilled.[147] Thus, it is proper to speak of a 'promise-fulfillment component' in Luke 24.50-53. While the effectiveness of the conclusion as a closural device may be questioned, it is nonetheless fitting to argue that the fulfillment in Luke 24.50-53 of the exodus and journey serves as an example of parallel closure.

This overall emphasis on prophecy and fulfillment in Luke is in keeping with the purpose of the document explicitly stated by the narrator to the explicit narratee, Theophilus. Luke speaks of 'a narrative concerning the events which have been fulfilled among us' (1.1). Basing his argument on evidence found in Luke 24, Dillon has suggested: 'It comes as no startling conclusion from all of this that the argument of prophecy fulfilled pervades Luke's composition from beginning to end and forms an important connective tissue between the two Lucan volumes'.[148] Dillon's suggestion may be taken one step farther by suggesting that this argument of prophecy fulfilled allows the narrator to bring his story to closure.

A final word needs to be said about the relationship between narrative time and plot in Luke–Acts. Most of the references cited above are internal prolepses which serve to create tension in the plot.

Their resolution produces subsequent release. Culpepper has noted that 'internal prolepses have the more exciting task of heightening dramatic intensity by anticipating coming events'.[149] The suspense created by prolepses, however, differs from the chronologically ordered narrative. Prolepses, Rimmon-Kenan claimed, 'replace the kind of suspense deriving from the question "What will happen next?" by another kind of suspense, revolving around the question "How is it going to happen?"'[150] Luke, more than the other Gospels, relies heavily on this narrative strategy to keep his story interesting and to bring his Gospel to closure.

The Central Section of Luke (9.51-19.44). A flood of literature has been written on the central section of Luke's Gospel in recent years.[151] Despite the spate of studies which have appeared, the judgment of I. Howard Marshall still rings true, 'the existence of this section in Luke is hard to explain, and it is doubtful whether the various recent studies of it have adequately accounted for its nature'.[152] The basic problem is the unbearable tension between form and content. The section is set in the framework of a journey to Jerusalem, but the confusing jumble of seemingly unrelated units of didactic material has sent more then one critic away sadly nodding his or her head.[153]

Scholars cannot even agree whether the section should end at 18.14, 19.27, or 19.44.[154] The number of titles assigned to this passage would rival royalty and is symptomatic of the problem. Thus, 'The Great Interpolation', 'The Travel Narrative', 'The Perean Section', 'The Samaritan Section', and 'The Gospel of the Journeys of Jesus' indicate the range of opinions.[155] Following B.H. Streeter, the innocuous title 'The Central Section' is accepted in this study.[156] And as the subheading indicates, the section is believed to extend to 19.44.[157]

James Resseguie has chronicled the history of interpretation of this section from 1856 to 1975, and there is no need to repeat that summary here.[158] More recently, however, David Moessner has classified the approaches to Luke's central section in four basic categories: (1) Adherents of the *Theological-Christological* category relate the central section's description of Jesus' ministry to the overarching scheme of the history of salvation;[159] (2) Closely related to (1) are those (*Ecclesiastical-Functional*) who claim 'the central section coheres because it exhibits a useful parallel between Jesus' journeying and the church's present journey';[160] (3) Those who argue from *Literary-Aesthetical* grounds assume 'the amorphous mass of

Luke's vast middle section in reality betrays a distinct literary pattern';[161] (4) And finally, those whom Moessner placed in the *Traditional-Logical* group find 'a logical progression of themes, or an ordering of catchwords or phrases, or polemics with opponents, etc., rather than a chronological progression of Jesus' journey-ministry is the prevailing modality'.[162]

While such grouping is necessarily arbitrary and the distinctness of some individual arguments is lost, overall Moessner has summarized previous scholarship well. Although he found something helpful in each approach, to one degree or another each emphasis tended to denigrate Luke's literary skill. Moessner concluded:

> All four approaches lead inevitably to one conclusion: Either Luke—at his best—has done a mediocre job in fulfilling his desire to give an 'ordered' account, or in 9.51ff. he shifts his aims entirely for grander theological, practical, or aesthetic pursuits.[163]

Such treatment by critics might qualify Luke's central section for what Henry James called 'the audacity of the misplaced middle'![164]

Despite the cul-de-sac which scholarship has encountered in discussion on this passage, several general conclusions may be drawn. First, however loosely plotted, the central section of Luke is presented in the setting of Jesus' journey to Jerusalem.[165] Second, the didactic material may serve to heighten the tension of the journey to the city where they kill prophets (13.33). Karl Schmidt expressed that experience thus: 'One cannot avoid being struck by the fact that although Jesus is travelling to Jerusalem all the time, he never really makes any progress'.[166] As Rimmon-Kenan has noted:

> In order to increase the reader's interest and prolong itself, the text will delay the narration of the next event in the story, or of the event the reader is now curious to learn about, or of the event which will temporarily or permanently close off the sequence in question.[167]

Third, regardless of the relationship between form and content in the central section, the entire middle section is couched in Luke's fulfillment scheme as noted above.

How does the final pericope of the Gospel and in a wider sense, the final chapter, provide closure to the central section of the narrative? In the larger resurrection narrative, Cleopas and his companion were on their way to Emmaus when Jesus himself drew near and went with them (24.15). The risen Lord is still journeying. But, while the journey to Jerusalem ends at 19.44ff. with the cleansing of the temple, the days of Jesus' *analempsis* have still not been fulfilled, nor has his exodus. Not until the last paragraph does the narrator bring Jesus' journey to completion.

The relationship between the central section and Luke's ending becomes even more significant if Talbert is correct in claiming that Mediterranean documents frequently have their key point at the center of the narrative.[168] If so, then everything from the mid-point of the story of Jesus moves toward the dénouement in 24.50-53. The delays caused by the long teaching material in the central section then serve to heighten the dramatic intensity.[169] Despite delays, setbacks, and disappointments, the journey is completed in the final scene. Jesus has been faithful to his journey, and God has been faithful to Jesus.

Openness and the Problem of Closure in Luke

After such a detailed analysis of the narrative strategies employed to bring closure to the Third Gospel, the temptation exists to overlook the narrative threads which continue to dangle. D.A. Miller has commented on this difficulty for the one interested in closure:

> Once the ending is enshrined as an all-embracing cause in which the elements of a narrative find their ultimate justification, it is difficult for analysis to assert anything short of total coherence. One is barred even from suspecting possible discontinuities between closure and the narrative movement preceding it, not to mention possible contradictions and ambiguities within closure itself.[170]

Part of the problem, of course, is that no matter how neatly a narrative ends, the possibility always exists that the narrator may re-open the story. As J. Hillis Miller has noted: 'The aporia of ending arises from the fact that it is impossible ever to tell whether a given narrative is complete. If the ending is thought of as a tying up in a careful knot, this knot could be untied again by the narrator or by further events, disentangled or explicated again'.[171] Fortunately, Torgovnick has provided the vocabulary in her model which also allows us to examine narrative openness as well as closure in the ending of Luke.[172]

Linkage. Another type of closural strategy, according to Torgovnick, involves those works which are part of a larger series of works or multi-volume work. 'Novels that form part of such a series sometimes end with the explicit message, "to be continued".'[173]

Torgovnick has labeled as *linkage* that closural strategy which 'links the novel not to its own beginning and middle, but to the body of another, often as yet unwritten, novel'.[174] In a way linkage is the counterpart to circularity. In both cases, the ending is linked to specific passages: in circularity, the link is to the beginning of the narrative; in linkage the connection is to a particular part of another story. Linkage is not a recent narrative strategy. Lucian of Samosa suggested that the principle of interlacing events (συμπεριπλοκῇ τῶν πραγματῶν) was an important narrative technique in writing history.[175]

There are several examples of linkage or interlacing in Luke 24. In fact, Tannehill claimed interlacing 'is clearest where the transition is clearest, at the juncture of Books 1 and 2'.[176] The most obvious linkage between the ending of Luke and the narrative of Acts is the departure of Jesus recorded in Luke 24.50-53 and Acts 1.9-11 (though with significant disagreements). The reference to 'repentance and forgiveness of sins' being preached by the apostles provides an obvious linking with Acts 2.38, 3.19, and 5.31. Jerusalem, named by Jesus as the locale for the inauguration of the missionary outreach in Luke 24.47, is interlaced with Acts 1.4. The reference to being witnesses in 24.48 provides a hinge to Acts 1.8, 22; 2.32; 3.15; 4.33; 5.32 and other parts of the narrative. Finally, Jesus' command that the disciples stay in the city until endowed with power from on high finds its indisputable linkage with the Pentecost narrative in Acts 2.

Such efforts at linkage between Luke and Acts have led Jacques Dupont to comment: 'Luc ne s'est pas contenté de juxtaposer l'un à l'autre ses deux livres *A Théophile*; il les a emboités l'un dans l'autre, faisant en sorte, comme le dit Lucien, "qu'ils soient mêlés par leurs extrémités"'.[177] Along with the closural strategies of circularity and parallelism, the narrator employs the strategy of linkage to underline the fact that while the story of Jesus is ending in Luke 24, the story of his followers and their struggle to implement the mission of God's saving purposes is just beginning.

Incompletion. At times, the fissures which are opened in a narrative defy attempts to bridge the gaps, producing a sense of *incompletion*.[178] Incomplete closure, in Torgovnick's words, 'includes many aspects that suggest circular or parallel closure, but omits one or more crucial elements necessary for full circularity or parallelism'.[179] This incompletion 'may result from deliberate authorial choices, or it may result from an inadvertent formal failure, or from some combination of the two'.[180] Despite the strong sense of closure detected in our study on parallelism, it is possible to argue that the narrative leaves 'unfinished business' which creates, in varying degrees, incomplete closure.

1. Conflict Scenes. The Third Gospel ends with the disciples in the temple blessing God. As noted above, this final line of the story provides some resolution to the conflict between Jesus' followers and the people of Israel. The narrative does not, however, fulfill expectations created at the beginning of the narrative for the pious people of Israel. While there are hints from the outset of the conflict within Israel which Jesus and his followers will produce (Luke 1.51-53; 2.34-35), there is a 'very strong emphasis on the view that Jesus means redemption for Israel, that is, for the Jewish people' (Luke 1.32-33, 54-55, 68-69, 71, 74; 2.38).[181] Tannehill has noted the incongruity between the initial expectation and final reality of the Jewish people and concluded: 'The story of Israel, so far as the author of Luke–Acts can tell it, is a tragic story'.[182] The conflicts between God's messenger and God's people are resolved by the final scene; the expectations regarding the pious people of God, however, remain unfulfilled even at the end of the narrative.

2. Promise and Fulfillment. The promises regarding the redemption of Israel made in the infancy narrative are not the only ones left unresolved by the end of the narrative. The eschatological sayings of Jesus (21.25-28; *passim*) obviously fall outside narrative time. The prophecy regarding the capture of Jerusalem (19.43-44; 21.22-24; 22.28-31) though fulfilled by the writing of the narrative is not realized within the time of the narrative itself. Likewise, the destruction of the temple (13.35a; 21.6) is foretold by Jesus but not fulfilled in the limits of the narrative (see Tables 7–9 for other examples). Simply put, there are a number of promises and prophecies which do not find resolution or fulfillment by either the end of Luke or the conclusion of Luke–Acts as a whole (or in the case of some of the eschatological sayings, the prophecies remain unfulfilled even at the time of the implied reader).

3. The Journey to Jerusalem. It was noted earlier that Jesus' journey to Jerusalem is couched in a promise-fulfillment schema. Since 9.51 'when the days were fulfilled for his *analempsis*', the reader has been preparing for the fulfillment of this promise. The promise of Jesus' *analempsis*, set as it is in the context of the journey narrative, does not find its fulfillment in the conclusion to the Gospel, or at least not the resolution expected by most readers. More

will be said about the ways readers respond to the ending of Luke in the section on the 'Informed Reader'. At any rate, while the story is brought to effective closure, substantial gaps remain which the reader struggles to bridge.

Closure and Viewpoint

A second set of terms was proposed by Torgovnick 'to describe the author's and reader's viewpoint on the novel's characters and major action at the novel's end'.[183] Torgovnick reduced the possibilities of this category to two: overview and close-up endings. An *overview ending* is one in which either the narrator's and reader's understanding is superior to the characters, or the conclusion is related 'from a point much later in or more cosmic in knowledge than that available to the novel's characters'.[184] The result is that the novel's major plot immediately makes sense to the reader.

In a *close-up ending*, on the other hand, there is no temporal gap between the body of the narrative and its conclusion. Rather, 'readers, like characters, will—at least initially—lack the overview made possible by temporal distance or by authorial glossing of the action'.[185] Luke 24.50-53 obviously falls under this category—no temporal distance separates the pericope from the body of the narrative. In fact, it is Acts, not Luke, which posits forty days between the resurrection and Jesus' ascension/departure.

Despite the usefulness of these two possible relationships in describing the viewpoint of narrator and reader on the story; by themselves, they tend to be too reductionistic. In order to understand better the dynamics at work in closure between the narrator's and reader's perspectives on the story, Torgovnick's second category of terms will be extended to include the relevant literature on point of view and focalization.

Point of View
Susan Lanser has already described the development of point of view in literary theory and no attempt will be made to reproduce her work here.[186] Rather, the seminal work of Russian formalist, Boris Uspensky, provides a working model for examining closure and point of view in the Third Gospel.[187]

The reader who first approaches a narrative assumes the stance of an alien onlooker. Gradually, however, the reader is enticed to enter the special world of the story and to view it internally rather than externally. At the end of the reading, the reader is faced with the task of exiting from the story world in order to return to his or her own point of view. Uspensky has labeled as *framing* this effort on the part of a text first to engage the reader in a point of view internal to the story and later to provide an exit from the story's point of view.[188] The purpose of the literary frame, much like its dramatic counterpart, is 'to provide a final transition from the internal point of view in the life of the tale to the external point of view belonging to the everyday world'.[189]

The narrator of Luke seems especially interested in framing his story in such a way that the reader could be afforded accessible entrance and exit. Uspensky argued that in some cases, the

> first-person narrator appears only at the beginning of the story, and then disappears. In terms of content, the narrator here would seem completely superfluous; indeed, his function, unrelated to the plot of the narrative itself, is only to provide a frame for the story.[190]

This is certainly the case in Luke 1.1-4 where the narrator addresses a named reader, Theophilus, for the first and only time in the Gospel. He uses a similar device to begin Acts. The opening paragraph seems, in fact, to be superfluous—the verses are an external prolepsis; that is, they are commentary not on the story which follows, but on the telling of the story, the narrative. According to Uspensky, what is really taking place is the narrator's effort to help the reader get into the story world which does not properly begin until verse 5, 'In the days of Herod the king'. The reader is being asked to assume a point of view internal to the narrative at the beginning of the narrative and a point of view external to the narrative at the end of the work. This framing is crucial for the transition to and from the story world.

Uspensky goes on to claim that 'the phenomenon of framing—of alternation between a point of view internal to the narrative and a point of view external to the narrative—may be observed on different levels of an artistic work'.[191] Those different levels are the familiar ones which he used to refine his understanding of point of view: psychological, spatial, temporal, phraseological, and ideological. On the psychological plane 'the authorial point of view relies on an individual consciousness (or perception)'.[192] The spatial plane examines the spatial position or location of the narrator,[193] while the temporal plane deals with the author's temporal position.[194] The phraseological plane measures the ways in which the author registers descriptions of characters or records speech.[195] The ideological plane is the most basic aspect of point of view and treats the narrator's evaluative system of ideas.[196] The ending of Luke's Gospel will be examined using these various planes in which point of view may be expressed.

Psychological Plane. At the beginning of a narrative text the narrator often begins as a detached observer, or as Uspensky has suggested: 'before the author adopts the perceptual point of view of a particular character, he first presents that character from the point of view of an external observer'.[197] Thus, in the first chapter of Luke, following the narrator's aside to his reader, the story begins from the point of view of an external observer who is describing a rather static and distant scene. Not until v. 12 is any inside view of any of the characters given; in this case, the reader is told that Zechariah was troubled and 'fear fell on him'.

Later in the narrative, the reader is made privy to certain characters' private thoughts, emotions, and intentions. In bringing closure to the story, however, this psychologically moored viewpoint may shift dramatically from an internal point of view to that of the external observer. Uspensky suggested:

> But even more striking may be the transition from internal to external positioning at the end of the story, when the detailed description of the feelings of the character is unexpectedly replaced by a description of that character from the point of view of an outside observer—as if the reader had never been familiar with that character.[198]

There are numerous examples in Luke's Gospel where the narrator gives an inside view of Jesus and the disciples (see Table 10 opposite).

The remarkable thing to note here is not the depth of the description of the thoughts and motives of the Lukan characters (the insight is usually quite shallow) but the frequency with which the narrator introduces such inside glimpses in the last chapter (24.8, 16, 28, 37, 38, 41). In fact, many Lukan scholars have long noted the intimacy and warmth of the Emmaus passage. These internal points of view on Uspensky's psychological plane make the conclusion of the Gospel stand out in sharp contrast. The shift from internal to external observer is seemingly completed on the psychological plane. There are no inside views of Jesus or the disciples in 24.50-53: they could be complete strangers as easily as the companions of the reader throughout the story.[199]

Table 10

Inside Views in the Gospel of Luke

4.1	'And Jesus, full of the Holy Spirit, returned from the Jordan'.
4.14	'And Jesus returned in the power of the Spirit'.
5.22	'When Jesus perceived their questions'.
6.8	'But he knew their thoughts'.
7.13	'And when the Lord saw her, he had compassion on her'.
9.47	'But when Jesus perceived the thought of their hearts'.
11.17	'But he, knowing their thoughts'.
19.11	'They supposed the kingdom of God was to appear immediately'.
22.61	'And Peter remembered the word of the Lord'.
24.8	'And they remembered his words'.
24.16	'But their eyes were kept from recognizing him'.
24.28	'But he pretended to be going further'.
24.37	'But they were startled and frightened and supposed that they saw a spirit'.
24.38	'Why do questionings rise in your hearts?'
24.41	'And while they still disbelieved for joy and wondered'.
24.45	'Then he opened their minds to understand the scriptures'.

Spatial Plane. Uspensky has argued: 'In terms of space, a point of view with a broad horizon ... which indicates an observer outside the action, is characteristically used in framing a narrative'.[200] Of particular interest for our study is Uspensky's reference to the silent scene. Again, according to Uspensky:

> In the silent scene, the observer, who is located at some distance from the action, can see the characters, but because of the distance, he seems unable to hear them. The remote position makes it possible for the author to present a general view of the whole scene.[201]

Following the preface in Luke 1.1-4, the narrative begins from a rather remote point of view. A summary statement describing Zechariah and Elizabeth is followed by a specific reference to Zechariah serving as priest. His choice to perform priestly rites and burn incense and the multitude of people outside praying are described with no dialogue. In fact, it is not until v. 13 that a character, the angel, speaks. The silence of the scene and the subsequent dialogue serve to move the reader from an external view to an internal one, at least on the spatial plane.

Luke 24.50-53 certainly fits this description. It is a silent scene in which the narrator 'employs a pantomimic description of the behaviour of the characters: the gestures are described, but not the words'.[202] The contrast between this scene and the rest of ch. 24 is striking: the resurrection narrative is permeated with dialogue between the women and the two men at the tomb, the travelers to Emmaus and Jesus, and the disciples and the risen Lord. In fact, the six verses immediately preceding the silent scene of 24.50-53 stand in sharp contrast to the rest of the Gospel where movement of the story-line, particularly in the central section, is often slowed and sometimes arrested by long discourses. The literary effect, then, from a spatial point of view is to create more distance than usual between the narrator/reader, on the one hand, and Jesus and the disciples, on the other. Strain as we might, we cannot hear the blessing of Jesus over the disciples, nor the singing of his followers in the temple. The narrator who so deftly beckons us to enter his world, now effectively shows us the way out![203]

Temporal Plane. Uspensky claimed that in temporal framing, often a narrative begins from a retrospective point of view, that is 'a point of view located in the future in respect to the time which unfolds within the narrative'.[204] Thus the narrative begins on a meta-textual temporal level. Likewise Uspensky suggested:

> The same phenomenon is also common in the epilogue, where a point of view synchronized with the time of a particular character may be replaced by an all-embracing temporal point of view. Acceleration (or condensation) of time related to the broadened temporal span of the ending of the narrative is also characteristic of the epilogue.[205]

The Gospel ends on just this sort of 'all-embracing temporal point of view'. The disciples are 'in the temple continually praising God'.[206] In a slightly different sense, this image of the disciples blessing God serves the function of a frame by giving the sense of the complete 'cessation of time brought about by the characters' freezing into poses'.[207] This *tableau vivant* forms an effective frame to the Gospel, leaving the reader with a sense of an ending created by the fixed image of the disciples continually in the temple.

Phraseological Plane. Uspensky has suggested that framing may be realized on the phraseological plane when 'a figure and a vehicle of the authorial speech, disappears from the text almost immediately after the introduction and reappears distinctly and in person very seldom' until the end.[208] While none of the characters figures in both beginning and closing frames of the Gospel narrative, the similarity between the priestly function of Zechariah in ch. 1 and the levitical priestly blessing of Jesus in 24.50 has already been noted.[209] The blessing which Zechariah was unable to complete on behalf of the people is completed by Jesus on behalf of the disciples.[210]

Ideological Plane. A narrative may suggest various ways of viewing the world. According to Uspensky, 'From the viewpoint of compositional possibilities, the simplest case (and for us, the least interesting) occurs when ideological evaluation is carried out from a single, dominating point of view'.[211] Luke's main character, Jesus, is the primary vehicle for the ideological stance of the narrator. And by the end, the disciples, who at times are employed as foils to Jesus' (and the narrator's) ideological evaluation (see Luke 22.24-27), also reflect the narrator's ideological viewpoint as they bless God, even in the absence of Christ.

Focalization

Genette championed the use of the term *focalization* to address the questions 'who sees?"' and 'who speaks?'[212] More recently, Rimmon-Kenan has clarified the issue even further with her own theory:

> Thus, speaking and seeing, narration and focalization, may, but need not, be attributed to the same agent. The distinction between the two activities is a theoretical necessity, and only on its basis can the interrelations between them be studied with precision.[213]

It is possible, therefore, for the narrator to be speaking, but for the action to be described from the perspective of one of the characters.

While neither Genette nor Rimmon-Kenan specifically addresses the issue of focalization and closure, one might follow Uspensky's line of reasoning and propose that in closure one would expect the

story both to be seen and spoken through the eyes and mouth of the
narrator, in order to create the needed distance between the reader
and the characters and plot. Hence, in terms of focalization, the
readers of Luke 24.50-53 watch the closing scene from a distance
because their guide refuses to draw any closer.[214]

Closure and the Relationship between Narrator and Reader

A third set of terms is needed, according to Torgovnick, to describe
the relationship between the narrator and reader during closure.[215]
M.H. Abrams has characterized the recent developments in literary
criticism as belonging to the 'Age of Reading'.[216] Still, while the work
by Ingarden, Eco, Fish, Culler, Tompkins, and others demonstrates
the shift of interest by varying degrees from text-oriented to reader-
oriented theory, we should appreciate Edgar McKnight's admirable
attempt in *The Bible and the Reader* to trace the inception of reader-
oriented literary criticism through the structuralist-formalist tradition,
the European contributions, and the American context.[217] Reader-
response criticism has coined a variety of terms to describe the
various emphases and nuances of the work of the reader.[218]

Discussion has clustered primarily around text-centered and
reader-centered models. The earlier and later writings of Stanley
Fish represent most clearly the two distinct answers given to Robert
Fowler's clearly articulated question: 'Does the text control the
reader or does the reader control the text?'[219] Rather than enter into
a rather lengthy discussion of the varying prominent views, and since
I believe there is value in both, this essay will consider both the
reader created by the text, i.e. Chatman and Booth's implied reader,
and the real reader who seeks to read the text creatively, i.e. Fish's
informed reader. In fact, the best model may be the mediating
position of Wolfgang Iser's implied reader who is produced in the
phenomenological interaction between text and reader and is, strictly
speaking, neither inside nor outside the text. The textual closural
structures of the implied reader will be taken up first, followed by a
discussion of the stance during closure which real readers take
when they read creatively.[220]

The Implied Reader and Redundancy

Seymour Chatman has suggested that the implied reader is 'the
audience presupposed by the narrative itself'.[221] Similar is Wayne
Booth's suggestion that the author 'makes his reader, as he makes his

second self'.[222] Iser goes a step further in defining the implied reader as 'a textual structure anticipating the presence of a recipient without necessarily defining him'.[223] These definitions, particularly Iser's, are helpful in our understanding the ways in which both the circular and parallel patterns of closure shape the response of the reader and produce the satisfaction of an ending in Luke.

A relatively recent development in reader-response criticism has been the exploration of *redundancy* and its shaping of implied readers. Emerging from information theory, which attempts to examine the ways in which information is transmitted from sender to receiver,[224] the purpose of redundancy, according to Janice Capel Anderson, is to 'increase predictability by decreasing the number of possible alternatives'.[225] Anderson has gone on to claim that redundancy may be examined in light of repetition in words, character groupings, plot, variation of the redundant or repeated details, and the context in which the information is couched.[226]

Culpepper has noted that redundancy may occur at any of several levels of the text: (1) verbal—the repetition of words and phrases at various points in the narrative; (2) formal—the repetition and variation of formal units or type scenes; (3) events (plot) and existents (characters, settings)—plot development and patterns of characterization can repeat (often with variation) the same information; (4) implicit commentary—symbolism, irony, and other devices 'may reinforce or challenge information or meanings which the reader obtains from other elements of the narrative'; (5) story and narrative—explicit commentary may be used to communicate information to the reader; (6) genre and canon—the canonical Gospels with significant variation and repetition are redundant.[227]

Of particular value for this study is Culpepper's third category of redundancy in events and existents. It is significant that the setting of Jesus' final departure in Luke is Bethany and that the characters involved include only Jesus and the disciples.[228] Both the setting and the cast occur together only once before in Luke at 19.28-40. The effect of redundancy on the level of events and existents will be examined employing Anderson's categories of repetition, variation, and context.

Repetition. The strongest repetitive link between Luke 19.28-40 and 24.50-53 is the geographical setting 'near Bethany' (19.29; 24.50). To be sure, in Luke 19, Bethany is mentioned in conjunction with Bethphage and the Mount of Olives, while in Luke 24, the reference stands alone. In both cases, however, the reference is somewhat ambiguous. In Luke 19, Jesus 'drew near unto Bethany' while in ch. 24 he led them out 'in the neighborhood of Bethany'.[229] While the narrator will refer again to the Mount of Olives in the narrative (21.37; 22.39; cf. 19.37), Bethany is not mentioned again until 24.50 and Bethphage is a *hapax* for Luke.[230]

Discussion of the place Bethany has usually been from a redactional perspective which tries to separate traditional elements from redactional creativity. Marshall and Lohfink exemplify the two extremes to which this particular approach leads. Marshall has argued that the reference to Bethany thwarts any contention that the ascension narrative (Marshall accepts the longer text) is a Lukan creation.[231] Lohfink, on the other hand, arguing that the passage is entirely redactional, is forced to claim that Bethany is the only geographical place outside Jerusalem known to Luke.[232] Both arguments seem unfortunately overdrawn. So much emphasis has been placed on proving or disproving the existence of a tradition behind the text that the obvious synchronic connection at the level of the text is missed.

In addition to the setting, the cast of characters and their actions are basically the same (the differences will be discussed below). Jesus and the disciples appear in both pericopae. Jesus is leading the way in both instances (19.28; 24.50). The disciples are rejoicing and blessing God on their way to Jerusalem (19.37-38; 24.52-53).[233]

Culpepper has suggested: 'Repetition contributes to *recognition*: the reader recognizes significant or typical settings, actions, pronouncements, and conflicts'.[234] In connecting the Triumphal Entry with the closing pericope by means of repeating the setting and the main group of characters, the narrator has, in a sense, identified Jesus' departure as a 'Triumphal Exit', albeit without parade or fanfare. Therefore, as the Triumphal Entry brings an end to the journey to Jerusalem, so the Triumphal Exit, for the implied reader, brings closure to Jesus' exodus and death-resurrection-exaltation (ἀνάλημψις).

Variation. Variation is very nearly as important as repetition in redundant patterns. According to Anderson: 'When the [redundant] pattern is broken new information appears which cannot easily be assimilated. It creates uncertainty and requires the implied reader to make choices'.[235] Most notable among the differences is the absence of the Pharisees from the ascension narrative. At the Triumphal Entry, Pharisees demand that Jesus rebuke the disciples for singing Hosannas, to which Jesus replies, 'I tell you, if these were silent, the very stones would cry out' (19.39-40). Removing the Pharisees from the final scene also removes conflict which would detract from the final departure scene of Jesus. Thus, this variation aids the implied reader in sensing a proper dénouement.

Second, the disciples are not the only ones who bless in the final episode. Here, as already noted, Jesus blesses his disciples, and this is his last act. The 'King who comes in the name of the Lord' (19.38) becomes the Priest who blesses his flock in a final farewell gesture.[236] Again, this variation helps produce a sense of ending.

Third, the disciples do not bless God until they are back in Jerusalem, more specifically in the temple. Again, this variation may be due to a narrative strategy which emphasizes the resolution of the conflict between Jesus and his disciples and the religious authorities.

Fourth, the dialogue which occupies nearly half the space of the first Bethany scene is completely missing from the second one. Again, this variation may be attributed to the fact that the final scene is a silent one designed not only to communicate the departure of Jesus but also to create distance between reader and story and to facilitate the departure of the reader from the story world.

'Variation', according to Culpepper, 'produces *movement*: the story introduces new elements, and the reader is required to integrate the new elements into the previous patterns'.[237] The movement in the case of the second Bethany scene contributes to the closing of the Gospel story. The demands on the implied reader to integrate the variations between these two stories are greater than at other places in Luke–Acts, but the reward is the satisfaction of knowing the Gospel threads—at least most of them—have been neatly tied and Luke's story of Jesus has been successfully concluded.

Context. Context serves to reduce alternatives for the reader.[238] Or to quote Culpepper again: 'Context allows *integration*: the more specific and informative the context the more successful the reader will be in evaluating a scene and integrating it, with its new elements, into the reading experience'.[239] The respective context of each Bethany scene helps establish certain limits. While the disciples travel to Jerusalem, the city of destiny in both passages, the narrative sandwiched between the two scenes radically alters one's understanding of that destiny. The immediate context for Jesus and the disciples in Luke 19 suggests Jerusalem is the city where prophets are killed, the site of Jesus' passion. Jesus' weeping over the city is a poignant example of what sort of image Jerusalem evokes for the reader of the Triumphal Entry.

In its immediate context, the Jerusalem to which the disciples return in Luke 24 is the site of the post-resurrection appearances of Jesus (24.36-43), the beginning of the preaching of repentance and forgiveness of sins (24.47), and the locale where the Father will endow the disciples with power from on high (24.49). The contextual differences between the two passages allows the implied reader to integrate this closing scene of the Gospel with the rest of the narrative.

An important function of any text is to shape its readers into good or informed readers, producing the desired result whether moral improvement or pure entertainment. Edgar Allan Poe once remarked: 'During the hour of perusal, the soul of the reader is at the writer's control'.[240] Hopefully, the control of the Gospel story over the soul of the implied reader extends beyond the construction of an implied reader from textual structures and shapes the perspectives of the real reader who is willing to become that implied reader.

The Informed Reader

The other side of the reader-response coin is equally important. This reader is roughly equivalent to Torgovnick's ideal reader 'who reads the text as it ought to be read'[241] or Fish's informed reader who is 'neither an abstraction, nor an actual living reader, but a hybrid—a real reader (me) who does everything within his power to make himself informed'.[242] In other words, the implied reader is not only the sum of all the reader clues derived from the clues; the term also describes real readers who attempt to be 'informed' readers by conforming their reading to the textual markers of the narrative.

Real readers, whether of the first or twentieth century, often are not able to make the moves the text requires. As Chatman has noted, 'Of course, the real reader may reject his projected role at some ultimate level'.[243] Twentieth-century readers are forced either to make sense of the text with sometimes contrived interpretations or accept the suggestion that one simply cannot make sense of a particular text. First-century readers of non-canonical religious texts had a luxury not now afforded the modern reader. If they did not like the way a text read, they could change it to suit them! Or as Kermode has noted:

> So long as a narrative was rewritable—that is, so long as it had not achieved canonical status—it was possible to change it, not only by excising elements no longer thought *convenable*, but by actual narrative intrusion. Once the canon was formed and the texts given

the sanctity that corresponds to the institution's desire to protect them, interpreters could not alter them but wrote commentaries instead.[244]

Such seems to be the case with Luke 24.50-53. Already I have argued on text-critical grounds that the reference to the ascension and the subsequent worship of the disciples are later interpolations into the text due to a christological tendency of the copyist(s).[245] One might also examine the problem in terms of reader response. To begin, let us take an obvious example of a textual variant which is generally agreed to be a later intrusion into the text. The Gospel ends with the reference to the disciples in the temple blessing God.[246] Several manuscripts (A B C² ΘΨ 063, f¹.¹³, M lat syᵖ·ʰ), however, add the word 'amen' at the conclusion. On this variant, Metzger has commented: 'The word, which is absent from the earliest and best representatives of both the Alexandrian and the Western types of text, is a liturgical addition introduced by copyists'.[247] This addition is not peculiar to Luke, for similar concluding elements are added to Matthew, Mark (both the intermediate and longer endings, though not after 16.8), John, and Acts. In one sense, these elements represent reader-response attempts to give solemnity to the Gospel.

Turning attention now to the more problematic passages, one might argue that the phrase 'and he ascended into heaven' (as well as 'they worshipped him') is also an example of reader response. That first phrase, 'and he ascended into heaven', may very well be the result of a real reader's inability to fulfill the role of the implied or ideal reader. Since 9.51 'when the days were fulfilled for his "lifting up"' the reader has been preparing for the fulfillment of this promise—and on first reading (if not also on subsequent readings), this reference seems to be to the 'taking up', that is, the ascension of Jesus. To use Petersen's metaphor, the first shoe is dropped at 9.51, and the reader anticipates the echo of the second shoe before a sense of closure is complete.[248] The shorter text, however, does not fulfill that tension. On the level of reader response, it is very easy to understand how a scribe could have added the reference to the ascension to bring the Gospel to what was believed to be its proper ending. As Petersen has observed: 'It is one thing to be dissatisfied with the end of a story, or not to believe that its end is the end, and quite another to substitute our own ending for the narrator's'.[249]

That this expectation would be true of the average first- (or fifth-) century reader has been ably demonstrated by Talbert. Talbert has shown that many of the documents which derive from Mediterranean antiquity employed 'functions of prophecy' or predictive material which anticipated later fulfillment. This narrative strategy is to be found both in Greek biographies and Jewish works alike.[250]

Regardless of how one interprets the ending, all would agree that at least for the real reader of today: 'The end of a text is not the end of the work when the narrator leaves unfinished business for the reader to complete, thoughtfully and imaginatively, not textually'.[251] It is possible to offer a plausible argument that the end of the Third Gospel is flawed and that the promise of 9.51 is simply left unfulfilled. While this is certainly a possible solution, readers would rather opt for the longer text and assign the flaw to a later, unknown, less inspired scribe![252]

Others might prefer to argue that the text is open-ended and does not bring the story to closure. While it will be held that the Gospel of Luke does not close so neatly as many suggest, the strong closural devices already discussed do suggest that the ending, however unexpectedly, does come. The thread left hanging, and admittedly it is a rather thick one, may be one way the narrator was able to prepare the reader for the continuation of the story in Acts.

Even if there were no longer text under whose shade we could take refuge, more than likely real readers, even those trying to be informed readers, would try to make sense of this passage as it stands. Kermode was surely right when he wrote:

> when we are looking for closure we may find in these parts evidence of that silent thickening of the texture, that occult tying of knots, which will quiet our anxiety (it is hardly too strong a word for our desire not to be fooled or disappointed by an ending).[253]

Susan Praeder has called this tendency of readers 'an old temptation, the temptation to make sense of the text'.[254] Being one of those readers, however, who likes to make sense of what is read, I have presented several alternatives for making sense of 24.50-53 as closure. The caution of Praeder to avoid the 'new temptation' to give the reader sovereignty over text and author is well taken: 'I would like to hear less about "the almighty reader" and more about "my reading", its strengths and weaknesses, the risks taken and not taken, and its relation to other readings'.[255] Below then is my reading of Luke 24.50-53, along with others, and the risks taken or not taken in any one of them.

One way to make sense of Luke's ending is by means of what

Barbara Herrnstein Smith called 'retrospective patterning'. Smith defined the process of retrospective patterning as 'readjusting perceptions of preceding expectations'[256] and claimed:

> certain thematic elements ... are brought into alignment, as it were, through what I have called 'retrospective patterning': that is, connections and similarities are illuminated, and the reader perceives that seemingly gratuitous or random events, details, and juxtapositions have been selected in accord with certain principles.[257]

Torgovnick has developed this process of retrospective patterning in her discussion of closure:

> Second or subsequent readings—when the question of 'what happens next' no longer pertains with urgency—differ fundamentally from first readings and resemble the ways in which we experience the past. Upon rereading, pattern and rhythm—connections between beginning, middle, and end—may be more easily discerned and more fully understood by the reader. Appreciating such connections through retrospective patterning provides the primary pleasure of rereadings, just as reliving the facts or perceiving the patterns in our lives forms the basis in which we regard our pasts.[258]

In the case of the ending of the Gospel of Luke, it seems that there are at least four ways of employing retrospective patterning to make sense of the text. First, one may interpret everything preceding 24.50-53, especially 9.51, in light of the ending. This reading would argue that the reference to ἀνάλημψις in 9.51 is not to the ascension of Jesus, but only to his death.[259] In particular, Plooij was an avid proponent of this view. In effect, Plooij, arguing from the shorter text, interpreted 9.51 in light of 24.51.[260]

Second, one may interpret the ending in light of everything that has preceded it, especially 9.51. In this category of readers would fall the work of Plummer,[261] S.M. Gilmour,[262] J.M. Creed,[263] the earlier work of Talbert,[264] and other older commentaries. This interpretation would hold that Luke 24.50-53 was a reference to the ascension, regardless of the text one read: the expectation created by the preceding narrative must be fulfilled at the end.

Third, one may interpret the end separate from the middle, either consciously or unconsciously accepting an incomplete conclusion with unfulfilled expectations or finding satisfactory dénouement in the ascension narrative of Acts. Into this category may be placed

A.R.C. Leaney,[265] and all those who have argued that Luke 24.50-53 and Acts 1.1-5 are later interpolations.[266]

Finally, one may interpret both middle and ending in light of one another through retrospective patterning. The first-time or casual reader of the Gospel of Luke would most probably first understand 9.51 as a reference to the ascension. This suggestion is strengthened by the fact that the word ἀναλαμβάνω is commonly used in ancient Jewish and pagan assumption stories, and is the favorite word of the New Testament to describe Jesus' ascension. Thus, the expectation that the day of Jesus' ascension will occur before the end of the Gospel arises from the text and is not an unreasonable expectation of the reader. When the reader arrives at the end, however, there is no explicit reference to the ascension. The reader is forced to do two things to gain a sense of satisfaction and closure. First, Luke 9.51 must be re-examined in light of the ending. What appears on first reading to be a reference to the ascension and nothing more must now be understood to include his death and resurrection as well. In fact, this reading is prominent in most of the recent commentaries, even those which accept the longer text.

Second, the reader must re-examine the ending in light of 9.51 and all that follows. Hence, the reader is led to understand that 24.50-53 contains at least a veiled reference to the ascension with the words 'and he departed from them'.[267] The result of such a reading is to strengthen the continuity between the crucified Christ, the resurrected Lord, and the Ascended One. The reader is unable to leap over Good Friday and Easter morning to the exaltation of Jesus. In addition, the significance of the ascension is drastically reduced, almost annihilated. In fact, some readers would never catch a hint of the ascension, especially if the narrative of Acts were unknown to them. Of far greater impact is the realization that Jesus is absent, yet the disciples still respond with joyful, obedient, and persistent faith. The real reader, desperately trying to fulfill the role of the implied reader, finds comfort in the fact that like the disciples he or she serves an absent Christ who has departed from them, and discovers courage in the response of the disciples.[268]

Categorizing the Ending of Luke

The relationship between narrator and reader during closure has been categorized by Torgovnick into four classifications. In the first, *complementary*, 'the reader accepts—more or less uncritically—both the ending itself and whatever meaning (or lack of meaning) the author wishes it to convey'.[269] A second relationship labelled by Torgovnick as *incongruent* exists 'when the author must more actively coax his reader into accepting an ending'.[270] The third category is closely related to the second; the relationship between narrator and reader may be called *congruent* if 'successful persuasion during closure results in the reader's acceptance of the ending'.[271] Here an incongruent relationship is converted to a congruent one. The last narrator-reader relationship, *confrontational*, describes the effort to confront the reader 'with the endings that deliberately thwart reader expectation, using the confrontation to achieve desired aesthetic and philosophical ends'.[272]

The relationship between narrator and reader in the closural process of Luke's Gospel may best be described as either incongruent or congruent. It is incongruent for those readers who are unable to make sense of the text and are forced to rewrite the ending or evoke extra-textual evidence to give the text proper closure. As Torgovnick has noted: 'Unsuccessful persuasion results in some continuing degree of incongruence, in some sense for the reader the ending is flawed'.[273] Those readers who are able to make sense of the text through retrospective patterning experience a congruent relationship when they accept the narrator's understanding of the cruciality of the 'lifting up' event (death-resurrection-ascension) for Luke's story of Jesus.[274]

Conclusion

From this analysis it may be concluded that the narrator of Luke has employed certain closural strategies to resolve the tensions of the major plot strategies of Luke's story of Jesus. Incomplete and complete priestly blessings, returning to Jerusalem, the timely appearance of angels, defining and redefining the pious people of God, and the temple and city of Jerusalem, are all literary devices which by virtue of their significance at the beginning and ending of the story draw a circle around the narrative. The literary circle depicts the limits of the story as effectively as the frame around a portrait. The painting evangelist has taken much care in framing the portrait he has so painstakingly produced.

The plot lines of the Gospel are effectively developed by such strategies as conflict scenes, prophecy and fulfillment, and the journey narrative of the central section. The threads of each of these plot devices in turn are neatly tied together by narrative closure. The temple, once the scene of heated confrontation between God's messenger, Jesus, and God's people, the Jewish leaders, has now become the site of God's new messengers, the disciples, blessing God unimpeded. Predictive materials from the Hebrew scriptures, heavenly messengers, and living prophets are used to create suspense and maintain interest in the story-line. Those prolepses become analepses in the final chapter, turning the expectations of the narrative inward and providing closure. The journey of Jesus is finally completed when he leads his followers out as far as Bethany, and then departs from them. At that point, a new journey begins and is the subject of Luke's subsequent volume.

The point of view of the narrator and the reader is also helpful in providing closure. In framing the narrative, the narrator has provided aids both to introduce and to exit the reader to and from the story. In varying degrees, the psychological, spatial, temporal, phraseological, and ideological levels of point of view all contribute to the ending of the Gospel. No inside views on the characters create distance between reader and text on the psychological plane. The silence of the final scene creates the feeling of distance and separation on the spatial plane. The fixed image of the disciples continually in the temple blessing God provides finality on the temporal level. Priestly references at beginning and end provide closure from the phraseological point of view. And the merging of viewpoints of narrator, reader, Jesus, and disciples, on the ideological plane strengthens the sense of closure.

The relationship between narrator and reader is equally important in creating a satisfactory dénouement. Employing the strategy of redundancy, the reader is coaxed to view the departure of Jesus as the Triumphal Exit corresponding to his Triumphal Entry. Both occur in the vicinity of Bethany and involve Jesus and the disciples. The variations in these two stories—the absence of the Pharisees, the blessing of Jesus, the presence of the disciples in the temple, and the suppression of dialogue—contribute significantly to the closural process in Luke. The fact that many real readers have been unhappy with the departure of Jesus, with no explicit reference to his ascension, indicates that Luke may well have been attempting to coax hesitant readers to accept his corrective of the significance of the ascension. Subsequent readings by the same reader, as well as different readers, may produce different readings—all of which are plausible. The most coherent one seems to be the one which finally conforms to the textual markers (almost hidden at times) that point to the inextricability of the death-resurrection-ascension of Jesus.

Despite the strong sense of closure, one must admit that there are numerous threads which remain untied, and several gaps which remain unfilled. Linkage is used to connect the story of Jesus in the Gospel with the story of his followers in Acts. Major events and themes like Jesus' departure, the mandate to witness, and the gift of the Holy Spirit, among others, are interlaced between the two narratives.

In terms of incomplete closure, conflict is resolved only to be re-opened in Acts—the fate of Israel still undecided by the end of Luke. Many prophecies and predictions do *not* find fulfillment within the narrative time of the Gospel. The journey of Jesus is finished; but his *analempsis* is 'to be continued' in Book II.

In the closural process, gaps do remain open. This fact has led J. Hillis Miller to conclude:

> Attempts to characterize the fiction of a given period by its commitment to closure or to open-endedness are blocked from the beginning by the impossibility of ever demonstrating whether a given narrative is closed or open. Analysis of endings leads always, if carried far enough, to the paralysis of this inability to decide.[275]

Others, and I place myself in this camp, are not quite so pessimistic about the reader's ability to sense an ending. As Barbara Smith has pointed out, 'no matter how weak the forces of closure are, the simple fact that its last line is followed by an expanse of blank paper will inform the reader that it is concluded'.[276]

The work of the narrative is over, but the work of the reader is unfinished. As Lou Silberman has noted: 'To be a teller of tales is no mean feat. To be a hearer of tales, too, is a high accomplishment, a noble art'.[277] So the reader is no less an artist than the author! While the readers are being ushered out the temple gate where they first entered the story, they glance over their shoulders and the image of disciples praising God, despite the absence of their Lord, is indelibly imprinted upon their hearts and minds. At that moment, the narrator/guide at their elbows whispers in their ears a command 'Go thou and do likewise!' and an invitation 'And please come again!'[278]

PART II
THE DEPARTURE OF JESUS IN ACTS

Chapter 4

ACTS 1.1-11 IN HISTORICAL CONTEXT:
A DIACHRONIC ANALYSIS

This chapter follows the same methodological path as Chapter 2. Using the tools of diachronic analysis, the opening verses are set in their historical context. First, the text of Acts 1.1-11 is established. Next, employing the insights of form criticism, the shape or genre of Acts 1.1-11 (especially vv. 6-11) is explored in light of other ancient ascension stories. Finally, the origins of the ascension narrative in Acts are probed in a brief tradition-history of the text.

Text-Critical Analysis:
Establishing the Text of Acts 1.1-11

Fitzmyer has recently written a stimulating and provocative article on the meaning of the ascension of Christ and Pentecost, and the relationship between the two.[1] In the course of his defense of the longer text of Luke 24.51, Fitzmyer commented:

> Yet, even if someone were to continue to question the [longer] reading, one would have to cope with the beginning of the Lucan second volume, which implies that the 'first volume'. . . ended with a mention of the ascension: 'until the day when he was taken up' (Acts 1.2), seemingly a reference to Lk. 24.51b.[2]

Having questioned the longer reading of Luke 24.51 in Chapter 2, I would like in this chapter to take up Fitzmyer's second challenge 'to cope with the beginning of the Lucan second volume' in order to show that the evidence of Acts 1 supports, rather than militates against, reading the shorter text at Luke 24.51. In fact, a close reading of the textual evidence and the texts themselves suggests such a conclusion is not only possible, but perhaps even probable.

History of Research

Research into the text of Acts has had a lively and colorful history. There are, of course, two distinct forms of the text of Acts. The Western text is nearly ten percent longer than the Alexandrian. More specifically, the text edited by A.C. Clark, a Western-type text, is eight and one-half percent longer than the text produced by Westcott and Hort, typically Alexandrian.[3] The Western text of Acts is 'generally more picturesque and circumstantial, whereas the shorter text is generally more colorless and in places more obscure'.[4]

This unusual phenomenon of two quite distinct texts led to several unique theories about the original text of Acts. As E.J. Epp has noted:

> For generations the striking text which Codex Bezae presents has been the object of extensive study, has evoked considerable controversy, has occasioned several novel theories, and has remained, all the while, at the center of the yet unsolved mystery of the 'Western' text.[5]

Below is a brief history of the research into the text of the Acts of the Apostles.[6] Major options will be presented and assessed. A summary of the current state of scholarship on the text of Acts will be followed by an extended analysis of the specific textual problems of Acts 1.1-11.[7]

Two Editions. The view that Luke had made two editions of the Acts was not original to Frederick Blass; rather, according to A.C. Clark, Jean Leclerc first argued for two editions coming from the same hand.[8] Blass was the first to popularize the argument.[9] Blass's contention was that Luke first produced a longer, rough draft of Acts in Rome which he later revised in the East, excising superfluous phrases and smoothing over awkward terminology.[10] This polished, second edition is preserved by the Alexandrian manuscripts, while the original rough draft was copied and preserved by the Roman church. The Western text is its main witness.

Blass's argument was immediately challenged in a scathing review by T.E. Page.[11] Page claimed the variants in the Western text 'bear traces of subsequent corrections of the text by a second-rate hand; that they were Luke's original version is incredible'.[12] Page identified four categories of the Western variants: (1) repeated exaggeration of emphasis; (2) introduction of religious formulae; (3) expansion of christological titles for Jesus; (4) heightening of the role of the Spirit.[13] He concluded that the variants of the Western tradition 'add practically nothing to our real knowledge of the Acts, while they frequently mar and spoil what they seek to improve'.[14]

Others also criticized Blass. In a work dedicated to the memory of Blass, A.C. Clark remarked: 'I gladly acknowledge my great debt to him ... I cannot, however, accept his attribution of both Z [Western] and G [Alexandrian] to the same author'.[15] Clark admitted that overall Blass's view was reasonable: 'Blass developed his theory with great skill and learning, and, if the Acts stood alone, it would possess considerable plausibility'.[16] Clark maintained that the problem, however, was not confined to Acts. In Luke, where Z is conspicuous for omissions, Blass was forced to reverse the roles and suggested the *editio Romana* was represented by G.

James Hardy Ropes also rejected Blass's proposal on the basis of what he called 'two fatal considerations'.[17] These were: (1) the theory insisted the author's revision resulted in a reduction of the serious and religious tone which had been adopted at first;[18] (2) there were major discrepancies in the two versions, with the Western text, in some cases, blatantly built on a misinterpretation of the Alexandrian.[19]

More recently, Haenchen has struck a similar vein of criticism. Haenchen has asserted Blass's 'hypothesis comes to grief, however, from the very fact that the texts often contradict each other'.[20] It might be noted at this point that this particular criticism, sounded by Clark, Ropes, and Haenchen, may not be as telling as once thought. Certainly the narrator of Luke–Acts, either through the use of sources or literary genius, was capable of retelling certain stories with both small and significant variations in detail.[21]

Despite such criticisms, Blass's theory has had some following. Eberhard Nestle,[22] Theodor Zahn,[23] J.M. Wilson,[24] and A.J. Wensinck,[25] all endorsed the two-edition theory. Most recently, Helmut Koester in his two-volume *Introduction to the New Testament* has apparently attempted to revive the theory that there were two ancient editions of Acts.[26] Blass's hypothesis is as impervious as it is indefensible; nevertheless, Metzger has noted 'most scholars today are reluctant to adopt Blass's theory of two editions of Acts'.[27]

Latinizations. In a study written near the end of the nineteenth century, J. Rendel Harris argued that 'the whole of the Greek text of Codex Bezae from the beginning of Matthew to the end of Acts is a re-adjustment of an earlier text to the Latin version'.[28] In fact, Harris concluded 'so extensively has the Greek text of Codex Bezae been modified by the process of Latinization that we can no longer regard D as a distinct authority apart from d'.[29]

Recent studies of bilingual codices, however, have shown that the influence is two-way.[30] A.C. Clark referred to the Latin d as a 'servile translation of D'.[31] Epp's conclusion seems cogent: 'the differences between D and d become less important because they are accounted for by the fact that it was largely d that suffered by assimilation'.[32]

Aramaisms. While others had suggested an underlying Semitic source for Acts (especially chs. 1-15), C.C. Torrey gave shape to the classic treatment of the Aramaic documentary hypothesis.[33] In a lengthy article Torrey argued that Luke himself had translated the infancy narrative from Hebrew into Greek.[34] Several criteria were employed in evaluating the data, the most important of which was 'the continued presence, in texts of considerable extent, of a Semitic idiom underlying the Greek'.[35]

This theory that Luke had used Semitic sources and had translated at least some of them himself was expanded in Torrey's *Composition and Date of Acts*.[36] Here Torrey argued for a written Aramaic source, literally translated by the Third Evangelist, underlying the first fifteen chapters of Acts.[37] Torrey contended:

> In short, the Greek of the first half of Acts differs widely and constantly from that of the second half, both in the idiom which it uses and in its literary structure. There is one obvious and satisfactory way of accounting for this fact, namely the hypothesis of translation in the first half.[38]

Torrey's investigation led him to disregard the textual variants of Codex Bezae since the Western text was 'later, and all but worthless'.[39]He also believed it impossible to recover or reconstruct Luke's Aramaic sources.

Torrey's hypothesis received mixed reviews.[40] Cadbury is typical of those who found difficulties with Torrey's view. Just a few of his more serious criticisms may be mentioned here. (1) Cadbury noted that Semitic expressions are found in Paul's writings and raised the question whether it were not possible for a Hellenistic Jew (or Christian) to compose a document 'as Semitic as that of Luke' without positing a translator.[41] (2) He also questioned many of Torrey's supposed mistranslations and suggested the discrepancies might be due to other reasons.[42] (3) Cadbury found Semitisms in Acts 16-28 which could not be dismissed as due to 'the influence of the translation-Greek which Luke had so extensively read and written'.[43] (4) Finally, the literary unity and integrity of the narrative of Acts was a decisive argument against Luke's use of a separate translated source for Acts 1-15.[44]

Despite such arguments, Torrey's Aramaic-document hypothesis did gain some limited support. Wilcox has perspicuously remarked on this bifurcation of opinion:

> Investigations seem to suggest that those who give support—though admittedly qualified support—to Torrey's position approach the material with a view to assessing the nature, extent, and intrinsic (historical) worth of such source-material as Luke may have used in the making of Acts; the other group makes its approach rather from the standpoint that Acts represents a literary whole; it is in the true sense not so much a compilation as a genuine literary composition.[45]

Metzger has concluded about Torrey's view: 'though such an hypothesis may account for certain linguistic phenomena, it offers no help in explaining how the Bezan text of Acts became nearly one-tenth longer than the Alexandrian text'.[46]

Black again took up the question of Aramaic sources in Acts in his work *An Aramaic Approach to the Gospels and Acts*, published in 1946.[47] Following his own evaluation of earlier work on Semitisms, Black suggested that Aramaisms did indeed 'contribute substantially to the solution of the great textual problems'.[48] Unlike Torrey, who believed D represented a translation of a hypothetical Aramaic version of the original text (Codex B),[49] Black asserted that the two distinct texts of B and D reflected 'different redactions of what was substantially, if not verbally, the same original Gospel text'.[50] The differences may be accounted for by recognizing that 'the redaction represented by the Bezan Codex has preserved more of the characteristics of the pre-Vulgate "fluid" textual period, the primitive type of text in earliest circulation, than the Vatican-Sinaitic redaction'.[51] In other words, Black would opt for an eclectic method in determining the original reading in a particular text.[52]

Max Wilcox drew conclusions similar to those of his teacher, Black.[53] Wilcox rejected Torrey's notion of a written Aramaic source:

> These 'little' knots of Semitic material surviving unrevised, although affording a rather strong indication of the general authenticity of the stories in which they are embedded, nevertheless do not permit us to argue in favour of translation of Aramaic or Hebrew sources by Luke.[54]

Wilcox distinguished three classes of Semitisms in Acts: (1) words, phrases, and verses which reflect some knowledge of the Hebrew Old

Testament textual traditions; (2) words and phrases which reflect affinity with the Septuagint; and (3) Semitic words and phrases which are not explained by LXX influence.[55]

J.D. Yoder arrived at conclusions much different from Torrey, Black, and Wilcox, in his study on the Semitisms in Codex D. He argued:

> (1) When one takes into account not only the instances of Semitic phenomena in codex Bezae, but also the Bezan variants which abandon Semitisms found in other MSS, the net increase of Semitisms is sometimes inconsequential, while in other respects this MS actually reveals fewer Semitisms than found in the B text; and (2) oft-times the data are concentrated in limited areas of the text, thus detracting from the supposed homogeneity of the Bezan text.[56]

While these theories about Semitisms in Bezae have much which commends them, on the whole, they have not provided the needed evidence to reconstruct a viable history of transmission for the Western text. The other options that remain are the classic statements which regard the Western and Alexandrian texts, respectively, as preserving the original text.

Western Text as Original Text. In a book published in 1914, A.C. Clark argued that the Western text reflected the original text and the Alexandrian was due to accidental omissions.[57] Ropes criticized this view claiming 'the theory . . . does not account for the facts . . . which show a rational, not merely an accidental, difference between the types of text'.[58] Later, Clark argued that the Alexandrian text was the result of deliberate excisions of the Western text.[59] By this time, Clark had abandoned his accidental-omission theory, claiming: 'The hypothesis of deliberate abbreviation clears up a number of difficulties which were left unexplained by the theory of accidental omission'.[60]

Clark's work received much attention but little support.[61] Because the Western text seemingly expands the typically colorless Alexandrian narrative and explains otherwise obscure passages, Clark's view has never carried scholarly consensus.

Alexandrian Text as Original Text. Ropes published *The Text of Acts* in 1926 as the third volume of the monumental five-volume work on Acts, *The Beginnings of Christianity*.[62] In the introduction to his study, Ropes claimed 'the creation of the "Western" text was the most important event in the history of the text of Acts, and the recovery of it . . . is an essential preliminary to a sound judgment on the textual criticisms of the book'.[63] Nonetheless, Ropes held that the Western text was not the product of the original author of Acts.[64] Rather, Ropes' hypothesis was:

> the 'Western' text was the original 'canonical' text (if the anachronism can be pardoned) which was later supplanted by a 'pre-canonical' text of superior age and merit. Such a theory involves many considerations, and would have grave consequences for the earliest history of the New Testament canon.[65]

Despite the fact that Ropes was willing to accept the Western text as an ancient tradition,[66] he found the Western text almost invariably inferior to the Old Uncials (Alexandrian).

For Ropes, as for Clark, the options were clear-cut: either the Western text preserved the primitive text and the Alexandrian was secondary or the opposite was true. While Ropes could imagine a reviser expanding the text to make it fuller, smoother, and more picturesque, he had considerable difficulty reasoning that a reviser would condense the Western text, sacrificing the vivid imagery and religious character of the text in the process.[67]

Haenchen, in his magisterial work on Acts, has also accepted the Alexandrian text as the more primitive. He argued that there are three categories of Western variants: (1) general alterations, found also in the Gospels and Pauline epistles, intended to polish and elucidate; (2) variants, peculiar to the Western text of Acts, which attempt to palliate redactional seams; (3) other variants, often resulting from Latinization, which belong peculiarly to Codex d and not to the Western text.[68] Haenchen concluded: 'In none of these three cases does the "Western" text of Acts provide us with the "original" text: that is the lesson we have been in gradual process of learning'.[69]

Eclectic Method. To date, no adequate theory of the transmission of the Western text has been presented. In fact, this lack of progress in textual theory, in general, has led Epp to speak of a 'twentieth-century interlude' in new Testament textual criticism.[70] The result has been that many scholars have been driven, some reluctantly, others jubilantly, to assume an eclectic methodology.[71] Typical is the remark made by the editorial committee in the *Textual Commentary* to the third edition of the UBS text:

> Since no hypothesis . . . to explain the relation of the Western and the Alexandrian texts of Acts has gained anything like general

assent, . . . the Bible Societies' Committee proceeded in an eclectic fashion, holding that neither the Alexandrian nor the Western group of witnesses always preserves the original text.[72]

While some have embraced this eclectic methodology with open arms,[73] Epp has warned that the eclectic method 'is as much a symptom of basic problems in the discipline as it is a proposed and widely applied solution to those problems'.[74] Epp distinguished between eclectic generalists, who recognize that no single criterion can be uniformly applied to all textual problems, and eclectic specialists who characteristically either favor external evidence or internal evidence in most text-critical judgments.[75]

Many eclectics who consider themselves to be generalists are, in fact, specialists. Epp cited the UBS Committee as an example. While the Committee pledged to proceed in 'an eclectic fashion' (see above), one finds a steady stream of such phrases as 'the preponderant weight of external attestation', 'the overwhelming weight of manuscript evidence', and 'superior manuscript support'. In fact, in their comment on Acts 2.17-21, they state: 'the possibility must be left open that occasionally the text of B represents a secondary development'.[76] While claiming to be eclectic generalists, they act as eclectic specialists, favoring external evidence in most readings.

The remainder of this chapter will examine the particular textual problems found in Acts 1.1-11. Since no new theory which would capture the elusive, pristine text is being offered here (such an endeavor is beyond the limitations of this work and this writer), I shall proceed to employ an eclectic methodology with due caution and recognition of its obvious limitations.[77]

The Textual Problems in Acts 1

The goal of this study is to recover as nearly as possible the text which best reflects that produced by Luke (or his community). This statement assumes, of course, that at some point in the early church, there existed a text of Luke–Acts which was the original text. Not all would agree,[78] nor would all share the same concern for its recovery.[79] With slight modification, I concur with Frank Stagg's statement: 'Although it runs against many currents today, I believe that the overriding task of textual criticism is the establishment of the text seemingly nearest authorial intention, not simply the gathering of variants'.[80] Authorial intent may be beyond recovery, even if the original manuscript were extant; however, the chief concern of Stagg remains intact: textual criticism is to recover the text which best reflects the oldest and best (and perhaps original) manuscript tradition. I am persuaded that all forms of Higher Criticism, particularly redactional studies, narrative criticism, and structuralism, are severely crippled (if not totally incapacitated) if the theology and literary style reflected in the document are that of a third-century scribe and not that of the author(s).[81]

Interpolation Theories. Before turning to the specific textual problems in Acts 1, it is necessary to consider the several theories which proposed either one or both ascension stories were later interpolations. Kirsopp Lake argued that the ascension narrative in Luke 24 had been added later when the two works were divided.[82] This view received the support of Wilder who maintained 'Luke 24.50-53, entire, is best seen as a summary of Acts 1.1-11, added to Luke when the two works were separated from each other'.[83] Conzelmann suggested: 'Luke xxiv, 50-53 is not an original part of the gospel. Luke's original account of the Ascension seems rather to be in Acts 1, even if it is amplified by an interpolation'.[84] Phillipe Menoud assumed both ascension accounts were interpolations added when the one-volume work of Luke–Acts was divided upon its acceptance into the canon.[85]

None of these proposals ever gained a broad following. Haenchen has argued against the supposition that Luke's work was originally one volume:

> First, the works were not taken into the canon by an ecclesiastical authority able to ensure the simultaneous alteration of all existing copies: their acceptance was, rather, a long drawn-out process. Nowhere have any traces come to light of the hypothetical older book. Second, it was daring enough to provide the gospel with a sequel in the shape of a book on the apostolic age, but is downright unthinkable that, instead of closing the gospel with the Resurrection and Ascension, Luke should prolong it until Paul's arrival in Rome; for him the life of Jesus was a self-contained epoch in the history of salvation, one distinct from the period which followed.[86]

These arguments for interpolation are also crippled by the fact that there is absolutely no manuscript evidence for such a hypothesis. Unless some archaeological discovery reverses that situation, these interpolation theories appear destined to float in the rarefied air of conjecture and guesswork.

Establishing a Text for Acts 1.1-11. Below are discussed the major textual problems found in Acts 1.1-11. An attempt is made to discuss

the evidence and adjudicate between the various readings.
1. Acts 1.2. In some Old Latin manuscripts ἀνελήμφθη is omitted. Augustine preserved this verse in *Acta cum Felice Manichaeo*: 'in die quo Apostolos elegit per Spiritum sanctum, et praecepit praedicare evangelium'.[87] A slightly different version is found in Augustine's *De unitate ecclesiae*: 'usque in diem quo Apostolos elegit per Spiritum sanctum, mandans eis praedicare evangelium'.[88] Similarly, Codex Gigas (gig) and Liber comicus (t) read: 'In die, qua praecepit apostolis per spiritum sanctum praedicare evangelium quos elegerat'.[89]

In Codex D, the Greek text reads: ἄρχι ἧς ἡμέρας ἀνελήμφθη ἐντειλάμενος τοῖς ἀποστόλοις διὰ πνεύματος ἁγίου οὓς ἐξελέξατο καὶ ἐκέλευσε κηρύσσειν τὸ εὐαγγέλιον. A similar text is attested by Thomas of Harkel for a Greek manuscript which he collated at the Enaton Monastery.[90] In addition, the Sahidic version also transposes ἀνελήμφθη earlier, but seems to have translated a Greek text that read κηρύσσειν τὸ εὐαγγέλιον οὓς ἐξελέξατο after ἁγίου.[91]

The text read by all other extant ancient Greek manuscripts, and found in most critical Greek editions, is: ἄχρι ἧς ἡμέρας ἐντειλάμενος τοῖς ἀποστόλοις διὰ πνεύματος ἁγίου οὓς ἐξελέξατο ἀνελήμφθη. The confusing evidence—with no fewer than six distinct variants—is diagrammed below in Table 11.

Table 11
Textual Evidence for Acts 1.2

Manuscript/Version	Text
Codex Vaticanus[a]	ἄχρι ἧς ἡμέρας ἐντειλάμενος τοῖς ἀποστόλοις διὰ πνεύματος ἁγίου οὓς ἐξελέξατο ἀνελήμφθη.
Codex Cantabrigiensis	ἄχρι ἧς ἡμέρας ἀνελήμφθη ἐντειλάμενος τοῖς ἀποστόλοις διὰ πνεύματος ἁγίου οὓς ἐξελέξατο καὶ ἐκέλευσε κηρύσσειν τὸ εὐαγγέλιον.
Sahadic Version	ἄχρι ἧς ἡμέρας ἀνελήμφθη ἐντειλάμενος τοῖς ἀποστόλοις διὰ πνεύματος ἁγίου κηρύσσειν τὸ εὐαγγέλιον οὓς ἐξελέξατο.
Harclean Version	ἄχρι ἧς ἡμέρας ἀνελήμφθη ἐντειλάμενος τοῖς ἀποστόλοις οὓς ἐξελέξατο διὰ πνεύματος ἁγίου καὶ ἐκέλευσε κηρύσσειν τὸ εὐαγγέλιον.

Augustine[b] *Acta c. Felice*	ἐν ᾗ ἡμέρᾳ τοὺς ἀποστόλους διὰ πνεύματος ἁγίου καὶ ἐκέλευσε κηρύσσειν τὸ εὐαγγέλιον.
Augustine *De unitate ecclesiae*	ἄχρι ἧς ἡμέρας τοὺς ἀποστόλους ἐξελέξατο διὰ πνεύματος ἁγίου ἐντειλάμενος αὐτοῖς κηρύσσειν τὸ εὐαγγέλιον.
Codex Gigas	ἐν ᾗ ἡμέρᾳ τοῖς ἀποστόλοις ἐξελέξατο διὰ πνεύματος ἁγίου κηρύσσειν τὸ εὐαγγέλιον οὓς ἐξελέξατο.

---

[a]Codex Vaticanus (B) represents here the vast majority of extant Greek manuscripts.

[b]The Greek text for the Old Latin has been reconstructed from the existing Latin texts.

These six different traditions represent three major variants: (1) readings which remove ἀνελήμφθη from their text (gig, t, Augustine[2/2]); (2) readings which place ἀνελήμφθη immediately after ἡμέρας (D, sa); (3) readings which place ἀνελήμφθη after ἐξελέξατο. In addition, readings 1 and 2 add the phrase 'and he commanded [them] to preach the gospel'.

Interpretations of the textual evidence and conjectural reconstructions of the text are almost as multifarious as the variant readings. The problem centers around ἀνελήμφθη and its presence, absence, or position in the text. Almost everyone has agreed that Codex D does not in this instance represent the original text, but is perhaps a conflation of the Old Latin and the Old Uncials.[92] Such consensus regarding the original text has been more difficult to attain.

Both Ropes and A.C. Clark (with slight variations) considered the text attested by the Old Latin witnesses, especially Gigas, as closest to the original, while the Alexandrian was corrupt.[93] Clark adopted the Old Latin text in its entirety. In other words, he excised ἀνελήμφθη and treated ἐκέλευσε κηρύσσειν τὸ εὐαγγέλιον as original. The resulting text read: ἐν ᾗ ἡμέρᾳ τοὺς ἀποστόλους ἐξελέξατο διὰ πνεύματος ἁγίου καὶ ἐκέλευσε κηρύσσειν τὸ εὐαγγέλιον. This theory, of course, is consonant with Clark's view of the Western text of Acts in general.[94]

Ropes conjectured an original ἐν ἡμέρᾳ ᾗ for ἄχρι ἧς ἡμέρας and suggested omitting οὓς and ἀνελήμφθη. He also rejected καὶ ἐκέλευσε κηρύσσειν τὸ εὐαγγέλιον as a Western substitute for the original ἐντειλάμενος. The text which he reconstructed, attested as a whole by no extant manuscript or version, read: ἐν ἡμέρᾳ ᾗ τοὺς ἀποστόλους ἐντειλάμενος διὰ πνεύματος ἁγίου.[95]

Ropes' colleague, Kirsopp Lake, expressed his dissent from Ropes' reconstruction in volume five of *The Beginnings of Christianity*. According to Lake, ἐξελέξατο can only refer to Luke 6.13ff. and the Gospel obviously neither began nor terminated at that point. Thus, the οὕς is to be retained. Further, Lake maintained that 'in a preface to the second book the important point to be noticed is that which was reached at the end of the first, so that ἄχρι is essential to the sense'.[96]

Lake did, however, accept Ropes' omission of ἀνελήμφθη. He met the grammatical difficulty by making a long parenthesis from διὰ πνεύματος ἁγίου to συναλιξόμενος. Lake's reconstructed text would be translated as: 'Until which day he ordered the apostles (whom he chose through the Holy Spirit; to whom also he presented himself living after his passion by many proofs, appearing to them during forty days, and speaking the things concerning God, and gathering together), he commanded them not to depart from Jerusalem'.

J.M. Creed has raised at least three objections to such a rendering: (1) the long parenthesis (which involves over twenty Greek words), is stylistically strained, and while grammatically possible does not appear to be grammatically probable; (2) the two words for command (ἐντειλάμενος and παρήγγειλεν), which would now stand in apposition, are badly redundant; (3) though the usual punctuation would connect συναλιξόμενος with παρήγγειλεν, Lake's proposal involves the linkage of παρήγγειλεν with the two preceding participles (ὀπτανόμενος and λέγων).[97] Creed further commented that removing the reference to the ascension from Acts 1.2 in no way solved the problem of the relationship of Luke 24 and Acts 1.[98]

Recently, Epp has argued that the Western text, represented by the Old Latin manuscripts and Latin Fathers, seemed to 'resist any description of Jesus as being "taken up into heaven"... even though our extant witnesses to that "Western" textual tradition do not show that this tendency was carried through with rigid consistency'.[99] Epp attempted to show that the omission of ἀνελήμφθη in Acts 1.2 was a part of the evidence that the 'Western' text was deliberately attempting to remove references to the ascension.[100]

Epp's article is most thought-provoking. He has marshalled evidence from five different texts: (1) the omission in Luke 24.51; (2) the omission of ἀνελήμφθη in Acts 1.2; (3) the use of *sublatus est* for *levatus est* in Acts 1.9; (4) the omission of εἰς οὐρανόν in 1.11; (5) the use of *receptus est* or *acceptus est* for the expected *assumptus est* in Acts 1.11; (6) the use of *receptus est* for *assumptus est* in Acts 1.22.[101]

Epp noted the two most damaging objections to his theory: (1) a lack of complete consistency; and (2) the presence of ascension in Western witnesses (D it vg cop Tertullian et al.) in the longer ending of Mark (16.19).[102] To these objections may be added several others: (1) If the contention of Chapter 1 is accepted (that the shorter reading in Luke 24.51 is original) and the longer reading in Acts 1.2 is omitted for reasons other than deobjectifying the ascension (see below), then the already inconsistent tendency in the Western text to deobjectify the ascension becomes fatally erratic. (2) It may be that what Epp is labeling a tendency in a hypothetical Western text could be better understood as a peculiar theological concern of just one Latin Father, Augustine, who is the only Western witness to read as many as five of the six variants identified by Epp. And even then Epp recognized that Augustine is not consistent in citing a given passage.[102]

Returning now to Acts 1.2, it is my contention that ἀνελήμφθη was, in fact, part of the original text and was intentionally, but mistakenly, removed from the text in an attempt at harmonizing Acts 1.2 with Luke 24.51. To make this assertion is to be open to the same criticism leveled at Westcott and Hort eighty years ago: 'it is surely illogical to do as Westcott and Hort did, namely, select a text of the gospel which does not mention the ascension, and a text of Acts which says that the gospel did mention it'.[104]

There are, however, reasons which are not altogether 'illogical' for accepting the shorter text of Western witnesses in Luke and the longer text of the Alexandrian witnesses in Acts. Much of the following argument revolves around Luke's use of the word ἀναλαμβάνω. In Luke–Acts the word occurs at Luke 9.51 (in its noun form); Acts 1.2, 11, 22; 7.43; 10.16; 20.13, 14; 23.31. Three distinct nuances seem to emerge in Lukan usage.[105] To begin at the end, the references in 20.13, 14; 23.31 all have the meaning of 'take along'.[106] The references in 1.11 and 10.16 are characterized by the addition of εἰς τὸν οὐρανόν, and indicate movement 'into heaven'. In the first instance, it is Jesus who is taken up into heaven; and in the second, the sheet in Peter's vision 'was taken up at once into heaven'.

Acts 1.22 should probably be included in this category. Although εἰς τὸν οὐρανόν is missing, the phrase ἀφ' ἡμῶν does give the word a directional connotation. The first two references emphasize motion toward (e.g. into heaven), while this one in Acts 1.22 suggests motion away from. In all three instances, however, the word has the distinct meaning of 'being taken up'.

The occurrences of ἀνάλημψις in Luke 9.51 and ἀνελήμφθη in Acts 1.2 present a different problem. On 9.51, Fitzmyer has questioned 'whether one should restrict it merely to the ascension or understand it in the still broader sense of Jesus' entire transit to the Father (via death, burial, and exaltation)'.[107] Marshall has claimed the reference is 'to the death of Jesus, but it is hard to resist the impression that there is also an allusion to Jesus being "taken up" or "taken back" to God in the ascension'.[108]

Still others have argued that ἀναλαμβάνω refers not to the ascension, but to Jesus' death or departure. G. Friedrich argued that the meaning of ἀνάλημψις in Luke 9.51 was 'death' not 'ascension'. He maintained:

> Die Entrückung ist nicht ein Kernpunkt der lukanischen Theologie, sondern ein geeignetes Schema, um die Trennung Jesu von seinen Jüngern zu beschreiben und den Einschnitt zwischen dem Wirken des irdischen Jesus und der von ihm beauftragten Boten in der Zeit der Kirche bis zur Parusie zu charakterisieren.[109]

Earlier, P.A. van Stempvoort had stressed 'the normal meaning of ἀνάλη(μ)ψις and ἀναλαμβάνομαι in the time of Luke and the first centuries: to die, to be taken up in the sense of to pass away, removal out of this world'.[110] Marshalling a legion of examples from Hellenistic and Jewish literature,[111] van Stempvoort concluded about 9.51: 'Here Luke indicates the whole process of his passing away and being taken up in the wide sense'.[112] Van Stempvoort extended his argument to include Acts 1.2 which is a reference to 'passing away and being taken up' in the sense of Luke 9.51.[113]

In a short study published in 1961, Jacques Dupont challenged van Stempvoort's understanding of ἀνελήμφθη in Acts 1.2. He is willing to concede 'le mot ἀνάλημψις ne s'applique pas uniquement à l'ascension, mais désigne le mystère pascal dans son ensemble: passion, mort, résurrection, ascension'.[114] But on Acts 1.2, he believed: 'on peut continuer à interpréter ἀνελήμφθη de Act. i. 2 comme on l'a fait jusqu'ici, en y voyant une mention de l'ascension de Jésus au ciel'.[115]

Dupont raised three basic objections to van Stempvoort's view:

(1) The fact that ἀναλαμβάνομαι designates 'death' in some Hellenistic literature does not preclude the New Testament literature from employing the word in a technical way to refer to a bodily ascension (Acts 1.11, 22; 1 Tim. 3.16; Mark 16.19). (2) There is a major discrepancy between 9.51, which refers to the plural '*days* of Jesus' taking up'—which lends itself to an understanding of the death, resurrection, and ascension *in toto*—and Acts 1.2, which refers to the singular *day* on which he was taken up—which seems explicitly to suggest the ascension. (3) Finally, by understanding ἀνελήμφθη to refer to the ascension, ἐντειλάμενος most naturally recalled the teachings of Luke 24.47-49.[116]

Despite these objections, it is my contention that van Stempvoort was correct in connecting Luke 9.51 with Acts 1.2. To be convincing, the criticisms raised by Dupont must be answered.

(1) First, the fact that the Hellenistic literature does understand ἀναλαμβάνομαι to designate 'death'[117] does not preclude the idea of 'ascension' in the New Testament. Dupont is certainly right on this point. But the significance of the material cited is not that it excludes ascension from the semantic field of ἀναλαμβάνομαι, but that it includes a much wider understanding.

(2) Upon first glance, this seems to be a devastating blow to van Stempvoort's theory, but a closer look will prove it less compelling than it appears. Does the singular ἡμέρας in Acts 1.2 rule out a reference to the whole passion, burial, and resurrection which obviously encompassed more than a twenty-four hour period? The evidence in Luke–Acts is inconclusive. At Luke 17.27 the reference is evidently to a single day: 'until the day Noah entered the ark'.

On the other hand, in Luke 1.20 where the phrase ἄχρι ἧς ἡμέρας occurs, another exact parallel to Acts 1.2 is found. In Luke 1.13, the angel of the Lord appeared to Zechariah and said to him: 'Do not be afraid, Zechariah, for your prayer is heard and your wife Elizabeth will bear you a son, and you shall call his name John'. Later in 1.20, in response to Zechariah's disbelief, the angel admonished: 'And behold, you will be silent and unable to speak until the day that these things come to pass'. And what are those things which must come to pass? The context indicates the birth and naming of John. But the reader learns later (1.57-64) that the process of delivering and naming takes place over eight days! Thus, the telescoping of events for dramatic effect is not unknown to Luke.

And so here, one may not be dogmatic in arguing that the reference in 1.2 is intended to express precise chronology. But neither may one argue conclusively that the reference simply points back to the passion, resurrection, and appearances of Jesus in the same way that 9.51 points forward to it.[118] In short, the singularity of ἡμέρας provides evidence that cuts both ways and may not be used to argue either case convincingly.

(3) If ἀνελήμφθη signifies the death and resurrection of our Lord to what does ἐντειλάμενος refer? The word may be a general reference to the teachings of Jesus since the choosing of the disciples (Luke 6.12-16). Or it may specifically refer to the teachings of the Lord to the disciples in the upper room before the arrest and crucifixion. It is interesting that in the Last Supper scene, the Lukan Jesus speaks more than in the other two Synoptic counterparts. Of particular note is the dispute about greatness and Jesus' subsequent command in 22.26: 'Let the greatest among you become as the youngest, and the leader as one who serves', and the distinctively Lukan sayings about the purse, bag, and swords.[119] This view also has the advantage of keeping the rest of the Acts preface in order. The passion-resurrection-exaltation is preceded by the commands given at the last supper (or during Jesus' ministry) and followed by the post-resurrection appearance stories, and then the commission of Luke in 24.49. Plooij came to a similar conclusion:

> It seems to me open to serious doubt whether the word ἀνάλημψις in Acts i.2 (whatever may be the meaning attached to the word by Luke) was meant to denote the ascension. That the series of events related in Acts i. 1, 2 intends to be the chronological order, seems evident . . . The ἀνάλημψις meant in v. 2 should accordingly precede the passion or at least, coincide with it.[120]

Another way of looking at the passage is to examine its surface structure. In the first work, Luke dealt with all that Jesus began 'to do' (ποιεῖν) and to teach' (διδάσκειν). These two functions, doing and teaching, seem to control the remaining two verses of the preface. Jesus *teaches* the disciples and then *acts* by being 'lifted up' (in the crucifixion and resurrection) (v. 2). Next, Jesus *acts* by presenting himself alive after the passion (!) and by appearing for forty days (not in Luke, however), and then he *teaches* them by speaking of the kingdom of God (v. 3). The structure may be diagrammed as in Figure 1.

This structure is no attempt to remove all the chronological problems from the narrative—several still remain.[121] Yet at the same time, this argument removes from the preface, which is highly stylized, several unnecessary difficulties. One may ask why Luke

Verse 1:	A—Jesus acts (ποιεῖν)
	B—Jesus teaches (διδάσκειν)
Verse 2:	B—Jesus teaches (ἐντειλάμενος)
	A—Jesus acts (ἀνελήμφθη)
Verse 3:	A—Jesus acts (παρέστησεν. . .ὀπτανόμενος)
	B—Jesus teaches (λέγων τὰ περὶ τῆς βασιλείας τοῦ θεοῦ)

Figure 1: The Surface Structure of Acts 1.1-3

would have written so obscurely—or, perhaps better, one may ask why we read so dimly!

Therefore, I would modify van Stempvoort's position in two significant ways. First, ἀνάλημψις in Luke 9.51 and ἀνελήμφθη in Acts 1.2 both refer not only to death or ascension, but to Jesus' entire journey back to God (burial, resurrection, exaltation).[122] Exaltation in the context of the Third Gospel does not refer to the ascension; rather, Luke's point is to show that Jesus is exalted in his death as well as his resurrection. The crucified Christ and Risen Lord are inextricably entwined in the narrative. Such an emphasis may be a corrective for Luke's readers who have emphasized the exaltation of the resurrection to the neglect of the crucifixion. Only after Luke impressed the connection of cross and resurrection upon his readers (Luke 24) is he ready to complete the reference to Jesus' exaltation with a narrated account of the ascension (Acts 1.9-11).

Second, a reason must be suggested for the omission of ἀνελήμφθη in 1.2 by Western witnesses. If the shorter text of Luke 24 were original, then Western scribes would have been puzzled by the presence of ἀνελήμφθη and would have mistakenly understood it as a reference to the ascension. The phrase was removed in an attempt to harmonize the text of Luke 24 with that of Acts 1.

Therefore, the word ἀνελήμφθη is treated (1) as original to the text, being erroneously omitted by certain Western scribes who had misread the subtle Lukan nuance and were attempting to harmonize the ascension accounts; and (2) as a reference to Jesus' passion, resurrection, and exaltation (the ascension being included in this exaltation in Acts 1.9-11). With this in mind, the following translation, in my opinion, would best capture the meaning expressed in Acts 1.1-2:

> In the first volume, O Theophilus, I dealt with everything which
> Jesus began both to do and to teach until which time he was

exalted, after he had given instructions to the apostles whom he
had chosen through the Holy Spirit.

2. Acts 1.9. Codex D and other Western witnesses (d cop^sa
Augustine) omit the words αὐτῶν βλεπόντων. In addition, D
changes ἐπήρθη to ἀπήρθη and transposes it after νεφέλη . . .αὐτόν.
While Augustine and the Coptic omit ἀπὸ ὀφθαλμῶν αὐτῶν, D
retains this after ἀπήρθη. This change seems to remove reference to
the disciples' watching the ascension. Plooij boldly asserted that the
reviser was unwilling to 'concede that, without an intervening cloud,
Jesus was lifted up from his apostles after having given them his
instructions. The "Ascension" was alright [sic], but a bodily
ascension was too much for him'.[123] In response to Plooij, Epp, who
also argued for an intentional Western omission, claimed:

> while the 'Western' formulation certainly does not *demand* an
> ascension in the usual sense, it also cannot be said to *preclude* such
> an understanding. Yet the reduction of the objectifying features is
> noticeable and significant.[124]

Again, it seems that Augustine, and not the 'Western' text, may be
the culprit wishing to remove allusions to a bodily ascension. Codex
D, while omitting the phrase 'as they were watching', includes the
phrase 'was removed from their sight'. Such oversight (!) by D seems
to eliminate the desired effect of excising the observable ascension
from the text.[125] Augustine, on the other hand, has the following text:
'cum haec diceret nubes suscepit eum et sublatus est ab eis'. ('After
he said this, a cloud enveloped him and he was taken away from
them'.) Here, Augustine successfully diminishes the ascension as an
observable event. The longer text should be read, and the shorter text
understood as the effort of Augustine.

3. Acts 1.11. While Epp suggested that the omission of εἰς τὸν
οὐρανόν might support the theory of the tendency of the Western
text to deobjectify the ascension,[126] the phrase more readily is
explained by accidental omission.[127] Haenchen suggested: 'Luke
probably wished to stress this aspect by including εἰς τὸν οὐρανόν
four times in rapid succession'.[128]

Below is my translation of Acts 1.6-11 which will serve as the
foundation for the following analyses in Chapter 5:

> [6]Indeed, after they had come together, they asked him, saying,
> 'Lord, at this time will you restore the kingdom to Israel?' [7]He said
> to them, 'It is not yours to know times or seasons which the Father

has set by his own authority; [8]but rather you will receive power after the Holy Spirit has come upon you, and you will be my witnesses in Jerusalem and all Judea and Samaria and until the end of the earth'. [9]And after he had said these things, while they were looking, he was lifted up and a cloud took him from before their eyes. [10]And as they were staring into heaven, while he was going, behold two men stood beside them in white robes, [11]and they said: 'Men of Galilee, why do you stand looking into heaven? This Jesus who was ascended from you into heaven, thus he will come in this way as you saw him going into heaven'.

Conclusion

Much of the difficulty in establishing a text for Acts lies in the enigma of the Western text. Despite grand and noble efforts, the conclusion of A.F.J. Klijn in 1969 still rings true: 'The riddle of the Western text has not been solved'.[129] Indeed, B.H. Streeter surely articulated a generation ago the frustration of the scholar who 'has met his Waterloo in the attempt to account for, or explain away, the existence of the Bezan text'.[13] While the quest for a coherent theory of the history of manuscript textual transmission must continue, textual criticism must limp on even if it is on the 'shifting sands of a serviceable but tentative and sometimes slippery eclecticism'.[131] Nonetheless, an attempt such as this one, which struggles with the maze of manuscripts and an interim methodology, is preferable to those studies which begin with literary criticism or exegesis, happily assuming that text-critical questions are answered once and for all.[132]

Form Analysis:
Establishing the Shape of Acts 1.1-11

In 1971, Lohfink published a significant work on the ascension narratives entitled *Die Himmelfahrt Jesu*.[133] His most important contribution was in the form-critical analysis of the ascension narratives in Luke–Acts. After pages of detailed analysis, Lohfink concluded: 'Die Himmelfahrt Jesu bei Lukas ist eine Entrückung'.[134] Though this assessment is judged to be essentially correct, at least one methodological judgment in this present study required modification of Lohfink's conclusions. Lohfink treated Luke 24.50-53 and Acts 1.1-11 together as the Lukan witness to the ascension of Jesus. Based on the previous text-critical decisions in this study, only the Acts pericope will be accepted as reflecting an explicit ascension scene with antecedents in other ancient ascension narratives. In fact, this nuance in method will cause conclusions to be slightly modified from Lohfink's astute form-critical analysis.

Common terminology and formal elements from ancient Greco-Roman ascension narratives will be compared to the Acts passage. Then the ascension in Acts will be compared with the constituent parts of translation scenes in the Old Testament and later Jewish writings. Finally, some judgment will be made regarding the probable type-scene upon which Acts 1.1-11 (especially vv. 9-11) is based.

Assumption Scenes in Ancient Greco-Roman Literature[135]
Below in Tables 12 and 13 are listed the most common verbs and elements associated with the Greco-Roman assumption story, along with several examples of texts which contain them.[136] Following each Table is a comparison of the Greco-Roman texts with Acts 1.1-11.

Table 12

Assumption Terminology in Ancient Greco-Roman Literature

Verb	Texts
1. ἀφανίζω	Antoninus, *Liberalis*, 25
ἀφανίζομαι	Isocrates, *Archidamus*, 18
	Strabo, VI.3.9
	Plutarch, *Romulus*, 27.3.4
	Herodotus, VII.166
	Josephus, *Antiquitates*, IX.2.2
	Diogenes Laertius, VIII.69
	Lysias, *Orationes*, II.11
ἀφανὴς γίγνομαι	Dionysius, *Antiquitates*, II.56.2
	Plutarch, *Numa*, 2.2
	Josephus, *Antiquitates*, IX.2.2
	Arrian, *Anabasis*, VII.27.3
	Apollodorus, *Bibliotheca*, III.1.1
ἀφαντὸς γίγνομαι	Diodorus, III.60.3; IV.58.6; IV.82.6
non (nusquam) compareo	Cicero, *De re publica*, II.10;

	Aurelius Victor, *De viris illustribus*, II.13
	Augustine, *De civitate Dei*, XVIII.21
2. ἁρπάζω	Homer, *Odyssey*, XV.250f.
	Theokrit, XVII.48
	Apollodorus, *Bibliotheca*, I.5.1
ἀναρπάζω	Dionysius, *Antiquitates*, II.56.2
	Plutarch, *Romulus*, 27.8
	Apollodorus, *Bibliotheca*, III.12.2
ἐξαρπάζω	Homer, *Iliad*, III.380; XX.443; XXI.597
συναρπάζω	Diodorus, III.60.3
rapio, rapior	Livy, I.16.2; XXXIX.13.13;
	Ovid, *Fasti*, II.701; *Metamorphoses*, IX.271f.
	Servius on Vergil, *Aeneid*, I.259.619
3. μεθίσταμαι	Diodorus, II.20.1; IV.38.5
	Dionysius, *Antiquitates*, I.64.4
	Apollodorus, *Bibliotheca*, II.8.1

Though there is an occasional text that may employ a different word, these three verb groups represent the most common terminology for describing a bodily assumption in the ancient Greek and Roman worlds.[137] Interestingly, none of the words favored by Luke in his description of Jesus' ascension play any noticeable role in the Greco-Roman texts.[13] In fact, only ἀναφέρω is a word employed with any degree of frequency in the pagan texts.[139] Since this word is believed to be part of a spurious text (see Chapter 2), it may be concluded that there is no viable contact between the terminology of the ascension account in Acts and the assumption stories of the ancient Greco-Roman world.

The relationship between the ascension in Acts and the characteristic features of Greco-Roman assumption stories is more difficult to assess than the assumption terminology.[140] It is certainly feasible that Luke or his tradition could have utilized some of these elements (mountain, cloud, worship of the cult) in the formation of the tradition of Jesus' ascension. To what degree, if any, have these pagan stories shaped the telling of Acts 1.9-11? The answer to this question can only be given after exploring the assumption stories in the Old Testament and later Jewish literature.

Table 13
Characteristic Features of Greco-Roman Assumption Stories

Feature	Text
Mountain	Lucian, *Hermotimus*, 7; Apollodorus, *Bibliotheca*, II.7.7; Minucius Felix, *Octavius*, 22.7 Diodorus Siculus, III.60.3 Aurelius Victor, *De viris illustribus* II.13
Funeral Pyre	Diodorus, IV.38.4 Juvenal, *Satirae*, XI.63 Apollodorus, *Bibliotheca*, II.7.7
Thunder-bolt(s)	Pindar, *Olympian Odes*, 2.25f. Philostratus, *Imagines*, 1.14 Nonnus, *Dionysiaca*, VIII.394–411 Minucius Felix, *Octavius*, 22.7
Whirlwind	Homer, *Odyssey*, XX.63–66 Sophocles, *Oedipus Coloneus*, 1659f. Dionysius, *Antiquitates*, II.56.2 Plutarch, *Romulus*, 27.7
Chariot	Ovid, *Metamorphoses*, IX.271f. Horace, *Carmina*, III.3.1316
Cloud(s)	Apollodorus, *Bibliotheca*, II.7.7 Dionysius, *Antiquitates*, I.77.2 Plutarch, *Numa*, 2.23
Heavenly Confirmation (Appearances of Ascended One)	Plutarch, *Romulus*, 28.13 Livy, I.16.58 Ovid, *Fasti*, II.499509 Lucian, *De Morte Peregrini*, 40 Philostratus, *Vita Apollonii*, VIII.31
Subsequent Worship of Cult	Diodorus, IV.10.7 Philostratus, *Vita Apollonii*, VIII.31 Apollodorus, *Bibliotheca*, II.4.11 Plutarch, *Romulus*, 27.8

Ascension Stories in the Old Testament and Later Jewish Literature
Assumption stories about Enoch, Elijah, Ezra, Baruch, and Moses, abound in the Jewish literature.[141] The characteristic terminology

and formal elements of these Old Testament and later Jewish assumption narratives are found in Tables 14 and 15. Again, following each Table is a comparison with Acts 1.

Table 14
Assumption Terminology in Ancient Jewish Literature

Verb	Text
1. ἀναλαμβάνω(-ομαι)	4 Kgdms 2.9-11 (Hebrew 2 Kgs 2.9-11 לקח)
	Sir. 48.9; 49.14
	1 Macc. 2.58
	4 Ezra 4.26; 12.9
	T.Abr. 4.4; 7.10, 16, 19
2. μετατίθεμαι	Gen. 5.24 (Hebrew לקח)
	Sir. 44.16
	Wis. 4.10

While the word μετατίθεμαι plays no role in Luke's description of Jesus' departure, the LXX translators' choice of ἀναλαμβάνω to describe the assumptions of Enoch (Sir. 49.14), and especially Elijah (4 Kgdms 2.9-11; Sir. 48.9; 1 Macc. 2.58), is a favorite Lukan term for Jesus' assumption/exaltation (Acts 1.2, 11, 22; cf. Luke 9.51). Other verbal parallels between the Elijah texts and Acts 1 are striking: the use of the preposition ἀπό with ἀναλαμβάνω (4 Kgdms 2.9; Acts 1.11); the phrase εἰς τὸν οὐρανόν (4 Kgdms 2.11; Acts 1.10, 11); the verb ἐπιστρέφω (4 Kgdms 2.13; Acts 1.12); the use of the substantive ὁ ἀναλημφθείς (Sir. 48.9; Acts 1.11); and the reference to πνεῦμα (Sir. 48.12; Acts 1.8). These points of contact are not sufficient to argue for a direct literary dependence of Luke on these Elijah texts,[142] but the cumulative effect of the parallels is certainly impressive.

Table 15
Characteristic Features of Jewish Assumption Stories

Feature	Text
Speech by the Spectators	4 Kgdms 2.9, 12
	Jub. 32.20
	Josephus, *Antiquitates*, 5.8.3

	T.Abr. 7.14
	Apoc. Mos. 13; 32-34
Whirlwind	4 Kgdms 2.1, 11
	Sir. 48.9, 12
Chariots	4 Kgdms 2.1, 11;
	Sir. 48.9
	4 Ezra 7.6
Cloud(s)	*T.Abr.* 8.3; 10.2; 12.1, 9
	4 Ezra 5.7
	[Rev. 11.12]
Angel(s)	*2 Enoch* 36.2; 55.1; 67.2
Subsequent Worship	*2 Enoch* 67.3; 68.5
	Tob. 12.22
Last Words of Ascended One	4 Kgdms 2.11
	Josephus, *Antiquitates*, IV.8.48

The characteristic features of the Jewish assumption stories show less connection with the salient features of Acts 1.1-11 than does the terminology of those stories. Though all of the characteristic elements in Acts (mountain, cloud, angels, last words of Jesus) are present in one or more Jewish texts, the number of witnesses which contain these elements in some cases is very slight.

The ascension of Jesus in Acts more closely resembles the Greco-Roman literature in terms of characteristic features—clouds, angels, and mountains seem to play a more significant role in the pagan texts than in the Jewish literature. The Lukan terminology, on the other hand, is much closer to the Jewish literature, particularly the Elijah texts. How to interpret this evidence is a source-critical question to be taken up in the next section. The overall conclusion to be drawn from the form analysis is that although no one pre-Lukan source contains all the salient features, the conceptual framework of the Lukan ascension narrative has been significantly shaped by the heavenly-assumption stories of antiquity.[143]

Source Analysis:
Establishing the Origins of Acts 1.1-11

Now that we have established the form of the ascension narrative in Acts to be that of a bodily assumption, several questions remain. Did

Luke create this ascension account or did he inherit it from the primitive tradition? If there was an ascension narrative in the traditional material, was it already based on a heavenly assumption story or did Luke shape the story with details borrowed from the pattern of other (Jewish or Greco-Roman) bodily assumptions? If Luke redacted the material, to what extent? And assuming a pre-Lukan tradition, is it possible to suggest a history of tradition through which the ascension story passed?

The answer to the first question, of course, determines the necessity of answering the others. Did Luke create the ascension narrative? After examining a variety of ascension texts in the early Christian literature,[144] Lohfink concluded that he did: 'wo in der frühen Kirche von einer sichtbaren Himmelfahrt Jesu gesprochen wird, die von der Auferstehung durch dazwischentretende Erscheinungen getrennt ist, liegt bereits Abhängigkeit von der lukanischen Konzeption vor'.[145] Others are not so certain. Dillon argued: 'we should rather keep an open mind towards the possibility, urged by others, that Luke was not the first to recount this terminal episode, hence that either his gospel's ending, or the Acts account, or both, rest upon the tradition he received'.[146]

To answer the question of a pre-Lukan ascension tradition, it is necessary to examine both internal and external evidence. Internally, is it possible to remove the Lukan redaction and so recover any traditional elements? Externally, are there any extra-canonical sources—either in the manuscript tradition or early Christian literature—which qualify as independent witnesses to a primitive ascension tradition? The examination will begin with the internal evidence.

A Primitive Tradition in Acts 1.1-11?
Tradition can only be recovered after a writer's style is known and redactional elements are removed or eliminated.[147] Separating redaction from tradition is often as much imagination as science since often the two are inextricably intertwined. The problem of recovering any traditional elements in Acts 1.1-11 is even more difficult due to the heavy redaction in this passage.[148] Nonetheless I will hazard an analysis of Acts 1.1-11 in the following paragraphs.

Actually Acts 1.1-5, though part of the narrative beginning, is not part of the ascension narrative proper and may be immediately dismissed from consideration.[149] Likewise Acts 1.6-8 may be omitted from discussion since it too is thoroughly Lukan in style, vocabulary, and themes.[150] Only the word ἀποκαθιστάνω could be considered as a possible remnant from an older tradition, and even here, though the terminology is not particularly characteristic of Luke–Acts, the theme is undisputedly Lukan (cf. Luke 19.11). The question of the fate (restoration or not?) of Israel will consume most of the narrative of Acts. Therefore, the most that could be said at this point about Acts 1.1-8 is that a primitive ascension tradition may have contained a dialogue regarding the restoration of Israel, the details of which are not recoverable. More probable, however, is Fuller's conclusion that 'all of verses 6-8 may therefore be safely assigned to the evangelist's redaction'.[151]

It is the ascension narrative proper, Acts 1.9-11, which deserves closest analysis. In Table 16, the frequency with which the vocabulary of Acts 1.9-11 occurs in Luke-Acts is compared with the other Gospels.[152] An analysis of the data follows the Table.

Table 16

A Comparative Analysis of the Vocabulary of Acts 1.9-11

Verse 9	Matthew	Mark	Luke	John	Acts
βλέπω	18	14	14	16	14
ἐπαίρω	1	0	6	4	5
νεφέλη	4	4	5	0	1
ὑπολαμβάνω	0	0	2	0	2
ὀφθαλμός	22	7	17	17	6
Verse 10					
καὶ ὡς	42	20	51	30	60
ἀτενίζω	0	0	2	0	10
καὶ ἰδού	17	0	17	0	3
εἰς τὸν οὐρανόν	1	3	6	2	7
πορεύομαι	29	3	51	13	37
ἄνδρες δύο	0	0	3	0	3
παριστάναι	1	6	3	2	13
ἐσθής	0	0	2	0	2
λευκός	3	2	1	2	1
Verse 11					
ἀνήρ	8	4	27	8	100

Γαλιλαῖοι	1	1	5	1	3
ἱστάναι	21	9	26	18	35
ἀναλαμβάνω	0	0	0	0	8
ὃν τρόπον	1	0	1	0	4
θεάομαι	4	2	3	6	3
καλούμενος	0	0	11	0	13

While the conclusions reached on the basis of any statistical analysis must be taken *cum grano salis*, the evidence does yield some rather interesting results. Obviously, the passage contains significant vocabulary which represents preferred Lukan terms, if not outright 'Lucanisms'.[153] However, it is possible to argue for the faint traces of a pre-Lukan ascension tradition, preserved particularly in v. 9. Leaving aside the first part of 1.9 as a redactional link to 1.6-8, the following observations may be made about the rest of Acts 1.9. (1) The phrase 'as they were watching' (βλεπόντων αὐτῶν) is not particularly Lukan as the analysis shows and may well be tradition preserved by Luke. (2) Of sixteen occurrences in the NT of the key word ἐπαίρω, eleven are found in Luke–Acts. It is significant, however, that only here in 1.9 is the word used in the passive voice with the literal sense of 'to be lifted up'.[154] (3) Likewise, ὑπολαμβάνω, a *hapax* found only in Luke–Acts, is used in its literal sense 'to take up someone or something' only here in Acts 1.9.[155] It is used elsewhere in Luke–Acts in a figurative sense of 'reply' (*taking up* what is said) or 'suppose'.[156] (4) The word for 'cloud' (νεφέλη) is also common to the synoptic tradition. (5) Finally, the word ὀφθαλμός enjoys common usage in all four Gospels and is not particularly Lukan.[157] A very good case can be made for arguing that practically all of Acts 1.9 (omitting the initial participial phrase as a redactional seam) reflects an earlier written (?) ascension tradition that read something like: 'And as they were watching he was taken up and a cloud took him [from their eyes]'.

Unfortunately, less can be said about 1.10-11. Here the vocabulary and style are distinctly Lukan (see Table 16 above). While it is possible that Luke's tradition has set the ascension in the context of the parousia—a possibility I would like to leave open—it is equally plausible that Luke, reminded both of the transfiguration (9.34) and the parousia (21.27; cf. Dan. 7.13),[158] has supplied what Fitzmyer has called the 'apocalyptic stage-props'.[159] By further additions of the angels, mountain locale, and the forty day instructions (all of which I take to be redactional elements), Luke has completed the shaping of Jesus' ascension into the form of a heavenly assumption story so common in the ancient world.

In summary, I conclude that the internal evidence favors the judgment that there was in Luke's tradition a brief narrative describing Jesus' ascension on a cloud from his disciples.[160] In re-evaluating the elements which have been identified as characteristic of heavenly assumption stories, I suspect that the presence of a cloud in this story is actually due more to the primitive tradition's expectations of the parousia based on Dan. 7.13 than to the presence of the cloud in (especially Greco-Roman) heavenly assumption stories. It is possible that Luke was inspired by the bodily ascension and presence of the cloud(s) in the early church's tradition and attempted to fill out the heavenly assumption story with elements common to that genre: (1) a mountain and (2) angels.

(1) The location on the Mount of Olives (rather than Bethany, cf. Luke 24.50) may be due to Luke's concern, among other things, to provide the setting of a heavenly assumption.[161] (2) The presence of the angels, on the other hand is more difficult to judge. It is possible that the angels are not simply 'apocalyptic stage-props', borrowed, as it were, from the common (Greco-Roman) heavenly assumption tradition. Rather the angels may serve to 'round off' the use of such divine confirmation at the high points of the narrative: the transfiguration, the resurrection, and the ascension. The evidence would support either view and it is finally impossible to adjudicate between the two of them. In fact, both concerns may have contributed to the shaping of Acts 1.9-11. The conclusion reached based on the internal evidence is that Luke inherited a brief narration of Jesus' ascension. He then both shaped it along the lines of an ancient heavenly assumption story (especially the assumption of Elijah, 2 Kgs 2) and couched it in eschatological expectations of the nature of Jesus' parousia.

Extra-Canonical Witnesses to Jesus' Ascension
Before a final conclusion can be reached, it is necessary to consider the external evidence for an ascension tradition, independent of Luke. First of all, the distinction needs to be drawn between what Lohfink called an exaltation kerygma (*Erhöhungskerygma*) and an ascension narrative (*Himmelfahrtserzählung*).[162] This first category of texts, exaltation kerygma, refers to (1) those passages which, following

his burial, reflect the exaltation of Christ to the glory of the Father, without describing the mode of transport (Phil. 2.8-11; 1 Tim. 3.16) and (2) texts which express this exaltation of Christ in terms of his being in heaven or at the Father's right hand, again with no specification of the mode (1 Thess. 1.10; 4.16; Rev. 1.12-18; 3.21b, 6.1b-7; 7.17).[163] In addition, there is a third category of NT passages which either allude to the ascension or motion upwards, without describing it (Heb. 4.14; 6.19-20; 9.24; 1 Pet. 3.22) or use the word 'ascend' in a non-narrative context (Rom. 10.6-8; Eph. 4.7-11; John 20.17; 17.15).[164] In other words, ascension language is used rather widely in the NT to describe the exaltation of Jesus. As Fitzmyer has observed: 'the exaltation is already pre-Lucan, even if the graphic details of its mode are not'.[165]

Only Luke in the NT has actually narrated the ascension. There are, however, a number of other extra-canonical sources which also provide a narration of Jesus' transfer from earth to heaven. Though a number of these texts (e.g. *Acta Pilati* 16.6; *Epist. apost.* 51) may be safely dismissed as derivatives of the Acts account,[166] at least three of those texts dismissed by Lohfink deserve reconsideration: Mark 16.19, Codex Bobiensis, and *Barnabas* 15.9.[167] The possible independent status of each of these passages will be discussed below.

Mark 16.19. The text reads: ὁ μὲν οὖν κύριος Ἰησοῦς μετὰ τὸ λαλῆσαι αὐτοῖς ἀνελήμφθη εἰς τὸν οὐρανὸν καὶ ἐκάθισεν ἐκ δεξιῶν τοῦ θεοῦ. Both external and internal evidence point to the non-Markan and secondary character of Mark 16.9-20, the so-called longer ending to the Gospel of Mark.[168] While it is almost axiomatic that 16.9-20 was not part of the original conclusion of Mark,[169] whether 16.9-20 contains any ancient traditional material independent of the canonical Gospels is a widely debated question. A number of scholars have tended to dismiss the entire postscript (16.9-20) as the result of a sustained raiding of the canonical Gospels with no independent status whatsoever.[170] Others, however, are less certain about evaluating the entire postscript as a mere compilation. Among those willing to consider each pericope on an individual basis, Mark 16.19 has continued to receive support as reflecting an independent, primitive tradition.[171]

A close examination of Mark 16.19 as a potential independent witness to an ancient ascension tradition, then, is warranted. With the exception of the common phrase εἰς τὸν οὐρανόν, there are a number of striking differences between Mark 16.19 and Acts 1.1-11:[172] (1) In Mark 16.19, 2(4) Kgs 2.11 (ἀνελήμφθη εἰς τὸν οὐρανόν) and Ps. 110.1 (καὶ ἐκάθισεν ἐκ δεξιῶν) are explicitly cited (cf. Acts 1.9-11);[173] (2) the ascension in Mark 16.19 occurs in Jerusalem (cf. Acts 1.12); (3) the ascension in Mark 16.19 apparently occurs indoors (cf. Acts 1.9); (4) there are no clouds or angelic interpreters in Mark 16.19.

It is entirely plausible that the author of this Markan postscript was composing freely from his tradition, which included the post-resurrection appearance stories of Matthew and Luke, but was by no means limited to them. In fact, some of this traditional material, including the ascension tradition, may have been from a rather primitive source.[174] This evidence leads me to concur with at least the last part of Reginald Fuller's conclusion:

> We conclude therefore that the canonical ending is not merely an artificial summary of the appearances in the other Gospels. In form it is modeled on the earlier lists of appearances (1 Cor. 15.5ff. and Mark 16.7), but with the substitution of longer summaries of the appearances in the other Gospels, *and an independent statement about the ascension* (emphasis mine).[175]

Codex Bobiensis on Mark 16.3. The Latin text reads: 'Subito autem ad horam tertiam tenebrae diei factae sunt per totam orbem terrae, et descenderunt de caelis angeli et surgent [surgentes?, surgente eo? surgit?] in claritate vivi Dei simul ascenderunt cum eo; et continuo lux facta est. Tunc illae accesserunt ad monumentum'.[176] In this variant the ascension is simultaneous with the resurrection and occurs before any of the appearances. Codex Bobiensis (k) is the most significant witness to the African Old Latin, though it contains roughly no more than half of Matthew and Mark.[177] Though the manuscript is usually dated around AD 400, there are significant agreements with St. Cyprian of Carthage (c. AD 250) and if E.A. Lowe's palaeographical analysis is correct, Bobiensis displays evidence of having been copied from a second-century papyrus.[178]

Lohfink has dismissed this remarkable variant as displaying dependence on the *Gospel of Peter*, 35-40.[179] This argument is bolstered by the conjectural emendation that *viri duo* (cf. *Gospel of Peter*) be included in the text.[180] Such emendation to the text of Bobiensis, as Metzger has pointed out 'appears to be unnecessary' and 'has been proposed in view of the account in the Gospel of Peter'.[181] At any rate, at least the question should be held open. For to accept or reject this variant as an independent witness to a narrated ascension would require further examination beyond that provided by either Lohfink or this study.

Barnabas 15.9. The text reads: διὸ καὶ ἄγομεν τὴν ἡμέραν τὴν ὀγδόην εἰς εὐφροσύνην, ἐν ᾗ καὶ ὁ Ἰησοῦς ἀνέστη ἐκ νεκρῶν καὶ φανερωθεὶς ἀνέβη εἰς οὐρανούς. Lohfink rejects this reference as dependent on the narration of events in Luke 24.[182] He argued that *Barnabas* was a 'schematizing' of Luke 24, following the pattern of 'resurrection—appearances—ascension'. This conclusion is subject to several criticisms.

First, it has been generally observed that the *Epistle of Barnabas* is from the hand of an author who ostensibly did not know 'any part of our present New Testament *in written form*'.[183] Second, and more specifically, it is odd that a schematization of Luke 24 in terms of resurrection, appearances, and ascension, would choose three terms that do not appear in Luke at all, much less in Luke 24 itself. The word for resurrection (ἀνέστη) is found neither in the longer or shorter text of Luke 24 nor in Acts 1.[184] Likewise, the word for appearance in *Barnabas* (φανερωθεὶς) is missing from the entirety of Luke–Acts. Finally the term for ascension (ἀνέβη) occurs only as an implicit reference to the ascension in Acts 2.34, not in Luke 24 or Acts 1.

In light of such tenuous connections on a literary level between Luke and *Barnabas*, Lohfink was forced to admit:

> Die Möglichkeit, dass die auffälligen Übereinstimmungen zwischen Lk 24 und Barn 15 vielleicht doch durch eine gemeinsame ältere Tradition mit Ostertermin bedingt sind, kann nicht ganz ausgeschlossen werden.[185]

The lack of any firm evidence for a literary dependence of *Barnabas* on Luke–Acts leads to the conclusion that, in fact, *Barnabas* reflects an ascension tradition of independent stature. This tradition may be a common, older one from which both *Barnabas* and Luke draw, but there is no convincing argument that one (*Barnabas*) was derived from the other (Luke).

In summary, this brief analysis of the extra-canonical sources for the ascension confirms the conclusion that there was a common tradition which narrated the ascension of Jesus. The traces of this tradition are remarkably slim. At most three sources could plausibly be accepted as independent witnesses to the ascension, and the number is more reliably two, Mark 16.19 and *Barnabas* 15.9 (excepting Bobiensis). In fact, the evidence is so delicately balanced that the prudent advice of Dillon must be heeded: 'One does have to admit that if there was a tradition of resurrection/appearances/ ascension comprising the paschal sequence independent of Luke's conception, such a tradition left remarkably few traces outside the Lucan sphere of influence'.[186] It is with due caution, then, that in the section which follows a tradition-history of the ascension narrative will be reconstructed from the few extant strands of tradition.

Tradition-History of the Ascension Narratives[187]

The development of a narrated ascension tradition has left few traces and it is safe to say without the canonical support of Acts 1, the tradition of Jesus' visible transfer from earth to heaven may not have survived in the history of the church.[188] The tradition seems to have passed through at least three identifiable stages.[189] The first stage of the tradition is represented by those texts which place the ascension at the end of the appearances to the disciples on Easter Sunday. Mark 16.19 and *Barnabas* 15.9[190] are the two texts which reflect this chronology.[191] Mark 16.19 with its explicit 'Elijah' christology and reference to Ps. 110 may well represent the more primitive tradition of the two, perhaps even reflecting a Palestinian setting.[192]

The second stage of the tradition history occurs when the ascension is separated from the resurrection by a short period of time, most notably forty (or fifty) days. It is at this point that the tradition becomes crystalized in the NT canon in Acts 1.[193] As noted before, the number forty is most probably a redactional element and introduced into the tradition for the first time by Luke and is closely related to the chronology of Pentecost. For liturgical reasons the Syriac *Doctrine of the Apostles* carried observance of the ascension forward to the fiftieth day, coinciding with the celebration of Pentecost.

The final stage, which lengthens the time between the resurrection and the ascension far beyond the forty- (or fifty-) day period, is represented in the main by later Gnostic texts. In the *Letter of James* (Jung Codex) the ascension takes place after 550 days.[194] According to Irenaeus, the Ophites and Valentinians argued that Jesus gave instructions to his disciples for eighteen months before ascending.[195] And finally, in the *Pistis Sophia*, Jesus does not ascend until twelve years after his resurrection.

Though the tradition history of the ascension narrative cannot be explained purely in temporal terms, it is helpful to note that the earliest traditions place the ascension on the day of the resurrection while the latest witnesses, particularly the second- and third-century

Gnostic texts separate the ascension from the resurrection anywhere from nearly two years to twelve. It only stands to reason that the Acts account which posits a forty-day interval would fall somewhere between these two poles.[196] Eventually, of course, this forty-day scheme would come to dominate the liturgical calendar of the Church.

Before concluding this diachronic analysis, a word should be said about the relationship of the kerygmatic tradition of exaltation to the tradition of a narrated ascension. The method of investigation suggested by Lohfink and others, and adopted here, of separating kerygmatic statements which allude to an ascension without narrating it and a narration which records a visible assumption (to which Acts bears the sole canonical witness) is surely correct. However, most scholars, whether they argue for a pre-Lukan ascension *narrative* or not, assume that the tradition of a narrated ascension derives from the exaltation kerygma.[197]

Following the lead of Alsup, who has argued that the post-resurrection appearance stories do not derive from the kerygmatic tradition of 1 Cor. 15.3-5 (contra Fuller),[198] I would merely like to suggest that the tradition of a narrated ascension did not *necessarily* derive solely from the exaltation kerygma. There are obvious points of contact between the exaltation kerygma and the ascension narratives (John 10.17; *Gospel of Peter* 9; Mark 16.19) and the importance of this interfacing should not be diminished. However, the early church had sufficient material close at hand in the Old Testament (ancient assumption stories, especially Elijah's translation; and apocalyptic material, especially Dan. 7.13) and more remotely in the ancient Greco-Roman assumption stories to formulate an ascension tradition quite apart from the exaltation kerygma. This suggestion is bolstered by the fact that with the possible exception of Mark 16.19 ('he sat down at the right hand of God'), none of the witnesses to a narrated ascension has as its central focus the exaltation of Jesus, Acts included.[199] One is able cautiously to conclude that the growth of the tradition of a narrated ascension is independent of direct influence from the exaltation kerygma, yet nevertheless informed by its basic message.

Conclusion

This diachronic analysis has established text, form, and source(s) for Acts 1.1-11. The text accepted is basically that of most critical editions of the Greek New Testament, with a suggestion as to the contextual meaning of ἀνελήμφθη in Acts 1.2, along with reasons for its omission in some manuscripts. The form-critical analysis confirmed Lohfink's contention that Luke's ascension narrative had the basic shape of a heavenly assumption story. The source analysis suggested that it is at least plausible to think that a pre-Lukan tradition of a narrated ascension did exist, though the tracks are admittedly faint and few.

When comparing the conclusions of diachronic analysis of Luke 24.50-53 with those here, several observations might be made. The brief ascension narrative at Luke's disposal was compressed even further at the end of the Gospel, removing any explicit reference to the ascension. At the level of the *Sitz in der Kirche*, Luke intended a veiled reference to the ascension in Luke 24.50-53 and intentionally suppressed any explicit mention of a heavenly assumption. In this way, he was able to instruct his community, who were living in the absence of Jesus, to pattern their behavior after the disciples who were obediently, joyfully, and continually blessing God, even after the departure of Jesus. In Acts, Luke expanded the ascension narrative by means of 'apocalyptic stage-props' so that the departure of Jesus in his sequel volume provides the impetus for the gift of the Spirit and the mission of the church. C.K. Barrett has commented on the relationship between accounts of the ascension of Jesus in Luke and Acts:

> Out of Luke's double understanding of the ascension arises a second double proposition of even greater importance. Since the ascension is for Luke both the end of the ministry of Jesus, in which His life finds the triumphant conclusion that gives it meaning, and the beginning of the Church, which makes the life of the Church both possible and intelligible, it follows that, in Luke's thought, the end of the story of Jesus is the Church; and, the story of Jesus is the beginning of the Church.[200]

Luke made creative use of his tradition by framing the ascension in Luke in the form of a benediction, bringing the closure appropriate to his readers' needs. Likewise in Acts, the ascension is recast as an invocation, providing the divine blessing on the church as a pneumatic community and on the outward expression of its mission to the world.

Chapter 5

ACTS 1.1-11 IN NARRATIVE CONTEXT:
A SYNCHRONIC ANALYSIS

The diachronic analysis of Acts 1.1-11 helped place the passage in historical context, examining the text, form, and origins of the ascension tradition found in Acts. Equally significant is the narrative context of the canonical form of the ascension. The synchronic analysis of this chapter attempts to be sensitive to the narrative function of Acts 1.1-11. Examination of the ascension narrative in the previous chapter focused on the *ascension*. Now attention is turned to the significance of the *narrative*.

History of Scholarship

Whatever else one might say about the ascension narrative in Acts, it must be recognized that the passage functions as a narrative beginning the story of Acts. Such a statement may sound simplistic, but in fact, many students of the ascension have overlooked this obvious truth. The ascension is not only *in* Acts, it stands at the outset to introduce the reader to the narrative. Therefore studies on narrative beginnings in literary criticism may shed new light on the function of the ascension in its narrative context in Acts.

Literary Theory and Beginnings in Narrative Literature
Only two major studies of narrative beginnings have appeared in the last twenty years. The first, *Romananfänge: Versuch zu einer Poetik des Romans*, edited by Norbert Miller, has made little impact on narratologists.[1] The second, *Beginnings: Intention and Method*, by Edward W. Said, has fared much better.[2] This work, published in 1975, has 'concentrated on beginnings both as something one does and as something one thinks about'.[3] Fashioned somewhat after

Kermode's *The Sense of an Ending*, Said examined the psychological (particularly Valery) and phenomenological (particularly Husserl) approaches to understanding beginnings.[4] Said has emphasized the beginning of writing (the literary process) more than the beginning of *the* writing (the literary product). Said's thesis was that:

> invention and restraint ... ultimately have *conserved* the novel because novelists have construed them together as *beginning* conditions, not as conditions for limitlessly expansive fictional invention. Thus the novel represents a beginning of a very precisely finite sort insofar as what may ensue from that beginning.[5]

While the breadth of Said's work is impressive and much appreciated, specific references to the strategies involved in constructing narrative beginnings are disappointingly few and hopelessly scattered.[6] Though Said has defined a beginning as something which 'methodologically unites a practical need with a theory, an intention with a method',[7] he has emphasized the intention to the denigration of the narrative method.[8] One contribution Said did make was the distinction between transitive and intransitive beginnings. The transitive beginning is one which is characterized by 'beginning with (or for) an anticipated end, or at least expected continuity'.[9] An intransitive beginning, on the other hand, is one 'which has no object but its own constant clarification' and is totally unrelated to the rest of the narrative, that is 'beginning *at* the beginning, *for* the beginning'.[10] The first, then, is 'projective and descriptive, the other tautological and endlessly self-mimetic'.[11] While certain modern literature may exhibit the intransitive beginning,[12] the beginnings of most ancient literature are inextricably entwined in some way with the rest of the narrative.

In addition to these studies, one might also mention the work by Meir Sternberg, *Expositional Modes and Temporal Ordering in Fiction*.[13] Sternberg's work is not devoted to an analysis of narrative beginnings, but he did evaluate the importance of commencements for the distribution of exposition, or information needed by the reader to make sense of the story. Sternberg's work will be treated in more detail under the relationship between narrator and reader during narrative entrance.

Despite the lack of full-length studies on narrative beginnings comparable to those on narrative closure by Torgovnick or Miller, numerous articles have been published in the last decade which have advanced the study of narrative beginnings. While many articles are concerned with the narrative beginnings of certain authors,[14] several others have addressed the problem in more general ways.

In 1978, George Watson published 'The Sense of a Beginning', an obvious challenge to Kermode's work a decade earlier.[15] Watson argued:

> These are among the reasons why beginnings count for more than endings. They require more concentration on the part of the author; more significant decisions, albeit personal ones, on the part of the reader; and they dominate the total texture of the works they initiate. I believe, too, that they are more various than endings.[16]

Robert Pope's 'Beginnings', published in 1982, is also helpful in analyzing openings in narratives.[17] He has written of the importance of the narrative voice in beginnings. Pope's work serves to complement, and in some respects correct, Watson's emphasis on the anticipatory role of beginnings. He claimed:

> Because, for the reader/listener, first words convey ... not a challenging puzzle which we must solve, but rather the manner and the authority of the voice in which any such fictional information will arrive. ... The reader may be cavalier unless he hears something in the writer's voice that prevents his escape, though to be so captured is the reader's profoundest desire.[18]

In addition to these two seminal articles, several other narratologists have written on the relationship of beginnings and endings in plot development. Most noteworthy of these are the article by Gerald C. Sorensen, which is doubly helpful because of its discussion of sequels, and Martin Kreiswirth's recent article, which is especially useful in the consideration of the beginning of Acts to the middle section of the narrative.[19]

Despite these works on narrative beginnings, it may be that many more scholars share the scepticism of Pope:

> I have too much of what beginnings must mean to the writer of fiction; I am always dissatisfied. In the background I hear a chorus: the flat, nasal voice of the journalism teacher whining her singsong cliché, *Well begun is half done*; the speech teacher who suggested that the speaker fire a pistol beside the inattentive ear of his unwilling listener; the writer of texts who referred to the first line and the first paragraph as the narrative hook; the writer of fiction who discussed the means of achieving tension within the first few lines, the first few paragraphs, asserting that many editors read no

further, imagining beginnings as a grand cleverness competition; even the writer who in passing insisted that each first sentence must be the seed from which every other sentence grows, for these are most often crafty considerations of craft.[20]

Pope's criticism is not of narrative beginnings themselves, but of the ways in which critics have trivialized their significance. Below is an attempt to take seriously the shape and function of the ascension story as a narrative beginning.

A Literary Model for Examining the Narrative Beginning of Acts

To examine the literary function of the ascension narrative in Acts, a modified form of Torgovnick's closural model will be employed. The opening passage will be examined in terms of (1) plot, that is, the relationship of the beginning to the end and the middle; (2) point of view, that is, the narrator's and reader's viewpoint on the novel's characters and major action; and (3) the relationship between the narrator and reader (implied reader and real reader) during entrance.

Several reasons may be offered to justify using basically the same model for examining the ending of Luke and the beginning of Acts. First, while the desired effects are certainly different, similar strategies are employed in beginning and ending narratives. The Apostolic Father who wrote, 'Behold, I make the last things like the first' (*Barnabas* 6.13), expressed not only a primitive eschatology, but a tried and tested literary tactic. Particular attention must be given to the reader during both processes, making sure the reader is properly introduced to the narrative and at the end that he or she is given an honorable discharge. How to get in and how to get out are vital issues in narrative beginnings and endings. This concern is reflected in the use of terms for both processes; they are mostly antithetical—beginning and ending, opening and closing, entrance and exit—but the language suggests these strategies are more alike than different.[21] The similarity between narrative beginnings and endings has been well articulated by Alexander Welsh:

> Beginnings and endings of narrative have much in common since both are arbitrary disjunctions in a sequence of events that is presumed continuous, extending before and after the events that are narrated. We also have to imagine a surrounding space for each narrative, so that one narrative is arbitrarily separated from another, these beginnings and endings from those.[22]

A second reason for employing the same model in the following analysis is that it affords the opportunity to test whether or not the previously stated presupposition is true, at least for Luke–Acts. Are there similar strategies involved in ending Luke and beginning Acts (or even, beginning Luke and ending Acts)? Can the differences between the two ascension narratives be explained, at least in part, by the divergent desired effects sought in narrative endings and beginnings? These questions may only be answered after a similar literary method has been applied to both the ending of Luke and beginning of Acts which brings out in bold relief the marked similarities in strategy and the stark contrasts in the results achieved in the two narratives.

Beginnings and Plot Development

Transitive beginnings are crucial to plot development.[23] Watson claimed: 'Opening sentences create expectations; they set a tone'.[24] Watson further suggested that there are three types of beginnings: (1) those in which the reader is discouraged from guessing the outcome, or encouraged to guess it wrong; (2) those in which the reader is encouraged to guess the ending, and guess it right; and (3) those in which one is simply told the ending.[24] It is this last category, where the end is told at the beginning, that Watson found 'supremely satisfying'.[26] Watson maintained: 'When the end is known in the beginning, we can think less of the Whether and more of the How. And the How, after all, concerns the deepest texture of literature'.[27]

The beginning of Acts, in its programmatic statement of 1.8, gives away its ending—the spread of the Gospel 'to the ends of the earth'. The reader is confident of the success of this mission because the narrator placed the words in the mouth of the most reliable of characters—Jesus. To be sure, the way Acts ends, with Paul in Rome, has plagued readers for centuries, but there can be little doubt that the narrative fulfilled its expectations expressed in its beginning, even though the ending does not come in quite the way expected. Throughout the narrative, the reader is preoccupied not with the question of *whether* or not the mission will be completed, but *how* that fulfillment will be achieved.[28] Below the relationship of the beginning of Acts to the end and middle of the narrative is explored, first in terms of circularity, then in terms of parallelism. Finally linkage between the two volumes will be discussed. Since incompletion is a word descriptive of the closural process rather than the beginning, it will be omitted from discussion here.

Circularity

The circular pattern of plot development in Acts is not nearly so strong as it is in Luke. In the Gospel, the story begins and ends in the temple in Jerusalem. Acts is a 'Tale of Two Cities', for the narrative begins in Jerusalem, but ends in Rome. In Luke, angels appear at beginning and end as framing devices. In Acts, angels appear at the beginning of the story and recur throughout the narrative, but are absent at the conclusion. In Luke, the disciples at the end are now the pious people of God, replacing the devout Jews of chs. 1 and 2. In Acts, Paul, not the disciples, occupies the place of protagonist at the ending.

Despite this lack of a neatly framed narrative, the beginning of Acts does in several ways anticipate its ending. In fact, several scholars have already worked on the relationship between Acts 1 and 28. Dupont has examined the conclusion of Acts (28.16-31) in light of the rest of the work, particularly the relationship between ch. 28 and Acts 2; 13; 21; Luke 1; 24, as well as Acts 1.[29] In addition, an unpublished dissertation written by Charles B. Puskas, Jr. under the supervision of Robert O'Toole, devoted several pages to the inter-connections between Acts 1 and Acts 28.[30] Puskas is right in claiming: 'While there is insufficient evidence for viewing Acts 1 and 28 as parallel texts, they both share common elements and have a special literary relationship'.[31] It should be recognized that the themes or ideas anticipated in the opening narrative are not, in most cases, simply resumed in the conclusion, but rather represent the final reference in a series of points throughout the text.

1. The Kingdom of God. Four of the eight occurrences of 'kingdom' in Acts are equally distributed in Acts 1.3, 6 and 28.23, 31.[32] The first reference is to Jesus speaking the things concerning the kingdom of God to the disciples, while he was staying with them. Interestingly, the last mention of the kingdom of God is also linked with 'abiding' in Acts 28.31: 'he remained there two whole years . . . preaching the kingdom of God'.[33] The second reference to the kingdom is actually the first in the narrative proper. The dialogue allows Jesus (and the narrator!) to correct some misunderstanding about the kingdom.

In every instance, the mention of 'the kingdom' or 'the kingdom of God' is accompanied by a word of preaching, exhorting, arguing, pleading, or testifying.[34] The kingdom of God, then, with its prominent position at the beginning and end of the narrative as well as strategic positioning throughout the story (Jerusalem, Samaria, Lystra, Ephesus, Miletus, and Rome) functions to move the plot along to its conclusion.[35] The kingdom is variously declared by Jesus himself, Philip, Barnabas, and Paul.[36] The context of each of these passages (as well as others in the Gospel) seems to bear out the conclusion reached by Maddox regarding the kingdom of God in Luke–Acts: 'Luke's real concern is not *when* the kingdom of God will come (as is generally assumed) but *who* will qualify to be admitted to it'.[37] The beginning anticipates the correction of the disciples' question in 1.6 and finds its final fulfillment at Acts 28.23, 31.[38]

2. Worldwide Missions. Puskas has noted: 'Studies in Luke–Acts have made frequent allusions to the relationship of Christ's commission (Acts 1.8) and Paul's mission in Rome (28.23-31)'.[39] This anticipated theme of worldwide missions finds satisfaction in the closing scene. Jesus informed his disciples that they would be witnesses, and at the close of the narrative Paul is found 'testifying of the kingdom of God'. The beginning of the narrative of Acts presents the last words of Jesus which concern the church's worldwide mission. A similar theme is struck in the last words of Paul (Acts 28.28).[40] In fact, most scholars see Paul's arrival in Rome as the fulfillment of Jesus' commission to his disciples to be witnesses 'to the ends of the earth'. On this point, Puskas has remarked:

> Concerning the theme of a world-wide mission, the relationship of Acts 28 to Acts 1 can be seen in the following manner: Paul, who is endued with the Holy Spirit (9.17-18; 13.2-3, 9; cf. 1.8), functions as Christ's witness in Rome (23.11; 28.23, 31; cf. 1.8), having brought the gospel to the Gentile world, to the 'ends of the earth'. In so doing the above, Paul has brought Christ's commission (1.8) to its completion in Acts.[41]

The connection between 'the ends of the earth' and Rome has been problematic. Again to quote Puskas:

> Caution should be taken in attempting to equate the designation 'ends of the earth' only with Rome (despite this apparent association in the Psalms of Solomon 8.15). The phrase 'ends of the earth' from Acts 1.8 is also employed in Acts 13.47/Isa. 49.6 to signify the Gentile world in general.[42]

Why does the narrative end with a reference to Paul in Rome for two years rather than with a more generalized reference to his

ministry in the gentile world or at least his death? Aside from the fact
that the real author probably knew of Paul's death in Rome which
prevented any mention of further missionary activity outside Rome,
the literary design of the plot makes the seemingly problematic
conclusion an appropriate ending to the narrative. To be sure, the
plot does not require the reference to Paul's ministry in Rome in Acts
28.30-31. Rather, the prophecy found at 23.11 that Paul must bear
witness to Christ in Rome is already fulfilled in Acts 28.16-29. To end
with a specific temporal reference to two years in a specific city may
be the narrator's only way of providing closure to a plot which is
ever-widening and expanding. Specificity of this kind facilitates the
closure of the narrative.[43] At any rate, there is an undeniable
connection between the prediction of the worldwide mission by Jesus
in Acts 1.8 and the activity of Paul in Rome, the center of the gentile
world in Acts 28.

   3. *Teaching*. The term διδάσκω occurs in the opening and closing
verses of Acts (1.1; 28.31) and, of course, is an important activity of
the apostles and Paul.[44] By framing the narrative with references to
teaching, the narrator has underscored the importance of the
teaching ministry and highlighted the parallel activities of Paul and
Jesus. Another shift has been completed in this last reference: Jesus is
no longer the teacher, but the subject matter, no longer the
proclaimer, but the proclaimed.

   4. *Last Words*. Dupont has pointed out an interesting contrast
between what is not to be made known and what is urged to be
understood: 'la réponse de Jesus commence par une négation:... Le
contraste est fort avec les mots qui introduisent la déclaration finale
de Paul'.[45] While the disciples are not to know the time or the season
which God has set, Paul expects the Jews to know that salvation is
now available to them. Couched in this 'knowing' context, the last
words of Jesus, 'witnesses ... to the ends of the earth', and the last
words of Paul, 'Let this be made known to you that to the Gentiles
has been sent this salvation of God' are complementary.[46]

   5. *Other Links*. Several other verbal and thematic links between
the beginning and ending of Acts may be mentioned, though at best
they seem secondary to the movement of the plot. The Holy Spirit is
actively involved in the pronouncement of Jesus (1.2) and Isaiah
(28.25). The anticipated empowering of the disciples by the Holy
Spirit is presupposed in Acts 28.[47] Dupont has cryptically suggested
that the 'restoration of the kingdom to Israel' in Acts 1.8 is connected
to the 'hope of Israel' in 28.20.[48] Dupont also added the novel

suggestion that just as the Third Gospel begins and ends in the temple, so Acts begins in an upper room with the disciples praying and ends in a lower room with Paul preaching.[49] Closely linked to these references to dwelling-places is the idea of 'abiding' which occurs at 1.4 and 28.30. Just as it is easier to board and disembark from a train which has stopped than one still in full motion, this mention of 'abiding' gives both beginning and ending a static texture which may assist the reader in entering into and exiting from a story which is momentarily stationary.[50]

A less compelling link suggested by some scholars is the use of Isaiah 6 in Acts 1 and 28. While Acts 28.26-27 is a direct quotation of Isa. 6.9-10, to say, as some do, that Acts 1.6-8 recalls in function Isa. 6.11-13 is to strain the evidence.[51] Equally unconvincing is R.H. Smith's thesis that: 'Paul's triumphant proclamation of the Gospel in Rome balances or rather completes the account of the ascension of Jesus at the beginning of Acts'.[52] Smith further asserted: 'By singling out Paul and focusing on his work in bringing the call to repentance and the word about Jesus to Rome, Luke is describing how the enthroned Jesus is Himself the answer to the question of distance from the earthly ministry of Jesus'.[53] Puskas has objected that 'the relevance of the enthroned Christ at Rome is at best an implicit theme in Acts 28'.[54]

In conclusion, as noted at the beginning of this section, the links between Acts 1 and 28, while numerous, are rather weak. With the exception of the gentile mission anticipated in Acts 1.8 and finally fulfilled in 28.25-31 (which may be more a parallel pattern than a circular one), the remaining verbal and thematic links between beginning and end are of secondary significance to the development and fulfillment of plot strategies in Acts.[55]

Parallelism
Modifying Torgovnick's definition, *parallelism* for narrative beginnings will be understood as occurring when the language, action, or grouping of characters refers not just to the end, but to a series of points in the text. Parallel plot development is much more prominent in Acts than circularity. Below is an attempt to analyze Acts 1.6-11 in relationship to the middle or body of the narrative, paying particularly close attention to the way the major plot strategies are anticipated in the narrative opening, developed in the middle, and later closed by the ending.[56]

Despite the number of ancillary plot strategies anticipated in Acts

1, this study is limited to the major one concerning the place of Israel in the gentile mission, reflected in the disciple's question and Jesus' response in 1.6-8.[57] Before engaging in a detailed analysis of the narrative, several concerns regarding method should be noted. First, a major methodological flaw of previous studies has been to wrench passages from the narrative in order to 'systematize' Luke's views concerning salvation history.[58] In order to correct this methodological error, this study will begin with the opening narrative and trace sequentially the response of the Jews to the gospel to determine if the order of events betrays any development in the plot of Acts. Second, as Tyson has noted: 'most of those scholars who have contributed to the discussion of Luke's attitude to the Jewish public ... have confined their attention to Acts'.[59] While space does not allow a full-length treatment of the Jewish populace in Luke, preliminary study shows that, although this same downward path of the Jews detected in Acts is present also in Luke, the plot strategies employed to move the story of the Jews are not the same.[60] Third, another inadequacy of previous studies has been their concentration on the response of only the Jews to the gospel. In order to capture the narrator's rich plot development, the response of those who accept the message of Jesus, the Christian community, must be examined, again for traces of plot development.[61]

Many of these methodological concerns have been expressed in a more general way by Luke Johnson who suggested that any study of Luke–Acts must be sensitive to the following factors:

> that Luke–Acts taken as a whole, is a story. It has a beginning and an end, and whatever the elements of circularity, the story is linear; things change and develop.... If this is a story, the reader must attend to the *place* in the story a passage occurs.... the story line has a consistent pattern of acceptance and rejection; ignoring the placement of passages within this pattern can lead to misreading.[62]

These two trajectories, the upward swing of those who teach and preach Jesus and the downward flight of those who have rejected him, are plotted side-by-side on the narrative graph of Acts. It is the major contention of this section that the worldwide mission and the rejection by the Jews and others are moved along from its prediction to its conclusion by what one literary critic has called the narrative patterning of the 'empty center'.

Martin Kreiswirth has suggested that the strategy of the 'empty center' describes the technique of employing a character at a novel's core who 'is characterized almost exclusively by means of . . . various monologues'.[63] In fact, this character 'functions primarily as a symbol of loss and evokes a similarly broad range of responses from those who come into contact with him'.[64]

This centripetal pattern of plot development employs a character who is 'absent but curiously present . . . around which both the major action and the various characters' thoughts revolve'.[65] The effect of such a narrative pattern is admirably summarized by Kreiswirth:

> These figures occupy their focal positions not only because all the circumferential characters obsessively look to them as a means of evaluating themselves and each other but also because they initiate and control their texts' sequence of incidents, its proairetic elements, as well as its sustaining enigmas, or hermeneutic elements. While the ramifications of their actions reverberate through time, they themselves are beyond time; they can only be interpreted, never understood and thus, like their counterparts in the other novels, they create gaps that the survivors vainly try to fill.[66]

This centripetal narrative patterning of the 'empty' center seems to describe aptly the plot strategy of the narrator of Acts. Jesus himself is gone; the message about him moves the plot. Like other main characters in open centers who are 'absent, but curiously present', Jesus does not make another on-stage appearance in the drama after he ascends in Acts 1. To be sure, Stephen sees him in a vision standing at the right hand of God and his voice is heard in the recounting of Paul's Damascus Road experience, but the 'earthly' Jesus himself does not re-appear. Jesus elicits a 'broad range of responses' and is the figure 'around which both the major actions and the major characters' thoughts revolve'. Jesus is the fulcrum of much of the conflict in the narrative. He becomes the dividing line between those who accept him and those who reject him. Those who reject him experience loss in the severest sense. The worldwide mission is to spread the gospel of Jesus Christ. He is interpreted in the sermons of Peter and proclaimed in the synagogues by Paul. The following pages are devoted to showing how the various plot strategies assist this centripetal narrative patterning.

Jesus' absence has led some to label Acts an example of 'absentee Christology'.[67] His name, however, occurs in the narrative of Acts no less than 69 times and in 24 of 28 chapters,[68] mostly in the sermons of Peter and Paul and in the narrator's comments. Here is the striking resemblance to what Kreiswirth has called the 'empty center'. O'Toole has also noticed that Jesus plays a significant role in Acts.

> The risen Lord acts and is present to the whole life of his church. He leads the Christians. Their mission is Christ's mission. He gives his followers their mission and directs them. When they are persecuted, he encourages, supports, and protects them. His power enables them to perform miracles. When they preach, he preaches; when they are heard, he is heard. Their salvation, a present experience and reality, comes only from him. They are baptized in his name and realize his presence in the Eucharist. Certainly, the Father and the Spirit are active, but a church without considerable activity on the part of the risen Christ is not Lukan.[69]

O'Toole still did not venture to say that the themes proposed in the preface are moved along distinct lines by references to Jesus. The intent here is to show how the plot of the acceptance or rejection of Jesus is moved by this pattern of the empty center.

The Jews in Acts. That there is a pattern of rejection of the gospel on the part of the Jewish populace is clear. The more pertinent question is: What type of rejection pattern emerges in the story of the Jews?[70] To answer that question, first those passages which record a positive response to the Gospel on the part of the Jews will be examined. This will be followed by an analysis of the rejection passages. The purpose here is to show that the gradual falling away and obduracy of Israel is anticipated in the disciples' question in 1.6 and developed by the plot stategy of the 'empty' center narrative patterning throughout the rest of the narrative.[71]

1. Jewish Acceptance of the Gospel. Within the course of the first nine chapters of Acts are recorded numerous conversions of Jews: 2.41, (47); 4.4; 5.14; 6.1; 7; and 9.42.[72] The narrator makes it clear that the first followers were Jewish (1.13-14, 21). Then, after Pentecost and Peter's sermon (addressed to 'men of Judea and all who dwell in Jerusalem'), about three thousand 'received his word and were baptized'. Though there were certainly some Gentiles among that group (see 2.9-11, especially the 'proselytes' of v. 10), the address of the sermon and the location in Jerusalem point to the overwhelming majority of 'converts' being Jews. Likewise, of the number of 'those who were being saved' mentioned in the summary statement of Acts 2.47, the context demands that a large number were Jewish.

In the fourth chapter of Acts, an even larger number (about 5,000 men) 'who heard the word, believed' (4.4). Again, the context of the temple area, while not excluding gentile God-fearers, would suggest that a prominent number were Jews. Likewise, the fifth and sixth chapters are couched in Jewish contexts. Chapter 5 is set in Solomon's portico: 'And more than ever believers were added to the Lord, multitudes of men and women' (5.14). Chapter 6 follows a reference to the apostles preaching in the temple and begins: 'Now in those days when the disciples were increasing in number'. A little later the reference is more explicit: 'and the number of the disciples multiplied greatly in Jerusalem', the narrative going so far as to record 'a great many of the priests were obedient to the faith' (6.7). In the city of Joppa (9.42) the narrator records that 'many believed in the Lord'.[73]

Jervell listed other passages as well which indicated 'mass conversions of Jews': 12.24; 13.43; 14.1; 17.10ff; (19.20); 21.20.[74] Recently, however, Sanders has challenged Jervell's interpretation of these passages.[75] Moving along chronologically in the narrative, we come first to Acts 12.24. On this passage Sanders noted: 'While it is possible that the note—entirely disconnected as it is from its context—refers to new conversions, it is markedly different from the previous summary statements that explicitly mention conversion'.[76]

It is possible that the narrator assumes by this point that the reader would understand his shorthand (see the fuller statements in 6.7; 7.18; 9.31).[77] Even if the reference is to the conversion of Jews as Jervell maintained, it is important to observe that the reference is implicit, not explicit, and except for 21.20 (discussed below) is the last reference to the mass conversion of Jews.

If we accept Jervell's suggestion that 'persuaded' implies conversion, then the next reference to Jewish converts is at 13.43.[78] Here the many Jews are joined by 'devout converts to Judaism', no doubt a reference to converted Gentiles. Before this point, the reader could only infer that the large numbers of converts included Gentiles, whereas here for the first time in the context of a Jewish affirmative response it is made explicit. Again, in the mission in the Diaspora, the references to the Jews who believed are now joined by references to Greeks or Gentiles as well (14.1; 17.10). Likewise in 18.4, Paul is recorded as having 'persuaded Jews and Greeks'. After the conversion of Crispus, the ruler of the synagogue, there are no other explicit references to Jewish conversion to Christianity in the context of the gentile mission.[79] At 19.26 Demetrius complains that Paul has 'persuaded' a sufficient crowd. The reference situated as it is in Ephesus, in the mouth of a Greek silversmith, at best only implies that part of the company is Jewish, much as the earlier references in Acts could only be assumed to include Gentiles.

Acts 21.20 is a reference to 'how many thousands there are among the Jews of those who have believed'. While Jervell took this verse as evidence of the growing Jewish responsiveness to the gospel,[80] Sanders argued for just the opposite: 'We are therefore able to arrive at the sum given in 21.20 without the assumption of a single Jewish convert in Jerusalem after 6.7'.[81] Given the development of the Jews' resistance to the Christian message, Sanders' remarks seem to reflect a more plausible reading of the text. The reference to the thousands of Jews who have believed is a poignant reminder to the reader who knows from a close reading what the elders in Jerusalem know: the glory days of mass Jewish conversions are over.[82]

The pattern of the 'empty center' surfaces even in these early references to the Jews. They are characterized positively because they have responded to Jesus affirmatively. The image of the Jews created at the beginning of the narrative is one of openness: early on, when the gospel is preached, they repent. The narrative beginning only sets the stage for apostasy and infidelity. This same Jesus and the message about him, will later evoke negative reactions and lead to a most tragic loss for Israel of dignity, status, and even salvation in Acts.

2. *Conflict Scenes*. At the same time the response of the Jews to the message about Jesus is being recorded as one of diminishing returns, the conflict scenes between the Jews and the Christian missionaries are increasing in intensity and frequency. Already we have seen what a significant role conflict scenes play as a plot device.[83] In the Gospel, Jesus is the one who comes into conflict with the religious leaders.[84] Below, the conflict scenes in Acts are examined sequentially, with particularly close attention paid to those which occur in the vicinity of the temple and synagogues (see Table 17).

The first skirmish occurs in the ascension narrative between Jesus and the disciples. They ask: 'Lord, will you at this time restore the kingdom to Israel?' Jesus' response does not imply that Israel is beyond restoration, but such restoration is not the primary task of the disciples. Tannehill remarked:

> Jesus' answer to the disciples' question denies that they can know
> the time and probably corrects their supposition that the restoration

may come immediately, but Jesus' reply is not meant to reject the possibility of a restoration of the kingdom to Israel.[85]

Rather, Jesus' response confirms that the inauguration of God's kingship among his people has now become the primary task for which the disciples have been deputized for proclaiming to the far corners of the world.[86] The process of restoration, if it is to happen at all, remains in the hands of God and his Messiah (Acts 1.7; 3.19-21); it is not the mission of the disciples, nor is it for them to know the details. The disciples' question and Jesus' response serve as the basis for the working of the rest of the narrative plot.[87]

Table 17

Conflict Scenes in Acts

Text	Context	God's People	God's Agent	Conflict
1.6-8	Mt of Olives	disciples	Jesus	1.6-8
2.13-42	Pentecost	those present	Peter	2.13ff.
3.1-4.21*	temple	priests/Sadducees temple captain	Peter, John	4.1-21
5.21-42*	temple	.. ..	apostles	5.28-32
6.8-8.1	Jerusalem	elders, scribes, people	Stephen	6.9-13, 7.54-8.1
9.29	Jerusalem	Hellenists	Paul	9.29
13.4-12	Cyprus	Bar-Jesus	Paul	13.10-12
13.13-52*	synagogue	Jews	Paul/Barnabas	13.45-52
14.1-5*	synagogue	Jews (Gentiles)	Paul/Barnabas	14.4-5
14.8-19	Lystra	Jews	Paul	14.19
17.1-9*	synagogue	Jews	Paul	17.4-5
18.1-11*	synagogue	Jews	Paul	18.6
21.26ff.*	temple	Jews of Asia	Paul	21.27ff.

Note: * indicates the conflict in the vicinity of the temple or synagogue.

The next conflict occurs in the Pentecost narrative between the disciples and those present (most of whom presumably are Jews). Mixed in with reactions of amazement and perplexity are words of mockery: 'They are filled with new wine' (2.13). Peter then uses the opportunity to correct their misunderstanding of the situation (2.14-21) and to deliver the message of Jesus whom they crucified and God raised from the dead (2.22-36).[88] Such preaching will later incur the wrath of the Jews; but at this point early in the narrative it leads to their repentance, conversion, and baptism (2.37-42).

In Acts 3–4 is recorded the first temple conflict scene. God's agents are Peter and John. The antagonists are the priests, the captain of the temple, and the Sadducees. The point of controversy, according to the narrator, is that the disciples were 'proclaiming in Jesus the resurrection from the dead' (Acts 4.2). The Jewish leaders warn them not to speak or teach in the name of Jesus (4.17, 18), but they fail to prevent the disciples' message from spreading further among the people (4.17). The end result is that the word of God is spoken openly (4.31). The plot of these two chapters is moved along by the various responses to Jesus, following the narrative of the empty center. The same message which was received by the Jewish people has been rejected by the leaders (priests, captain of the temple, and the Sadducees).

The second temple conflict scene is set in Solomon's portico (5.12ff.). The number of participants and the level of intensity increase. God's messengers this time include all the apostles. The antagonists are led by the high priests and the Sadducees. After escaping, the apostles are found again in the temple and brought before the council (5.27). The warning issued by the high priest is that the apostles should not 'teach in this name'. Their intention, so the high priest charges, is 'to bring this man's blood upon us' (5.28). As in the conflict in ch. 4, Peter (and here the apostles) responds with a christocentric message (5.29-31). The conflict intensifies and the accusers would have killed them had not the cool counsel of Gamaliel prevailed (5.34-40). Having beaten the apostles, the opponents again charge them not to speak in 'the name of Jesus' (5.40). The result again is that the apostles were every day preaching and teaching Jesus as the Christ.

The intensity of the conflict continues in 6.9 when diaspora, or more specifically, Asian Jews, dispute with Stephen.[89] They plot his death and manage to stir up support not only from the elders and scribes but also from the people who until this time had either responded affirmatively to the Jesus message or at most expressed astonishment or wonder at the apostles' teachings and deeds (6.12).[90] Stephen's last remark 'And they killed those who announced beforehand the coming of the Righteous One, whom you have now betrayed and murdered' (7.53), agitates the Jews into a state of rage.[91] In the heat of their anger, Stephen's vision of 'Jesus standing at the right hand of God' (7.44) serves to underline the fact that Jesus, though absent from the dialogue, is still a part of the narrative world and in fact is the prime mover of the plot in the conflict scenes between Jews and Christians. Stephen dies a martyr's death like Jesus, asking for forgiveness against his persecutors.[92]

Acts 8 begins with a reference to a 'great persecution' against the church in Jerusalem culminating with believers being scattered all over Judea and Samaria, except the apostles (8.1-2). This reference concludes the section of Acts devoted to Christian mission in Jerusalem. A sharp contrast is to be noted in the early references to those Jews who responded to the message of Jesus and this passage which indicates a widespread persecution in Jerusalem against the church. After an interlude which involves the witness to Samaritans, the narrator reminds the reader that Paul is still breathing threats against the church (9.1). After Paul's conversion, he is found at Jerusalem preaching openly (9.29) and disputing with the Hellenists who were seeking to kill him (9.29).[93]

At the beginning of ch. 12 is the cryptic note that the death of James, John's brother 'pleased the Jews' (12.3). Significant here is the fact that the distinction made earlier between the Jewish leaders and the indeterminate crowds of Jews is missing. The tragic reversal of the special status of the Jews as God's people is slowly being effected.

With Acts 13, we have the beginning of the missionary endeavors of Paul and a series of synagogue scenes. Richard has noted about these synagogue scenes: 'In practically every synagogue episode the outcome is negative: expulsion, persecution, or withdrawal'.[94] Acts 13.4-12 is the account of the conversion of Sergius Paulus at Paphos. There, a Jewish false prophet named Bar-Jesus is not only obdurate in his stance towards the gospel, he stands against Paul, Barnabas, and John, 'seeking to turn away the proconsul from the faith' (13.8). The punishment of Bar-Jesus or Elymas, who is too spiritually blind to recognize the gospel of Jesus, is to be struck with blindness.

The next synagogue conflict scene occurs in Antioch of Pisidia. This time Paul is God's representative, the Jews are the adversaries. The Jews protest Paul's teaching, which was again a christocentric message (13.16-41).[45] Here we have the first of three warnings that the mission of the gospel is to turn to the Gentiles. Implicit again is the fact that Jesus is the source of contention and the cause of loss for Jews.

After being driven out of Antioch by 'the Jews', Paul and Barnabas encounter trouble at Iconium when 'unbelieving Jews' stir up the Gentiles and attempt to stone Paul and Barnabas (14.5). At Lystra these persistent Jews from Antioch and Iconium join forces and persuade the people to stone Paul, leaving him for dead (14.19). The next synagogue conflict scene is set in Thessalonica. Again, Paul's preaching of Jesus (17.3) persuaded some and caused the Jews to become jealous (see 5.17; 13.45) and, following the typical pattern, incite a riot. This time the narrator adds the interesting detail that the Jews took 'some wicked fellows of the rabble' indicating no doubt the depths which the Jews' depravity had reached. The scene is repeated in Berea when the Jews of Thessalonica come over to stir up the crowds against Paul and Silas. Paul leaves Berea and is recorded as arguing in Athens 'in the synagogue with the Jews' (17.17).

The last synagogue conflict scene occurs at 18.1-11 in Corinth. Paul preaches to the Jews that the Christ was Jesus. Again the 'Jews' oppose him. Paul responds with the second warning, 'From now on I will go to the Gentiles' (18.6). At this point a new element is introduced into the conflict scenario: Paul goes next door and the scene ends with Crispus the ruler of the synagogue, and all his household, believing in the Lord and being baptized (18.8). This scene is the last specific record of the conversion of a Jew.

The impenitence of the Jews continues to heighten as the narrative draws to a close. In 19.8-10, Paul is, as usual, speaking boldly in the synagogue at Ephesus. After three months Paul withdrew from them because 'some were stubborn and disbelieved' (19.9). Usually the narrator records some positive response to the gospel, as well. Such is not the case here. Only the negative results are registered. Here is another sign that the Jews have forfeited their status.[96] Later in ch. 20, Paul learns of another plot against him by the Jews (20.3).

One final temple scene, 21.26ff., has the Jews from Asia stirring up the crowds. Paul was dragged from the temple, and the people attempted to kill him.[97] During his defense addressed in Hebrew to the 'people' (21.40), the Jews interrupt with the strong vituperation: 'Away with such a fellow from the earth! For he ought not to live' (22.22).[98]

The fractious nature of the Jews is exploited by Paul during his trial when theological controversy causes such an upheaval that the tribune removed Paul from the premises for fear that he 'would be torn in pieces by them'. (23.10) The desperate attitude of the Jews is poignantly conveyed by the narrator when he records their suicide pact 'neither to eat nor drink until they had killed Paul' (23.13; see 23.13-22). The collaboration of the Jews with their high priest is not unnoticed by narrator and reader (24.9; 25.7). Later, the Roman governor Festus charged that Paul was 'this man about whom the whole Jewish people petitioned me, both at Jerusalem and here, shouting that he ought not to live any longer' (25.24). On this passage, Tyson remarked: 'Perhaps Luke wished to emphasize the total rejection of Paul in Acts 25.24'.[99]

The remainder of ch. 25, along with 26, 27, and much of 28, is preoccupied with Paul's trial[100] and his voyage to Rome. The last scene of the narrative, however, is problematic for our consideration of the course of the Jews in Acts. Paul receives a large number of the local leaders of the Jews and tries to convince them about Jesus and the kingdom. The result was that 'some were convinced by what he said, while others disbelieved' (28.24). Paul's speech ends with the third warning against the Jews and the promise again that 'this salvation of God has been sent to the Gentiles' (28.29).[101] While Jervell maintained that the way is open to Jews who respond positively to the gospel, the way in which the story has developed seems to argue otherwise.[102] On the conclusion of Acts, Tyson has argued:

> Endings not only conclude stories, but they also resolve tensions
> that were developed in the body. They tell how the story turned
> out. Although Acts suggests a continuation of the story, with Paul
> in Rome, the ending nevertheless functions in the usual way.
> Despite the bright happiness of the early chapters, it is the end of
> the story that is the most impressive.... At the end, Jewish
> acceptance of Jesus and the early Christians has been either
> neglected or suppressed. The Jewish public has heard but rejected
> the gospel.[103]

The mission to 'the ends of earth' is complete by Acts 28.31; the promise of Israel restored, however, is unfulfilled.[104] By the end of the narrative, the narrative patterning of the empty center (in which the characters variously respond to an absent, but curiously present Jesus) depicts the 'Jews' as representative of all those who have rejected the gospel of Jesus, and the 'Gentiles' are those who have accepted salvation in his name, or at least seem willing to do so.

The Christian Community in Acts. At the beginning of the

narrative, the Christian community in Acts is presented as unified and like-minded. After the ascension, the disciples, along with the women and the family of Jesus, 'with one accord devoted themselves to prayer' (1.14). Judas' successor is chosen with no difficulty; even Matthias' competition, Joseph Barsabbas, does not raise a dissenting voice.[105] Acts 2.1 records that they (the believers) were all in one place. In the summary statement of 2.44-45, believers are described as being together and having all things in common. And in 4.24, the disciples lifted their voices, in chorus fashion, in harmonious praise to God.

This ostensible unity of the Christian community is fractured early on by internal divisions. Ananias and Sapphira deceive the apostles by withholding funds and disrupt the fellowship (5.1-11); the Greek-speaking Jewish Christians murmur and complain that the Hebrews, or Aramaic-speaking Jewish Christians,[106] are neglecting the Hellenists' widows (6.1-16). Both of these conflicts are quickly resolved: Ananias and Sapphira are struck dead (!); seven men are appointed to 'serve tables'.

Later, in 9.26, the newly converted Paul receives a cool reception on the part of the disciples in Jerusalem, and the conversion of Cornelius creates problems for Peter with the 'circumcision party' in Jerusalem (11.1-18). Again, these two skirmishes are soon stopped: Barnabas bears witness to the authenticity of Paul's conversion. The last major conflict occurs at the council at Jerusalem (ch. 15). Peter, Paul, and Barnabas argue the case for the inclusion of the Gentiles in the Church without the rite of circumcision; other believers, especially those of the Pharisee party (15.4), dissented. The Apostolic Decree represented the agreed compromise (15.22-30).

Interestingly, following each one of these conflict scenes, the narrator records a summary statement which describes the harmony and growth of the church. Following the account of Ananias and Sapphira, one reads in 5.14: 'And more than ever believers were added to the Lord, multitudes both of men and women'. After the dispute between the Hellenists and Hebrews the text narrates: 'And the word of God increased; and the number of the disciples multiplied greatly in Jerusalem' (6.7). Again, following Paul's attempt to join the disciples at Jerusalem, one finds: 'So the church . . . had peace and was built up . . . and in the comfort of the Holy Spirit it as multiplied' (9.31). And in the immediate context following the dispute between Peter and the circumcision party is recorded: '. . . and a great number that believed turned to the Lord' (11.21).

Finally, in the narrative subsequent to the council at Jerusalem, Judas and Silas who read the Apostolic Decree to the congregation at Antioch 'were sent off in peace by the brethren to those who had sent them' (15.31).

There are no other major conflicts in the Christian community following the resolution of the gentile issue in ch. 15.[107] The statements about the church's concord and converts, however, continue throughout the rest of the narrative, at least up to the point of Paul's journey to Rome and his defense before the Roman authorities (16.5; 17.4; 18.23, 27; 19.20).

The conflict scenes between the Jews and Christians and those disputes which are internal to the Christian community have distinct literary functions. At the beginning of the narrative, both groups are presented as harmonious and responsive to the gospel. The Jewish-Christian conflict scenes record the downward flight of the Jews. The story of Israel is all the more tragic because of the impressions created in the narrative beginning. There the Jewish populace are depicted as open and pliant to the gospel. As the plot continues to develop, however, the major issue stands out in bold relief: rejection or acceptance of Jesus is the focal point of the narrative. The reader is aware of the presence of Jesus from the opening scene where he is actually onstage and that presence continues to be felt as Jesus functions as an absent character who moves the plot line along.

The conflicts within the Christian community, however, serve the plot function of propelling the Church to new heights. Each conflict within the community allows the narrator the opportunity to emphasize the growth, harmony, and success of the community which responds to the gospel of Jesus. The success story of the Church is plotted alongside the tragic story of Israel—the difference between the two revolves around their response to the risen Christ.

Reverse Linkage

Torgovnick defined *linkage* as that which links a narrative 'not to its own beginning and middle, but to the body of another, often as yet unwritten, novel'.[108] *Reverse linkage*, then, would be the phenomenon of a sequel referring to its predecessor. The inter-textualities, that is, the verbal, formal, and thematic correspondences, between Acts 1 and the narrative of the Third Gospel have been widely noted. This statement is not to suggest that the plot of Acts is so dependent on Luke that it could not be understood by itself. Gerald Sorensen has noted: 'both the sequel and its predecessor are complete in themselves—that is, 'closed,'. . . its plot is in no way dependent on its antecedent'.[109] Rather, one problem of any sequel is determining where to begin, or as Sorensen put it: 'A fundamental problem of the sequel' is 'that of its beginning'.[110] The problem of beginning the sequel of Acts is examined below.

1. Acts 1 and Luke 24. Talbert has performed the yeoman's task of compiling the content and verbal links of Luke–Acts.[111] In addition to noting parallels within the Third Gospel and within Acts, Talbert listed the correspondences between Luke 24 and 9, and Acts 1. On Luke 24 and Acts 1, Talbert wrote: 'The remarkable similarities between the end of the Gospel according to Luke and the beginning of the Acts of the Apostles have been widely recognized'.[112] The most significant linkage is between Acts 1.4 and Luke 24.49. In both accounts, Jesus commands the disciples to 'stay in the city' (Luke 24.49); 'not to depart from Jerusalem' (Acts 1.4) and wait for 'the promise of the Father' (24.49; Acts 1.4). Also the gentile mission and the mandate to witness are unfolded. Luke 24.47-48 reads: 'repentance and forgiveness of sins should be preached in his name to all nations, beginning from Jerusalem. You are witnesses of these things'. Likewise, in Acts 1.8, Jesus charges: 'and you shall be my witnesses in Jerusalem and in all Judea and Samaria and to the end of the earth'. One might also mention the departure of Jesus (Luke 24.51; Acts 1.9) and the return of the disciples to Jerusalem (Luke 24.52; Acts 1.12).[113]

2. Acts 1 and Luke 9. J.G. Davies first noted the similarities between the ascension narrative in Acts 1 and the transfiguration story in Luke 9 in a short article published in 1955.[114] Davies drew attention to no less than fourteen points of contact between these two chapters. Talbert has pared the list down to three.[115] Here, just two are mentioned. In Acts 1.9 the narrative records that a cloud took Jesus out of the disciples' sight. Likewise, in Luke 9.34-35, 'a cloud came and overshadowed them'. Also, both the transfiguration (9.28) and the ascension (1.12) took place on a mountain.

3. In addition to those elements of reverse linkage which are peculiar to Luke 24 and 9, there are several verbal correspondences common to the transfiguration, resurrection, and ascension narratives. Most obvious is the presence of the 'two men' in all three accounts. In fact, the verbal correspondence is exact for all three stories contain the phrase 'and behold two men' (καὶ ἰδοὺ ἄνδρες δύο) (see Luke 9.30; 24.4; Acts 1.10). It is striking that at three of the most exalted

moments of Jesus' ministry—his transfiguration, his resurrection, and his ascension—these two men are present.[116] There is no need to argue that these two men at the empty tomb and the ascension are Moses and Elijah, but that the appearance of these two at the transfiguration is part of this 'two men' motif seems unquestionable. What is significant is that these witnesses have the literary function of affirming and interpreting the event for the characters present and for the reader. The fact that the two men are missing in the ascension narrative in the Gospel adds strength to my argument that the account, at best, only opaquely refers to the ascension and that only careful and repeated readings yields this rather obscure reference. In addition to the two men, all three narratives mention white garments: in Luke 9.29, the garments belong to Jesus and in Luke 24.4 and Acts 1.10, the garments are those of the two men.

Ancient sequels often employed the literary technique of recapitulating a previous book at its beginning.[117] Talbert has argued that the correspondences go beyond this ancient literary device:

> These correspondences are due only partially to the Lucan appropriation of antiquity's custom of recapitulating an earlier book at the beginning of the next...Acts 1.1-5 is indeed a recapitulation but the correspondences go through vs. 12. One may, therefore, say that Luke has expanded a custom of antiquity due to his stylistic tendency.[118]

At any rate, the narrative beginning of Acts has sufficient reverse linkage with the Gospel that the readers are constantly called upon to remember the story of Jesus, while learning about the story of the early church.

Beginnings and Viewpoint

Just as the end of a narrative should function to exit the reader from the story world to the real world, so the beginning of a text should provide access from the world of the reader to the world of the text. Uspensky has borrowed the term *framing* from the arena of pictorial art to label this process of entrance to and exit from the narrative world. He claimed:

> The importance of the problem of the frame, that is, of the borders of the artistic work, is evident. In a work of art, whether it be a work of literature, a painting, or a work of some other art form, there is presented to us a special world, with its own space and

time, its own ideological system, and its own standards of behavior. In relation to that world, we assume (at least in our first perceptions of it) the position of an alien spectator, which is necessarily external. Gradually, we enter into it, becoming more familiar with its standards, accustoming ourselves to it, until we begin to perceive this world as if from within, rather than from without. We, as readers or observers, now assume a point of view internal to the particular work.[119]

Point of View

The ways in which the narrator aids the reader to enter and leave the gospel story have already been analyzed. The concern here is to examine how the narrator coaxes the reader to re-enter the story world (now Acts), with some attention paid to the exiting procedure at the end of the narrative. As Uspensky has pointed out: 'The phenomenon of framing—of alternation between a point of view internal to the narrative and a point of view external to the narrative—may be observed on different levels of an artistic work'.[120] Again, the relationship of narrator to reader during entry into the narrative world will receive consideration based on Uspensky's various levels of point of view: psychological, spatial-temporal, phraseological, and ideological planes of point of view. This discussion will be followed by an examination of the focalization of Acts 1.1-12.

Psychological Plane. Uspensky has noted, 'on the psychological plane, before the author adopts the perceptual point of view of a particular character, he first presents that character from the point of view of an external observer'.[121] A close reading of Acts 1.1-12 reveals that there are no inside views of the disciples in this passage. In fact, the first inside view of the disciples as a group does not occur until Acts 2.46: 'they partook of food with glad and generous hearts'. The inside views on the disciples afforded by the narrator may be diagrammed as in Table 18.

The first inside view in the whole narrative is only slightly earlier than the first 'plunge' into the minds of the disciples. In the Pentecost narrative the multitude was 'bewildered . . . and they were amazed and wondered' (2.6-7).[122] The narrative of Acts, then, begins from an external point of view.[123] Both narrator and reader are external observers at the beginning, but as Uspensky noted: 'The position of the external observer suddenly disappears; we forget about it in the same way as we forget about the frame when we look at a painting'.[124] Thus, the narrative begins rather removed from the

Table 18

Inside Views on the Disciples in Acts

2.46	'they partook of food with glad and generous hearts'.
4.32	'those who believed were of one heart and soul'.
5.5	'And great fear came upon all who heard of it'.
5.11	'And great fear came upon the whole church, and upon all who heard of these things'.
6.5	'And what they said pleased the whole multitude'.
10.45	'And the believers from among the circumcised who came with Peter were amazed'.
12.16	'and when they opened, they saw him and were amazed'.
15.22	'Then it seemed good to the apostles and the elders, with the whole church, to choose'.

story world and while the narrator and reader never get too involved in the thoughts and emotions of the characters, gradually the reader's eyes do become adjusted to the lighting of the story world created by the Third Evangelist. Entry into the narrative world from the psychological point of view is slow, but sure.

Spatial Plane. Often, when an author wishes to describe a particular scene 'from some single, very general, point of view', the narrator will imply what Uspensky has called 'the bird's-eye point of view'.[125] The observer from the 'bird's-eye view' 'has assumed a specific position, not abstract, but real; that position is indicated by the fact that there are some things that the observer cannot see from his vantage point'.[126] This statement is certainly true in Acts 1.9-11. There the observer sees from the vantage point of the disciples. When Jesus is lifted up and a cloud removes him out of the sight of the disciples, he is also removed out of the sight of the narrator and reader as well. Hence the scene is described in general terms from a specific spatial point of view, that of the disciples. Already then the reader is aligned with the main characters of this story—the disciples.[127]

Uspensky has suggested: 'Frequently, the bird's-eye view is used at the beginning or the end of a particular scene, or even at the beginning or end of a whole narrative'.[128] He went on to remark: 'This elevated viewpoint, then, used at the beginning and end of the narration, serves as a kind of "frame" for the scene, or for the work as a whole'.[129] Luke has used the bird's-eye view on the spatial plane of point of view as a framing device to entice the reader to become involved in the story of the expansion of the church, beginning from the ascension of Jesus.

Temporal Plane. Point of view on the temporal plane may also be used to frame a narrative. Again, Uspensky argued:

> Temporal framing may be realized by the use at the beginning of a narrative of the retrospective point of view and subsequently, as the narrative proceeds, of the synchronic point of view. In fact, the narrative often begins with hints about the denouement of the plot which has not yet begun; this indicates the use of a point of view external to the story, a point of view located in the future in respect to the time which unfolds within the narrative.[130]

Acts certainly begins from this retrospective point of view with its direct address to Theophilus. In addition, 'hints about the dénouement of the plot' are given in the foreshadowing of Pentecost in 1.6 as well as in the programmatic statement of 1.8.[131] Just as cessation of time may be used as a closing device in literary framing so: 'Fixation of time at the beginning of a narrative . . . may also be realized by the use of the imperfective aspect of the past tense (in *verba dicendi*)'.[132]

This use of the imperfect occurs sparingly in the opening verses of Acts, but it does occur at a strategic point in the ascension narrative, 1.10, in the form of an imperfect periphrastic, 'while they were gazing into heaven', and again later at 1.13 'where they were staying', and 1.14 'and all these were praying'. This use of the imperfect, which in Greek denotes continuous past time, allows the reader to enter the story. To quote Uspensky again: 'the imperfective aspect enables the author to carry out his description from within the action—that is, synchronically, rather than retrospectively—and to place the reader in the very center of the scene he is describing'.[133] Again, point of view on the temporal plane invites the reader to view the action from within the story, looking, as it were, over the narrator's shoulder.[134]

Phraseological Plane. There are at least two examples of framing on the plane of phraseology in the opening lines of Acts. The first is the presence of a first-person narrator in the preface. Only in the preface to Luke does the narrator speak in the first-person singular,[135] and as Uspensky perspicuously remarked about the intrusion of first-person narrators in texts narrated in third person: 'this first-person narrator appears only at the beginning of the story, and then disappears. In terms of content, the narrator here would seem completely superfluous; indeed, his function, unrelated to the plot of the narrative itself, is only to provide a frame for the story'.[136] Hence, the first-person narrator serves as a framing device at the beginning of each narrative, though his presence is missing at the close of both. Walworth correctly observed: 'The narrator of Acts will not again emerge from the narrative world in such a self-conscious manner'.[137] Nonetheless, he has served the purpose of helping the reader gain access to the story world.

Second is the use of Theophilus as an overt narratee.[138] Again, the figure of Theophilus occurs only in the prefaces to the double work of Luke–Acts. Luke created the literary figure of Theophilus as 'an hermeneutical bridge between the narrative world of the text and the "real world" of the actual readers'.[139] Evoking Theophilus, then, at the beginning of the narrative is a literary technique by which the narrator enables the reader to gain entrance to the narrative on the phraseological plane.

Ideological Plane. The narrator moves the reader into the story on the ideological plane by means of what some have considered to be a 'smooth transition'[140] while others have called it 'an awkward change'.[141] The verse in question is 1.4 where the narrator slips from indirect to direct discourse with no warning. The phrase is reminiscent of the Gospel of John where the voice of the narrator and the voice of Jesus are so similar as to be indistinguishable.[142] The reader is required to accept the viewpoint of Jesus almost immediately. Walworth has admirably described this shift from external to internal point of view on the evaluative plane:

> The narrator of the prologue of Acts effects the transition from external to internal point of view in a subtle manner. Readers are scarcely aware where the prologue ends and the continuation of the story begins.
> ... By 1.4b the narrator completes the lure into the story world by breaking into direct discourse in the middle of his quotation of Jesus' saying. The reader passes imperceptibly from the narrator's armchair audience to direct witness of the events of Acts.[143]

While the readers are led to identify with the values of Jesus, whom they have already learned to trust from the Gospel, some distance is created between reader and disciples by the disciples' question of Jesus and his response, as well as the reproof by the two angelic figures.[144] Talbert has pointed out that the surface structure of Acts 1.4-8 and 1.9-11 are formally similar. Acts 1.4-8 contain (a) the risen Jesus' word not to depart from Jerusalem, but to wait for the promise of the Father (1.4-5); (b) the disciples' query (1.6); (c) the risen Jesus' response in two parts: a reproof (1.7), and a promise (1.8). Likewise, 1.9-11 is comprised of similar elements: (a) the risen Jesus' action, being taken into heaven (1.9); (b) the disciples' behavior (1.10a); (c) and the angelic response in two parts: a reproof (1.11a), and a promise (1.11b).[145]

Despite the reproaches, both dialogues end with promises to the disciples, thus inviting the reader to assume the disciples' ideological stance. In fact, from this group emerges the protagonist for much of the first half of the narrative, Peter. The identification of reader with disciples is strengthened by what precedes and what follows the ascension narrative. At 1.2, we learn that Jesus chose the apostles through the Holy Spirit. In Acts 1.3, we find that Jesus appeared to them for forty days.[146] Following the ascension, Acts 1.12-14 'sets out the exemplary behavior of those who are fully instructed. *They pray!*'[147] The result is that when Jesus exits from the scene, the reader is still left with a group of characters who have been chosen by Jesus through the Holy Spirit, who have been witnesses of his post-resurrection appearances and ascension,[148] who have been deputized as ambassadors with a divine mandate, and who, in a few short verses, will receive the promise of the Father in the gift of the Holy Spirit at Pentecost. To be sure, the disciples are not perfect—Philip will have to fulfill their assignment to take the gospel to Samaria,[149] Peter will vacillate in his dealings with the Gentiles—but the disciples, especially Peter, carry 'the reader's perspective and identity in the early chapters of Acts', and function 'for the narrator to shape the reader subtly toward a particular view of discipleship'.[150] The point of view at the beginning of Acts serves to frame the narrative on all five levels of Uspensky's model.

Focalization

Focalization, according to Rimmon-Kenan, 'has both a subject and an object'.[151] The subject, the focalizer, may take either an external or an internal perceptual position to the story. External focalization occurs when the narrator 'is the agent whose perception orients the presentation'.[152] In other words, if the narrator is the focalizer, that is the subject who perceives, then focalization is external to the story.

Luke 24.50-53 is an example of external focalization. The reader can get no closer than the narrator takes him or her, and the scene is viewed from the perspective of the narrator. This strategy, as has been mentioned, helps the reader exit from the story. Internal focalization, on the other hand, 'generally takes the form of a character-focalizer'.[153] Here the locus of focalization is *inside* the represented events.

The ascension narrative in Acts is a good example of internal focalization. Here the story is told, not from the perspective of a remote narrator, but from the perspective of the disciples. The reader is, in a sense, looking over the shoulders of the disciples, hearing what they hear and seeing what they see. When Jesus ascends, he not only ascends into heaven (which again is described in earth-bound terms), he is also taken from their eyes by a cloud. And when Jesus is gone, the reader is left standing beside the disciples, gazing into heaven. The gentle rebuke of the two messengers is meant as much for the ears of the reader as for the disciples—*all* eyes are heaven-fixed. Again, this internal focalization is a means by which the reader gains sure access into the story.

While the focalizer may be external or internal to the story, the object of focalization, the focalized, may be seen, according to Rimmon-Kenan, either from without or within. That is, the external focalizer may see only the outward manifestations of the story (without). Or the external focalizer (narrator-focalizer) may present 'the focalized from within, penetrating his feelings and thoughts'.[154] Likewise, an internal focalizer may see the story from 'within', that is, have inside views on the objects' feelings and emotions, to use Uspensky's terminology. Or the internal focalizer may 'also be confined to the outward manifestations of the focalized'.[155] The Acts account fits this category. The story is seen from the perspective of the disciples, focalizers internal to the story. The focalized event, the ascension, is seen only from without—there is no record of how Jesus or the disciples felt about the farewell meeting, no hidden thoughts, no display of deep emotions. In Luke, on the other hand, the story is told by an external focalizer, the narrator, from without the story.

Again, focalization is a tool employed by the narrator to assist the reader in entering or leaving the story. In the case of Acts, the story is seen from the perspective of the disciples drawing the reader into the story. Nonetheless, the depth of that 'internal' perspective is shallow, never plunging beneath the surface of outwardly visible actions and clearly audible speech.

In summary, then, the relationship of narrator and reader to the events and existents of the ascension story in Acts moves from external to internal. This transition may be detected on every plane of Uspensky's model of point of view and in focalization. The narrator who worked so diligently to enable the reader to emerge from the narrative world of Luke is equally persistent in coaxing him or her to enter again!

Beginnings and the Relationship between Narrator and Reader

The last relationship to be examined in this study of narrative beginnings is that between the narrator and the reader during the process of entrance into the narrative world. Iser's twofold definition of the implied reader is again helpful in this study. An implied reader is the property of the text; the reader is encoded in the text. Reader-response criticism describes the attempt by real readers to follow more or less successfully the clues and textual markers in the text, thereby producing meaning through the reading process.

The Implied Reader

The term *implied reader* will designate the reader created by the text; here are explored the ways in which the text places limits on the meanings created in the reading process. In particular, the strategies of defamiliarization and primacy effect shape the reading of the ascension story in Acts as a narrative beginning.[156]

Defamiliarization. Iser defined defamiliarization as the use of techniques and strategies 'to set the familiar against the unfamiliar'.[157] When dealing with the story of Jesus and his followers, so familiar to the Christian community, it is necessary to defamiliarize the all-too-familiar elements of the story. As Iser has noted elsewhere: 'Communication would be unnecessary if that which is to be communicated were not to some extent unfamiliar'.[158] By the use of defamiliarization, the narrative beginning of Acts evokes a response on the part of its implied reader.

Recently, Resseguie has explored the ways in which the synoptic Gospels employ defamiliarization as a textual strategy to negate certain social, cultural, and religious norms.[159] If the norms are held by opponents of Jesus, according to Resseguie, 'the process of defamiliarization seeks to depragmatize the norms, i.e. to take them out of their original context in which they had validity and a frame of reference, and to question the underlying assumptions of the norms'.[160] If the norms are held by favorable characters, then defamiliarization not only negates the norms, but 'creates sympathy on the part of the reader for a character who expresses a deficient norm. This allows the reader to align himself sympathetically with a character, and the resultant negation of a familiar norm is more forceful'.[161] This latter technique is of greatest interest for the analysis of Acts 1.

Deficient norms held by favorable characters are defamiliarized in the biblical narrative by: (1) portraying the character in a favorable or sympathetic way, increasing the degree of identification between reader and character; (2) creating distance between reader and character through Jesus' negation of the norm; (3) creating tension between identification with the character and negation of the character's behavior.[162]

Applying this model of defamiliarization to Acts 1.6-11, the favorable characters are clearly the disciples. Identification with the disciples is encouraged from the very beginning of the narrative. In addition to the favorable information shared in the opening verses about the disciples, it has been shown already that the narrative is focalized from the perspective of the disciples, thus bringing reader and disciples even closer together.

Resseguie has also suggested:

> distance may be reduced between a character and the reader by the type of question or request posed to Jesus. At times a request not only seems reasonable, but it even appears unreasonable to the (implied) reader for Jesus to refuse the request.[163]

Before the ascension, the disciples ask: 'Lord, will you at this time restore the kingdom to Israel?' This question does not seem unreasonable, particularly in light of the narrative of Luke–Acts as a whole.[164] In fact, several readings of this text are plausible. The disciples may have mistakenly assumed that the impending Pentecost experience would be the parousia or they may have wrongly supposed that the ascension was to be identified with the parousia.[165]

Jesus' response does not suggest that restoration of Israel is impossible, but it does challenge the norms of the disciples and the implied reader.[166] The burning issue is not 'When will the kingdom be restored to Israel?'; rather it is 'Who is commissioned to spread the good news on worldwide missions?' Hence, the narrator employs the process of defamiliarization to remove the focus of the implied reader from the destiny of Israel and re-directs it to the gentile mission. Israel in Luke–Acts is cast in an important, but supporting, role to the story of the unhindered growth of the church.[167] The evaluative judgment of the significance of Israel is challenged and corrected by the narrator through Jesus.

Another device often used in the defamiliarization process is the rhetorical question. Resseguie commented: 'A rhetorical question seeks not only a response . . . in the text but also from the reader of the gospel'.[168] The narrative strategy of rhetorical questions, according to Fish, 'draws us into its rhythm and creates in us the expectation of an answer'.[169] In Acts 1.10, the two messengers ask this type of rhetorical question: 'Men of Galilee, why do you stand looking into heaven?' Again, just as the disciples' words seemed reasonable in their question to Jesus, so also their actions seem most natural. What else should one do when Jesus ascends except stand and look into heaven after him!

Again, the narrator has employed defamiliarization, this time in the form of a rhetorical question to correct the deficient norms of the disciples and the implied reader. Idly gazing into heaven is an inappropriate reaction to Jesus' ascension. The messengers assure the disciples (and reader) that Jesus will return in just the same way he left. Implicit in the angels' words, of course, is that the disciples ought to busy themselves in light of and because of Jesus' absence. At least one could easily infer such a conclusion by the disciples' reaction to the angels: they returned to Jerusalem and 'devoted themselves to prayer' (1.14).

Thus, one may conclude that the narrator has employed the narrative strategy of defamiliarizing the familiar in order to correct at least two insufficient values held by the disciples (the place of Israel in the kingdom of God and the significance of the ascension), and more importantly, by the implied reader.

Primacy Effect. Despite the fact that the disciples' words and actions are corrected in the opening scene of Acts, the disciples are cast in an overwhelmingly favorable light in the opening chapters of the text. They are appointed as witnesses; they are endowed with the Holy Spirit at Pentecost; they heal; they are courageous in the face of persecution, etc. First impressions go a long way in shaping the reader's response to a character or group of characters. Sternberg has labeled this doctrine of 'first impressions' the *primacy effect*.[170] For Sternberg, the primacy effect involves 'the sequential manipulation of the reader's attitudes and sympathies, norms and hypotheses'.[171] Using this control strategy of primacy effect, the literary artist:

> can manoeuvre his reader into regarding the same character either as a good fellow with some human frailties or as an ugly customer surprisingly possessed of a few attractive or redeeming traits by doing little more than presenting a given aggregate of motifs in different sequences.[172]

The application of this literary theory to Acts is obvious. The narrator could have chosen to portray the disciples as unreliable, fractious, or self-serving. In fact, had the narrative begun at a point in time earlier, depicting the disciples' pettiness at the Lord's Supper, or faithlessness in prayer on the Mount of Olives, or even a point later in time with the Jerusalem Council in Acts 15 or the inept elders in Acts 21, the primacy effect would have altered the implied reader's perception of the apostles. Instead, the apostles are presented in a very favorable light; their values are corrected, but they are *still* Jesus' chosen witnesses and spokespersons. The reader is so impressed by this initial exposure to disciples, that questionable behavior in later parts of the narrative is overlooked or absorbed into the reader's otherwise positive attitude toward the apostles. As Rimmon-Kenan put it:

> The text can direct and control the reader's comprehension and attitudes by positioning *certain* items before others... Thus, information and attitudes presented at an early stage of the text tend to encourage the reader to interpret everything in their light. The reader is prone to preserve such meanings and attitudes for as long as possible.[173]

A good example of the impact the primacy effect has had on the reader's perception of the disciples may be found in the title of the narrative. The title, 'The Acts of the Apostles', which goes back at least to the second century,[174] has puzzled scholars for centuries. Typical are the comments of Krodel:

> The title itself is misleading, because it does not indicate that Acts is volume two of our author's literary work. Moreover, this book does not deal with the acts of the apostles, plural. Its two main figures are Peter and Paul, and the latter is not really an apostle according to Luke.[175]

Likewise, F.F. Bruce has conjectured: 'The title *The Acts of the Apostles* may have been intended to point out that Paul was not the only faithful apostle of Christ (even if much more is said about him than about the others in Acts)'.[176] It may very well be the case that the title of Acts is the result of the primacy effect on real readers. Because of the prominence of the apostles at the beginning of the narrative, they seem to occupy a place of much greater significance than they actually do in the course of the narrative.

At any rate, the primacy effect is important in the narrative beginning of Acts. In fact, the decision to begin with the ascension may involve more than the traditional view that the end of the story of Jesus is the beginning of the story of the church. In addition to this concern, the text spends a generous portion of its narrative space confirming the apostles as worthy successors of Jesus.[177] The effect of these first impressions continues to shape the implied reader's perception to the very end of the narrative.

Reader Response

Robert Pope has described the role of the real reader who accepts the role of the implied reader created by the text:

> the searching mind discovers a dark entrance in the side of an unknown and moves down the mysterious passage of voice. This requires the ability to recognize the entrance, the courage to enter the throat of that cave, and the craft to balance this new knowledge.[178]

The real reader, of course, must choose whether or not to follow the narrator-guide and make the moves suggested by the textual markers. Here, reader-response criticism makes its real contribution. Rather than searching for a static meaning within (or in some cases behind) a text, reader-response criticism 'attempts to describe what a text *does* to a reader, i.e., what assumptions the reader is making, what expectations he or she is forming, what conclusions he is reaching'.[179] That process is never cut-and-dried. As Iser has suggested: 'We look forward, we look back, we decide, we change our decisions, we form expectations, we are shocked by their non-fulfillment, we question, we muse, we accept, we reject; this is the dynamic process of recreation'.[180]

Analyzing how the ascension narrative would have shaped the perception of the character of Jesus by real readers of the first century would be most profitable. Unfortunately, such studies are subjective and any conclusion must be labeled 'tentative'. Nevertheless, such an undertaking is crucial for properly placing the ascension within Lukan theology. To understand the impact the ascension narrative in Acts would have had on a first-century reader, one must understand the multiplicity of ascension, translation, and bodily assumption stories which pervaded Jewish, Greek, and Roman literature. Lohfink has provided the most exhaustive and detailed analysis of these bodies of ancient literature and their relationship to the ascension in the two volumes Luke–Acts.[181]

Lohfink examined ascension stories in the world of the New Testament (Greek and Roman literature, the Old Testament, and Jewish writings) and compared those findings with the ascension in Luke–Acts and concluded that the ascension of Jesus was a heavenly translation story. These bodily translation stories (*Entrückung*) were characterized by the following distinctive elements: a mountain as the site of the assumption, an address by the one ascending, witnesses present who viewed the bodily ascent, and often clouds which escorted the ascending figure into the heavens.[182] Of course, all of these elements are found in the ascension narrative in Acts and a first-century reader with any degree of familiarity with Greek or Jewish literature could not miss the obvious parallels with the Lukan account. But what meaning would such a first-century reading produce?

Talbert has argued that the ascension in Acts is reminiscent of the stories from Mediterranean antiquity of immortals at career's end, when they are taken up into heaven.[183] The first-century reader would, no doubt, have understood this last episode in the earthly life of Jesus to be divine confirmation of his ministry. The ascension is the coronation of Jesus' ministry; the ascension narrative ushers in the gentile mission, foreshadows the parousia, and anticipates the gift of the Holy Spirit at Pentecost. Maddox insisted 'the ascension is for Luke the point of intersection of Christology, eschatology and ecclesiology'.[184]

A real reader, whether of the first or twentieth century, attempting to become an 'ideal' reader of the text, must take into account the rich imageries which color the ascension. Real readers must also grapple with the multifarious roles the ascension plays within the narrative of Luke–Acts, concluding the ministry of Jesus and anticipating the ministry of the church. The ascension, then, describes the journey of Jesus into heaven and the journey of the church into the world.[185]

Conclusion

To engage in reading the book of Acts is to enter a strange, new world. Or as Pope has expressed it:

> We have come to a universe with new rules and a language so ancient that we cannot possibly understand—only fascination and delight keep us going, and only the narrative voice knows where we are headed. We must pick our way through this world of darkness behind our guide, led by the voice that knows these things.[186]

As our eyes grow accustomed to the darkness, however, we recognize some well-known terrain: the Mount of Olives, Jerusalem, the upper room. And the faces are familiar: the apostles, the women, the two heavenly messengers, and before the cloud sweeps him away, we even get a glimpse of the resplendent Christ. Despite the similarities, this new narrative world is full of unexpected twists and turns and we 'have great fears and proceed tentatively, but with what high hopes'.[187]

The crucial importance of a narrative beginning in engaging the reader in the reading act cannot be overemphasized. A variety of literary strategies may be employed to create and sustain interest at the very beginning. Some techniques may be obvious, like the reverse linkage between Luke and Acts.[188] Others, like focalization, defamiliarization, and the primacy effect, cast their spell ever so subtly and quietly. From the beginning question and answer period, the main plot-line of the rise of the church and the fall of Israel is anticipated; it is moved along through the text by an empty center narrative patterning.

The ascension story as a narrative beginning is indispensable in focusing the reader's still blurry vision on this new world. To chance being a spectator is to risk becoming a participant! Or to quote Pope again: 'We understand from first words, entrance, just how deeply we must be prepared to delve and whether or not we wish to risk our minds and hearts, if not our souls, our time . . . in the reading of a work of fiction'.[189] The stakes to enter the narrative world of Acts are high—hearts and minds, souls and time—but the rewards of walking again with an old and trusted friend are well worth the risk.

CONCLUSION

Chapter 6

THE DEPARTURE OF JESUS IN CANONICAL CONTEXT:
A COMPARATIVE ANALYSIS

Gerard Sloyan called Luke 'the great storyteller of Christendom; without his tales . . . we would be much the poorer'.[1] The painting evangelist is a master at his art; subtle shades and hues are delicately and meticulously placed on the Gospel canvas. With a sure and steady hand, he has sketched the story of Jesus and the early church. Luke is no mean writer, no ivory-tower theologian, no dispassionate historian. His is no cool, evenly reported piece of journalism. Rather, the twin volumes of Luke and Acts are the confessional statement of a deeply pious *littérateur*—so much so, that over a hundred years ago, the poet Dante Rossetti was inspired to write:

> Give honor unto Luke Evangelist;
> For he it was (the aged legend say)
> Who first taught Art to fold her hands and pray.[2]

Relationship between Luke 24 and Acts 1

Luke's literary prowess is at its best in the ascension narratives at the end of the Third Gospel and the beginning of Acts. Paradoxically, readers of Luke–Acts who are bent on historical investigations or obsessed with consistency in details have accused Luke of 'botching the job'. Numerous attempts have been made to explain the similarities and differences between these two accounts. These arguments are summarized and evaluated below, followed by yet another proposal drawn from this diachronic and synchronic study of the ascension narratives.[3]

Interpolation Theories

The interpolation theory that the ascension narrative was appended to Luke–Acts (or just Luke) has already been discussed and found wanting. Conzelmann, Kirsopp Lake, Menoud, Wilder, and others, have proposed theories which, though they differ in details, basically assume that the ascension narrative was interpolated into the text when Luke and Acts were divided upon acceptance into the canon. Besides lacking any textual evidence to support this theory, redactional studies have shown that the themes, vocabulary, and style of both ascension stories are thoroughly Lukan.[4] In addition, this study has attempted to show that these two accounts are indispensable to their respective narrative contexts and hardly represent an afterthought.[5]

Source Theories
Others have suggested that Luke was familiar with two distinct traditions about the ascension, each of which is reflected in his writings.[6] This particular proposal has taken various twists. C.F.D. Moule suggested that after completing the Gospel, Luke received new traditions about the ascension which he incorporated into Acts.[7] Others have surmised that Luke knew both traditions and preserved them both without making a value judgment between them.[8]

Such assumptions have been challenged from several sides. First, many scholars would deny that any primitive, pre-Lukan ascension tradition existed, much less two of them. Lohfink, for example, has argued: 'Nirgendwo finden sich auch nur die kleinsten Indizien einer sichtbaren Himmelfahrt beziehungsweise einer Entrückung, wie wir sie von Lukas her kennen'.[9] Still others, willing to admit the possibility of an ascension tradition in the primitive church, think such source theories do not adequately explain the inclusion of the ascension narratives in Luke–Acts.[10] Talbert has remarked:

> Any explanation which thinks of Luke as a historian in the modern sense whose concern for factual accuracy is uppermost also must be discarded. Nor is it likely that the author of Luke–Acts can be thought of as the type of historian who would include all traditions known to him in order to be fair.[11]

Theological Concerns
That the two ascension narratives are the product of some theological concern is a view held by many Lukan scholars today. Fitzmyer wrote that no small reason for referring to the ascension in both Luke and Acts was 'the emphasis that the double reference gives to the ascension as the line of demarcation for two periods of Lucan

salvation-history'.[12] J.G. Davies, on the other hand, suggested Luke may have shaped his stories around a Raphael typology in Luke 24 and an Elijah typology in Acts.[13]

By far the most popular explanation of theological concerns is the one first offered by P.A. van Stempvoort in 1959. The narrative in Luke, with its blessings and Jesus' priestly gesticulation, gave what Stempvoort called a 'doxological' interpretation of the ascension.[14] The Acts account, on the other hand, with its emphasis on the activity of the Holy Spirit in the Church, van Stempvoort dubbed an ecclesiastical-historical interpretation.[15] These categories have won wide acceptance.[16] S.G. Wilson slightly modified van Stempvoort's views, suggesting that the Acts account is Luke's 'pastoral' interpretation of the ascension: it is the author's way of dealing with the problem of the delayed parousia.[17] H. Flender, using van Stempvoort's interpretation as a springboard, argued that the ascension in Luke is told from an earthly viewpoint, while the Acts narrative is from a heavenly viewpoint.[18]

While van Stempvoort's position has many merits, particularly in noticing that the two accounts have very distinct interpretations of the same event, he gave little attention to the function of each passage in its narrative context. That, of course, has been of primary concern for this study. Before one can begin to understand the theological import of these passages, their literary distinctiveness must be appreciated.

Literary Perspectives
Certainly this study is not the first to suggest that the differences between the ascension narratives in Luke and Acts should be understood from a literary perspective. About the ascension narratives in Luke–Acts, Talbert concluded a decade ago: 'In the light of modern study of the Lucan writings, that explanation is most probable which posits the creative hand of the author'.[19] Talbert sought to provide an answer to the problem by investigating the *structure* or *architecture* of the passages.

Narrative Strategies and Redundancy
This study has attempted to examine the *function* of the pericopae within their narrative contexts. A literary model which considered plot, point of view, and reader response was employed to examine Luke 24.50-53 as a narrative ending and Acts 1.6-11 as a narrative beginning. A comparison of the two accounts will brush back the

foliage and lay bare the fruits of this study.

Most helpful for the literary comparison of the two ascension narratives is the study of redundancy already employed in Chapter 3.[20] It is recalled that *redundancy*, according to Culpepper, may occur not only in the repetition of words, type scenes, plots, and implicit commentary, but even at the level of the canon where the canonical Gospels are redundant.[21] Viewing redundancy from this level is even more appropriate for Luke–Acts because the two works share a common author.

Redundancy in Luke–Acts has several functions, according to Tannehill: (1) it combats the tendency to forget information over a long narrative; (2) it is a means of emphasis; (3) it has a persuasive effect; (4) it allows for character development; (5) it confirms expectations reached through the reading process; (6) it allows changes in the pattern to be noted; (7) it provides a sense of unity in the narrative; and (8) it encourages interaction among characters and events in the reading process.[22] What is needed is a model to measure this rich literary technique so freely used in Luke–Acts, especially in the ascension narratives. According to Janice Capel Anderson, redundancy may be examined according to repetition, variation, and context.[23] Below, then, is a comparison of the ascension narratives in Luke–Acts with an eye to explaining both the correspondences and the variations.

Repetition. Three elements provide the strongest links of repetition between the ascension narratives. First, the characters are the same in both accounts—Jesus and the disciples.[24] Second, in both accounts, this scene is the last appearance of Jesus to his disciples.[25] Third, both accounts share in common Jesus' commission to his disciples to preach to 'all the nations' or 'the ends of the earth'. Also, there is the exact verbal correspondence of 'the promise of the Father'.[26] By so connecting these two accounts, the narrator strengthens the retrospective patterning of the reader who understands the cryptic reference to 'he departed from them' as an opaque reference to the ascension.

Tannehill remarked: 'The use of repetitive patterns preserves a sense of unity of purpose and action in spite of significant developments'.[27] This is no more crucial than in the narrative which binds Luke and Acts together. By repeating the ascension in Acts, the narrator has identified the story of Jesus with the story of the Church. C.K. Barrett has given eloquent testimony to the inextricable link between these two accounts when he claims that 'in Luke's thought, the end of the story of Jesus is the Church; and the story of Jesus is the beginning of the Church'.[28]

Certainly Luke could have ended his Gospel otherwise. None of the other Gospel writers narrated an ascension. And certainly Acts could have begun elsewhere, for none of the other apocryphal Acts begins with the ascension narrative. Or as Maddox put it: 'The ascension is the major bridge from volume one to volume two: it is the necessary climax of the one and starting-point of the other'.[29] This fact is hardly new, and it creates little problem for the reader of Luke–Acts. What is troublesome for the reader is not the similarities, but the dissimilarities between the two accounts.

Variation. Anderson claimed variation 'creates uncertainty and requires the implied reader to make choices'.[30] That the variations in the ascension narratives have created uncertainty among real readers is evinced by the above theories explaining the dissimilarities. Plainly speaking, there are more elements of variation between these two accounts than of repetition. Culpepper has noted: 'The degree of dissonance between new and old and the ratio of variation to repetition determine whether the story will give the reader a smooth ride or a rough one'.[31] Haenchen has claimed: 'It must be admitted that the two-fold account of the Ascension constitutes a . . . stumbling-block'.[32] Judging from the history of reader response to these two passages, the 'major bridge from volume one to volume two' has seemed to some to be little more than a single-cable, swinging bridge suspended high above the narrative chasm. Some have attempted to dismantle it; others have paused to examine the craftsmanship before crossing over; still others have passed with eyes tightly shut or dashed recklessly ahead; but all of them have had a 'rough ride'.

The major variations between the two ascension narratives may be listed as follows: 1. Most obvious of the discrepancies is the chronological difference between Luke and Acts. The Gospel appears to date the final departure of Jesus on Easter Sunday night; Acts allows for a period of forty days during which Jesus appeared to the disciples. 2. The site of the ascension is slightly different. In the Gospel, the ascension takes place 'in the neighborhood of Bethany'; in Acts, the Mount of Olives is the locale of Jesus' departure. The fact that Bethany was located on the Mount of Olives,[33] while easing historical concerns, serves only to heighten the literary significance of the variation. Each location has a specific function in its literary context. 3. Though both narratives register that the disciples return to Jerusalem, their specific destination and the activity which occupies them varies between the two. In Luke, of course, the disciples return with joy to the temple and are incessantly blessing God. In Acts, on the other hand, the disciples return to the upper room where they 'with one accord devoted themselves to prayer' (Acts 1.14). 4. There is no dialogue in the Gospel account; one only sees, not hears, the action. On the other hand, the greatest portion of the Acts narrative is devoted to questions and answers.[34] 5. The 'raising of the hands' and the repeated references to 'blessing' are missing from Acts. 6. Luke has the cryptic note 'he departed from them', while Acts explicitly records 'he ascended into heaven'. Whether the two refer to the same event is unclear on first readings. 7. Mention of the cloud which enveloped Jesus and of two heavenly messengers who interpreted the event for the disciples, so prominent in Acts, is missing in Luke.

Variation produces movement. The reader, according to Culpepper, 'is required to integrate the new elements into the previous patterns'.[35] The movement produced in these variations is striking. Repetition reaffirms the link between the Gospel and Acts; variation impels the reader to leave the Gospel story and move on to the story of the church. Or as Tannehill phrased it: 'The same or related characters may be presented in similar situations in order to highlight an important change'.[36] It is at the point of understanding the variations between the two accounts that redundancy theory makes its greatest contribution.

Context. The narrative context reduces the number of choices available to the reader for understanding the passages and facilitates the integration of the scene into the reading experience.[37] The ascension story in Luke functions in its narrative context as an ending which brings closure to the Gospel, while the ascension account in Acts serves in its context as a narrative beginning. The differences in detail between these accounts may be accounted for largely by the role of each in its respective narrative context. Below, each unit of variation is examined in terms of context.

1. From a historical point of view, the difference of the 'forty days' between Luke and Acts seems intolerable. Momentarily suspending those historical concerns, the temporal discrepancy is readily explained on literary grounds. To end the Gospel with a reference to forty days of appearances by the risen Lord would be to change the

ending of the Gospel from a close-up scenic ending to an overview epilogue. In Torgovnick's words, in a close-up ending 'no temporal distance separates ending from the body of the novel'.[38] In these endings, readers often discover the appropriateness of the ending only through retrospective analysis. An overview epilogue, on the other hand, has two formal characteristics: 'it sets the perspective by a shift in time-scale or orientation; it provides some element of *Nachgeschichte* (after-history) for the major characters'.[39]

If the narrator is attempting in the closing scene to educate his readers concerning the relationship between the crucifixion and exaltation, then a close-up scenic ending is the most appropriate to use. It forces the reader, through close and retrospective reading, to either share the understanding of Jesus' exaltation to include death-resurrection-ascension (a congruent ending) or to reject such a view (an incongruent ending).[40] An overview ending which gave the after-history of Jesus or the disciples would not only radically change the content of the Third Gospel as it now stands; more importantly, it would also destroy the effect of the ending of Luke.[41]

Forty days of appearances in Acts, on the other hand, is entirely appropriate in its narrative context. Establishing the disciples as reliable and legitimate successors of Jesus is a major task of the opening narrative in Acts.[42] It will be recalled that the primacy effect, that is, the effect that positioning certain material first has on the reader, is important in establishing a positive identity for the disciples in the book of Acts.[43] The period of forty days is needed in Acts, not to allow Jesus enough time to make appearances, but to assure the reader that the disciples are 'fully instructed' (see Acts 20.20, 27, 31).[44] During this period of time, then, Jesus spoke to them about 'the things concerning the kingdom of God' (1.3).[45]

The specific reference to 'forty days' may be explained by recognizing: (a) the number forty has a rich biblical heritage (see Exod. 24.12-18; *2 Baruch* 76.1-4);[46] and (b) the dating of the Pentecost requires that the hiatus between Easter and Pentecost be filled—this Luke does by the forty days of instruction and ten days (implied) in which the disciples pray and choose a successor for Judas.[47] By being taught by the risen Lord, praying together with one accord, and performing the delicate and crucial task of selecting Judas' replacement without incident, the disciples are presented in the opening scene as educationally, spiritually, and organizationally prepared to undertake the task of worldwide missions to which they have been assigned.

2. The locale of Jesus' final departure varies between the two accounts. The reference in Luke to Bethany is appropriate because it closely links the closing scene with the Triumphal Entry scene at 19.28-40.[48] The closing scene of the Gospel, set as it is in Bethany, becomes Jesus' Triumphal Exit. In the same way that the Triumphal Entry closes the journey of Jesus to Jerusalem, so the Triumphal Exit brings an end to Jesus' exodus and *analempsis*.

The Mount of Olives, on the other hand, is the site of the ascension in Acts (1.12). Here the reference not only recalls the Triumphal Entry scene (19.29, 37), but also 21.37 and 22.39. The reference at 21.37 is to Jesus teaching in the temple during the day and lodging at the Mount of Olives at night. More significant is the reference in 22.39: 'And he came out, and went, as was his custom, to the Mount of Olives; and the disciples followed him'. Interestingly, Luke alone of the Evangelists records that the place to which Jesus withdrew was the Mount of Olives.[49] Important here is the narrator's effort to inform the reader that the Mount of Olives was a familiar place to Jesus; and the specific reference to 'the place', indicates he has prayed here before. In other words, Jesus has retreated to a place of prayer familiar to him; whether the disciples have been here before is unclear. Jesus commands the disciples to pray and then withdraws a short distance from them to pray himself.[50] The disciples fail to pray and are found 'sleeping for sorrow' (22.45).

The next (and last) reference to the Mount of Olives in Luke–Acts is in the ascension account at 1.12. By means of redundancy, the narrator has reminded the reader not of the Triumphal Entry so much as the prayer scene on the mountain.[51] Jesus has again taken his disciples to that favorite place—here is an element of repetition. The disciples still enjoy that special status of Jesus' messengers. This time, however, when they return from Jerusalem they do what they were unable to accomplish prior to the arrest—they pray![52] Again, the reader is assured of the disciples' readiness and competence to be witnesses of the gospel.

3. Closely related to (2) above is the specific place to which the disciples return after the departure scene. In Luke, the disciples return to the *temple* and are continually blessing God. It will be recalled that depicting the disciples in the temple is a strong closural device which emphasizes that the conflicts between Jesus and the religious authorities have been resolved, at least in the Gospel.[53] In addition, locating the disciples in the temple is reminiscent of the

beginning of the Gospel. The last line of Luke, then, provides an effective parallel *and* circular strategy of closure.

In Acts the disciples return to 'the upper room'. This word is not the same used to describe the room where Jesus ate the Passover meal with his disciples (Luke 22.12), yet the identification of the two seems most natural.[54] If one assumes the two rooms are the same, then the reference serves to strengthen the connection made above between the prayer scene on the Mount of Olives and the ascension in Acts. The argument remains intact regardless and the temple may be more important to the narrative context in Luke than the upper room is in Acts.[55]

4. The scene at the end of Luke is a silent one. The significance of this silence is that it creates distance between the reader and the characters and effects closure.[56] The reader can 'see' Jesus and the disciples, but is unable to hear them. This framing device creates the literary illusion of space between reader and story and effectively assists the reader in leaving the story world.

The Acts account, on the other hand, is more than half dialogue— and the dialogue is important. Three speeches help anticipate the unfolding of the rest of the narrative. (a) Jesus promises the disciples that 'before many days you will be baptized with the Holy Spirit' (Acts 1.5). This word finds fulfillment in the Pentecost narrative (see Acts 1.8). (b) In response to the disciples' question about the kingdom, Jesus gives his commission which, in effect, serves to outline the rest of the narrative. Haenchen has noted:

> Luke has in fact described the contents of Acts through the words of Jesus in verse 8 . . . the whole action of Acts becomes the fulfillment of Jesus' word, and this is much more than a mere table of contents: it is a promise![57]

(c) The other speech is that of the angels in 1.10-11. They first reprove the disciples for standing and gazing into the heavens after Jesus. They then reassure the disciples that Jesus' ascension is an earnest of Jesus' parousia, but implicit in their description is that the two events are separate.

5. The 'raising of the hands' and blessing, again, are strong closural devices appropriate in the context of Luke 24.50-53 as a narrative ending.[58] These elements are missing in Acts 1.6-11. The variation again is due simply to the fact that what is appropriate or necessary for a narrative ending is not always appropriate or necessary for a narrative beginning.

6 and 7. Variations (6) and (7) may be taken together. First, the reference to Jesus' departure in Luke 24 is the concise statement, 'and he departed from them'. Any allusion to the ascension is seen only through retrospective patterning or second and subsequent readings of the text. The variant 'and he ascended into heaven' would certainly make sense in the context, but again would remove the 'teachable moment' from the narrative when the narrator encourages the reader to see the continuity between the crucified Christ, the risen Lord and the Exalted One.

Acts, on the other hand, not only has the explicit reference to the ascension 'and he ascended into heaven'; it also has the accompanying apocalyptic stage-props of the messengers and the cloud. The messengers remind the reader of the transfiguration and empty tomb and accentuate Jesus' glorification by providing witnesses. The cloud is also a common element in assumption stories and again suggests the transfiguration story. The narrative context of the ascension in Acts is an appropriate place to make such links and explicit references to the ascension, while Luke is not.

All of these variations may be explained by their narrative context. Some elements which are appropriate to the narrative ending of Luke are not so for the narrative beginning of Acts, and vice versa. In fact, the presence of these discrepancies, rather than hindering narrative development, is the factor which moves the plot along. The ascension narratives then become what Tannehill has called an expanding symbol:

> Repetition may lead us to deepening discovery of such symbols, as familiar material returns in new contexts and with new significance. Having experienced the power of the symbol to expand in the story, the reader is more likely to believe that it hides residues of meaning which call for further exploration.[59]

The narrator of Luke–Acts has employed the ascension narrative to bring closure to one narrative and provide entrance into its sequel. Even if the author had two traditions of the ascension before him, he still had to choose which would fit best at the end, and which at the beginning, of the two works. The ascension narratives represent Luke at his literary best. Through the literary device of redundancy in the ascension narrative, he both ties his two volumes together with repetition, yet moves ahead to tell the tale of the early church by expanding the symbol.

Conclusion

On beginnings and endings, T.S. Eliot once remarked:

> What we call the beginning is often the end
> And to make an end is to make a beginning.
> The end is where we start from.

The end of this work is, in some ways, a beginning. Tottering, first steps have been taken to apply in tandem diachronic and synchronic analyses to the narratives of Jesus' departure in Luke and Acts. In so doing, it is hoped that the narratives of Luke and Acts received just treatment both as ancient writings of the first century and as timeless literary structures. These two divergent methodological paths of synchronic and diachronic examination have led to the same conclusion: For literary and theological reasons, Luke chose to end the Gospel with an implicit reference to the ascension of Jesus and to begin Acts with an explicit depiction of that same scene. The differences between the two accounts are as theologically and literarily significant as are the similarities. Still, much has been left undone—but then, 'the end is where we start from'. Ascension Day may never find its proper place in the Church Calendar. More lamentable would be for the literary masterpiece of the painting evangelist to remain in obscurity. Heart and hands lovingly fashioned these ascension narratives from the 'raw' materials which the early church saw fit to preserve. No doubt close examination of the work yields flaws which in a lesser *objet d'art* would prove fatal. But in this literary *chef d'œuvre* even the blemishes enhance its beauty.

NOTES

Notes to Chapter 1

1. *In die dominica Paschae*, 52-54. On other patristic reflections on the ascension, see V. Larrañaga, *L'Ascension de Notre-Seigneur dans le Nouveau Testament* (Rome: Biblical Institute, 1938), pp. 12-17.

2. J.N.D. Kelly, *Early Christian Creeds* (London: Longman, 1972), p. 369. The Latin text reads: 'tertia die resurrexit a mortuis, ascendit ad coelos, sedet ad dexteram dei patris omnipotentis, inde venturus est iudicare vivos et mortuos'.

3. *Ibid.*, p. 216.

4. Eusebius is typical of this period in suggesting that the Ascension be celebrated on Whitsunday; see *Vita Const.* 4. 64; *De solemn. pasch.* 5.

5. See E.J. Epp, 'The Ascension in the Textual Tradition of Luke–Acts', *New Testament Textual Criticism: Its Significance for Exegesis*, ed. E.J. Epp and G.D. Fee (Oxford: University Press, 1983), pp. 131-34, for references in the New Testament to the ascension and exaltation of Christ.

6. The longer ending of Mark 16.9-20 does, of course, narrate the ascension of Jesus; but this text is generally considered to be a later addition to the Gospel. The passage will, however, be considered in the diachronic analysis of Acts 1.1-11.

7. J.G. Davies, *He Ascended Into Heaven: A Study in the History of Doctrine* (New York: Association Press, 1958), p. 9.

8. Commentaries on Luke and articles on the ascension are too numerous to mention here. For additional bibliography, see: François Bovon, *Luc le théologien: Vingt-cinq ans de recherches (1950-1975)* (Paris: Delachaux & Niestlé, 1978); Erich Grässer, 'Acta-Forschung seit 1960', *TRu* 41 (1976), pp. 141-94, 259-90 and *TRu* 42 (1977), pp. 1-68; also Earl Richard, 'Luke—Writer, Theologian, Historian: Research and Orientation of the 1970's', *BTB* 13 (1983), pp. 3-15; Jerome Kodell, 'The Theology of Luke in Recent Study', *BTB* 1 (1971), pp. 115-44; Robert O'Toole, 'Why Did Luke Write Acts (Lk-Acts)?' *BTB* 7 (1977), pp. 66-76.

9. See for example, H.B. Swete, *The Ascended Christ: A Study in the Earliest Christian Teaching* (London: Macmillan, 1910); William Hanna, *The Forty Days After Our Lord's Resurrection* (New York: Robert Carter, 1866).

10. Bruce M. Metzger, 'The Ascension of Jesus Christ', *Historical and Literary Studies: Pagan, Jewish and Christian* (Grand Rapids: Eerdmans, 1968), p. 86. Such concerns are also found in the writings of Peter Toon who

delivered the W.H. Griffith Thomas Memorial Lectures at Dallas Theological Seminary, April 12-15, 1983. The four lectures were entitled 'Historical Perspectives on the Doctrine of Christ's Ascension' and were subsequently published in the Seminary's journal, *Bibliotheca Sacra*.

11. Reginald H. Fuller, *The Formation of the Resurrection Narratives* (Philadelphia: Fortress, 1980), p. 6. Fuller noted in his Preface that his manuscript had been completed before C.F. Evans' *Resurrection and the New Testament* (London: SCM, 1970) appeared.

12. *Ibid.*, p. vii. Other works include: Edward L. Bode, *The First Easter Morning*, AnBib, 45 (Rome: Biblical Institute, 1970); Willi Marxsen, *The Resurrection of Jesus of Nazareth*, trans. Margaret Kohl (Philadelphia: Fortress, 1970); J.E. Alsup, *The Post-Resurrection Appearance Stories of the Gospel Tradition*, Calwer theologische Monographien 5 (Stuttgart: Calwer Verlag, 1975); George E. Ladd, *I Believe in the Resurrection of Jesus* (Grand Rapids: Eerdmans, 1977); Ulrich Wilckens, *Resurrection. Biblical Testimony to the Resurrection: An Historical Examination and Explanation* (Edinburgh: Saint Andrews Press, 1977); J.-M. Guillaume, *Luc interprète des anciennes traditions sur la résurrection de Jésus* (Paris: Gabalda, 1979); Herman Hendrickx, *Resurrection Narratives*, Studies in the Synoptic Gospels (London: Geoffrey Chapman, 1984); Pheme Perkins, *Resurrection: New Testament Witness and Contemporary Reflection* (Garden City, NY: Doubleday, 1984). For additional bibliography, see Hendrickx, pp. 132-50 and Perkins, pp. 453-79.

13. The major commentaries on Luke–Acts divide along these same lines. For example, I. Howard Marshall, *Commentary on Luke*, NIGTC (Grand Rapids: Eerdmans, 1978), employed the historical method to demonstrate the historical reliability of the Gospel. On the other hand, Ernst Haenchen, *The Acts of the Apostles: A Commentary*, trans. Bernard Noble *et al.* (Philadelphia: Westminster, 1971), argued for the redactional creativity of the author.

14. Typical perhaps is Willi Marxsen's concluding comment (*The Resurrection of Jesus of Nazareth*, p. 54) in his brief discussion of the ascension narratives in Luke–Acts: 'Numerous attempts have been made to find a solution to the questions which arise here. I cannot go into all the possible answers; nor do they play a particularly important part in connection with our present theme'.

15. See C.H. Dodd, 'The Appearance of the Risen Christ: An Essay in Form Criticism of the Gospels', *Studies in the Gospels*, ed. D.E. Nineham (Oxford: Blackwell, 1955), pp. 16ff. Xavier Léon-Dufour, *Resurrection and the Message of Easter*, trans. R.N. Wilson (New York: Holt, Rhinehart & Winston, 1974), pp. 164-67.

16. Fuller, *Formation*, pp. 122-23, for example.

17. Strictly speaking, of course, there are no post-resurrection appearance stories in Mark, only the promise of such. Here I agree with Reginald Fuller

and others who view 16.7 as a reference to a post-resurrection appearance, contra those who see here a reference to the parousia (R.H. Lightfoot, W. Michaelis, W. Marxsen, N. Perrin, etc.) or as a promise of the Gentile mission (J. Weiss, E.C. Hoskyns, C.F. Evans, etc.). See Fuller, *Formation*, pp. 57-64, for discussion and bibliography.

18.   One of the strongest advocates for the modified two-source hypothesis is Joseph Fitzmyer. He presented his case in 'The Priority of Mark and the 'Q' Source in Luke', *Jesus and Man's Hope*, Vol. I, ed. D.G. Miller (Pittsburgh: Pittsburgh Theological Seminary, 1970), pp. 131-70, and employed the method rigorously in his massive commentary, *The Gospel According to Luke*, AB, 2 vols. (Garden City, NY: Doubleday, 1981 and 1985).

19.   See especially Farmer's *The Synoptic Problem: A Critical Analysis* (New York: Macmillan, 1964); 'A "Skeleton in the Closet" of Gospel Research', *BR* 9 (1961), pp. 18-42; and 'The Two-Document Hypothesis as a Methodological Criterion in Synoptic Research', *ATR* 48 (1966), pp. 1204-1206.

20.   See the works by Fitzmyer and Farmer already cited; also William R. Farmer, 'Modern Developments of Griesbach's Hypothesis', *NTS* 23 (1977), pp. 283-93. These two scholars have maintained a continuous debate regarding the validity of the two-source and Griesbach hypotheses for studies in the Synoptic Gospels.

21.   Fitzmyer, however, has argued that this 'loss of confidence' is 'characteristic of a small group of students of the Synoptic relationships, mostly American, a few British, and still fewer Continental scholars' (*Luke*, Vol. II, p. x).

22.   Charles H. Talbert and Edgar V. McKnight, 'Can the Griesbach Hypothesis Be Falsified?', *JBL* 91 (1972), pp. 338-68.

23.   C.H. Talbert, 'Shifting Sands: The Recent Study of the Gospel of Luke', *Int* 30 (1976), pp. 393-94. Talbert's own problems with the procedures could be traced through his writings. In the article, 'The Redactional Critical Quest for Luke the Theologian', *Jesus and Man's Hope*, Vol. I, ed. D.G. Miller (Pittsburgh: Pittsburgh Theological Seminary, 1970), pp. 171-222, Talbert challenged many of Hans Conzelmann's conclusions which were based on a redaction-critical model which was in turn based on the two-source hypothesis. In a book, *Literary Patterns, Theological Themes, and the Genre of Luke–Acts* (Missoula: Scholars Press, 1974), p. 14, Talbert admitted to 'being caught in a crossfire' between those who accept or oppose the two-source hypothesis and those who would discard source analysis as unnecessary. With the publication of *Reading Luke*, Talbert has moved much closer to the latter camp than the former.

24.   Joseph B. Tyson, 'Conflict as a Literary Theme in the Gospel of Luke', *New Synoptic Studies: The Cambridge Gospel Conference and Beyond*, ed. William R. Farmer (Macon, GA: Mercer University Press, 1983), p. 303.

25. One could also say the same for most commentaries on Luke.

26. Gerhard Lohfink, *Die Himmelfahrt Jesu: Untersuchungen zu den Himmelfahrts- und Erhöhungstexten bei Lukas* (Munich: Kösel, 1971), pp. 150-51. For a review of Lohfink's study, see Ferdinand Hahn, '*Die Himmelfahrt Jesu*: Ein Gespräch mit Gerhard Lohfink', *Bib* 55 (1974), pp. 418-26.

27. As the section on 'Methodology' will show below, however, I believe Lohfink's study in no way renders the present investigation superfluous. This study addresses issues not only ignored by Lohfink, but issues which I consider crucial to a proper understanding of the narratives of Luke and Acts.

28. Richard J. Dillon, *From Eye-Witnesses to Ministers of the Word: Tradition and Composition in Luke 24*, AnBib, 82 (Rome: Biblical Institute, 1978), pp. 170-82.

29. See Murray Krieger, *A Window to Criticism: Shakespeare's Sonnets and Modern Poetics* (Princeton, NJ: Princeton University Press, 1984), pp. 3-4; cited by R. Alan Culpepper, 'Story and History in the Gospels', *Review and Expositor* 81 (1984), p. 468.

30. Terence J. Keegan, *Interpreting the Bible: A Popular Introduction to Biblical Hermeneutics* (New York: Paulist Press, 1985), p. 167.

31. See for example R.A. Culpepper, 'Story and History', pp. 467-77; Leander E. Keck, 'Will the Historical-Critical Method Survive? Some Observations', *Orientation by Disorientation: Studies in Literary Criticism and Biblical Literary Criticism, Presented in Honor of William A. Beardslee*, ed. Richard A. Spencer (Pittsburgh: Pickwick Press, 1980). Walter Wink, *The Bible in Human Transformation* (Philadelphia: Westminster, 1973), went so far as to call historical-critical scholarship bankrupt. The way this shift in biblical scholarship has specifically affected Lukan studies will be explored in Chapter 3.

32. Culpepper, 'Story and History', p. 471.

33. See R.J. Karris, 'Windows and Mirrors: Literary Criticism and Luke's Sitz im Leben', *SBL Seminar Papers* (Missoula: Scholars Press, 1979).

34. Keegan, *Interpreting the Bible*, p. 30.

35. *Ibid.*, p. 38.

36. A point made by Brevard S. Childs, *Introduction to the Old Testament as Scripture* (Philadelphia: Fortress, 1979).

37. Redaction criticism will not be utilized in any rigorous way for several reasons. First, as has already been noted, *Redaktionsgeschichte* is dependent upon a now questionable two-source hypothesis. Second, since there are no parallels to the departure of Jesus in the other Synoptics, narrative analysis, not redaction or composition criticism, is more helpful in understanding the movement of the text.

38. B.S. Childs, *The New Testament as Canon: An Introduction* (Philadelphia: Fortress, 1985), p. 523.

39. *Ibid.*, p. 527.
40. *Ibid.*, p. 528.
41. *Ibid.*
42. *Ibid.*, pp. 527-28.
43. *Ibid.*, p. 525. In a sense, the goal which Childs suggests is not far removed from the purpose espoused here. And while I am deeply sympathetic with Childs' overall program (especially see my indebtedness in Chapter 6), I find his discussion of New Testament textual criticism to be one of the weakest links in his argument. In a way, Childs has imposed his understanding of textual criticism of the Old Testament upon his understanding of the New Testament text and the chaffing effect is predictable. Childs is certainly correct in noticing that textual criticism is a discipline much in need of renewal. The loss of prominent textual critics to retirement or administrative positions, coupled with the disappearance of geographical centers of text-critical work, have led Epp ('New Testament Textual Criticism in America: Requiem for a Discipline', *JBL* 98 [1979], pp. 94-98) to write a requiem for New Testament textual criticism in America. Epp (p. 98) claimed:

> I may have pushed too far the figure of speech in the subtitle of this paper when I chose the expression, '*Requiem* for a Discipline'. Yet, that ominous eventuality is all too likely should the clear trends of the recent past continue even into the near future.

In a sense, Childs' canonical model may have the effect of driving the final nail into the coffin of New Testament textual criticism as a scholarly discipline, at least on the American scene. A fuller statement of my concern for the practice of textual criticism will be found in Chapter 4.

44. See Chapter 3 for a list of those scholars who have broken the ground in the application of literary theory to biblical texts.
45. Tyson, 'Conflict as a Literary Theme', pp. 304-305.
46. To some extent such autonomy of the text may be more congenial to the conservative, evangelical scholar who already has a 'high' view of scripture. The problem a conservative scholar has is accepting the suspension of historical questions while the narrator tells the tale.
47. See R.A. Culpepper, *Anatomy of the Fourth Gospel: A Study in Literary Design* (Philadelphia: Fortress, 1983), pp. 8-11, for a list of some objections and Culpepper's response. The question of methodology is one addressed by Culpepper.
48. W.C. van Unnik, 'Luke's Second Book and the Rules of Hellenistic Historiography', *Les Acts des Apôtres: Traditions, rédaction, théologie*, ed. J. Kremer (Gembloux: Leuven University Press, 1979), pp. 37-60. Comparing Acts with ancient historiography, van Unnik noted (p. 60) 'how much fruit the comparison of Luke with ancient historiography can yield'. See also W.C. van Unnik, 'Éléments artistiques dans l'évangile de Luc', *L'Évangile de Luc: Problèmes littéraires et théologiques*, ed. Frans Neirynck (Gembloux: Leuven University Press, 1973), pp. 129-40.

49. C.H. Talbert, *What is a Gospel? The Genre of the Canonical Gospels* (Philadelphia: Fortress, 1977). For an example of the way in which reading Luke as an ancient biography can inform the reader, see C.H. Talbert, 'Prophecies of Future Greatness: The Contribution of Greco-Roman Biographies to an Understanding of Luke 1.5-4.15', *The Divine Helmsman*, ed. J.L. Crenshaw and Samuel Sandmel (New York: KTAV, 1980), pp. 129-41.

50. Richard I. Pervo, 'The Literary Genre of the Acts of the Apostles' (Th.D. dissertation, Harvard University, 1979); see also Stephen P. and Marla J. Schierling, 'The Influence of the Ancient Romances on *Acts of the Apostles*', *ClassBul* 54 (1978), pp. 81-88.

51. *Ibid.*, p. 41.

52. Susan Praeder, 'Luke–Acts and the Ancient Novel', *SBL Seminar Papers*, ed. Kent H. Richards (Missoula: Scholars, 1981), p. 292. For more information on the ancient novel, one might consult G.N. Sandy, 'Recent Scholarship on the Prose Fiction of Classical Antiquity', *ClassWorld* 67 (1974), pp. 321-59; B.P. Reardon, 'Aspects of the Greek Novel', *GR* 23 (1976), pp. 118-31; B.P. Reardon, ed., *Erotica Antiqua, Acta of the International Conference on the Ancient Novel* (Bangor, Wales: University College Press, 1977).

53. R.J. Karris, 'Windows and Mirrors', p. 52.

54. *Ibid.*, p. 53.

55. *Ibid.*

56. I still would prefer to see examples of certain literary techniques and patterns drawn from ancient literature which shares a common language and cultural setting with the Gospels; but at least, the biblical scholar should be alert to the pitfalls of such studies.

57. Culpepper, *Anatomy*, p. 9.

58. Robert H. Smith, 'The Theology of Acts', *CTM* 42 (1971), p. 527.

59. Allen J. Walworth, 'The Narrator of Acts' (Ph.D. dissertation, The Southern Baptist Theological Seminary, 1984). Walworth (*ibid.*, p. 8) claimed: 'Granted that the same author stands behind both works, his narrator is not necessarily the same in both works'.

Notes to Chapter 2

1. B.F. Westcott and F.J.A. Hort, *The New Testament in the Original Greek*, Vol. II (London: Macmillan, 1881), p. 1.

2. A. Westcott, *Life and Letters of Brooke Foss Westcott*, Vol. I (London: Macmillan, 1903), p. 250.

3. Westcott and Hort, *The New Testament*, p. 210.

4. *Ibid.*, p. 225.

5. *Ibid.*, p. 176.

6. WH identified an intermediate class of Western omissions that may or may not be non-interpolations: Matt. 6.15, 25; 9.34; 13.33; 21.44; 23.26; Mark 2.22; 10.2; 14.39; Luke 5.39; 10.41; 12.19, 21, 39; 22.62; 24.9; John 3.32; 4.9.

7. The following examples are not intended to be exhaustive of the works influenced by WH, but representative of the pervasive impact their text-critical judgments had on their contemporaries and immediate successors. In addition to the translations, commentaries, and critical editions of the Greek New Testament, one could also cite a spate of older journal articles which simply assumed the text-critical judgments of WH.

8. Jack R. Lewis, *The English Bible/From KJV to NIV: A History and Evaluation* (Grand Rapids: Baker, 1981), pp. 71-72.

9. Alfred Plummer, *A Critical and Exegetical Commentary on the Gospel According to St. Luke*, ICC (New York: Scribner 1903).

10. Henry Balmforth, *The Gospel according to St. Luke* (Oxford: Clarendon, 1930).

11. William Manson, *The Gospel of Luke* (New York: R.R. Smith, 1930).

12. John M. Creed, *The Gospel according to Luke: The Greek Text with Introduction, Notes, and Indices* (London: Macmillan, 1950).

13. Norval Geldenhuys, *Commentary on the Gospel of Luke* (Grand Rapids: Eerdmans, 1951).

14. S.M. Gilmour, 'The Gospel according to St. Luke', *IB* Vol. VIII (Nashville: Abingdon, 1952), pp. 1-434.

15. A notable exception is A.R.C. Leaney who argued for the authenticity of 24.12. See Leaney, *A Commentary on the Gospel According to St. Luke* (London: A. & C. Black, 1958).

16. Merk (1933, 1964[9]) and Bover (1943, 1968[5]) read the longer texts with no brackets.

17. I.H. Marshall, *Commentary on Luke*, NIGTC (Grand Rapids: Eerdmans, 1978).

18. J.A. Fitzmyer, *The Gospel According to Luke*, AB, 2 vols. (Garden City: Doubleday, 1981 and 1985).

19. C.H. Talbert, *Reading Luke: A Literary and Theological Commentary* (New York: Crossroad, 1983).

20. Marshall, *Luke*, pp. 884-910.

21. Fitzmyer, *Luke*, I, pp. 128-33.

22. *Ibid.*, I, p. 131. See also his article, 'The Ascension of Christ and Pentecost', *TS* 45 (1984), pp. 409-40.

23. *Ibid.*, II, pp. 1544, 1545, 1547, 1575, 1576, 1590.

24. Talbert, *Reading Luke*, p. 227.

25. E. Haenchen, *The Acts of the Apostles: A Commentary*, trans. Bernard Noble, *et al.* (Philadelphia: Westminster, 1971), p. 59.

26. E. Schweizer, *The Good News According to Luke* (Atlanta: John Knox

Press, 1984); E. Earle Ellis, *The Gospel of Luke* (Grand Rapids; Eerdmans, 1981).

27. Kurt Aland *et al.*, *The Greek New Testament*, 1st edn (Stuttgart: United Bible Societies, 1966), p. xli.

28. The printed text for UBS[3] is the same as N-A[26]. A similar phenomenon took place between the 25th and 26th editions of Nestle-Aland.

29. These reasons were brought indirectly to my attention by Klyne Snodgrass, who argued for the longer text in 'Western Non-Interpolations', *JBL* 91 (1972), pp. 369-79. Snodgrass (p. 378) appealed both to Jeremias and to p[75] in order to conclude: '. . . the "Western non-interpolations" . . . have little claim to authenticity'.

30. Joachim Jeremias, *The Eucharistic Words of Jesus*, trans. Norman Perrin (Philadelphia: Fortress, 1966), pp. 149-59.

31. *Ibid.*

32. Marshall, *Luke*, pp. 884, 888, 901-902, 909.

33. p[75] contains (with lacunae) Luke 3-24 and John 1-15.

34. V. Martin and R. Kasser, eds., *Papyrus Bodmer XIV-XV: Évangiles de Luc et Jean* (Cologny-Genève: Bibliothèque Bodmer, 1961), p. 5.

35. K. Aland, 'The Significance of the Papyri for Progress in New Testament Research', *The Bible in Modern Scholarship*, ed. J.P. Hyatt (Nashville: Abingdon, 1965), p. 135.

36. *Ibid.*, p. 334.

37. K. Aland, 'Neue neutestamentliche Papyri II', *NTS* 12 (1965-66), pp. 193-210.

38. B. Metzger, 'The Bodmer Papyrus of Luke and John', *ExpT* 73 (1962), p. 203.

39. Carlo Martini, 'Problema recensionalitatis codicis in luce papyri Bodmer XIV (p[75])', *VD* 44 (1967), p. 196. See also *Il Problema della recensionalità del codice B alla luce del papiro Bodmer XIV*, AnBib, 26 (Rome: Biblical Institute, 1966).

40. The final step of acceptance of the longer text would entail changing the rating of the texts in the UBS from D ('a very high degree of doubt concerning the reading selected for the text') to a higher grade. This move is imminent according to Fitzmyer, 'Ascension and Pentecost', p. 417 n. 21: 'I have been told that the ratings of many of the Western Non-Interpolations are to be upgraded in the next edition of UBSGNT (oral communication of B. Metzger)'.

41. Westcott and Hort, *The New Testament*, p. 71.

42. Plummer, *Luke*, p. 548.

43. Ignace de la Potterie, 'Le titre *kurios* appliqué à Jésus dans l'évangile de Luc', *Mélanges bibliques en hommage au R.P. Béda Rigaux*, ed. A. Descamps and A. de Halleux (Gembloux: Duculot, 1979), p. 124.

44. B. Metzger, *A Textual Commentary on the Greek New Testament*

(London: United Bible Societies, 1971), p. 183.

45. Snodgrass, 'Western Non-Interpolations', p. 375.

46. Jeremias, *The Eucharistic Words*, p. 149; Aland, 'Neue neutestament-liche Papyri II', p. 197.

47. Westcott and Hort, *The New Testament*, p. 71; Plummer, *Luke*, p. 548.

48. Robert Mahoney, *Two Disciples at the Tomb: The Background and Message of John 20.1-10* (Bern: Herbert Lang, 1974), p. 60. In his discussion of the sources which underlie John 20.1-10, Mahoney devoted several pages to the non-interpolations.

49. Metzger, *A Textual Commentary*, p. 184; Jeremias, *The Eucharistic Words*, p. 149; Marshall, *Luke*, p. 886.

50. Snodgrass, 'Western Non-Interpolations', p. 375.

51. Westcott and Hort, *The New Testament*, p. 71.

52. Raymond E. Brown, *The Gospel According to John*, AB; Vol. II (Garden City: Doubleday, 1970), p. 969.

53. K.P.G. Curtis, 'Luke xxiv.12 and John xx.3-10', *JTS* 22 (1971), p. 515.

54. *Ibid.*

55. Mahoney, *Two Disciples at the Tomb*, p. 67.

56. *Ibid.*, p. 68.

57. Jeremias, *The Eucharistic Words*, p. 150.

58. *Ibid.*

59. *Ibid.*

60. Metzger, *A Textual Commentary*, p. 184; Marshall, *Luke*, p. 888.

61. Frans Neirynck, 'The Uncorrected Historic Present in Lk XXIV.12', *ETL* 48 (1972), pp. 548-53; see also 'The "Other Disciple" in Jn 18, 15-16', *ETL* 51 (1975), pp. 113-41.

62. R.H. Fuller, *The Formation of the Resurrection Narratives* (Philadelphia: Fortress, 1980), pp. 101-102.

63. Plummer, *Luke*, p. 559.

64. K.P.G. Curtis, 'Linguistic Support for Three Western Readings in Luke 24', *ExpTim* 83 (1971-72), p. 344.

65. Mahoney, *Two Disciples at the Tomb*, p. 61.

66. Neirynck, 'The Uncorrected Historic', pp. 551-53. Herman Hendrickx, *Resurrection Narratives*, Studies in the Synoptic Gospels (London: Geoffrey Chapman, 1984), p. 46.

67. Marshall, *Luke*, p. 901.

68. Snodgrass, 'Western Non-Interpolations', p. 375.

69. Plummer, *Luke*, p. 559.

70. Curtis, 'Linguistic Support', p. 334.

71. Metzger, *A Textual Commentary*, p. 187.

72. K. Aland, 'Die Bedeutung des p[75] für den Text des Neuen Testaments. Ein Beitrag zur Frage der "Western non-interpolations"', *Studien zur*

Überlieferung des Neuen Testaments und seines Textes (Berlin: de Gruyter, 1967), p. 169.

73. Westcott and Hort, *The New Testament*, p. 38.
74. Plummer, *Luke*, p. 559.
75. Metzger, *A Textual Commentary*, p. 189.
76. *Ibid.*
77. *Ibid.*
78. Westcott and Hort, *The New Testament*, p. 38.
79. Metzger, *A Textual Commentary*, p. 190.
80. *Ibid.*
81. E.C. Colwell, *Studies in Methodology in Textual Criticism of the New Testament* (Grand Rapids: Eerdmans, 1969), p. 156.
82. Mahoney, *Two Disciples at the Tomb*, p. 49.
83. *Ibid.*, p. 50.
84. *Ibid.*
85. E.J. Epp, 'The Twentieth Century Interlude in New Testament Textual Criticism', *JBL* 93 (1974), p. 393.
86. Snodgrass, 'Western Non-Interpolations', p. 369.
87. Aland, 'Bedeutung', p. 158.
88. Metzger, *A Textual Commentary*, pp. 192-93.
89. *Ibid.*
90. *Ibid.*, p. 193.
91. It may be reasonably assumed that Matthew Black represented the minority view of the Committee and argued for the authenticity of the Western readings in Luke 24 as he has done elsewhere for key passages in Acts; see Matthew Black, 'Notes on the Longer and Shorter Text of Acts', *On Language, Culture and Religion: In Honor of Eugene A. Nida*, ed. Matthew Black and W.A. Smalley (Paris: Mouton, 1974), pp. 119-31; also 'The Holy Spirit in the Western Text of Acts', *New Testament Textual Criticism: Its Significance for Exegesis*, ed. E.J. Epp and G.D. Fee (Oxford: Clarendon, 1981), pp. 159-70.
92. Metzger, *A Textual Commentary*, p. vii.
93. It is at this point that I part company with WH (Westcott and Hort, *The New Testament*, p. 282) who claimed: 'even among the numerous unquestionable spurious readings of the New Testament there are no signs of deliberate falsification of the text for dogmatic purposes'.
94. For a detailed study of Codex D in modern scholarship, see A.F.J. Klijn, *A Survey of the Researches into the Western Text of the Gospels and Acts* (Utrecht: Kemink, 1949); and *A Survey of the Researches into the Western Text of the Gospels and Acts: 1949-69* (Leiden: Brill, 1969).
95. Frederick Wisse, *The Profile Method for Classifying and Evaluating Manuscript Evidence*, SD, Vol. 44 (Grand Rapids: Eerdmans, 1982), p. 91, has recently challenged this position and argued: 'D is clearly related to Gr B in Luke though it is an exceptional member'.

96. L.W. Hurtado, *Text-Critical Methodology and the Pre-Caesarean Text: Codex W in the Gospel of Mark*, SD, 43 (Grand Rapids: Eerdmans, 1981), p. 68.

97. For a categorization of such terms as 'singular', 'significant', 'sub-singular', etc., see E.J. Epp, 'Toward the Clarification of the Term "Textual Variant"', *Studies in New Testament Language and Text*, ed. J.K. Elliott (Leiden: Brill, 1976), pp. 153-73.

98. Hurtado, *Text-Critical Methodology*, pp. 69-80. These categories were deduced inductively by Hurtado and should not be viewed as exhaustive or invariable.

99. While based on thorough and detailed research, the proposed methodology is far removed from the caricature of the text-critic, locked in an ivory tower, stooped over an aging and obscure manuscript, peering through blood-shot eyes, trapped in a world of minutiae!

100. Colwell, *Studies in Methodology*, p. 156.

101. Hurtado, *Text-Critical Methodology*, p. 69.

102. Kenneth W. Clark, 'The Theological Relevance of Textual Variation in Current Criticism of the Greek New Testament', *JBL* 85 (1966), p. 16.

103. E.J. Epp, *The Theological Tendency of Codex Bezae Cantabrigiensis in Acts* (Cambridge: Cambridge University Press, 1966). Cf. C.K. Barrett's critique of Epp in 'Is there a Theological Tendency in Codex Bezae?', *Text and Interpretation: Studies In the New Testament Presented to Matthew Black*, ed. Ernest Black and R.McL. Wilson (London: Cambridge University Press, 1979).

104. George E. Rice, 'The Alteration of Luke's Tradition by the Textual Variants in Codex Bezae' (Ph.D. dissertation, Case Western Reserve University, 1974).

105. *Ibid.*, p. iii.

106. It should be noted that Rice sometimes appealed to variants which may not reflect a theological bias; see for example 2.40, where the variant may well be due to a Latinism.

107. B.H. Streeter, *The Four Gospels* (London: Macmillan, 1961), p. 143; Kirsopp Lake, *Landmarks in the History of Early Christianity* (London: Macmillan, 1920), p. 120.

108. Rice, 'The Alterations of Luke's Tradition', p. 100. Whether D makes the same corrections in Matthew is unknown, since the first chapter of Matthew in D is lost. See also 'Luke 3.22-28 in Codex Bezae: The Messianic King', *AUSS* 17 (1979), pp. 203-208.

109. *Ibid.*, p. 103. See also the variant at 9.20.

110. *Ibid.*, pp. 120-21.

111. *Ibid.*

112. G.E. Rice, 'Western Non-Interpolations: A Defense of the Apostolate', *Luke–Acts: New Perspectives from the Society of Biblical Literature Seminar*, ed. C.H. Talbert (New York: Crossroad, 1984), pp. 1-15.

113. *Ibid.*, p. 3.

114. Cf., however, Rice's most recent article, 'Is Bezae a Homogeneous Codex?', *PersRelSt* 11 (1984), pp. 39-54. Rice (p. 54) concluded: 'Bezae is not a homogeneous codex. Although the Bezan text of Matthew and Mark do reflect some variants that may be attributed to a bias, they are insignificant in the comparison with the text of Luke/Acts'. Rice offered no reason which would explain why the scribal editorial activity is limited to Luke–Acts. It is easier to understand why a scribe would redact Acts, which has no parallel in the canon; one is harder pressed to justify the choice of Luke over the other Gospels, unless a scribe intended to alter the writings of Luke only. See also, Michael W. Holmes, 'Early Editorial Activity and the Text of Codex Bezae in Matthew' (Ph.D. dissertation, Princeton University, 1984).

115. Colwell, *Studies in Methodology*, p. 117. Colwell has overstated his case by asserting *all* variants in p^{75} can be explained 'as the result of a single force'.

116. *Ibid.*

117. For differing evaluations of the scribal habits of p^{75}, cf. Clark, 'The Theological Relevance', pp. 1-16; G.D. Fee, 'p^{66}, p^{75}, and Origen: The Myth of Early Textual Recension in Alexandria', *New Dimensions in New Testament Study*, ed. Richard N. Longenecker and Merrill C. Tenney (Grand Rapids: Zondervan, 1974), pp. 19-45.

118. In addition to the idiosyncrasies mentioned above, Marchant King, 'Notes on the Bodmer Manuscript of Luke', *BSac* 122 (1965), p. 235, has conjectured that 'for all its beautifully careful production, the manuscript gives evidence of having been a book of the people'.

119. Clark, 'The Theological Relevance', p. 15.

120. Fee, 'The Myth of Early Textual Recension', p. 32.

121. It is mentioned here only to show how difficult the task is, even for the experienced text-critic!

122. King ('Notes', p. 240) suggested: 'It rather neatly shows how prominent was the thought of resurrection in the mind of this scribe or some previous one. Certainly some unknown believer there in Egypt was really occupied with the core of Christian thinking!'

123. Walter Bauer, *A Greek-English Lexicon of the New Testament and Other Early Christian Literature*, ed. F. Danker and trans. William Arndt and F. Wilbur Gingrich (London: University of Chicago, 1979), p. 705.

124. *Ibid.*, p. 713.

125. The other problem, a compound with a third singular verb is not so difficult. The 'crowd' is separated enough from the verb that a scribe might overlook this grammatical error.

126. King, 'Notes', p. 239.

127. See also Luke 11.39; 13.13.

128. James M. Robinson, *The Story of the Bodmer Papyri* (Philadelphia: Fortress, forthcoming).

129. Earlier, Albert Pietersma had also identified the Dishna Papers with the Bodmer Papyri, based on three photographs of the Dishna Papers; see Robinson, *ibid.*

130. These two significant finds are named after the respective main towns in the vicinity, Dishna and Nag Hammadi. Neither, however, is the nearest hamlet to its respective site of discovery.

131. E.J. Epp, 'A Continuing Interlude in New Testament Textual Criticism?', *HTR* 73 (1980), p. 146. Addressing the significance of the papyri for New Testament research, Epp (*ibid.*) remarked in passing: 'papyrus survives almost exclusively in the hot climate and dry sands of Egypt'.

132. See J.M. Robinson, ed., *The Nag Hammadi Library* (San Francisco: Harper & Row, 1981).

133. R.McL. Wilson, *The Gospel of Philip* (London: Mowbray, 1962), p. 32. See also Logion 90.

134. For additional references to second- and third-century Gnostic views of the resurrection and ascension, see C.H. Talbert, 'An Anti-Gnostic Tendency in Lucan Christology', *NTS* 14 (1968-69), pp. 259-71; *Luke and the Gnostics* (Nashville: Abingdon, 1966). It should be noted, however, that Talbert assigned these anti-Gnostic tendencies to the author of Luke and not a later scribe. It seems more likely, at least in Luke 24, that such an emphasis was due largely to the concerns of later scribes.

135. Barrett ('Is there a Theological Tendency?' p. 26) noted about Codex D: 'The essential characteristic of the MS, or text, is to exaggerate existing tendencies'. The same is certainly true here for p^{75}. The scribe is not creating new christological categories, but rather accentuating the ones already there.

136. K.W. Clark, 'The Text of the Gospel of John in Third-Century Egypt', *NovT* 5 (1962), p. 23.

137. An impressive amount of work has already been done in this area. This study barely touches the periphery of the field and does not pretend to solve the problem. For summaries of research into this area, see Mgr. de Solages, *Jean et les Synoptiques* (Leiden: Brill, 1979); Frans Neirynck, *Jean et les Synoptiques: Examen Critique de l'exégèse de M.-É. Boismard* (Leuven: Leuven University Press, 1979).

138. K. Weiss 'ἀναφέρω', *Theological Dictionary of the New Testament*, ed. Gerhard Kittel and trans. G.W. Bromiley (Grand Rapids: Eerdmans, 1964), IX, p. 60.

139. Contra P.A. van Stempvoort, 'The Interpretation of the Ascension in Luke and Acts', *NTS* 5 (1959), pp. 30-42, who claimed the liturgical element was introduced by the author, not a later scribe.

140. E.J. Epp, 'Ascension in the Textual Tradition of Luke–Acts', *New Testament Textual Criticism: Its Significance for Exegesis*, ed. E.J. Epp and G.D. Fee (Oxford: Clarendon, 1981), pp. 131-46.

141. Colwell, *Studies in Methodology*, pp. 117-18; G. Fee, 'The Significance

214   *The Departure of Jesus in Luke–Acts*

of Papyrus Bodmer II and Papyrus Bodmer XIV-XV for Methodology in
New Testament Textual Criticism' (Ph.D. dissertation, University of
Southern California, 1966); also Fee, 'The Myth of Early Textual Recension',
pp. 19-45.

142. This statement, of course, is not true for 24.51 where Codex D is
joined by א.

143. G.D. Fee, 'Rigorous or Reasoned Eclecticism—Which?', *Studies in
New Testament Language and Text*, ed. J.K. Elliott (Leiden: Brill, 1976),
p. 35.

144. Epp, 'Toward the Clarification', p. 164.

145. Perhaps the strongest argument against this position is the most
obvious one. p[75] is not the only witness to the longer text and thus may not
be responsible for the changes even if they are later interpolations. This is a
difficult, but not insurmountable, problem. If the longer passages were, in
fact, later additions, their presence in so many and varied witnesses would
necessitate their inclusion in the text at a very early date. In effect, one would
search for an early witness to the changes and p[75] may very well provide that
testimony.

146. While not all may agree with the text-critical conclusions drawn here,
on a more practical level, a plea may be entered. While the jury is still out, I
ask that the editors of the critical Greek editions consider reinstating single
or double brackets around the non-interpolations to indicate a serious
textual problem. The text, now found in most classrooms and sure to be the
basis for most forthcoming translations and commentaries, has its problems.
Without a careful reading of the critical apparatus, the neophyte to textual
criticism—whether student, pastor, or bible translator—will probably not
even be aware of the textual difficulties that exist in Luke 24. Even those
who are able to move through the critical apparatus with some competence,
work from the presupposition that the editors of the text are much more
proficient in the field of textual criticism. Yet situations arise, as in the case
of the Western non-interpolations, where the opinions of the leading textual
critics are sharply divided. In either case, the printed text wins by default.

147. Aland, 'The Significance of the Papyri', p. 346.

148. Fee, 'The Myth of Early Textual Recension', p. 45.

149. On the thoroughly Lukan content and vocabulary of Luke 24.50-53,
see Jean-Marie Guillaume, *Luc interprète des anciennes traditions sur la
résurrection de Jésus* (Paris: Librairie Lecoffre, 1979), pp. 228-34. Guillaume
(p. 234) concluded: 'l'analyse confirme l'hypothèse que la finale du troisième
évangile (Lc., 24, 50-53) est lucanienne d'expression, d'idées et de
composition'.

150. This study is not the first to note the difficulties of establishing the
form of Luke 24.50-53. At the conclusion of his now classic form-critical
treatment of the post-resurrection appearances, C.H. Dodd, 'The Appearances
of the Risen Christ: An Essay in Form Criticism of the Gospels', *Studies in*

the Gospels, ed. D.E. Nineham (Oxford: Blackwell, 1955), p. 26, dismissed the ascension narrative in Luke as 'scarcely more than an editorial winding-up of the series of incidents following the resurrection'.

151. Because text-critical considerations have led me to reject the longer text of Luke 24.51, the comparison between the Lukan ascension narrative and the heavenly assumption stories in the ancient Greco-Roman and Jewish literature will be addressed in the diachronic analysis of Chapter 4.

152. J.E. Alsup, *The Post-Resurrection Appearance Stories of the Gospel-Tradition* (Stuttgart: Calwer Verlag, 1975).

153. *Ibid.*, p. 264.

154. *Ibid.*

155. B.J. Hubbard, *The Matthean Redaction of a Primitive Apostolic Commissioning: An Exegesis of Matthew 28.16-20* (Missoula, Montana: Scholars Press, 1974).

156. *Ibid.*, pp. 32-62.

157. *Ibid.*, p. 64. Hubbard notes that the commissioning accounts generally either have a response to the presence of the commissioner (reaction) or to his commission (protest), but rarely both.

158. *Ibid.*, pp. 62-64.

159. *Ibid.*, p. 64. Of the twenty-seven passages Hubbard examined as commissioning accounts, only Isa. 6.11b-13b, 49.5f.; Jer. 1.10 lack this formal conclusion.

160. T.Y. Mullins, 'New Testament Commission Forms, Especially in Luke–Acts', *JBL* 95 (1976), p. 603, argued that the confrontation, commission and reassurance are the only indispensable elements in biblical commissions. Mullins also argued that the commissioning form was a remarkably common form in the NT and occurred more frequently in non-resurrection contexts than it did in the resurrection narratives themselves (pp. 605-606).

161. Hubbard, *Matthean Redaction*, p. 122.

162. B.J. Hubbard, 'Commissioning Stories in Luke–Acts: A Study of their Antecedents, Form and Content', *Semeia* 8 (1977), pp. 103-126; *idem*, 'The Role of Commissioning Accounts in Acts', *Perspectives on Luke–Acts*, ed. C.H. Talbert (Danville, VA: ABPR, 1978), pp. 187-98. This second article was written in part as a response to Mullins' article, 'New Testament Commission Forms', which has recently questioned whether or not Hubbard's *Gattung* does not apply better to non-resurrection contexts of the NT than to the appearance stories.

163. Hubbard, 'Commissioning Stories', pp. 114-22.

164. Of the two places (Acts 22.17-21; 23.11) where no conclusion occurs, Hubbard, 'Commissioning Stories', p. 120, observed that in one of them (Acts 22.17-21), Paul, recounting the christophany in the first person, is interrupted by his audience.

165. For some reason, Hubbard does not list a 'Conclusion' for this pericope in his discussion (pp. 116-17), though it is clear from Table 3

(p. 122) that he does in fact understand 24.50-53 to be the concluding element of this christophany; cf. also 'The Role of Commissioning Accounts', p. 190.

166.   Compare, for example, the concluding elements of the commissioning stories identified by Hubbard (p. 122) in Luke–Acts: Luke 1.5-25, 26-38; 2.8-20; Acts 5.17-21; 9.1-9, 10-17; 10.1-8, 9-23; 16.9-10; 18.9-11; 22.6-11; 26.12-20; 27.21-26.

167.   *Ibid.*, p. 122.

168.   Pseudo-Mark 16.14-20, which does have this formal element of conclusion, will be examined in Chapter 4.

169.   See Lohfink, *Die Himmelfahrt Jesu*, p. 168.

170.   There is also the similarity in the usage of προσκυνέω in both pasages if one reads the longer text in Luke 24.51.

171.   Van Stempvoort, 'Interpretation of the Ascension', p. 34.

172.   Dillon, *Eye-Witnesses*, p. 223.

173.   *Ibid.*, p. 179.

174.   *Ibid.*, p. 180.

175.   J. Munck, 'Discours d'adieu dans le Nouveau Testament et dans la littérature biblique', *Aux Sources de la tradition chrétienne* (Paris: Delachaux & Niestlé, 1950).

176.   *Ibid.*, p. 168.

177.   See Hubbard's critique of Munck's position in *Matthean Redaction*, pp. 14-15.

178.   W.S. Kurz, 'Luke 22.14-38 and Greco-Roman and Biblical Farewell Addresses', *JBL* 104 (1985), pp. 251-68.

179.   *Ibid.*, p. 253.

180.   *Ibid.*, p. 259.

181.   R. Alter, *The Art of Biblical Narrative* (New York: Basic Books, 1981), p. 51.

182.   Several of the farewell scenes themselves have liturgical echoes. See, for example, the death of Debora in Pseudo-Philo's *Biblical Antiquities*, 33.

183.   Contrast this reaction with that of the disciples recorded in Acts 1.10!

184.   Alter, *Art of Biblical Narrative*, p. 62.

185.   See, for example, J. Dupont, *Le Discours de Milet: Testament Pastoral de Saint Paul (Actes 20, 18-36)* (Paris: Cerf, 1962); H.-J. Michel, *Die Abschiedsrede des Paulus an die Kirche Apg 20,17-38* (Munich: Kösel, 1973).

186.   This investigation of farewell addresses has been limited to *biblical* departure scenes because Kurz ('Luke 22.14-38 and Farewell Addresses', p. 261) has explored the form of Greco-Roman farewell addresses and concluded that farewell scenes in Luke–Acts 'are clearly in the biblical tradition of farewell speeches, and in tone and content and style have more in

common with biblical rather than with secular farewell addresses'. See Kurz, pp. 253-55, for a discussion of Greco-Roman departure addresses.

187. Cf. Dillon, *Eye-Witnesses*, p. 173; B. Hubbard, 'Commissioning Stories in Luke–Acts', pp. 103-26; Lohfink, *Die Himmelfahrt Jesu*, pp. 147-51.

188. Dillon, *Eye-Witnesses*, p. 173. For most scholars who accept the longer text of 24.51, the major source-critical problem is whether there was a pre-Lukan tradition of the ascension. This analysis probes whether or not there was a pre-Lukan last blessing by Jesus in the context of a leave-taking scene. The question of the ascension is addressed in Chapter 4. That Luke 24.50-53 is a final departure scene whether or not ἀναφέρετο. . .οὐρανόν is original has been recognized by a number of scholars; e.g. Dillon, *Eye-Witnesses*, p. 172; J.M. Creed, *The Gospel according to St. Luke: The Greek Text with Introduction, Notes, and Indices* (London: Macmillan, 1950), p. 302; H. Schlier, *Besinnung auf das Neue Testament. Exegetische Aufsätze und Vorträge*, II (Freiburg: Herder, 1964), pp. 228, 230; J. Kremer, *Die Osterbotschaft der vier Evangelien. Versuch einer Auslegung der Berichte über das leere Grab und die Erscheinungen des Auferstandenen* (Stuttgart: Verlag Katholisches Bibelwerk, 1969), pp. 78f.

189. Lohfink, *Die Himmelfahrt Jesu*, p. 150.

190. *Ibid.*

191. *Ibid.*

192. *Ibid.* In fact, this evidence could be used to support the shorter text in Luke 24.51. Nowhere does Luke record a double departure scene as we have in Luke 24. One finds heavenly apparitions departing and in some cases going into heaven (Luke 2.15; Acts 1.11), but never together. So, to say 'Jesus departed from them, and was carried into heaven' seems to be a redundancy Luke was unwilling to commit.

193. In cinema, the difference might be likened to a distinct change in scene, whereby transition is made by a brief, but significant, moment of blackout on screen. The viewer knows that the action—whether plot, place, or person—has taken a distinct turn. This is contrasted to the fade-out in which the former scene slowly dissipates into the background, while the next scene continues. A visual 'echo' is created which serves to remind the viewer of the significance of the last scene for the current one.

194. Are these characters to be understood as angelic messengers? It certainly seems so. Lohfink presumably understood the two men in Luke 9.33 to be heavenly visitors. And while there is no need to identify the two men at the empty tomb and on the Mount of Olives as Moses and Elijah, as some have done, it is evident that in all three instances, the two serve to clarify for the witnesses and the readers what is taking place. In 9.33, Moses and Elijah discuss Jesus' exodus; in 24.6 the two men explain the empty tomb; in Acts 1.11 they explain the significance of the ascension for the parousia. So if Luke 9.33 is to be considered as evidence for a Lukan tendency to excuse heavenly messengers from the stage, then Luke 24.8 and

Acts 1.11 serve as counter-evidence to show this procedure is not rigorously followed.

195. On the textual problem in 28.29, see B.M. Metzger, *A Textual Commentary*, p. 502.

196. Lohfink, *Die Himmelfahrt Jesu*, p. 150.

197. Dillon, *Eye-Witnesses*, p. 174.

198. G.R. Osborne, *The Resurrection Narratives: A Redactional Study* (Grand Rapids: Baker, 1984), pp. 266-70. Some even suggest that Luke learned of a second, longer ascension account between the writing of the Gospel and the composition of Acts.

199. Marshall, *Luke*, p. 908.

200. See Chapter 3. This argument is much more satisfactory than that offered by Lohfink, *Die Himmelfahrt Jesu*, pp. 202-207, which suggests that Bethany is the only place known to Luke outside Jerusalem.

201. Lohfink, *Die Himmelfahrt Jesu*, p. 209. Likewise P. Perkins, *Resurrection: New Testament and Contemporary Reflection* (Garden City: Doubleday, 1984), p. 168, has argued: 'Both passages appear to be Luke's own composition'.

202. R. Bultmann, *History of the Synoptic Tradition*, trans. John Marsh (New York: Harper & Row, 1963), p. 286.

203. Dillon, *Eye-Witnesses*, p. 220.

204. See the discussion on source analysis of Acts 1 in the diachronic examination of Chapter 4.

Notes to Chapter 3

1. B.H. Streeter, *The Four Gospels* (London: Macmillan, 1924), p. 548.

2. See Dorothee Klein, *St. Lukas als Maler der Madonna: Ikonographie der Lukas-Madonna* (Berlin: n.p., 1933), p. 8; cited by E. Haenchen, *The Acts of the Apostles: A Commentary*, trans. Bernard Noble *et al.* (Philadelphia: Westminster, 1971), p. 90.

3. C.H. Talbert, *Literary Patterns, Theological Themes and the Genre of Luke–Acts* (Missoula: Scholars Press, 1974), pp. 1-5.

4. More comprehensive summaries of the work on Luke–Acts may be found in Haenchen, *Acts*, pp. 14-132; J.A. Fitzmyer, *The Gospel According to Luke, I-IX*, AB, Vol. I (Garden City: Doubleday, 1981), pp. 3-127.

5. C.H. Talbert, 'Shifting Sands: The Recent Study of the Gospel of Luke', *Int* 30 (1976), p. 395, has correctly observed: 'Prior to 1950 ... research on the Third Gospel focused on source criticism'. Vincent Taylor's work, *Behind the Third Gospel: A Study of the Proto-Luke Hypothesis* (Oxford: Clarendon, 1926), was the best-known of these source analyses in Luke. For a survey of research in source-criticism on Luke, see Fitzmyer, *Luke*, I, pp. 63-106. On the book of Acts, see Haenchen, *Acts*, pp. 14-50.

6.   The form-critics, K.L. Schmidt, *Der Rahmen der Geschichte Jesu* (Berlin: Trowitsch & Son, 1919); M. Dibelius, *Die Formgeschichte des Evangeliums* (Tübingen: J.C.B. Mohr, 1919); and R. Bultmann, *Die Geschichte der synoptischen Tradition* (Göttingen: Vandenhoeck & Ruprecht, 1921), served as precursors to the development of redaction criticism in Gospel studies. In Luke, the first major redactional study was Hans Conzelmann's *Die Mitte der Zeit: Studien zur Theologie des Lukas* (Tübingen: Mohr, 1953) (ET *The Theology of St. Luke*, trans. Geoffrey Buswell [Philadelphia: Fortress, 1982]). Chronologically, Conzelmann's watershed work was published between two other landmark redactional studies by Günther Bornkamm, 'Die Sturmstillung im Mattäusevangelium', *W&D* 1 (1948), pp. 49-54; and Willi Marxsen, *Der Evangelist Markus: Studien zur Redaktionsgeschichte des Evangeliums* (Göttingen: Vandenhoeck & Ruprecht, 1956). Jerome Kodell in 'The Theology of Luke in Recent Study', *BTB* 1 (1971), p. 126, claimed that Conzelmann's work represented 'the accepted battlefield for current debate'. For an exhaustive and judicious study of the history of redaction criticism, see Joachim Rohde, *Rediscovering the Teaching of the Evangelists*, trans. Dorothea M. Barton (London: SCM, 1968). The radical break which these scholars precipitated is even more remarkable when one considers the perspicacious judgment of Rohde, *The Teaching of the Evangelists*, p. 16: 'It is a striking fact that redaction-critical work has been decisively advanced above all by the work of beginners. Conzelmann's book consists of his dissertation and inaugural lecture, Marxsen's study is his inaugural dissertation'.

7.   On the matter of historicity, see W. Ward Gasque's, *A History of the Criticism of the Acts of the Apostles* (Tübingen: Mohr, 1975). Though an exhaustive account of the ebb and flow of the historicity debate, it is slanted by his effort to vindicate the historical reliability of Acts. I.H. Marshall's *Luke: Historian and Theologian* (Grand Rapids: Zondervan, 1970) is a slightly more balanced, though still conservative, effort which tried to defend Acts' reliability. One might also mention H. Flender, *St. Luke: Theologian of Redemptive History* (Philadelphia: Fortress, 1967); W.C. Robinson, Jr, *The Way of the Lord* (privately published doctoral dissertation submitted to the University of Basel); and E. Franklin, *Christ the Lord: A Study in the Purpose and Theology of Luke–Acts* (Philadelphia: Westminster, 1975). These last three works were written in reaction to what the writers considered to be the unwarranted skepticism on the reliability of the Luke–Acts by Conzelmann and others.

8.   Acclaimed 'the doyen of Anglo-Saxon research on Acts' (Haenchen, *Acts*, p. 43), H.J. Cadbury displayed remarkable sensitivity to the style, vocabulary, and composition of Luke–Acts. Because of his typically careful and balanced treatments of his subject, Cadbury's *The Making of Luke–Acts*, as well as his contribution to the magisterial five-volume work, *The Beginnings of Christianity*, must still be consulted by serious students of

Lukan style and vocabulary. His destruction of the Hobart/Harnack thesis that Luke and Acts were written by Luke the physician allowed scholarly focus to return to the stylistic characteristics of Luke–Acts. Cadbury's students used to jest that Cadbury earned his doctorate by wresting Luke's away from him. See Amos Wilder, 'In Memoriam: Henry Joel Cadbury', *NTS* 21 (1975), pp. 313-17.

Other attempts to continue the search for Lukan literary patterns include: M.D. Goulder, *Type and History in Acts* (London: SPCK, 1964); J.G. Davies, 'The Prefigurement of the Ascension in the Third Gospel', *JTS* 6 (1955), pp. 229-33; Paul S. Minear, 'Luke's Use of the Birth Stories', *Studies in Luke–Acts: Essays Presented in Honor of Paul Schubert* (Nashville: Abingdon, 1966), pp. 111-30; Robert Morgenthaler, *Die lukanische Geschichtsschreibung als Zeugnis: Gestalt und Gehalt der Kunst des Lukas*, 2 vols. (Zürich: Zwingli-Verlag, 1949). Haenchen, *Acts*, p. 47, commented that Morgenthaler's work 'threw a new idea into the debate: the Lucan writings are a work of art! Unfortunately this fruitful idea was reduced to the simple implication that Luke deliberately followed the "rule of duality"'.

Despite the work by Cadbury and others, the work of the redaction critics, particularly Conzelmann, dropped with sledge-hammer swiftness upon an unsuspecting spate of Lukan scholars and led W.C. van Unnik, 'Luke–Acts, a Storm Center in Contemporary Scholarship', *Studies in Luke–Acts*, p. 16, to label Luke–Acts one of the great 'storm centers' of New Testament scholarship. The eye of the storm was to be found in the varying estimations of Luke's theology and the questions raised about the historical reliability of Luke–Acts. Of concern here is that such interest in what the Evangelist intended by what he wrote (his theology) and whether or not his writings can be considered historically trustworthy served to diminish the energy spent on the Evangelist as a *littérateur*.

9. Talbert, *Literary Patterns*, p. 7.

10. He referred to *Die Apostelgeschichte* in *Reading Luke: A Literary and Theological Commentary on the Third Gospel* (New York: Crossroad, 1982), p. 244. Talbert (pp. 1-2) dismissed the use of the two-source theory so fundamental for redactional studies and relied instead on non-biblical literary criticism. See Mikeal C. Parsons, 'Review of Charles H. Talbert's *Reading Luke*', *PersRelSt*, 10 (1984), pp. 283-85.

11. A.N. Wilder, 'Semeia, An Experimental Journal for Biblical Criticism: An Introduction', *Semeia* 1 (1974), p. 2. In this article, Wilder has described the literary and historical context from which the journal arose.

12. L.T. Johnson, *The Literary Function of Possessions in Luke–Acts*, SBLDS 39 (Missoula: Scholars Press, 1977); R.J. Karris, *Luke: Artist and Theologian, Luke's Passion Account as Literature* (New York: Paulist Press, 1985). On the effect of narrative criticism on the traditional historical-critical method of biblical studies, see R.A. Culpepper, 'Story and History in the Gospels', *R&E* 81 (1984), pp. 467-77. See also L.E. Keck, 'Will the

Historical-Critical Method Survive? Some Observations', *Orientation by Disorientation: Studies in Literary Criticism and Biblical Literary Criticism, Presented in Honor of William A. Beardslee,* ed. Richard A. Spencer (Pittsburgh: Pickwick, 1980), pp. 115-17.

13. See J.B. Tyson, *The Death of Jesus in Luke–Acts* (Columbia, S.C.: University of South Carolina Press, 1986); R.C. Tannehill, *The Narrative Unity of Luke–Acts: A Literary Interpretation* (Philadelphia: Fortress, 1986).

14. Aristotle, *The Poetics,* trans S.H. Butcher (New York: Hill & Wang, 1968), p. 65.

15. Henry James, 'The Art of Fiction', *Approaches to the Novel: Materials for a Poetics,* ed. Robert Scholes (San Francisco: Chandler, 1961), p. 295. The article originally appeared in *Longman's* magazine in 1884.

16. E.M. Forster, *Aspects of the Novel* (San Diego: Harcourt, Brace, & Jovanovich), p. 27.

17. Réné Girard, *Deceit, Desire, and the Novel,* trans. Yvonne Freccero (Baltimore: Johns Hopkins, 1965).

18. *Ibid.,* p. 294.

19. *Ibid.*

20. *Ibid.,* p. 296.

21. Marianna Torgovnick, *Closure in the Novel* (Princeton: Princeton University Press, 1981), p. 9, has written, 'Girard's thesis obscures the differences that count as much as the similarities in novelistic closure'.

22. Alan Friedman, *The Turn of the Novel* (New York: Oxford University Press, 1966), p. xi. Friedman (p. xv) defined *open* in the following way: 'I use "open" to refer to an ending which does not contain or "close off" the rising pressure of conscience in a novel'.

23. *Ibid.,* p. 188.

24. Frank Kermode, *The Sense of an Ending: Studies in the Theory of Fiction* (New York: Oxford University Press, 1967).

25. Alexander Welsh, 'Foreword', *Nineteenth-Century Fiction* 33 (1978), p. 1.

26. For criticisms of Kermode at this point, see Roy Pascall, 'Narrative Fictions and Reality', *Novel* 11 (1977), pp. 40-50; also Torgovnick, *Closure,* pp. 7-8.

27. Barbara Herrnstein Smith, *Poetic Closure: A Study of How Poems End* (Chicago: University of Chicago Press, 1968), p. viii.

28. *Ibid.,* pp. 117-21.

29. Such 'borrowing' has been encouraged by Smith herself (*ibid.,* p. 15): 'Although in this section I continue to speak specifically of poetry, the distinction offered here separates not verse from prose but fictive from nonfictive speech. Novels are also imitations of discourse: the narrative itself, not only the events narrated, is "fictional"'.

30. David H. Richter, *Fable's End: Completeness and Closure in Rhetorical*

Fiction (Chicago & London: University of Chicago Press, 1974), p. vii.
31. *Ibid.*
32. See *Nineteenth-Century Fiction* 33 (1978), pp. 1-158; *Narrative Endings* (Berkeley: University of California Press, 1979).
33. J. Hillis Miller, 'The Problematic of Ending in Narrative', *Nineteenth-Century Fiction* 33 (1978), p. 3.
34. *Ibid.*, p. 7.
35. Frank Kermode, 'Sensing Endings', *Nineteenth-Century Fiction* 33 (1978), p. 144. Welsh, 'Opening and Closing *Les Misérables*', *Nineteenth-Century Fiction* 33 (1978), p. 9, argued that 'the main difference between my point of view and Miller's is that I see the "impossibility". . . of the endings of most nineteenth-century novels, as resulting not from violations of logic but from contradictions of desire'.
36. Torgovnick, *Closure*, p. 10.
37. *Ibid.*
38. *Ibid.*, pp. 3-4.
39. *Ibid.*, p. 5.
40. *Ibid.*
41. *Ibid.*, p. 13.
42. *Ibid.*, p. 14.
43. *Ibid.*, p. 16.
44. *Ibid.*, p. 18.
45. One other work should be noted in passing before leaving this section. *Narrative and its Discontents: Problems of Closure in the Traditional Novel* (Princeton: Princeton University Press, 1981) by D.A. Miller is another attempt to deal with the problematic of closure. Published simultaneously with Torgovnick's work (by the same publisher), Miller's book was evidently written independently of Torgovnick—neither mentions the other in text or bibliography. As Miller (p. xii) has noted: 'Although most of twentieth-century narratology pivots on the priority of ending, or narrative closure, it also takes nothing so much for granted'. Miller's basic argument (p. xiv) is 'not that novels do not "build" toward closure, but that they are never fully or finally governed by it'. Miller made several good points and will be utilized as a corrective to Torgovnick and others who understand the ending as always providing unity and coherence.
46. Torgovnick, *Closure*, p. 13.
47. *Ibid.*
48. *Ibid.*, p. 14.
49. *Ibid.*
50. *Ibid.*, p. 198.
51. *Ibid.*, p. 13.
52. See the citations of Aristotle on plot in D.A. Russell and M. Winterbottom, eds., *Ancient Literary Criticism: The Principal Texts in New Translations* (Oxford: Clarendon, 1972). For a critical and historical survey

of the use of plot and story in the novel, see Robert L. Caserio, *Plot, Story, and the Novel: From Dickens and Poe to the Modern Period* (Princeton: Princeton University Press, 1979).

53. E.M. Forster, *Aspects of the Novel* (San Diego: Harcourt, Brace, & Jovanovich, 1955; 1st edn, 1927), p. 27.

54. Shlomith Rimmon-Kenan, *Narrative Fiction: Contemporary Poetics* (London: Methuen, 1983), p. 16.

55. R.S. Crane, 'The Concept of Plot', *Approaches to the Novel*, ed. Robert Scholes (San Francisco: Chandler, 1961), p. 165. Norman Friedman, 'Forms of the Plot', *The Theory of the Novel*, ed. Philip Stevick (New York: Free Press, 1967), pp. 146-66, has subdivided Crane's basic plots into fourteen subplots.

56. Frank Kermode, *The Sense of an Ending*, p. 45.

57. Kieran Egan, 'What Is a Plot?', *New Literary History* 9 (1978), p. 461. Egan (pp. 455-60) sought to chart various understandings of plot from those who saw plot concretely as 'the outline of events' in the narrative itself to those who looked to the mind of the reader for evidence of organization.

58. M.H. Abrams, *A Glossary of Literary Terms* (New York: Holt, Reinhart, & Winston, 1971), p. 127.

59. Culpepper, *Anatomy*, p. 80.

60. Rimmon-Kenan, *Narrative Fiction*, p. 135.

61. Culpepper, *Anatomy*, pp. 84-98.

62. Stevick, *The Theory of the Novel*, p. 140.

63. Rimmon-Kenan, *Narrative Fiction*, p. 18.

64. Kermode, *The Sense of an Ending*, p. 45.

65. Edgar Allan Poe, 'The Philosophy of Composition', *The Complete Works of Edgar Allan Poe*, ed. James A. Harrison, Vol. XIV (New York: George D. Sproul, 1902), p. 193. Culpepper, *Anatomy*, p. 84, argued: 'Whereas we can only guess at the meaning of events we actually experience, events in a narrative have a definite meaning because they are part of a story which has an ending'.

66. Girard, *Deceit, Desire, and the Novel*, p. 307.

67. Miller, *Narrative and its Discontents*, pp. xiii-xiv.

68. One need only consider the problematic ending of Mark's Gospel to demonstrate this point.

69. Torgovnick, *Closure*, p. 13.

70. Minear, 'Luke's Use of the Birth Stories', pp. 111-30; R.E. Brown, *The Birth of the Messiah: A Commentary on the Infancy Narratives in Matthew and Luke* (Garden City: Doubleday, 1979); see also Alfred Plummer, *The Gospel According to St. Luke*, ICC (New York, Scribner, 1896), pp. xli-lxx. Plummer (p. lxix) identified the following elements in Luke 1–2 as occurring with high frequency in the rest of the Gospel: the construction of compound verbs; the use of the periphrastic; the repeated use of the articular infinitive; the frequency of πρός and the accusative with verbs of dialogue; the use of

the optative mood in indirect questions; the attraction of the relative pronoun; a characteristic use of ἐγένετο and αὐτός.

71. Torgovnick, *Closure*, p. 6.

72. E. Schweizer, *The Good News According to Luke*, trans. D.E. Green (Atlanta: John Knox Press, 1984), p. 378. Similarly, Fitzmyer, *Luke*, II, p. 1590, has noted: 'What Zechariah (1.22) could not do, that Jesus does to his silent followers'.

73. H. Hendrickx, *The Resurrection Narratives of the Synoptic Gospels* (London: Geoffrey Chapman, 1984), p. 98. Hendrickx concluded:

> Luke's intention of concluding with a priestly blessing can also be gathered from his repeated use of 'to bless/blessing' at the beginning (Lk. 1.42, 64; 2.28, 34) and at the end of his gospel (24.30, 50, 51, 53). The important difference is that, whereas in the first texts we are in a Temple context, at the end the blessing takes place outside the Temple, possibly symbolizing the beginning of the new age of the Church.

74. Torgovnick, *Closure*, p. 199.

75. R.J. Dillon, *From Eye-Witnesses to Ministers of the Word: Tradition and Composition in Luke 24*, AnBib, 82 (Rome: Biblical Institute, 1978), p. 176. I.H. Marshall, *Commentary on Luke*, NIGTC (Grand Rapids: Eerdmans, 1978), p. 909, has argued: 'The idea of Jesus as a priest does not seem to play any role in Lk.'

76. Fitzmyer, *Luke*, II, p. 1590.

77. This is not to suggest that the real author of the Third Gospel necessarily had this particular device in mind when he wrote the Gospel, nor is it necessary to argue so. Certainly, the Evangelists were not schooled in modern literary theory, but if the text itself allows for, or in fact demands, such interpretation, then such an understanding is quite legitimate.

78. Of the 38 occurrences of the word in the New Testament, 34 occur in Luke–Acts.

79. The parallel phrase occurs also at Acts 1.12.

80. At this point, one might note the *way* in which the disciples return to Jerusalem—'with great joy'. The theme of joy is a common one in Luke–Acts, particularly in the infancy narrative (1.14; 2.10). Both the coming of Jesus (his birth) and the going of Jesus (his departure) are occasions for great joy. See Marshall, *Luke*, p. 910.

81. D.M. Stanley, *Jesus in Gethsemene: The Early Church Reflects on the Suffering of Jesus* (New York: Paulist Press, 1980), p. 206.

82. The angel mentioned in Luke 24.43-44 occurs in a serious textual problem. External evidence is overwhelmingly in favor of omitting the passage as a later addition. Metzger, *A Textual Commentary*, p. 177, argued that it is more likely an interpolation 'added from an early source, oral or written, of extra-canonical traditions concerning the life and passion of Jesus' rather than an attempt to remove a reference to the humanity of Jesus which 'was incompatible with his sharing the divine omnipotence of the

Father'. Stanley, *Jesus in Gethsemene*, p. 207, while accepting the 'inspired character' of the passage, recognized that 'the opinion favoring non-authenticity of the verses is more than probable'. See Stanley's excellent discussion of the reasons for considering the verses 'an intrusion into the account' on pp. 205-207; also J.A. Fitzmyer, 'Papyrus Bodmer: Some Features of Our Oldest Text of Luke', *CBQ* 24 (1962), pp. 170-79; Jean Duplacy, 'La préhistoire du texte in Luc 22.43-44', *New Testament Textual Criticism: Its Significance for Exegesis: Essays in Honor of Bruce M. Metzger*, ed. E.J. Epp and G.D. Fee (Oxford: Oxford University Press, 1981), pp. 81-86; B.D. Ehrman and M.A. Plunkett, 'The Angel and the Agony: The Textual Problem of Luke 22.43-44', *CBQ* 45 (1983), pp. 401-16. Ehrman and Plunkett (p. 416) argued from external evidence, transcriptional (theological) and intrinsic (structural) probability 'that the problem is best resolved by considering the verses an interpolation into the text of Luke's Gospel, made sometime before AD 160'. To these arguments may now be added the one above drawn from narrative analysis of the whole Gospel. For the alternative view which accepts the verses as original, cf. Talbert, *Reading Luke*, p. 214. Talbert believed the passage 'fits with the overall tendency in Luke to depict Jesus as a martyr'. The shorter reading is preferred here and thus the reference to the angel is not dealt with in our treatment above.

83. While some might argue that the two men at the transfiguration scene are angels, they are explicitly identified as Moses and Elijah (9.30). The two men who appear at the empty tomb, however, are explicitly identified as angels at 24.23. What function do they serve? In Luke, the angels are used to introduce the birth of Jesus and to interpret that event to Mary and the shepherds. They are also used to introduce the resurrection of Jesus (24.4-7). These two men will reappear in Acts 1.10-11 with a similar function—to interpret the ascension for the disciples.

84. Torgovnick, *Closure*, p. 199.

85. This is what Tannehill has called a 'tragic story'. See R. Tannehill, 'Israel in Luke–Acts: A Tragic Story', *JBL* 104 (1985), pp. 69-85.

86. For a list of the references to 'temple' in Luke–Acts, see F.D. Weinert, 'The Meaning of the Temple in Luke–Acts', *BTB* 11 (1981), pp. 85-89. Literature on the temple in Luke–Acts is rather uneven. The more recent and important works are listed below: M. Bachmann, *Jerusalem und der Tempel: Die geographisch-theologischen Elemente in der lukanischen Sicht des jüdischen Kultzentrums* (Stuttgart: Kohlhammer, 1980); K. Baltzer, 'The Meaning of the Temple in the Lukan Writings', *HTR* 58 (1965), pp. 263-77; T. Brodie, 'A New Temple and a New Law: The Unity and Chronicler-based Nature of Luke 1.1-4.22a', *JSNT* 5 (1979), pp. 21-45; W. Horbury, 'New Wine in Old Skins: IX—The Temple', *ExpTim* 86 (1974), pp. 36-42; Naymond Keathley, 'The Temple in Luke–Acts' (Ph.D. dissertation, The Southern Baptist Theological Seminary, 1971); R. Laurentin, *Jésus au Temple: Mystère de pâques et foi de Marie en Luc 2, 48-50* (Paris: Gabalda,

1966); C. Van der Waal, 'The Temple in the Gospel according to Luke', *Neotestamentica* 7 (1973), pp. 44-59.

87.   Culpepper, *Anatomy*, pp. 85-86. Fitzmyer *Luke*, I. p. 164, dubbed Jerusalem 'the city of destiny for Jesus and the pivot for the salvation of mankind'.

88.   Henry James, *The Art of the Novel*, ed. R.P. Blackmur (New York: Scribner, 1907, rpt 1962), p. 6.

89.   Other references in the last chapter of Luke might be mentioned in passing as contributing to the closural effect by pointing the reader back to the first chapters, but those mentioned above seem to cover the most important ones and certainly provide sufficient evidence for the following conclusion: Luke 24, particularly 24.50-53, serves to give a sense of completion, and thus closure, to the Gospel.

90.   Torgovnick, *Closure*, p. 13.

91.   V.S. Bann and J.E. Bowlt, eds., *Russian Formalism: A Collection of Articles and Texts in Translation* (Edinburgh: Scottish Academic Press, 1973), pp. 6-19.

92.   Joseph Tyson has offered an initial sounding for a literary analysis of the theme of conflict. See his 'Conflict as a Literary Theme in the Gospel of Luke', *New Synoptic Studies: The Cambridge Gospel Conference and Beyond*, ed. William R. Farmer (Macon, GA: Mercer University Press, 1983), pp. 303-27. Tyson did not confine his study to temple or synagogue conflict scenes, though they did comprise the greatest number of his examples. Tyson also made no attempt to address the resolution of these conflict scenes in the Gospel.

93.   On conflict as a literary strategy in the Gospels, see Rhoads and Michie, *Mark as Story*, p. 191; J.D. Kingsbury, *Matthew as Story* (Philadelphia: Fortress, 1986), pp. 2-9.

94.   On settings in literary theory, see Chatman, *Story and Discourse*, pp. 138-45; Wesley Kort, *Narrative Elements and Religious Meanings* (Philadelphia: Fortress, 1975), pp. 20-39. On settings in the Gospels, see Rhoads and Michie, *Mark as Story*, pp. 63-72; Kingsbury, *Matthew as Story*, pp. 27-29.

95.   The distinction between public and private settings is made by Rhoads and Michie, *Mark as Story*, p. 67. Unlike Mark, however, the conflicts between Jesus and the religious authorities in Luke do not always occur in public settings.

96.   Here I use the categories employed by Elizabeth Struthers Malbon in *Narrative Space and Mythic Meaning in Mark* (San Francisco: Harper & Row, 1986), pp. 131-36.

97.   *Ibid.*

98.   Historically speaking, the category 'religious authorities' encompasses some very diverse groups—scribes, Pharisees, and synagogue rulers. I have chosen to distinguish between the settings of the conflict between Jesus and

the Jewish leaders rather than the character groupings of scribes, Pharisees, and synagogue rulers because, from a literary perspective, these categories of leadership are essentially collapsed in the narrative. On the ways in which these groups fulfill the same narrative role in Luke, see Tannehill, *The Narrative Unity of Luke–Acts* pp. 169-99. On the way in which the Jewish leaders function as a 'single character' in the other Gospels, see Rhoads and Michie, *Mark as Story*, pp. 117-22; Kingsbury, *Matthew as Story*, pp. 13-17; Culpepper, *Anatomy*, 125-32.

99. These meal-time conflicts may be heightened in the narrative by the conflict in the Levi story (19.1-10) where the narrator reports that they *all* grumbled against Jesus, not just the Pharisees.

100. This passage is also the third and last Sabbath-healing controversy in Luke. The other two are set in the synagogue (6.6-11; 13.10-17).

101. This passage also has remarkable similarities to the feeding of the multitudes in 9.10-17. See Tannehill, *Narrative Unity of Luke–Acts*, pp. 289-90.

102. Dillon, *Eye-Witnesses*, p. 104.

103. The word οἶκος does not occur in the pericope, but is, of course, implied by the narrative.

104. If Dillon, Tannehill, and others are correct in suggesting that Luke 24.41-43 is a meal scene, then this meal scene provides the context for instruction—a typical element of the other meals. Thus, this last meal with the disciples would add to the sense of resolution of the meal-time conflicts. See Tannehill, *Narrative Unity of Luke–Acts*, pp. 291-92: Dillon, *Eye-Witnesses*, pp. 189-203.

105. On Luke 24.47, see Jacques Dupont, 'La portée christologique de l'évangélisation des nations d'après Luc 24.47', in *Neues Testament und Kirche: Für Rudolf Schnackenburg*, ed. Joachim Gnilka (Freiburg: Herder, 1974), pp. 125-43.

106. Tannehill, *Narrative Unity of Luke–Acts*, p. 293, has noted about 24.41: 'This statement is evidently intended to describe an ambiguous response'.

107. I am indebted in this section to an unpublished response by Tannehill to my paper 'Narrative Closure and Openness in the Plot of the Third Gospel: The Sense of an Ending in Luke 24.50-53', *Society of Biblical Literature 1986 Seminar Papers*, ed. Kent Harold Richards (Atlanta: Scholars Press, 1986), pp. 201-23.

108. N.R. Petersen, *Literary Criticism for New Testament Critics* (Philadelphia: Fortress, 1978), p. 83. Petersen's language has the advantage of describing the narrative strategy of both Luke and Acts. Cf., however, Arland J. Hultgren, *Jesus and his Adversaries: The Form and Function of the Conflict Stories in the Synoptic Tradition* (Minneapolis: Augsburg, 1979), who argued that conflict stories had *less* significance for Luke than for the other Synoptics.

109. The six confrontation incidents according to Petersen (*ibid.*, p. 89), are found in Luke 4.16-30; 20.1-19; Acts 3–4; 5.12-42; 13.13-52; 18.1-11.

110. Tyson, 'Conflict as a Literary Theme', p. 314.

111. The information that the visitor was an angel of the Lord had already been given to the reader at 1.11.

112. Luke placed the temple episode third and last in the series of temptations, perhaps to underscore the significance of this trial in comparison to the other two. Compare Matt. 4.1-11, where the narrator has placed the temple scene second, reserving the mountain temptation (mountains being as significant in Matthew as the temple is in Luke).

113. Tyson, 'Conflict as a Literary Theme', p. 315.

114. No attempt will be made here to deal with the resolution of these confrontation scenes in Acts, though it should be noted that what seems to be resolved for the Gospel is re-opened in the conflict scene in the temple at Acts 3–4.

115. R.J. Karris, *Invitation to Luke: A Commentary on the Gospel of Luke with Complete Text from the Jerusalem Bible* (Garden City: Image Books, 1977), has admirably captured the finality of the closing scene of Luke:

> I can still recall the powerful emotions which pulsed through me when I finished reading John Steinbeck's *The Grapes of Wrath*. Its last chapter harnessed all the themes of the book into one overwhelming image, that of a nursing mother giving suckle and life to a starving adult. This example of the summarizing character of a book's last chapter leads us down the road to appreciating Luke's achievement in chapter 24.

116. Tyson, 'Conflict as a Literary Theme', p. 326.

117. This statement, of course, assumes the text-critical position of Chapter 2 that προσκυνήσαντες αὐτόν is a later interpolation.

118. Obviously, none of the Gospels ends in the same way. Because Luke has so emphasized the temple as the place of conflict, it is appropriate that the Gospel end there with conflict resolved.

119. Torgovnick, *Closure*, p. 13, has commented: 'Often less obvious than circularity, parallelism becomes clear only upon retrospective analysis'. Such a statement is supported by a perusal of the commentaries, monographs, and articles on this passage, the majority of which notice the circular concordance between the beginning and end of the story, while few argue that the disciples in the temple in any way resolves a major tension developed throughout the narrative.

120. The scene may not close as neatly as first appears, particularly when the reader recalls Jesus' statement that he had been teaching in the temple daily and no one had bothered him. The least one might expect in a sequel is that the major conflicts would occur outside the temple. Such, of course, is not the case with Acts.

121. Paul Schubert, 'The Structure and Significance of Luke 24', *Neutestamentliche Studien für Rudolf Bultmann*, ed. W. Eltester (Berlin: Töpelmann, 1957), pp. 165-86.

122. P. Minear, 'Luke's Use of the Birth Stories', pp. 111-30. Minear (pp. 119-20), while accepting the basic theme of prophecy and fulfillment, criticized Schubert's understanding of what was being fulfilled; N.A. Dahl, 'The Story of Abraham in Luke–Acts', *Studies in Luke–Acts: Essays presented in honor of Paul Schubert*, ed. L.E. Keck and J. Louis Martyn (Nashville: Abingdon, 1966), pp. 139-59; L. Johnson, *Possessions in Luke–Acts*; R.J. Karris, *What Are They Saying About Luke and Acts?* (New York: Paulist Press, 1979). See also J. Dupont, 'L'utilisation apologétique de l'ancien Testament dans les discours des Actes', *ETL* 29 (1953), pp. 289-327; E. Lohse, 'Lukas als Theologe der Heilsgeschichte', *EvT* 14 (1954), pp. 256-75; S. Schulz, 'Gottes Vorsehung bei Lukas', *ZNW* 54 (1963), pp. 104-16; Christoph Burchard, *Der dreizehnte Zeuge* (Göttingen: Vandenhoeck & Ruprecht, 1970), p. 185; Karl Löning, *Die Saulustradition in der Apostelgeschichte* (Münster: Aschendorff, 1973); G. Schneider, 'Zur Bedeutung von *kathexēs* im lukanischen Doppelwerk', *ZNW* 68 (1977), pp. 128-31; D.L. Tiede, *Prophecy and History in Luke–Acts* (Philadelphia: Fortress, 1980); O.C. Edwards, *Luke's Story of Jesus* (Philadelphia: Fortress, 1981).

123. C.H. Talbert, 'Promise and Fulfillment in Lucan Theology', *Luke–Acts: New Perspectives from the Society of Biblical Literature Seminar*, ed. C.H. Talbert (New York: Crossroad, 1984), pp. 91-103. At this point, we will deal only with Talbert's summary and critique of the 'proof-from-prophecy' school (pp. 91-96). The second half of his argument, that 'in Luke–Acts the prophecy-fulfillment schema functions very much as it does in its Mediterranean milieu' (p. 101), will be addressed below under 'Reader Response'.

124. *Ibid.*, p. 93.

125. *Ibid.*, p. 95.

126. *Ibid.*, p. 94. These helpful categories are expanded in 'Excursus A: The Fulfillment of Prophecy in Luke–Acts', of Talbert's *Reading Luke*, pp. 234-40.

127. *Ibid.*, p. 93.

128. R. Maddox, *The Purpose of Luke–Acts* (Göttingen: Vandenhoeck & Ruprecht, 1982), p. 155, made a similar point when he argued: 'These passages pointing to the fulfilment of *prophecies* in Scripture are different from those where *commands* of Scripture are deliberately obeyed: Luke 2.22-24; 10.26f.; Acts 23.5; and from those where theological argument is supported by reference to Scripture: Luke 19.46; 20.17, 28, 37, 42'. See further, J.A. Sanders, 'Isaiah in Luke', *Int* 36 (1982), pp. 144-55.

129. Talbert, 'Promise and Fulfillment', p. 94. Recently, Charles H. Cosgrove, 'The Divine *DEI* in Luke–Acts: Investigations into the Understanding of God's Providence', *NovT* 26 (1984), pp. 168-90, has argued along similar lines. According to Cosgrove (pp. 172-73), of the forty occurrences of *dei* in Luke–Acts, at least thirteen reflect an ordinary usage for ethical obligation or claims for better judgment and not divine necessity. Cosgrove, (p. 189) concluded: 'The term *dei* is not a *terminus technicus* in Luke–Acts

but carries a wide range of meaning. There is, however, within this circle of broad usage a motif of the divine "must" that is crucially important to Luke'. Cosgrove, like Talbert, recognized that while the term *dei may* reflect divine necessity, it does not necessarily do so! For other studies on the divine *dei* in Luke–Acts, consult: H.J. Cadbury, *The Making of Luke–Acts*, pp. 303-305; Erich Fascher, 'Theologische Beobachtungen zu *dei*', *Neutestamentliche Studien für Rudolf Bultmann*, ed. W. Eltester (Berlin: Töpelmann, 1954), pp. 228-54.

130. Talbert, 'Promise and Fulfillment', p. 101. With this statement there seems to be an *opinio communis*. See Maddox, *The Purpose of Luke–Acts*, p. 139; Fitzmyer, *Luke*, I, pp. 179-80.

131. The term *narrator* is employed to refer to the one who tells the story. The narrator is a rhetorical device whose purpose it is to introduce the reader to the narrative world and the characters which populate it. Also, masculine pronouns are consistently used when referring to the narrator. While the gender of the narrator cannot be established, Susan Lanser, *The Narrative Act: Point of View in Prose Fiction* (Princeton: Princeton University Press, 1981), p. 16 reasonably argued 'writers and narrators are presumed male unless the text offers a marking to the contrary'.

132. The distinction between 'narrative time' and 'story time' was popularized by Gerard Genette in *Narrative Discourse: An Essay in Method*, trans. Jane E. Lewin (Ithaca: Cornell University Press, 1980). Story time refers to the passage of time within a particular story-frame; in our case, the passing of time between the annunciation of the birth of John the Baptist and the departure of Jesus in Luke. Narrative time on the other hand, is determined by what Genette called order (sequence), duration (relationship of length of narrative to the length of the story), and frequency.

133. On Luke's reference to καθεξῆς in his preface, R.J. Dillon, 'Previewing Luke's Project from his Prologue (Luke 1.1-4)', *CBQ* 43 (1981), p. 219, argued that of the three types of sequence available to this word (temporal, geographical, and logical), 'we prefer to apply at Luke 1.3 the sense that emerges in Acts 11, that of logical or idea-sequence'. Likewise, M. Völkel 'Exegetische Erwägungen zum Verständnis des Begriffs *kathedzēs* im lukanischen Prolog', *NTS* 20 (1973-74), p. 294, has claimed: '*kathedzēs* as depicting the modality of a literary presentation therefore refers not to the events recorded, either by way of chronological exactitude or factual completeness, but to that which constitutes the correct understanding of the events'.

134. Genette, *Narrative Discourse*, p. 40.

135. *Ibid*.

136. The analepses and prolepses could be clarified further. Internal analepses which recall an earlier part of the narrative already narrated are called *repeating* analepses. Those which refer to events which have already happened, but which are not narrated are known as *completing* analepses.

Similarly, internal prolepses which point forward to events which will eventually be narrated within the time of the narrative are repeating prolepses, while those which prefigure events not described in the narrative are completing prolepses. These categories, while helpful, are not necessary to the task here. See Genette, *Narrative Discourse*, pp. 40-76.

137. Cosgrove, 'The Divine *DEI* in Luke-Acts', p. 174. Similarly, Fitzmyer, *Luke*, I, p. 180, noted: 'Often enough, Luke interprets OT passages, which were not in themselves prophetic, not only as prophetic, but even as predictive'.

138. Maddox, *The Purpose of Luke-Acts*, p. 142.

139. *Ibid.*

140. The exception, Luke 24.47, will be discussed below under 'Linkage'.

141. Maddox, *The Purpose of Luke-Acts*, p. 142. Maddox (p. 155) noted that Acts 1.16-20 (the betrayal and death of Judas) is an 'exception to this concentration on the main lines of the story of Jesus'.

142. Contrast the external prolepsis in Mark 16.7.

143. Note, however, the important prophecy of Simeon 'for glory to your people Israel' (2.32) which creates expectations about Israel which are repeatedly thwarted and frustrated throughout Luke and Acts. See Tannehill, 'A Tragic Story', pp. 74-76.

144. A phrase used by Kermode, *The Sense of an Ending*, p. 3. Petersen, 'When is the End not the End?', p. 158, has remarked: 'By communicating information about the implied reader's present in the form of predictions made in the past, the narrator also objectifies the reader's tumultuous present as having been predictively past'.

145. See below under 'The Central Section of Luke (9.51-19.44)'.

146. Talbert, 'Promise and Fulfillment', p. 92.

147. For a succinct summary of the various interpretations of ἔξοδος at Luke 9.31, see Sharon H. Ringe, 'Luke 9.28-36: The Beginning of an Exodus', *Semeia* 28 (1983), pp. 92-94.

148. Dillon, 'Prologue', p. 212. In this article, Dillon, 'Prologue', p. 223, argued:

> Luke is conscious of the overarching and compelling logic of the divine plan at every step of his two-volume work, and the 'order' of each happening— where and when he locates it—expresses how it obeys that logic and fits that plan. Since, moreover, the divine plan guides history according to the rhythm of 'promise and fulfillment', the 'directional thrust' of an event, displayed by its 'ordering', will often involve the manifest way it brings the prophecies to realization, or points forward to such realization in the future.

149. Culpepper, *Anatomy*, p. 70; Rimmon-Kenan, *Narrative Fiction*, p. 48.

150. Rimmon-Kenan's position is a modification of Genette who claimed prolepsis was incompatible with suspense. See Genette, *Narrative Discourse*, p. 105.

151. Only the most recent and important are mentioned here: J.H. Davies, 'The Purpose of the Central Section of Luke's Gospel', *SE* II (=*TU* 87; Berlin: Akademie, 1964); J. Drury, *Tradition and Design in Luke's Gospel* (Atlanta: John Knox Press, 1976), pp. 138-64; H.L. Egelkraut, *Jesus' Mission to Jerusalem: A redaction critical study of the Travel Narrative in the Gospel of Luke, Lk 9.51–19.48* (Frankfurt: Peter Lang, 1976); C.F. Evans, 'The Central Section of St. Luke's Gospel', *Studies in the Gospels: Essays in Memory of R.H. Lightfoot*, ed. D.E. Nineham (Oxford: Blackwell, 1955), pp. 37-53; J.A. Fitzmyer, 'The Composition of Luke, Chapter 9', *Perspectives on Luke–Acts*, ed. C.H. Talbert (Danville: ABPR, 1978), pp. 149-52; W. Gasse, 'Zum Reisebericht des Lukas', *ZNW* 34 (1935), pp. 293-99; D. Gill, 'Observations on the Lukan Travel Narrative and Some Related Passages', *HTR* 63 (1970), pp. 199-221; W. Grundmann, 'Fragen der Komposition des lukanischen Reiseberichts', *ZNW* 50 (1959), pp. 252-70; M. Miyoshi, *Der Anfang des Reiseberichts: Lk 9.51–10.24*, AnBib, 60 (Rome: Biblical Institute, 1974); David P. Moessner, 'Luke 9.1-50: Luke's Preview of the Journey of the Prophet like Moses of Deuteronomy', *JBL* 102 (1983), pp. 575-605; G. Ogg, 'The Central Section of the Gospel according to St. Luke', *NTS* 18 (1971-72), pp. 39-53; P. von der Osten-Sacken, 'Zur Christologie des lukanischen Reiseberichts', *EvT* 33 (1973), pp. 476-96; B. Reicke, 'Instruction and Discussion in the Travel Narrative', *SE* I (=*TU*) 73, 1959, pp. 206-16; J.L. Resseguie, 'Interpretation of Luke's Central Section Luke 9.51-19.44) since 1856', *StBibTh* 5 (1975), pp. 3-36; W.C. Robinson Jr, 'The Theological Context for Interpreting Luke's Travel Narrative (9.51ff.)', *JBL* 79 (1960), pp. 20-31; F. Stagg, 'The Journey Toward Jerusalem in Luke's Gospel', *R&E* 64 (1967), pp. 499-512; G.W. Trompf, 'La section médiane de l'évangile de Luc: l'organisation des documents', *RHPR* 53 (1973), pp. 141-54; J.W. Wenham, 'Synoptic Independence and the Origin of Luke's Travel Narrative', *NTS* 27 (1980-81), pp. 507-15. See Egelkraut, *Jesus' Mission to Jerusalem*, pp. 238-57 for additional bibliography.

152. Marshall, *Historian and Theologian*, pp. 149-50.

153. Marshall, *Luke*, pp. 401-402, claimed; 'the general themes of the section are hard to define and it is even more difficult to find any kind of thread running through it'.

154. For a summary of the positions taken on the extent of the section, see J.L. Resseguie, 'Interpretation of Luke's Central Section', p. 3.

155. *Ibid.*, p. 4.

156. B.H. Streeter, *The Four Gospels*, p. 203. Streeter described the nomenclature 'The Central Section' as 'a title which states a fact but begs no questions'.

157. For arguments for and against this view, see Resseguie, 'Interpretation of Luke's Central Section', p. 3.

158. *Ibid.*, pp. 3-36. Resseguie, however, provided a helpful summary with little or no critique.

159. Moessner, 'Luke 9.51', p. 577.

160. *Ibid.*

161. *Ibid.*, p. 588.

162. *Ibid.*

163. *Ibid.*, p. 582. Moessner went on to ask: 'Can we be satisfied with an evangelist whose literary felicity does not include a credible picture at the level of the story of Jesus' words and deeds? Can we dismiss the undramatic flair of more than one-third of Luke's storytelling artistry as simply an adherence to a normative unpatterned gospel pattern? When all is said and done, is the journey motif merely a convenient silo for a farrago of tradition?'

164. Henry James, 'Initial Intentions and Final Forms', *The Theory of the Novel*, ed. Philip Stevick (New York: Free Press, 1967), p. 168. In the second half of his essay, Moessner argued ('Luke 9.51', p. 579): 'Luke has dynamically structured his story-stuff by integrating his plot devices around a fourfold movement or plot motivation, namely, the calling and fate of Moses in Deuteronomy'. Though Moessner's conclusions could be questioned, his effort to determine the plot devices which motivate the story through the travel scenes must be applauded.

165. Moessner, 'Luke 9.51', p. 579.

166. Cited by Stagg, 'The Journey Toward Jerusalem', p. 499.

167. Rimmon-Kenan, *Narrative Fiction*, p. 126.

168. Talbert, *Literary Patterns*, p. 112.

169. See the above comments by Rimmon-Kenan on the effects of delay in narrative.

170. D.A. Miller, *Narrative and its Discontents*, p. xiii.

171. J. Hillis Miller, 'The Problematic of Ending in Narrative', *Nineteenth-Century Fiction* 33 (1978), p. 3.

172. Torgovnick, *Closure*, p. 14. I am indebted to Robert Tannehill, whose correspondence, questions, and writings have provided much of the stimulation for this section. Gratitude is expressed also for his willingness to make available to me the pertinent parts of his then unpublished manuscript, *The Narrative Unity of Luke–Acts*.

173. Torgovnick, *Closure*, p. 15.

174. *Ibid.*

175. Lucian, 52-54, 63-64; cited by J. Dupont, 'La Question du plan des Actes des Apôtres à la lumière d'un texte du Lucien de Samosate', *NovT* 21 (1979), pp. 220-31.

176. See Tannehill, *Narrative Unity of Luke–Acts*, p. 295.

177. Dupont, 'La Question du plan des Actes', p. 225. For the ways in which 24.47-49 also connects with earlier parts of the Acts narrative, see Tannehill, *Narrative Unity of Luke–Acts*, pp. 293-98.

178. On the ambiguity involved in gapping and closure, see Meir Sternberg, *The Poetics of Biblical Literature: Ideological Literature and the Drama of*

Reading (Bloomington: Indiana University Press, 1985), pp. 258-63.

179. Torgovnick, *Closure*, p. 13.

180. *Ibid.* Some studies would label such incomplete closure as 'anti-closural'. See Smith, *Poetic Closure*.

181. Tannehill, 'Israel in Luke–Acts', p. 72.

182. *Ibid.*, p. 85. Tannehill (p. 81) distinguished between the emotions of anguish, pity, and fear aroused by tragedy (see Aristotle, *Poetics* 1450-1453) and the hatred of anti-Judaism to argue that the story of Israel, for Luke, is tragic not bitter (cf. Jack Saunders, *et al.*).

183. Torgovnick, *Closure*, p. 14.

184. *Ibid.*, p. 15.

185. *Ibid.* The appropriateness of the ending and its implications for meaning are usually available to the reader after reflection and perhaps even some emotional distance from the story.

186. Susan Lanser, *The Narrative Act*, pp. 12-63. Lanser (pp. 3-4) remarked: 'Who we are, what we know, desire, and believe, what we have learned to notice and value, how we interact with other beings and things, all provide an intricate nexus of conditions, an unavoidable (though not unalterable) context, within which individuals and groups of people see the world. This means that human perception is always structured upon a relationship of perceiver to perceived—upon a *point of view*.'

187. B. Uspensky, *A Poetics of Composition. The Structure of the Artistic Text and Typology of a Compositional Form*, trans. Valentina Zavarin and Susan Wittig (Berkeley: University of California Press, 1973). The choice of Uspensky was made even more confidently because he includes a fifteen-page section on framing and point of view; see pp. 137-51.

188. *Ibid.*, p. 137.

189. *Ibid.*, p. 146.

190. *Ibid.*, p. 147.

191. *Ibid.*, p. 148.

192. *Ibid.*, p. 81. See also pp. 81-100.

193. *Ibid.*, pp. 58-65.

194. *Ibid.*, pp. 65-75.

195. *Ibid.*, pp. 17-55.

196. *Ibid.*, pp. 8-16.

197. *Ibid.*, p. 148.

198. *Ibid.*, p. 149.

199. One might argue that the reference to the disciples returning to Jerusalem 'with joy', could be an inside view; one could, on the other hand, argue that such joy was quite visible on the part of the disciples by the looks on their faces and the songs on their lips. At any rate, this reference, if an inside view, is negligible when compared with the earlier reference to the disciples 'disbelieving' for joy.

200. *Ibid.*, p. 149.

201. *Ibid.*, p. 65.

202. *Ibid.*

203. Uspensky's silent scene modifies Torgovnick's close-up ending. To be sure, the closing scene of the Gospel is a close-up and not an overview ending. Nevertheless, it is not close enough to allow the reader to hear precisely what was said or see exactly where Jesus went!

204. *Ibid.*, p. 149. Uspensky went on to cite the Gospel of Luke as an example of a narrative 'which begins from a retrospective position with a direct address to Theophilus'.

205. *Ibid.*

206. According to W. Bauer, *A Greek-English Lexicon of the New Testament and Other Early Christian Literature*, ed. F. Danker and trans. William Arndt and F. Wilbur Gingrich (London: University of Chicago Press, 1979), p. 179, διὰ παντός indicates 'extension over a whole period of time, to its very end'.

207. Uspensky, *A Poetics of Composition*, p. 150. Uspensky also noted: 'Fixation of time at the beginning of a narrative... may also be realized by the use of the imperfective aspect of the past tense (in *verba dicendi*)'. This phenomenon may be observed in Luke 1 where we find an imperfect periphrastic 'the multitude of people were praying at the hour of incense'. In both cases, at the beginning and the end, in sharp contrast to the middle of the narrative, time is static—a typical framing device.

208. *Ibid.*

209. One might also mention the angels in chs. 1 and 24 if the larger infancy and resurrection narratives are taken into consideration.

210. This suggestion differs from what Uspensky has described on the phraseological plane. Uspensky spoke of characters figuring only in the frame of a narrative and not the text. This argument supposes a characteristic which appears at beginning and end but not in the middle.

211. Uspensky, *A Poetics of Composition*, p. 8.

212. Genette, *Narrative Discourse*, p. 186. This distinction dispels the problem of other studies of point of view which treat the two questions as one.

213. Rimmon-Kenan, *Narrative Fiction*, p. 72.

214. This observation will gain significance when later it is argued that the ascension scene in Acts is seen from the perspective of the disciples.

215. Torgovnick, *Closure*, p. 16. Torgovnick distinguished between real author, implied author, and narrator; here reference will be to the narrator of Luke unless otherwise indicated.

216. M.H. Abrams, 'How to do Things with Texts', *Partisan Review* 46 (1979), p. 566.

217. E.V. McKnight, *The Bible and the Reader: An Introduction to Literary Criticism* (Philadelphia: Fortress, 1985). For a review of McKnight's work, see Mikeal C. Parsons, '*The Bible and the Reader*: A Reader's Response', *PersRelSt* 14 (1987), pp. 79-82.

218. For a description and definition of these various terms, see Culpepper, *Anatomy*, pp. 205-207.

219. Robert M. Fowler, 'Who is "the Reader" in Reader Response Criticism?', *Semeia* 31 (1985), p. 13.

220. For other literature on reader response criticism, see the Bibliography in Fowler, 'Who is "the Reader"?', pp. 22-23. Especially note the distinction made between 'critic' and 'reader' by George Steiner, 'Critic/Reader', *New Literary History* 10 (1979), pp. 423-52.

221. S. Chatman, *Story and Discourse: Narrative Structure in Fiction and Film* (Ithaca: Cornell University, 1978), p. 150.

222. W. Booth, *The Rhetoric of Fiction* (Chicago: University of Chicago, 1979), p. 138.

223. W. Iser, *The Implied Reader* (Baltimore: Johns Hopkins, 1974), p. 34. See also *The Act of Reading* (Baltimore: Johns Hopkins, 1978).

224. On information theory see Colin Cherry, *On Human Communication* (Cambridge, Mass.: M.I.T. Press, 1957); J.P. Pearce, *Symbols, Signals and Noise: The Nature and Process of Communication* (New York: Harper & Row, 1961); C.L. Book, *et al.*, *Human Communication Principles, Contexts and Skills* (New York: St. Martin Press, 1980).

225. J.C. Anderson, 'Double and Triple Stories, the Implied Reader, and Redundancy in Matthew', *Semeia* 31 (1985), p. 82. See also Susan Rubin Suleiman, 'Redundancy and the "Readable" Text', *Poetics Today* 1 (1980), pp. 119-42; Susan Wittig, 'Formulaic Style and the Problem of Redundancy', *Centrum* 1 (1973), pp. 123-36. Wittig (p. 127) suggested that redundancy could also be detected in terms of plot as well as in syntactical and metrical patterns: 'many of the narratives will be seen to be structurally redundant in terms of plot as well as verse-form; that is, having heard or read the first scene, made up of a number of obligatory motifs, an audience familiar with several narratives in the same genre can predict the composition of the second scene, and so on, through the course of the narrative'. R.A. Culpepper, 'Redundancy and the Implied Reader in Matthew: A Response to Janice Capel Anderson and Fred W. Burnett' (Seminar Response Paper, SBL Literary Aspects of the Gospels and Acts, 1983), p. 3, defined redundancy as 'essentially the superfluity of means for conveying important information in any communication process'.

226. Anderson, 'Double and Triple Stories', pp. 84-85.

227. Culpepper, 'Response', p. 4. Suleiman, 'Redundancy', p. 120, has also noted that redundancy may occur at various levels and is not limited to simple verbal repetition within the text.

228. That the reference to the disciples involves a much larger group than the Twelve (or Eleven in ch. 24) is clear in both passages. At Luke 19.37 mention is made of an 'entire multitude of disciples', while the witnesses of the final appearance and departure of the Risen Christ included at least the two travelers to Emmaus (24.13), the Eleven and those with them (24.33),

and most probably the women who were at the empty tomb (24.11). For a detailed argument favoring this view, see Quentin Quesnell, 'The Women at Luke's Supper', *Political Issues in Luke–Acts*, ed. R.J. Cassidy and P.J. Scharper (Maryknoll: Orbis, 1983), p. 60. See also Rosalie Ryan, 'The Women from Galilee and Discipleship in Luke', *BTB* 15 (1985), pp. 56-69; Elizabeth Schüssler-Fiorenza, *In Memory of Her* (New York: Crossroad, 1983), p. 138; Ben Witherington, 'On the Road with Mary Magdalene, Joanna, Susanna and Other Disciples', *ZNW* 70 (1979), pp. 243-48.

229. G. Lohfink, *Die Himmelfahrt Jesu: Untersuchungen zu den Himmelfahrts- und Erhöhungstexten bei Lukas* (Munich: Kösel-Verlag, 1971), p. 166, translated ἔχω ἕως as 'in Richtung auf'.

230. It is interesting to note that Mark made free use of Bethany (11.1, 11, 12; 14.3) and that where Luke has recorded (21.37) that Jesus 'lodged on the mount called Olivet', Mark's narrative recorded Jesus lodging at *Bethany* with the twelve (11.11). Matthew, however, made no mention of Bethany at the Triumphal Entry, only Bethphage and the Mount of Olives (21.1), but did record Jesus lodging not at the Mount of Olives, but at Bethany. In addition, both Mark and Matthew recounted the anointing at Bethany which is missing in Luke.

231. Marshall, *Luke*, p. 908.

232. Lohfink, *Himmelfahrt*, pp. 202-207.

233. Interestingly, neither the Marcan account (Mark 11.1-10) nor the Matthean account (21.1-9) explicitly identify as disciples those who are lining the way with coats or palm branches.

234. Culpepper, 'Response', p. 2.

235. Anderson, 'Double and Triple Stories', p. 85.

236. See Chapter 2.

237. Culpepper, 'Response', p. 2.

238. Anderson, 'Double and Triple Stories', p. 85.

239. Culpepper, 'Response', p. 2.

240. Edgar Allan Poe, 'Tale-Writing—Nathaniel Hawthorne', *The Complete Works of Edgar Allan Poe*, XIII, p. 153.

241. Torgovnick, *Closure*, p. 16.

242. S. Fish, 'Literature in the Reader: Affective Stylistics', *New Literary History* 2 (1970), p. 145. There is a debate among literary theorists whether interpretation should be text-controlled or reader-controlled. E.D. Hirsch, *Validity in Interpretation* (New Haven: Yale University Press, 1967); M.H. Abrams, 'How to do Things with Texts', pp. 566-88; and to some extent the earlier work by Iser, *The Implied Reader*; represent those who advocate text-centered controls of interpretation. Supporters of reader-generated interpretations have found an able spokesperson in Fish, *Is There a Text in This Class?: The Authority of Interpretive Communities* (Cambridge: Harvard University Press, 1980). See also Iser, *The Act of Reading*. The view taken here is that meaning is generated in the act of reading (Fish, Iser), but that

wild subjectivity is checked by the presence of a text. Interpretations are no longer to be judged as 'correct' or 'incorrect' but interpretations must be measured by the standard of the text as more or less plausible. And interpreters must stand ready to accept the fact that multiple meanings may be plausible interpretations of the same text.

243. Chatman, *Story and Discourse*, p. 150.

244. Kermode, 'Sensing Endings', p. 151. Commenting on the ending of Mark, Kermode (pp. 147-48) noted: 'If you do not like the ending of the gospel, you can no longer make up your own conclusion, but you can invent a prehistory to explain why it is unsatisfactory'.

245. See Chapter 2.

246. Some MSS read 'praising God' (D it). Others have conflated the two readings and have 'praising and blessing God' (A C² W 063 f¹·¹³ M lat syᵖ·ʰ *et al.*).

247. Metzger, *A Textual Commentary*, p. 191.

248. N. Petersen, 'When is the End not the End? Literary Reflections on the Ending of Mark's Narrative', *Int* 34 (1980), pp. 151-66.

249. *Ibid.*, p. 151.

250. Talbert, *Reading Luke*, p. 236. Talbert (pp. 236-37) cited Lucian's *Alexander the False Prophet*, Suetonius' *Life of Vespasian*, and the ancient novel by Apuleius, *The Golden Ass*. From Jewish works, Talbert (pp. 237-38) listed the deuteronomic history of the Hebrew Scriptures, Qumran commentaries on Isaiah, Micah, Psalm 37, Habakkuk, and Josephus' *Antiquities*. Talbert (p. 237) employed this evidence in a slightly different manner than here, arguing that in each case the fulfillment of oracles 'legitimates the religious or political authority of the person to whom the prophecy referred or of the god who gave it'.

251. Petersen, 'When is the End not the End?' p. 153.

252. Discussion from this point will involve only the variant 'and he ascended into heaven'. Similar arguments could be made for the variant 'and they worshipped him'; however, since this variant is more ancillary to the closural strategies in Luke 24.50-53 and since it has already been considered in some detail in Chapter 2, it is omitted from consideration here.

253. Kermode, 'Sensing Endings', p. 148. Kermode's words on the ending of Mark are equally appropriate in consideration of the ending of Luke: 'we are left with a choice betwen saying that Mark was simply incompetent, or that the ending, though strange, is right if rightly (finely) interpreted'.

254. S. Praeder, 'Jesus–Paul, Peter–Paul, and Jesus–Peter Parallelisms in Luke–Acts: A History of Reader Response', *SBL Seminar Papers* (Missoula: Scholars Press, 1984), p. 38.

255. *Ibid.*, p. 39.

256. Smith, *Poetic Closure*, p. 13. Later, Smith (pp. 35-36) suggested: 'Although stability implies composure and the absence of further expectations, this does not mean that our experience of the work ceases abruptly at the last

word. On the contrary, at that point we should be able to re-experience the entire work, not now as a succession of events, but as an integral design'.

257. *Ibid.*, p. 119.

258. Torgovnick, *Closure*, p. 8. It should be noted that Torgovnick included retrospective patterning in her discussion of the relationship of the end to the beginning and middle of a narrative. I have modified Torgovnick's model by reserving examination of the role of retrospective patterning until this point since the process is more the responsibility of the reader than the text.

259. See the discussion of this passage in Chapter 4.

260. Daniel Plooij, *The Ascension in the 'Western' Textual Tradition* (Amsterdam: Koninklijke Akademie, 1929), p. 11.

261. A. Plummer, *The Gospel According to St. Luke*, ICC (New York: Scribner, 1903). Plummer (p. 202) argued that 9.51 was a reference to Jesus' 'assumption, i.e. the Ascension', and then later (p. 565), commenting on 24.51 wrote: 'This refers to the Ascension, whatever view we take of the disputed words which follow'.

262. S.M. Gilmour, 'The Gospel according to St. Luke', *IB* Vol. VIII (Nashville: Abingdon, 1952). Gilmour (p. 181) called 9.51 'a reference to the Ascension' and argued (p. 434) about 24.51 'there are no reasonable grounds for doubting that this is the story of the Ascension'.

263. J.M. Creed, *The Gospel according to Luke: The Greek Text with Introduction, Notes, and Indices* (London: Macmillan, 1950), pp. 141, 302.

264. Talbert, *Literary Patterns*, p. 122, claimed: 'Regardless of whether one prefers the longer or the shorter text, the verse still refers to the ascension'. Talbert has recently endorsed the longer reading in *Reading Luke*, p. 233.

265. A.R.C. Leaney, *The Gospel According to St. Luke* (London: A. & C. Black, 1958), pp. 172, 295-96.

266. See e.g. H. Conzelmann, *The Theology of St. Luke*, trans. Geoffrey Buswell (Philadelphia: Fortress, 1961), p. 94; Phillipe Menoud, 'Remarques sur les textes de l'ascension dans Luc–Actes', *Neutestamentliche Studien für Rudolf Bultmann*, ed. Walther Eltester (Berlin: Alfred Töpelmann, 1957), pp. 148-56.

267. The verb διίστημι is found only in Luke–Acts in the New Testament, here and elsewhere at Luke 22.59 and Acts 27.28. John Gerhard Lygre, 'Exaltation: Considered with Reference to the Resurrection and Ascension in Luke–Acts' (Ph.D. dissertation, Princeton Theological Seminary, 1975), argued for a spatial-temporal nuance of the word from the context of Luke 22 and Acts 27, and thus an undisputed spatial-temporal reference to the ascension in Luke 24. His arguments fail to convince.

268. This description of the effect of closure on the reader is similar to Torgovnick's suggestion, *Closure*, p. 209, that 'effective endings command a novel to "stand still here" in a way that defamiliarizes and makes us feel anew the artfulness of a fictional structure, the essence of some human experience, or both'.

269. *Ibid.*, p. 17.
270. *Ibid.*
271. *Ibid.*
272. *Ibid.*, p. 18.
273. *Ibid.*, p. 17.
274. Though one might argue that Luke ends in a complementary relationship with the reader (as, in fact, it actually does in the longer text), Torgovnick's distinction (*ibid.*, p. 18) between the two is instructive: 'The distinction between a complementary relationship and a congruent one depends upon the degree of resistance the author anticipates from the reader, and the degree to which an author works hard during closure to minimize such resistance'. Though it is impossible to suggest how much resistance the real author anticipated from his audience, it is clear that little was done to minimize that resistance and hence the relationship is better described as incongruent/congruent.
275. J. Hillis Miller, 'The Problematic of Ending', p. 7.
276. Smith, *Poetic Closure*, p. 211.
277. L. Silberman, '"*Habent Sua Fata Libelli*": The Role of Wandering Themes in Some Hellenistic and Rabbinic Literature', *The Relationship Among the Gospels*, ed. W.O. Walker (San Antonio: Trinity University, 1978), p. 218.
278. I am reluctant to use the phrase 'absentee christology' because of the theological baggage the term carries with it, but in a sense this idea of an absent Christ along with the idea of an ascended Lord paints in broad strokes at least part of Luke's characterization of Jesus in Luke–Acts.

Notes to Chapter 4

1. J.A. Fitzmyer, 'The Ascension of Christ and Pentecost', *TS* 45 (1984), pp. 409-40.
2. *Ibid.*, pp. 416-17.
3. According to F.G. Kenyon, *The Western Text in the Gospels and Acts, Proceedings of the British Academy*, XXIV (London: n.p., 1939), p. 26, Clark's text has 19,983 words compared to 18,401 words in Westcott and Hort's edition.
4. B. Metzger, *A Textual Commentary on the Greek New Testament* (London: United Bible Societies, 1971), p. 260.
5. E.J. Epp, *The Theological Tendency of Codex Bezae Cantabrigiensis in Acts* (Cambridge: Cambridge University Press, 1966), p. 165.
6. Summaries of the research on Acts may be found in A.F.J. Klijn, *A Survey of the Researches into the Western Text of the Gospels and Acts* (Drubkerij: Utrecht, 1949); Klijn, *A Survey of the Researches into the Western Text of the Gospels and Acts, Part Two 1949-1969* (Leiden: Brill, 1969); Epp, *The Theological Tendency*, pp. 1-21.

7. While these verses extend beyond the ascension narrative proper, there are textual problems here crucial for understanding the significance of the ascension.

8. A.C. Clark, *The Acts of the Apostles* (Oxford: Clarendon, 1933), p. xxi.

9. F. Blass, *Acta apostolorum, sive Lucae ad Theophilum liber alter* (Göttingen: Vandenhoeck & Ruprecht, 1895). See even earlier, J.B. Lightfoot, *On a Fresh Revision of the English New Testament* (London: Macmillan, 1871), p. 29.

10. *Ibid.*, pp. 1-36.

11. T.E. Page, 'Review of Frederick Blass' *Acta apostolorum*', *ClassRev* 11 (1897), pp. 317-20.

12. *Ibid.*, p. 320.

13. *Ibid.*, pp. 319-320.

14. *Ibid.*, p. 320.

15. Clark, *The Acts of the Apostles*, p. xi.

16. *Ibid.*, p. xxi.

17. J.H. Ropes, *The Text of Acts, The Beginnings of Christianity*, Vol. III, ed. F.J. Foakes Jackson and Kirsopp Lake (London: Macmillan, 1926), p. ccxxvii.

18. *Ibid.*, p. ccxxix.

19. *Ibid.* See pp. ccxx-ccxxi for specific examples.

20. E. Haenchen, *The Acts of the Apostles: A Commentary*, trans. Bernard Noble *et al.* (Philadelphia: Westminster, 1971), p. 51.

21. The ascension narrative itself, if it were original in Luke (and both Ropes and Haenchen accept the longer text in Luke 24), is a good example of Luke's apparent disinterest in detail. See also the accounts of Paul's call on the Damascus Road (Acts 9.1-9; 22.6-11) and Peter's vision in Joppa (Acts 10.9-16; 11.4-10) for example. These variations are extremely important in our discussion of 'redundancy' in Chapters 3 and 6.

22. E. Nestle, 'Some Observations on the Codex Bezae', *Expos* 2 (1895), pp. 235-40. Nestle (p. 235) claimed Codex Bezae reflected an underlying Semitic original. Max Wilcox, *The Semitisms of Acts* (Oxford: Clarendon, 1965), p. 2, suggested: 'The importance of Nestle's work lay in its influence upon Blass, who now observed a number of grammatical forms and idioms of an apparently Semitic nature'.

23. T. Zahn, *Introduction to the New Testament* (New York: Scribner, 1917), pp. 8ff.

24. J.M. Wilson, *The Acts of the Apostles, Translated from the Codex Bezae, with an Introduction on its Lucan Origin and Importance* (London: SPCK, 1923).

25. A.J. Wensinck, 'The Semitisms of Codex Bezae and their Relation to the Non-Western Text of the Gospel of St. Luke', *BBC* 12 (1937), pp. 11-48.

26. H. Koester, *Introduction to the New Testament: History and Literature of Early Christianity*, Vol. II (Philadelphia: Fortress, 1982), pp. 20, 26, 51.

See also, M.E. Boismard, 'The Text of Acts: A Problem of Literary Criticism?', *New Testament Textual Criticism: Its Significance for Exegesis*, ed. E.J. Epp and G.D. Fee (Oxford: Clarendon, 1981), pp. 147-57.

27. Metzger, *A Textual Commentary*, p. 264. A similar hypothesis was made by George Salmon, *Some Thoughts on the Textual Criticism of the New Testament* (London: John Murray, 1897), p. 140, which suggested that the Western text preserves explanatory notes made by Luke for readings of his work. This thesis has failed to gain scholarly attention, much less consensus.

28. J. Rendel Harris, *Codex Bezae: A Study of the So-Called Western Text of the New Testament*, Texts and Studies, 2 (Cambridge: Cambridge University Press, 1891), p. 41.

29. *Ibid.*, p. 114.

30. E.J. Epp, *The Theological Tendency*, p. 8.

31. A.C. Clark, *The Acts of the Apostles*, p. 219. J.A. Findlay, 'On Variations in the Text of D and d', *BBC* 9 (1931), p. 11, made a count of the variations in the text of D and d, with the following result: Matthew 107, John 106, Luke 176, Mark 469, Acts 607. He suggested that 'possibly a corrector has been at work assimilating Greek to Latin in the Gospels, but has tired of his work by the time he reached Mark–Acts'.

32. Epp, *The Theological Tendency*, p. 10.

33. Earlier, F.H. Chase, *The Old Syriac Element in the Text of Codex Bezae* (London: Macmillan), postulated that the deviations so common in Codex Bezae were the result of the influence of an old Syriac version on the Greek text of D.

34. C.C. Torrey, 'The Translations made from the Original Aramaic Gospels', *Studies in the History of Religions, Presented to Crawford Howell Toy*, ed. D.G. Lyon and G.F. Moore (New York: Scribner, 1912), pp. 269-317.

35. *Ibid.*, pp. 283-84.

36. C.C. Torrey, *Composition and Date of Acts* (Cambridge, Mass.: Harvard University, 1916).

37. *Ibid.*, pp. 5-6. Torrey distinguished I Acts (chs. 1-15) from II Acts (16-28) which showed no evidence for an underlying Semitic document. Because of common vocabulary and style, Torrey (*ibid.*, p. 5) also believed 'that the author of 16-28 was the translator of 1-15'.

38. *Ibid.*, pp. 8-9.

39. *Ibid.*, p. 40.

40. Unlike his earlier article, 'The Translations', which Torrey (*ibid.*, p. 5) remarked 'was not reviewed or noticed in print, so far as I am aware', there were numerous responses to his later monograph. See C.H. Dodd *The Apostolic Preaching and its Development* (New York: Harper, 1944); F.J. Foakes-Jackson, 'Professor C.C. Torrey on the Acts', *HTR* 10 (1917), pp. 352-61; F.J.M. Voste, 'Torrey, C.C., *The Composition and Date of Acts*

(Review)', *RB* 14 (1917), pp. 300-303; A.A. Vazakas, 'Is Acts i–xv. 35 a Literal Translation from an Aramaic Original?', *JBL* 37 (1918), pp. 105-10; W.J. Wilson, 'Some Observations on the Aramaic Acts', *HTR* 11 (1918), pp. 74-99; F.C. Burkitt, 'Professor C.C. Torrey on Acts', *JTS* 20 (1919), pp. 321f.; C.A.A. Scott, 'An Aramaic Source for Acts i–xv', *ExpTim* 31 (1919-20), pp. 220-23; H.J. Cadbury, 'Luke—Translator?', *AJT* 24 (1920), pp. 436-55; E.J. Goodspeed, 'The Origin of Acts', *JBL* 39 (1920), pp. 83-101; J.W. Falconer, 'The Aramaic Source of Acts I–XV and Paul's Conversion', *Expos* 19 (1920), pp. 271-85; G.A. Barton, 'Professor Torrey's Theory of the Aramaic Origin of the Gospels and the First Half of the Acts of the Apostles', *JTS* 36 (1935), pp. 357-73; H.F.D. Sparks, 'The Semitisms of Acts', *JTS* 1 (1950), pp. 16-28.

41. Cadbury, 'Luke—Translator or Author?', p. 446.

42. *Ibid.*, p. 447.

43. *Ibid.*, p. 448.

44. *Ibid.*, pp. 448-51. See also Goodspeed, 'The Origin of Acts', p. 87; Voste, 'Review', p. 302.

45. Wilcox, *The Semitisms of Acts*, p. 11.

46. Metzger, *A Textual Commentary*, p. 269.

47. M. Black, *An Aramaic Approach to the Gospels and Acts* (Oxford: Clarendon, 1946). In subsequent editions, Black considered the then newly discovered Dead Sea Scrolls.

48. *Ibid.*, p. 6.

49. C.C. Torrey, *Documents of the Primitive Church* (New York: Harper, 1941), pp. 121, 147-48.

50. Black, *An Aramaic Approach*, p. 214.

51. *Ibid.*, p. 215.

52. M. Black, 'The Longer and the Shorter Text of Acts', *On Language, Culture, and Religion: In Honor of Eugene A. Nida*, ed. M. Black and W.A. Smalley (Paris: Mouton, 1974), p. 120, claimed: 'it may well be, in the end, that A.C. Clark was right that the scribe or scribes responsible for the "B" textual tradition, now exemplified in P75-B, were, in many cases, deliberately abbreviating the tradition of the "Western" text'. On the eclectic method in textual criticism, see the discussion below.

53. M. Wilcox, *The Semitisms of Acts* (Oxford: Clarendon, 1965).

54. *Ibid.*, p. 181.

55. *Ibid.*, p. 180.

56. James D. Yoder, 'Semitisms in Codex Bezae', *JBL* 77 (1959), p. 317; see also 'The Language of the Greek Variants of Codex Bezae', *NovT* 3 (1959), pp. 241-48.

57. A.C. Clark, *The Primitive Text of the Gospels and Acts* (Oxford: Clarendon, 1914).

58. Ropes, *The Text of Acts*, p. ccxxvii. Elsewhere Ropes (*ibid.*, pp. ccxxi-ccxxii) had argued: 'A careful reading of any appropriate form of the

"Western" text of Acts, such as that of Codex Bezae ... will be likely to convince the student that on the whole ... he has before him a definite integral text not explicable as the mere accumulation of scribal errors and incidental modifications'.

59. A.C. Clark, *The Acts of the Apostles*, p. viii.

60. *Ibid.*, p. ix. This view represents a shift from Clark's former position. Clark (*ibid.*, p. xxxi) claimed: 'In view of the new evidence as to the methods of abbreviators, I now think that many of them may have been deliberate'.

61. Cf., however, Black, 'Notes', pp. 119-32, who seems to suggest sympathy for Clark's Western text.

62. In this volume, Ropes gathered both the critical text and the principles upon which he based his text-critical judgments.

63. Ropes, *The Text of Acts*, p. viii.

64. *Ibid.*

65. *Ibid.*, pp. ccxlv-ccxlvi. A.C. Clark, *The Acts of the Apostles*, p. xxiv, crisply retorted: 'I do not feel quite sure what is meant by these remarks, and would only say that possible "consequences to the history of the N.T. canon", whether grave or otherwise, should not deter us from seeking for the truth. It is more important to discover this than to bolster up antiquated theories'.

66. More recently, this view has been argued by R.P.C. Hanson, 'The Provenance of the Interpolator in the "Western" Text of Acts', *NTS* 12 (1965-66), pp. 211-30.

67. Ropes, *The Text of Acts*, p. ccxxv. Ropes, p. ccxxvi, argued: 'If choice has to be made between the theory that the "Western" text was the original ... and the theory that the Old Uncial was the original ... the answer seems to me clearly in favour of the latter'.

68. Clark, *The Acts of the Apostles*, p. xxii.

69. Haenchen, *Acts*, pp. 50-56.

70. E.J. Epp, 'The Twentieth-Century Interlude in New Testament Textual Criticism', *JBL* 93 (1974), pp. 386-414.

71. E.J. Epp, 'The Eclectic Method in New Testament Textual Criticism: Solution or Symptom?', *HTR* 69 (1976), p. 212, has defined the eclectic method as one: '(1) that treats each text-critical problem ... separately and largely in isolation from other problems, (2) that "chooses" or "selects" (*eklegomai*) from among available and recognized text-critical criteria those that presumably are appropriate to that particular text-critical situation, and (3) that then applies the selected criteria in such a way as to "pick" or "choose" (*eklegomai*) a reading from one or another manuscript and thereby arrive at a text-critical decision for that particular variation-unit'.

72. Metzger, *A Textual Commentary*, pp. 271-72.

73. See. e.g., G.D. Kilpatrick, 'An Eclectic Study of the Text of Acts', *Biblical and Patristic Studies in Memory of Robert Pierce Casey*, ed. J. Neville Birdsall and R.W. Thompson (Freiburg: Herder, 1963), pp. 64-77; A.F.J. Klijn,

'In Search of the Original Text of Acts', *Studies in Luke–Acts: Essays Presented in Honor of Paul Schubert*, ed. L.E. Keck and J.L. Martyn (Nashville: Abingdon, 1966), p. 104.

74. E.J. Epp, 'The Eclectic Method', p. 212.

75. *Ibid.*, p. 254.

76. Metzger, *A Textual Commentary*, p. 295.

77. I also recognize that I am an 'eclectic specialist' who characteristically prefers internal over external evidence. At the same time, however, using Fee's categories, I consider myself to be a rational rather than a rigorous eclectic.

78. In particular, those scholars who maintain Blass's two-edition hypothesis, or some modification of it, would claim two texts which deserve 'original text' status. Still, as E.C. Colwell, 'Biblical Criticism: Lower and Higher', *JBL* 67 (1948), pp. 6-7, has observed: 'The autographs of the New Testament perished; they perished early. There is nothing mysterious or puzzling about this. They were written on papyrus. They were written to be read. They were read till the pages fell out or were torn. . . . the originals of the New Testament books were copied before they perished, and in the first one hundred and fifty years of Christian history copies of copies multiplied'.

79. E.J. Epp, *The Theological Tendency*, p. 165, sought 'simply to understand the D-text of Acts in its own terms without reference to the questions of origin or originality'.

80. F. Stagg, 'Establishing a Text for Luke–Acts', *SBL Seminar Papers* (Missoula: Scholars Press, 1978), p. 47.

81. Cf., however, Merrill M. Parvis, 'The Nature and Tasks of New Testament Textual Criticism: An Appraisal', *JR* 32 (1952), p. 172, who suggested that some variants added by scribes to the Gospel texts may reflect oral tradition earlier than that preserved in the NT. He asked: 'Why should the fact that one form was reduced to writing have given it authority over other existent forms when all were the products of the understanding and interpretation of the primitive church?' See also F.C Grant, 'Where Form Criticism and Text Criticism Overlap', *JBL* 59 (1940), pp. 11-21.

82. Kirsopp Lake, *The Beginnings of Christianity*, Part 1, *The Acts of the Apostles*, Vol. V (London: Macmillan, 1933), p. 3; also Vol. III, pp. 256-61.

83. A. Wilder, 'Variant Traditions of the Resurrection in Acts', *JBL* 62 (1943), p. 311. Wilder (*ibid.*) believed the omission by the Western text of 'and was carried up into heaven' was 'due to a desire thus to minimize the difficulty presented by the forty days interval of Acts 1.3'.

84. H. Conzelmann, *The Theology of St. Luke*, trans. Geoffrey Buswell (Philadelphia: Fortress, 1961), p. 94.

85. P. Menoud, 'Remarques sur les textes de l'ascension dans Luc-Actes', *Neutestamentliche Studien für Rudolf Bultmann*, ed. Walther Eltester (Berlin: Alfred Töpelmann, 1957), pp. 148-56.

86. Haenchen, *Acts*, p. 99.

87. Cited by Ferdinand Graefe, 'Der Schluss des Lukasevangeliums und der Anfang der Apostelgeschichte', *TSK* 61 (1888), p. 537.

88. Graefe, 'Der Schluss des Lukasevangeliums', p. 538.

89. Cited by E.J. Epp, 'The Ascension in the Textual Tradition of Luke–Acts', *New Testament Textual Criticism: Its Significance for Exegesis*, ed. E.J. Epp and G.D. Fee (Oxford: Clarendon, 1981), p. 136.

90. J.M. Creed, 'The Text and Interpretation of Acts i 1-2', *JTS* 35 (1934), p. 176. Creed noted that in this manuscript διὰ πνεύματος ἁγίου probably followed ἐξελέξατο.

91. Metzger, *A Textual Commentary*, p. 274.

92. *Ibid.*, pp. 275-77.

93. These two scholars are strange text-critical bedfellows, especially in light of their divergent views on the text of Acts!

94. Clark, *The Acts of the Apostles*, pp. 2, 250.

95. Ropes, *The Text of Acts*, pp. 256-61.

96. Kirsopp Lake, *The Acts of the Apostles*, p. 2.

97. Creed, 'The Text and Interpretation of Acts i 1-2', p. 180.

98. *Ibid.*, p. 181.

99. Epp, 'The Ascension', p. 141.

100. Earlier, Ferdinand Graefe, 'Der Schluss des Lukasevangeliums', pp. 524-41 and Daniel Plooij, *The Ascension in the 'Western' Textual Tradition* (Amsterdam: Koninklijke Akademie, 1929), pp. 39-58, tried to explain some of the Western readings on the basis of doctrinal concerns.

101. Epp, 'The Ascension', p. 141. Epp (*ibid.*) also showed that of the six variants, Augustine supports five, Codex Gigas supports four (of five), and Codex Bezae, p, t, *De promissionibus*, and Vigilius each support two.

102. *Ibid.*, pp. 142-43.

103. *Ibid.*, p. 141.

104. Kirsopp Lake, 'The Practical Value of Textual Variation: Illustrated from the Book of Acts', *BibWorld* 19 (1902), p. 363. This passage is quoted approvingly by Metzger, *A Textual Commentary*, pp. 275-76.

105. Acts 7.43 is not considered here as reflecting special Lukan usage, since Luke is quoting the septuagintal form of Amos 5.25-27 where ἀναλαμβάνω is used.

106. W. Bauer, *A Greek-English Lexicon of the New Testament and Other Early Christian Literature*, ed. F. Danker and trans. W. Arndt and F.W. Gingrich (London: University of Chicago, 1979), p. 57, more precisely identified the usage in 20.13, 14 as 'take on board'.

107. J. Fitzmyer, *The Gospel According to Luke*, AB, Vol. I (Garden City: Doubleday, 1981), p. 828.

108. I.H. Marshall, *Commentary on Luke*, NIGTC (Grand Rapids: Eerdmans, 1978), p. 405.

109. G. Friedrich, 'Lukas 9.51 und die Entrückungschristologie des Lukas', *Orientierung an Jesus: Festschrift für J. Schmid*, ed. P. Hoffmann *et al.* (Freiburg: Herder, 1973), p. 52.

110. P.A. van Stempvoort, 'The Interpretation of the Ascension in Luke and Acts', *NTS* 5 (1959), p. 32.

111. *Ibid.*, pp. 32-33.

112. *Ibid.*, p. 33.

113. *Ibid.*, It should be noted at this point that van Stempvoort did accept the longer Alexandrian text at Luke 24.51.

114. J. Dupont, "ΑΝΕΛΗΜΦΘΗ (Act. I. 2)', *NTS* 8 (1961), p. 156.

115. *Ibid.*, p. 157.

116. *Ibid.*, pp. 155-57.

117. See van Stempvoort, 'The Interpretation of the Ascension', p. 32.

118. The same may not be true for 1.22 where ἕως replaces ἄχρι (note the textual variant where א A 81 *et al.* retain ἄχρι) and ἡμέρας is made more 'definite' by the presence of the article τῆς.

119. Those who believe Acts 1.2 describes the ascension hold that the commands mentioned in 1.2 refer to Jesus' appearance before the disciples narrated in Luke 24.36-49. Interestingly, if one were to take the reference to 'commands' literally, there are six imperatives in the Lord's Supper discourse and only four in the last appearance scene!

120. Plooij, *The Ascension in the 'Western' Textual Tradition*, p. 11. I see no reason to accept Plooij's (*ibid.*, p. 12) further supposition of accepting a common Aramaic source underlying Luke 9.51 and Acts 1.2.

121. The forty days in Acts 1.3 and the quotation of Jesus in 1.4b-5 are two obvious *cruces interpretationis*.

122. Fitzmyer, *Luke*, I, p. 828.

123. Plooij, *The Ascension in the 'Western' Textual Tradition*, p. 15.

124. Epp, 'The Ascension', p. 138.

125. Notice also that Latin d has *levatus est* ('lifted away from their sight').

126. Epp, 'The Ascension', p. 139.

127. Metzger, *A Textual Commentary*, p. 283.

128. Haenchen, *Acts*, p. 150.

129. Klijn, *A Survey of the Researches, Part Two*, p. 64.

130. B.H. Streeter, 'Codices 157, 1071 and the Caesarean Text' *Studies Presented to Kirsopp Lake* (London: Macmillan, 1937), p. 150.

131. Epp, 'A Continuing Interlude?', p. 15.

132. Epp, 'The Twentieth Century Interlude', p. 414, has lamented the dearth of serious students of textual criticism: 'In short, NT textual criticism is an area seriously affected by decreasing attention, diminishing graduate opportunities, and dwindling personnel'.

133. G. Lohfink, *Die Himmelfahrt Jesu: Untersuchungen zu den Himmelfahrts- und Erhöhungstexten bei Lukas* (Munich: Kösel, 1971).

134. *Ibid.*, p. 75.

135. Lohfink distinguished between the 'heavenly journey' (Himmelsreise), often of an apocalyptic seer, and the ancient assumption or removal story.

He concludes (*ibid.*, p. 41) that 'der Entrückungstyp die grössere Ähnlichkeit der lukanischen Himmelfahrt aufweist'. Among his arguments that the ancient assumption story is a more likely candidate for the formal background to the Lukan material is the fact that the heavenly journey narrative is often the travels of a spirit (psyche) and often the *terminus ad quem* of the narration is the arrival of the spirit in the heavenly world. For other reasons, see Lohfink, *Die Himmelfahrt Jesu*, pp. 32-42.

136. See *ibid.*, pp. 41-49. Of course no one assumption narrative contains all of these verbs or formal elements. These tables are not intended to be exhaustive; for additional texts, see Lohfink, pp. 42-46; J.G. Davies, *He Ascended Into Heaven: A Study in the History of Doctrine* (New York: Association, 1958); P.W. van der Horst, 'Hellenistic Parallels to the Acts of the Apostles: 1-26', *ZNW* 74 (1983), pp. 17-26; A.S. Pease, 'Some Aspects of Invisibility', *Harvard Studies in Classical Philology* 53 (1942), p. 136.

137. The substantive form of these verbs (ἀφανισμός; ἁρπαγή; and μετάστασις) also occurs in a number of texts. See Lohfink, *Die Himmelfahrt Jesu*, p. 42.

138. The words employed by Luke to describe Jesus' departure include: διίσταμαι (Luke 24.51); ἀναλαμβάνομαι (Acts 1.2, 11, 22); ἐπαίρομαι (Acts 1.9); πορεύομαι (Acts 1.10, 11).

139. It is always accompanied by the phrase εἰς τὸν οὐρανόν. See Plutarch, *Numa*, 2.3; Antoninus, *Liberalis*, 25. For other texts, see Lohfink, *Die Himmelfahrt Jesu*, p. 42 n. 72.

140. It should be noted in passing that Lohfink observed additional phenomena that occurred less frequently in the assumption narratives of the pagan texts. The sun darkening, the earth quaking, lightning flashing, a light appearing in a nocturnal sky, thunder crashing, and a voice speaking, all occur sporadically throughout these texts, but not often enough to qualify them as a *characteristic* feature (see Lohfink, *Die Himmelfahrt Jesu*, p. 45).

141. Lohfink (p. 53) argued that the 'heavenly journey' narratives in Jewish literature are indistinguishable from the assumption stories and thus did not treat them as a possibly separate influence on Acts. Lohfink also concluded (p. 54) that the form of 'translation of the soul' (Aufnahme der Seele) stories is relatively late and does not provide the immediate background to the Lukan concept of ascension.

142. Pace Lohfink, *Die Himmelfahrt Jesu*, p. 58; Dillon, *Eye-Witnesses*, p. 177; contra R. Pesch, 'Der Anfang der Apostelgeschichte: Apg. 1, 1-11. Kommentarstudie', *EKK* Vorarbeiten 3 (1971), pp. 16f.

143. See Dillon, *Eye-Witnesses*, p. 176. Likewise, Lohfink, *Die Himmelfahrt Jesu*, p. 79, concluded: 'wenn die lukanische Himmelfahrtsgeschichte auch nicht von einer uns bekannten *individuellen* Entrückungserzählung abhängig ist, so doch von der *Form* der Entrückung *im ganzen*'.

144. Lohfink, *Die Himmelfahrt Jesu*, pp. 115-34, considered John 20.17; Mark 16.19; *Barnabas* 15.9; *Aristides* 2.8; *T. Abr.* 3.8-11; *Gospel of Peter* 9f.;

Codex Bobiensis on Mark 16.3; *Ascension of Isaiah* 3.13-18; *Epistula Apostolorum* 51; and *Acts of Pilate* 16.6. For various reasons, Lohfink (pp. 115-34 passim; esp. p. 134) concluded that none of these texts reflected an ascension tradition independent of Luke.

145. *Ibid.*, p. 134.

146. Dillon, *Eye-Witnesses*, p. 174.

147. A point made by Bruce Chilton in 'Announcement in Nazara: An Analysis of Luke 4.16-21', *Gospel Perspectives*, Vol. II, ed. R.T. France and D. Wenham (Sheffield: JSOT Press, 1981), pp. 149ff.

148. I.H. Marshall has evaluated the relationship between tradition and redaction in a helpful, albeit conservative way in *Luke: Historian and Theologian* (Grand Rapids: Zondervan, 1971).

149. See Jean-Marie Guillaume, *Luc interprète des anciennes traditions sur la résurrection de Jésus* (Paris: Gabalda, 1979), pp. 234-39, for a detailed literary analysis of common Lukan vocabulary, style and themes. On the meaning of ἀνελήμφθη in Acts 1.2, see the text-critical analysis earlier in this chapter.

150. Again, Guillaume, *ibid.*, pp. 239-45, has provided a thorough and persuasive discussion of the passage and his results need not be reproduced here.

151. Fuller, *Formation*, p. 127; contra Osborne, *The Resurrection Narratives*, p. 270, who maintained the primitive tradition 'included a farewell address (vv. 6-7 and a primitive form of v. 8)'. It may also be noted that Acts 1.6-8 may be more closely associated with commissioning scenes than with the farewell speeches of an ascending hero.

152. The analysis found in Guillaume, *Luc interprète des anciennes traditions*, pp. 239-43, is supplemented with additional material in Table 16.

153. The categories of 'preferred vocabulary' and 'lucanisms' are those of Guillaume, *ibid.*, pp. 239, 241.

154. See Bauer *A Greek-English* p. 282. The closest parallel is in 18.13 where the passive voice is also used, this time to describe the reluctance of the 'publican' to 'lift his eyes into heaven'. See Luke 6.20; 11.27; 16.23; 18.13; 21.28; 24.50(!); Acts 2.14; 14.11; 22.22; 27.40.

155. *Ibid.*, p. 845.

156. See Luke 7.43; 10.30; Acts 2.15.

157. The preposition ἀπό is very Lukan (241 of 441 occurrences in the Gospels) and may warrant further investigation into the phrase 'from their eyes'.

158. In fact, Eric Franklin, 'The Ascension and the Eschatology of Luke-Acts', *SJTh* 23 (1970), pp. 191-200, has argued that Luke's eschatological perspectives were shaped, not by the parousia, but by Jesus' ascension.

159. Fitzmyer, 'Ascension and Pentecost', p. 419. Unlike Fitzmyer, I am willing to accept the presence of the cloud as part of the tradition Luke inherits.

160. See the paragraph above for the reconstruction of this narrative. Whether the ascension provided the pattern for the expectations of the parousia in the early church, or whether the process was vice versa, is an historical question tangential to this study and not addressed here.

161. The significance of the reference to the Mount of Olives will be discussed in Chapter 5.

162. Lohfink, *Die Himmelfahrt Jesu*, pp. 242f.

163. Fitzmyer, 'Ascension and Pentecost', p. 410. Because they are of secondary significance for this study, I have mentioned only NT passages which reflect the ascension kerygma. For extra-canonical references in the manuscript tradition amd among the early church witnesses, see Davies, *He Ascended into Heaven* (*op. cit.*).

164. These texts actually represent an intermediary category between ascension kerygma and ascension narratives. Fitzmyer (*ibid.*, pp. 414-15) included these passages as evidence of Jesus' ascension in the NT, though without describing it in spatial-temporal terms. Here I agree with Lohfink in distinguishing these passages which mention ascension in the context of exaltation kerygma and those (namely Luke–Acts) which narrate the ascension as a visible transfer from earth to heaven.

165. Fitzmyer, 'Ascension and Pentecost', p. 420. What remains unexamined is the relationship between ascension kerygma and ascension narrative. This question will be addressed at the end of this section under the 'History of Tradition'.

166. See Lohfink's discussion in *Die Himmelfahrt Jesu* for a list and evaluation of these texts.

167. Since the longer ending of Luke 24.51 has been judged as spurious in this study, it would be possible to suggest that p^{75} also reflects an independent ascension tradition. To avoid circular reasoning, p^{75} will be considered only of secondary significance.

168. See Metzger, *A Textual Commentary*, pp. 122-26 for a detailed discussion of both external and internal evidence.

169. The notable exception is W.R. Farmer, *The Last Twelve Verses of Mark* (Cambridge: Cambridge University Press, 1974), who argued that 16.9-20 (with the possible exception of 16.10) was a Markan composition. Similarly, Eta Linnemann, 'Der (wiedergefundene) Markusschluss', *ZThK* 66 (1969), pp. 255-78, argued that 16.15-20 was original to Mark, but 16.9-14 was not. For the majority view regarding the secondary nature of Mark 16.9-20, see Kurt Aland, 'Bemerkungen zum Schluss des Markusevangeliums', *Neotestamentica et Semitica: Studies in honour of Matthew Black* (Edinburgh: T & T Clark 1969), pp. 157-80.

170. See among others J.G. Davies, *He Ascended into Heaven*, pp. 42-49; Hans Grass, *Ostergeschehen und Osterberichte* (Göttingen: Vandenhoeck & Ruprecht, 1970), p. 15; E. Lohmeyer, *Galiläa und Jerusalem*, FRLANT 52 (Göttingen: Vandenhoeck & Ruprecht, 1936); Lohfink, *Die Himmelfahrt*

Jesu, pp. 119-21; Alsup, *Appearance Stories*, pp. 117-24. Contra Metzger, *A Textual Commentary*, p. 126, who speaks of the 'evident antiquity of the longer ending'.

171. See especially C.H. Dodd, 'The Appearance of the Risen Christ: An Essay in Form Criticism', *Studies in the Gospels*, ed. D.E. Nineham (Oxford: Blackwell, 1957), pp. 9-35; Reginald Fuller, *The Formation of the Resurrection Narratives* (Philadelphia: Fortress, 1980), pp. 155-57; Fitzmyer, *Luke*, II, p. 1586.

172. These differences also exist between Mark 16.19 and the longer text of Luke 24.50-53.

173. The Greek text of 2 Kgs 2.11 reads: καὶ ἀνελήμφθη Ἠλίου... ὡς εἰς τὸν οὐρανόν. The Greek text of Ps. 110 (109) reads: εἶπεν ὁ κύριος τῷ κυρίῳ μου κάθου ἐκ δεξιῶν μου.

174. See the following 'History of Tradition' for an evaluation of the antiquity of the material.

175. Fuller, *Formation*, p. 157. See also Fitzmyer, *Luke*, II, p. 1586, who argued that he was 'inclined to regard it [Mark 16.19] as a separate tradition'.

176. The translation which follows was taken from Metzger, *A Textual Commentary*, pp. 121-22:

> But suddenly at the third hour of the day there was darkness over the whole circle of the earth, and angels descended from the heavens, and as he [the Lord] was rising [reading *surgente eo*] in the glory of the living God, at the same time they ascended with him; and immediately it was light. Then the women went to the tomb.

177. Metzger, *Text of the New Testament*, p. 73.

178. Cited by D. Plooij in *BBC* 11 (1936), p. 11.

179. Lohfink, *Die Himmelfahrt Jesu*, p. 129 concluded: 'Die Gründe sind die gleichen wie beim Petrusevangelium'.

180. *Ibid.* Lohfink is here following the earlier lead of von Harnack and Bultmann.

181. Metzger, *A Textual Commentary*, p. 122.

182. R.A. Kraft, *The Apostolic Fathers*, Vol. III (New York: Nelson, 1965), pp. 19f.

183. Lohfink, *Die Himmelfahrt Jesu*, pp. 122-23.

184. The word is used with reference to the resurrection of Jesus in Acts (2.24, 32; 8.26; 13.33, 34; 17.31).

185. Lohfink, *Die Himmelfahrt Jesu*, p. 125.

186. Dillon, *Eye-Witnesses*, p. 174

187. I am aware that the recent, provocative study by Werner Kelber, *The Oral and Written Gospel* (Philadelphia: Fortress, 1983) radically re-evaluates the relationship between oral tradition and written narratives. Kelber suggests that the written Gospel, especially Mark, is a counterform to oral tradition and serves a disorienting and re-orienting function. Kelber's work

calls into question the whole program of form and source analyses as practiced in the last fifty years. While I am sympathetic to Kelber's concerns, I justify my attempt at a tradition history here because Kelber himself (p. 209) has noted that Matthew and Luke 'reverse some aspects of Mark's anti-oral bias'. In other words, while it is unlikely that Mark has passively or even perhaps amicably passed on the apostolic tradition, it may not be as difficult to trace the history of a tradition in Luke. Nonetheless, I consider the work done here provisional until there is some methodological advance made in response to the 'bombshell' Kelber has dropped on biblical scholarship.

188. On the way in which the Acts' account of the ascension finally prevailed in the Church, see Morton S. Enslin, 'The Ascension Story', *JBL* 47 (1928), pp. 60–73.

189. If one were willing to accept the testimony of Bobiensis, the first stage would be those texts which placed the ascension at the same time as the resurrection (cf. also *Gospel of Peter* 10). In this case the appearances would follow the assumption. This is the argument of Fuller, *Formation*, p. 129. Though the resurrection and ascension may have been easily interchanged in the exaltation *kerygma*, the ascension *narrative* seems to be another case altogether (see below).

190. The phrase 'on the eighth day' is a polemic against Jewish Sabbath worship and most probably refers to the day of the resurrection, the day after the Sabbath. See Lohfink, *Die Himmelfahrt Jesu*, p. 121.

191. These two are joined by the longer text of Luke 24.51 found in p^{75}. Cf. also *Epistola Apostolorum* 62.

192. See J.D.G. Dunn, *Christology in the Making* (Philadelphia: Westminster, 1980), p. 305.

193. Cf. also Tertullian, *Apol.*, 21. Acts 13.31 may reflect the more ancient and ambiguous reference to 'after many days' which Luke redacts to the number 'forty days'.

194. Likewise in *Asc. Isa.*, a Jewish work redacted by a later Christian hand, the ascension of Jesus occurs after 545 days (9.16).

195. Irenaeus, *Adv. Her.*, I.3.2.

196. That this tradition-history must be taken with due caution may be seen from the fact that a reconstruction of the tradition based on pure chronological concerns would be forced to include also those manifestly late witnesses which place the ascension at the time of the transfiguration (*Apocalypse of Peter*) or at the Crucifixion (*Gospel of Peter* 5.19; *Acts of John* 102). Likewise, if we were willing to accept John 20.17 as a witness to a narrated ascension tradition, we would have a witness which places the ascension between the appearances of Jesus.

197. E.g. Lohfink *et al.*, who argue for the ascension as a Lukan creation, and Fuller *et al.*, who believe the passage has an underlying tradition.

198. See J.E. Alsup, *The Post-Resurrection Appearance Stories of the Gospel Tradition* (Stuttgart: Calwer, 1975).

199. The focus in Acts 1 is on the parousia and especially the response of the disciples.

200. C.K. Barrett, *Luke the Historian in Recent Study* (London: Epworth, 1961), p. 57.

Notes to Chapter 5

1. N. Miller, ed., *Romanfänge: Versuch zu einer Poetik des Romans* (Berlin: n.p., 1965).

2. E.W. Said, *Beginnings: Intention and Method* (New York: Basic Books, 1975).

3. *Ibid.*, p. xi.

4. J. Kucich, 'Action in the Dickens Ending: *Bleak House* and *Great Expectation*', *Nineteenth-Century Fiction* 33 (1978), p. 90, has noted the similarity (and differences) between the work by Kermode and Said: 'Both Kermode and Said assume that the task the novelist sets himself is to uncover the philosophical truth about our relationship to our experience, to fix once and for all the relative positions of human freedom and human necessity. In this way, they both see the novel as fundamentally epistemological'.

5. Said, *Beginnings*, p. 83.

6. Said included numerous allusions to and quotations from the Bible and (pp. 215-23) an eight-page discussion of the impact of Renan's *Life of Jesus*! At one point, Said (pp. 372-73) summarized his argument: 'The state of mind that is concerned with origins is, I have said, theological. By contrast, and this is the shift, beginnings are eminently secular, or gentile, continuing activities'.

7. *Ibid.*, p. 380.

8. I may be too hard at this point on Said. Obviously his intentions and methods are not the same as mine in a quest for understanding narrative beginnings. Still, the critique seems to be justified by the failure of Said to answer his own questions in the beginning paragraph of his work (*ibid.*, p. 3): 'Is a beginning the same as an origin?... To what extent is a beginning ultimately a physical exigency and nothing more than that?... By what sort of approach, with what kind of language, with what sort of instruments does a beginning offer itself up as a subject for study?'

9. *Ibid.*, pp. 72-73.

10. *Ibid.*, p. 73.

11. *Ibid.*

12. Employing Said's categories of intransitive and transitive beginnings, Donald Pease has argued for intransitive beginnings in Purdy's writings in 'False Starts and Wounded Allegories in the Abandoned House of Fiction of James Purdy', *Twentieth-Century Fiction* 28 (1982), pp. 335-49.

13. M. Sternberg, *Expositional Modes and Temporal Ordering in Fiction* (Baltimore: Johns Hopkins, 1978).

14. See for example Heinz-Joachim Mullenbrock, 'Modes of Opening in the Work of E.M. Forster: A Contribution to the Poetics of His Novels', *Modern Philology*, 70 (1973), pp. 216-29; M.M. Lay, 'Temporal Ordering in the Fiction of Margaret Drabble', *Critique: Studies in Modern Fiction* 21 (1980), pp. 73-84; K. Hume, 'Beginnings and Endings in the Icelandic Family Sagas', *Modern Language Review* 68 (1973), pp. 593-606; D.M. Wyatt, 'Hemingway's Uncanny Beginnings', *Georgia Review* 31 (1977), pp. 476-501.

15. G. Watson, 'The Sense of a Beginning', *Sewanee Review* 86 (1978), pp. 539-48.

16. *Ibid.*, p. 541.

17. R. Pope, 'Beginnings', *Georgia Review* 36 (1982), pp. 733-51.

18. *Ibid.*, p. 734.

19. G.C. Sorensen, 'Beginnings and Endings: *The Virginians* as a Sequel', *Studies in the Novel* 13 (1981), pp. 109-21; M. Kreiswirth, 'Centers, Openings, and Endings: Some Faulknerian Constants', *American Literature* 56 1 (1984), pp. 38-50; also see A. Welsh, 'Opening and Closing *Les Misérables*', *Nineteenth-Century Fiction* 33 (1978), pp. 8-23.

20. Pope, 'Beginnings', p. 733. Sir John Henry Moore expressed his disdain for beginnings themselves in his poem, 'The Duke of Benevento', cited by Sternberg, *Expositional Modes*, p. 42:

> I hate the prologue to a story
> Worse than the tuning of a fiddle,
> Squeaking and dinning;
> Hang order and connection,
> I love to dash into the middle;
> Exclusive of the fame and glory,
> There is a comfort on reflection
> To think you've done with the beginning.

21. In fact, each of these three couplets of terms is more appropriate to one of the elements of our models than the others. Opening and closing best describe the phenomenon of plot development—it is opened in the beginning, sustained in the middle, and closed in the ending. Beginning and ending define the relationship of viewpoint between narrator, reader, and text which determines whether or not the reader enters the narrative with the sense of beginning and leaves with a sense of ending. Entrance and exit characterize the relationship of reader to text for the reader who enters into and exits from the narrative world.

22. A. Welsh, 'Opening and Closing', p. 10. This 'surrounding space', of course, is what Uspensky described as the frame. While Kermode, 'Sensing Endings', p. 156 objected to Welsh's terminology, he did not question the close alliance of beginnings and endings: 'But I think it is wrong to call

beginnings and endings "arbitrary disjunctions in a sequence of events that is presumed continuous". . . . When the story begins, time goes into a fit of relative synchronicity. The completion of the plot is the completion of all that is demanding our attention; and earlier time is relevant only insofar as it is said to be so'.

23. Said distinguished between transitive and intransitive beginnings. Intransitive beginnings are unrelated to the narrative which follows; transitive beginnings are inextricably linked with its middle and end. Acts 1, of course, is a transitive beginning. General discussion of plot and literary theory may be found in Chapter 3. Familiarity with that material is assumed here.

24. Watson, 'The Sense of a Beginning', p. 541.

25. *Ibid.*, pp. 542-43.

26. *Ibid.*, p. 548.

27. *Ibid.*

28. This is not to say that other expectations created later in the narrative are not left unfulfilled, i.e., the outcome of Paul's trial in Rome. Barbara Thiering, 'Opening and Closing Narratives in the Gospels and Acts', *AbrN*, 4 (1963-64), p. 50, has perspicuously remarked: 'Luke leaves Paul in Rome because he has thereby reached the summit of the geographical-theological plan of Luke-Acts. Yet . . . the reader naturally expects to be told the outcome of the trial, and not to be left in contemplation of St. Paul in comfortable captivity'.

29. J. Dupont, 'La conclusion des Actes et son rapport à l'ensemble de l'ouvrage de Luc', *Les Actes des Apôtres: Traditions, rédaction, théologie*, ed. J. Kremer (Gembloux: Leuven University Press, 1979), pp. 359-404. The literature on the ending of Acts is quite extensive, perhaps because of the problem caused by the failure of Luke to narrate Paul's death. On Acts 28, see H.J. Hauser, *Strukturen der Abschlusserzählung*; S.M. Praeder, 'The Narrative Voyage: An Analysis and Interpretation of Acts 27-28' (Ph.D. dissertation, Graduate Theological Union, 1980); G. Delling, 'Das letzte Wort der Apostelgeschichte', *NovT* 15 (1973), pp. 193-204; R.H. Smith, 'The Theology of Acts', *CTM* 42 (1971), pp. 527-35; F. Stagg, 'The Unhindered Gospel', *R & E* 71 (1974), pp. 451-62; H.J. Cadbury, 'The Summaries in Acts', *Beginnings of Christianity*, Vol. V, pp. 392-402.

30. C.B. Puskas, Jr, 'The Conclusion of Luke-Acts: An Investigation of the Literary Function and Theological Significance of Acts 28.16-31' (Ph.D. dissertation, St. Louis University, 1980).

31. *Ibid.*, p. 92.

32. The other occurrences may be found in Acts 8.12; 14.22; 19.8; 20.25. In Luke, see 1.33; 4.5, 43; 6.20; 7.28; 8.1, 10; 9.2, 11, 27, 60, 62; 10.9, 11; 11.2, 17, 18, 20; 12.31, 32; 13.18, 20, 28, 29; 14.15; 16.16; 17.20(2), 21; 18.16, 17, 24, 25, 29; 19.11, 12, 15; 21.10, 31; 22.16, 18, 29, 30; 23.42, 51.

33. Maddox, *The Purpose of Luke-Acts*, p. 133, noted in passing: 'Acts

begins and ends on this note: in Acts 1.3 the risen Jesus tells the Apostles, during the forty days before the ascension, "the things about the Kingdom of God"; in Acts 28.31 the very last thing Luke tells us is that Paul was freely and openly "proclaiming the Kingdom of God and teaching the things about Lord Jesus Christ"'. On 'remaining', Dupont ('La conclusion', p. 390) suggested: 'En 1,4, les apôtres doivent ne pas quitter Jérusalem, mais y "attendre" (περιμένειν); en 28,30 Paul "demeura" (ἐνέμεινεν) deux années entières dans son logis'.

34. It is interesting to note that within the immediate context of each mention of the kingdom of God, some sort of conflict or confrontation arises between God's messengers and those listening to the preaching of the kingdom, thereby focusing more clearly the Jew-Christian contention.

35. Maddox, *The Purpose of Luke–Acts*, p. 133, suggested: 'It is true that in Acts "the Kingdom of God" has become more or less synonymous with "the Christian message": but we should nor [sic] prejudge the significance of this with an adverb like "merely"'.

36. It is noteworthy that one of the famed 'we' passages, 14.22, is involved in the discussion of the kingdom of God, perhaps underscoring the necessity for the reader to 'enter the kingdom of God'.

37. Maddox, *The Purpose of Luke–Acts*, p. 106.

38. This statement is contrary to Arthur Wainwright's judgment in 'Luke and the Restoration of the Kingdom to Israel', *ExpT* 89 (1977), p. 76: 'The story of Jesus' ascension ends with a prophecy that he "will come in the same way as you saw him go into heaven" (Ac 1.11), and this is the real answer to the disciples' question about the restoration of the kingdom. Jesus will return at an unknown date in the future, which will be the time for Israel's restoration'.

39. Puskas, 'The Conclusion of Luke–Acts', pp. 91-92.

40. Dupont, 'La conclusion', p. 390.

41. Puskas, 'The Conclusion of Luke–Acts', p. 93.

42. *Ibid.*, p. 92.

43. That many have found this closure insufficient is evident from the literature in which various reasons for the ending of Acts are put forward.

44. The word also occurs at 4.2, 18; 5.21, 25, 28, 42; 11.26; 15.1, 35; 18.11, 25; 20.20; 21.21, 28. In one instance the teaching is false. Acts 15.1 refers to those from Judea who were teaching circumcision. Though primarily the activity of the apostles, it is not confined to them. Acts 15.35 indicates that 'many others' were also teaching and preaching with Paul and Barnabas.

45. Dupont, 'La conclusion', p. 390.

46. *Ibid.* Dupont maintained: 'En se rendant compte du sens réel de l'expression de Act I, 8 on perçoit en même temps le lien étroit qui unit la dernière parole de Paul à la dernière parole de Jésus.... Le témoignage à Jésus que les apôtres doivent porter jusqu'à l'extrémité de la terre coïncide avec le salut que Dieu envoie aux Gentils'.

47. Puskas, 'The Conclusion of Luke–Acts', p. 92.

48. Dupont, 'La conclusion', p. 390. Puskas ('The Conclusion of Luke–Acts', pp. 94-95) criticized Dupont's suggestion: 'To equate the two concepts (in 1.6 and 28.20) as synonymous is to ignore the distinct meaning of the hope of Israel as hope in the resurrection of the dead (Acts 23.6; 24.15; 26.6-8; 28.20)'. A close reading of the texts mentioned by Puskas may judge his criticism to be too harsh.

49. *Ibid.*, p. 363. Dupont proposed: 'Si le troisième évangile commence et se termine dans le Temple de Jérusalem (Lc 1, 8ss.; 24.53), on peut dire que les Actes commencent dans une chambre haute pour se terminer dans une chambre louée'.

50. *Ibid.*, p. 390.

51. This hypothesis is held by A. Garcia Del Moral, 'Un posible aspecto de la tesis y unidad del libro de los Hechos', *Est. Bibl.* 23 (1964), pp. 41-92; cited by Dupont, 'La conclusion', p. 390. It is much more fruitful to examine the way in which Acts 28.26-27 brings to closure a parallel plot development which begins in Acts 1.

52. R.H. Smith, 'The Theology of Acts', p. 531.

53. *Ibid.*, p. 535.

54. Puskas, 'The Conclusion of Luke–Acts', p. 94.

55. These links do, at least, serve to bring a sense of closure to the narrative of Acts.

56. Discussion of the literary theory on plot may be found in Chapter 3. That discussion is assumed in the application here.

57. After the bulk of research for this section was finished, an important article was published by R.C. Tannehill, 'Israel in Luke–Acts: A Tragic Story', *JBL* 104 (1985), pp. 69-85. Tannehill's effort (p. 69) was 'an attempt to understand Luke–Acts as a unitary narrative in which the episodes receive their meaning through their function within the larger whole'. Tannehill's work confirmed the initial soundings of this study: the story of Israel is one of gradual degeneration. There are several differences between the two studies, however. This study focuses more detailed attention on the ways in which the conflict stories move the plot line, while Tannehill relied on previous Old Testament quotations, and the missionary speeches to investigate the story of Israel in Luke–Acts. Certainly, if one is to describe the plot of Acts in a comprehensive fashion, the speeches in Acts must be taken into consideration. I am concerned only to trace through Acts the narrative thread which begins in Acts 1.1-11. Also, Tannehill's study did not recognize that while the story of the demise of Israel runs throughout Luke–Acts, the strategies employed to convey that story differ in Luke and Acts. Therefore it is necessary both to examine Luke–Acts as a whole for plot development (as Tannehill did) and to consider both stories separately to allow the various plot strategies to surface.

58. In addition to Tannehill, 'Israel in Luke–Acts', the most striking

exceptions to this methodology are the works by J.B. Tyson, 'The Jewish Public in Luke–Acts', *NTS* 30 (1984), pp. 574-83; and J.T. Sanders, 'The Salvation of the Jews in Luke–Acts', *Luke–Acts: New Perspectives from the Society of Biblical Literature Seminar*, ed. C.H. Talbert (New York: Crossroad, 1984), pp. 104-28. See also now the papers by J.T. Sanders, R.C. Tannehill, and D.L. Tiede, collected in the 1986 Seminar Papers. These articles were published after this chapter was completed.

59. Tyson, 'The Jewish Public in Luke–Acts', p. 575. Tyson mentioned the studies by J.C. O'Neill, *The Theology of Acts in its Historical Setting* and J. Jervell, *Luke and the People of God* as leaning heavily on Acts to the neglect of Luke. Conversely, the works by J. Kodell, 'Luke's Use of *Laos*, "People", Especially in the Jerusalem Narrative (Lk 19, 28-24, 53)', *CBQ* 31 (1969), pp. 327-43 and P. Minear, 'Jesus' Audiences, According to Luke', *NovT* 14 (1974), pp. 81-109, are examples of works which focus almost exclusively on Luke.

60. I have alluded to some strategies employed to show the reversal of the status of the 'people' in the Gospel in Chapter 3. In Luke, there is the same gradual hardening to Jesus until the pious Jews in the opening chapters of the Gospel have been replaced in the temple by pious Christians. These confrontation scenes in which the participants debate over an action or attitude of one of those present are very different from this empty center pattern in Acts where the character responsible for the division is not present.

61. A. Walworth, ('Narrator', pp. 110-27), who, in his study of characterization, included not only the opposition of the Jews, but also internal opposition within the Christian community, Roman opposition and Gentile opposition, concluded that in all these groups the response to the Gospel was divided. These findings are a helpful corrective to Jervell who insisted that the Jews are divided, but paid no attention to the response of other groups in the narrative. Walworth did not, however, examine the ways in which the responses of these various groups moves the major story-line of world-wide missions. Since no characters from these last two groups (Romans and Gentiles) are represented in the opening verses of Acts, reference to them will be confined to footnotes to show how they, too, either accept or reject the Jesus message.

62. L.T. Johnson, 'On Finding the Lukan Community: A Cautious Cautionary Essay', *SBL Seminar Papers* (Missoula: Scholars Press, 1979), pp. 87-100.

63. M. Kreiswirth, 'Centers, Openings, and Endings: Some Faulknerian Constants', *American Literature* 56, 1 (1984), p. 39. Kreiswirth is writing on specific plot strategies found in Faulkner, but several of his suggestions fit Acts remarkably well.

64. *Ibid.*

65. *Ibid.*, pp. 39-40. On Thomas Sutpen and Carothers McCaslin,

characters in Faulkner's *Absalom, Absalom!* Kreiswirth (p. 40) commented: 'They too are thus depicted essentially through the subjective impressions of the surrounding characters and similarly serve as the armatures around which their texts' major tensions and meanings are generated'.

66. *Ibid.*, p. 40.

67. C.F.D. Moule, 'The Christology of Acts', *Studies in Luke–Acts: Essays Presented in Honor of Paul Schubert*, ed. L. Keck and J. Louis Martyn, (Nashville: Abingdon, 1966), pp. 159-85. O'Toole has also attacked this view of 'absentee Christology' in his article, 'Activity of the Risen Jesus in Luke–Acts', *Bib* 62 (1981), pp. 471-98.

68. The name 'Jesus' occurs in every chapter in Acts except chs. 12, 14, 23, and 27.

69. O'Toole, 'Activity of the Risen Jesus', p. 497. G. MacRae, '"Whom Heaven Must Receive Until the Time": Reflections on the Christology of Acts', *Int* 27 (1973), p. 160, allowed for an absentee christology but argued: 'For our emphasis on the "absentee" character of the Christology of Acts is only half the story. How does the growing Christian community relate to the Christ who is exalted in heaven? Or to put the question differently, Is there any sense in which the "absent" Christ is nevertheless present to his church?' MacRae (pp. 160-63) then argued that while much of the church's activity was done in the absence of Jesus, his presence was still conveyed through the Holy Spirit, the name of the Lord, recalled history and the lives of his followers. MacRae's arguments for both Jesus' absence and his presence is testimony to our contention that Jesus, 'though absent, is curiously present'. Cf., however, J.A. Ziesler, 'The Name of Jesus in the Acts of the Apostles', *JSNT* 4 (1979), pp. 28-41, who argued Luke did not use the concept of 'the name of Jesus' to convey the presence of an otherwise absent Lord.

70. E. Richard, 'The Divine Purpose: The Jews and the Gentile Mission (Acts 15)', *Luke–Acts: New Perspectives from the Society of Biblical Literature Seminar*, ed. C.H. Talbert (New York: Crossroad, 1984), p. 198.

71. N. Petersen, *Literary Criticism for New Testament Critics* (Philadelphia: Fortess, 1978), pp. 83-91, has correctly pointed out that this analysis of the sequential composition of Luke–Acts must accompany any examination of the parallel composition. This parallel composition or *redundancy*, as it is called in Chapter 3, will be examined in Chapter 6 for what Tannehill has termed the 'echo effect'. See Tannehill, 'The Composition of Acts 3–5: Narrative Development and Echo Effect', *SBL Seminar Papers* (Chico: Scholars Press, 1984), pp. 217-40.

72. The list is compiled by Jervell, *Luke and the People of God* (Minneapolis: Augsburg, 1972), p. 44, and accepted by Sanders, 'The Salvation of the Jews', p. 111.

73. Whether or not to include the baptizing activity of Philip in Samaria depends on whether Luke is believed to number Samaritans among the Jews.

Among those who count the Samaritans as Gentiles in Luke–Acts are: M.S. Enslin, 'Luke and the Samaritans', *HTR* 36 (1943), p. 281; J. Bowman, *Samaritanische Probleme* (Stuttgart: Kohlhammer, 1967), p. 62; and H.J. Cadbury, *The Making of Luke–Acts* (London: SPCK, 1961), p. 257. Jervell, in his essay 'The Lost Sheep of the House of Israel: The Understanding of the Samaritans in Luke–Acts', *Luke and the People of God*, p. 123, claimed: 'There ought to be no doubt that Luke regards the Samaritans as Jews. Luke's interest in them and explicit references to them are related to their special status within Israel'. Cf. however, R.J. Coggins, 'The Samaritans and Acts', *NTS* 28 (1982), pp. 423-34, who is less certain where Samaritans should be placed in the division between Jews and Gentiles in Acts.

74.   Jervell, *Luke and the People of God*, p. 44.

75.   Sanders, 'The Salvation of the Jews', pp. 108-13.

76.   *Ibid.*, p. 111.

77.   J. Kodell came to the same conclusion, albeit using different evidence, in '"The Word of God grew". The Ecclesial Tendency of *Logos* in Acts 6, 7; 12, 24; 19, 20', *Bib* 55 (1974), pp. 505-19.

78.   J. Sanders has tried to make an argument against Jervell based on the meaning of the word 'persuade'. He claimed ('The Salvation of the Jews', p. 108):

> Of the numerous places in Acts where the word πείθω occurs, only in the three accounts of Paul's turning to the Gentiles (13.43; 18.4; and 28.23-24) and in 17.4 and 19.26 may this 'persuasion' be understood as referring to conversion to Christianity.... The fact that ... belief/conversion is mentioned later, after the announcement of turning to the Gentiles, supports the contention that the earlier 'persuasion' is not conversion.

Sanders' contention, well-argued to this point, seems to stretch the evidence and is not supported by a close reading of the texts. Particularly in the case of 28.24, Sanders overlooks the obvious contrast in the οἱ δέ clause, where 'convinced' stands in contrast to 'disbelieved'. Sanders' argument is in disagreement with the findings of H.J. Hauser, *Strukturen der Abschlusser-zählung der Apostelgeschichte, (Apg 28, 16-31)*, An Bib, 86 (Rome: Biblical Institute, 1979), pp. 62-66. Hauser (p. 66) concluded:

> Das Lexem lässt die Erfolgsbeschreibung bei einem Teil der Juden verschwommen und mehrdeutig. Offenbar kommt es nicht so sehr auf das konkrete Schicksal dieses Teiles der Juden an, sondern besonders auf die Tatsache, dass die Predigt die Hörerschaft in zwei Lager gespalten hat. Daran knüpft die Beschreibung des V. 25a an.

At best, Sanders' arguments may serve to soften Jervell's hard-line stance that the conversion of the Jews is present throughout the Acts narrative. The subtle distinction between convinced and believed, while perhaps too fine to press the non-salvific nature of 'persuade' as Sanders did, may be a literary device to aid the reader in understanding the gradual, and at points imperceptible, descent of the Jewish people in the narrative.

79. Sanders, 'The Salvation of the Jews', p. 109.
80. Jervell, *Luke and the People of God*, p. 46.
81. Sanders, 'The Salvation of the Jews', p. 112. Sanders criticized Jervell for including 21.20 in his list of reported mass conversions: 'It is therefore not proper to assume, as Jervell does, that 21.20 refers to such additional converts *when* that is the very point that needs to be proved'. (Though he mentioned 21.20, I could find no discussion by Jervell which would merit Sanders' severe criticisms at this point.)
82. The degree to which the Christian elders are out of touch with the Jewish community is seen when Paul, in the temple on the 'good' advice of the elders, is dragged from that place and beaten.
83. See Chapter 3, also Petersen, *Literary Criticism*, p. 83. Tyson is in basic agreement with Petersen regarding the importance of conflict as a plot device. He claimed in 'The Opposition to Jesus in the Gospel of Luke', *PersRelSt* 5 (1978), p. 146: 'Structuralists and other literary critics claim that the theme of conflict lies at the heart of any dramatic narrative.... Luke–Acts contains a series of conflicts, with Jesus and later the apostles and Paul occupying one side'. See also J.B. Tyson, 'Conflict as a Literary Theme in the Gospel of Luke', *New Synoptic Studies: The Cambridge Gospel Conference and Beyond*, ed. William R. Farmer (Macon: Mercer University Press, 1983), pp. 303-27.
84. The major conflicts in Acts have already been identified by Petersen, *Literary Criticism*, p. 89: Acts 3–4; 5.12-42; 13.13-52; 18.1-11. In addition to these conflict scenes with the Jews, it should be noted that there are several gentile conflict scenes (cf. Acts 16 and 19).
85. Tannehill, 'Israel in Luke–Acts', p. 76. Tannehill buttressed his argument by appealing to Peter's speech in Acts 3.19-21. L.E. Keck, 'Listening To and Listening For: From Text to Sermon (Acts 1.8)', *Int* 27 (1973), p. 188, remarked: 'The apostles are not to understand themselves on the verge of a restored kingdom but on the verge of power and mission'. Contra Maddox, *The Purpose of Luke–Acts*, FRLANT, 126 (Göttingen: Vandenhoeck & Ruprecht, 1982), p. 106, who has argued about 1.6-8: 'Jesus' answer includes an indirect denial that it is Israel to whom the Kingdom will be given'.
86. D.L. Tiede, 'Acts 1.6-8 and the Theo-Political Claims of Christian Witness', *Word and World* 1 (1981), p. 41. Tiede further suggested about Acts 1.6-11:

> The depiction is highly stylized, replete with stock features of the dramatic last appearance of the great leader: the poignant question or leading comment which summarizes the hopes and fears of the followers: 'Lord, will you at this time restore the kingdom to Israel?' the final oracle which at once corrects and redirects all short-sighted understanding into the service of the mission; the dramatic 'departure'.

D. Hill, 'The Spirit and Church's Witness: Observations on Acts 1.6-8',

IrBibSt 6 (1984), pp. 16-26, saw a much tighter structure in these verses with each phrase of the disciples' question being explicitly addressed by Jesus' response.

87. Haenchen, *Acts*, p. 143, claimed: 'Here we have the first mention of the problem of the Gentile mission, which will make itself felt again and again in Acts right up to 28.28'.

88. It should be noted that the first half of Peter's Pentecost speech, the explanation (2.14-21), is addressed to 'men of Judea and all those who dwell in Jerusalem'. The second half, the exhortation (2.22-36), is spoken specifically to 'men of Israel'. On the christological content of the speeches in Luke–Acts, W.S. Kurz has argued that Luke has followed the commonly accepted rules of the Hellenistic art of rhetoric. See W.S. Kurz, 'Hellenistic Rhetoric in the Christological Proof of Luke–Acts', *CBQ* 42 (1980), pp. 171-95. A full examination would need to take into account the information supplied by the speeches in Acts. See especially, Sanders, 'The Jewish People in Luke–Acts', pp. 110-29.

89. J. Polhill, 'The Hellenistic Breakthrough: Acts 6-12', *R&E* 71 (1974), pp. 474-86, correctly saw these chapters depicting Christianity's emergence from the chrysalis of Judaism to its worldwide mission.

90. The narrator even lists the 'people' first so that the reader does not miss this change in their plot function.

91. E. Richard argued that Stephen's speech both acknowledged Christianity's heritage in Judaism and the fact that it cannot be limited to any one place. See Richard, 'The Polemical Character of the Joseph Episode in Acts 7', *JBL* 98 (1979), pp. 255-67; *Acts 6.1–8.4: The Author's Method of Composition* (Ann Arbor: Scholars Press, 1978).

92. See C.H. Talbert, 'Martyrdom and the Lukan Social Ethic', *Political Issues in Luke–Acts*, ed. R.J. Cassidy and P.J. Scharper (Maryknoll: Orbis, 1983), pp. 98-100, for a treatment of the significance of the deaths of Jesus and Stephen for Luke–Acts.

93. R. Pesch, E. Gerhart, and F. Schilling, '"Helenisten" und "Hebräer": Zu Apg 9,29 und 6,1', *BZ* 23 (1979), pp. 87-92, made the helpful observation that the Hellenists of Acts 6.1 were Greek-speaking Jewish-Christians, while the Hellenists mentioned in 9.29 were Greek-speaking Jews in Jerusalem.

94. Richard, 'The Divine Purpose', p. 197.

95. See R. O'Toole, 'Christ's Resurrection in Acts 13, 13-52', *Bib* 60 (1979), pp. 361-72. O'Toole argued that a major portion of Paul's speech dealt with the resurrection.

96. Richard, 'The Divine Purpose', p. 198, overstated his case when he argued: 'owing to the disbelief and abuse of some, Paul withdraws from the synagogue and teaches two years at the hall of Tyrannus with great success among Jews and Greeks'. To say, as the narrator does, that both Jewish and Greek residents of Asia heard the word hardly implies great success if one is talking about a positive response to what was heard—a fact which can by no means be assumed from even a cursory reading of Acts.

97. Tyson, 'The Jewish Public in Luke–Acts', p. 583, held Luke 'does not consistently indicate that the actions of diaspora Jews were different from those of Palestinian Jews. For example, the plot against Paul that is described in Acts 23.12-22 is probably to be understood as devised by Palestinian Jews'. This argument is contra that of Walworth ('Narrator', p. 126) who claimed: 'The narrator of Acts reserves his harshest characterization of rejection for the Asian Jews'.

98. This reference was noticed by Tyson (*ibid.*, p. 581). Although no speakers are explicitly identified in 22.22, Tyson (p. 583) reasoned: 'the third person plural refers to the people who were being addressed, last mentioned in 21.40'.

99. *Ibid.*, p. 581.

100. See R. O'Toole, *Acts 26: The Christological Climax of Paul's Defense* (Rome: Biblical Institute, 1978).

101. Another profitable way of looking at these passages would be to investigate them for evidence of redundancy, i.e., repetition, variation, and context. To take one very important example, the three warnings against the Jews (13.46; 18.6; 28.28) share a basic element: the message of salvation will now be taken to the Gentiles. The variation in context is significant; in each case, the Jews do less and less to provoke this invective from Paul. In chapter 13, the Jews are filled with jealousy, contradict what Paul says, and revile him. In chapter 18, they oppose and revile, but there is no mention of jealousy. In chapter 28, all the Jews do is disagree among themselves. The door which is being opened to the Gentiles (14.27) is slowly being closed on the Jews, until finally it slams shut in Rome.

102. Jervell, *Luke and the People of God*, pp. 63-64.

103. Tyson, 'The Jewish Public in Luke–Acts', p. 583. Even Tannehill ('Israel in Luke–Acts', p. 85), who pointed out several places in Acts where there is 'a lingering hope for the salvation of the Jews', admitted: 'the indications of hope for the salvation of the Jews which point beyond the end of Acts are few and brief, whereas Jewish rejection dominates the final scene in Acts and is emphasized in other major scenes of the narrative. The story of Israel, so far as the author of Luke–Acts can tell it, is a tragic story'.

104. The above statements are made on the basis of narrative analysis, with no thought given to the actual historical situation. Some who have dealt with the narrative on the level of historicity have lodged charges of anti-Semitism against the author of Luke–Acts. J. T. Sanders, 'The Parable of the Pounds and Lucan Anti-Semitism', *TS* 42 (1981), pp. 660-68, has been particularly vehement in his protests (p. 667):

> The entire geographico-theological plan of Luke-Acts is predicated on the simple evangelical premise that the Jews rejected Jesus and that the gospel was then taken to the Gentiles, who accepted it. While such a notion is the backbone of Luke's theology, however, it is hardly reliable history. It is, in fact, so patently untrue. . . that we recognize it for the anti-Semitic lie that it is. Without that lie we would not have Lucan theology.

On the other extreme are those scholars, like Jervell and Tiede, who maintain a continuity between faithful Israel and the 'new' faithful Israel, the Church. Others who recognize that Acts records the rejection of the Gospel by the Jews are willing to allow Luke's intention to be that of individual conversion of Jews to the faith. Evidence for both views is easily found. It may be that Talbert ('Martyrdom and the Lukan Social Ethic', p. 101), was most sensitive to the narrative when he claimed:

> It is incorrect to say *only* that for Luke it is when the Jews have rejected the gospel that the way is open to the Gentiles. It is equally incorrect to say *only* that when Israel has accepted the gospel that the way to the Gentiles is opened. Both, indeed, are parts of the total view of Luke.

Aligning with Talbert is Tannehill ('Israel in Luke–Acts', p. 81) who admitted that the tale of Israel in Luke–Acts is a 'tragic story', but countered charges of anti-Semitism by claiming:

> The emotions of anguish, pity, and sorrow aroused by tragedy are not the same as the hatred of anti-Semitism, nor does the negative stereotyping of anti-Semitism fit the emphasis on the great hopes and honors of the Jews, which is essential to Luke's tragic story.

On the level of the text, this narrative analysis tends to agree with Tannehill and no attempt is made to evaluate the historical reliability of the account or the author's intention beyond the parameters of the story.

105. In fact, several scribes attempted to identify the Joseph in Acts 1.23 with the Joseph who sold a field and laid the money at the apostles' feet (4.36-37). Codex D and a few others harmonized the names by changing βαρσαββᾶν in 1.23 to βαρναβᾶν (see 4.36). Similarly, MS 181 changed βαρναβᾶς in 4.36 to conform to βαρσαββῆς. These attempts probably reflect more scribal harmonization than Christian harmony: nonetheless, they represent real readers' response to the Christian unity depicted in the narrative.

106. Haenchen, *Acts*, p. 260, made this distinction between the Hellenists and Hebrews mentioned in 6.1. See also E.C. Blackman, 'The Hellenists of Acts 6.1', *ExpT* 48 (1936-37), p. 524; C.F.D. Moule, 'Once More, Who Were the Hellenists?' *ExpT* 70 (1959), pp. 100-102; Pesch, 'Hellenisten', pp. 87-88.

107. One last conflict is recorded between Paul and Barnabas over John Mark. Rather than representing a major conflict which threatened the unity of the Church or the Gentile mission, it may well be that the division, in the words of Walworth ('Narrator', pp. 111-12), 'allows the narrator to pursue the career of Paul without the presence of Barnabas siphoning off the reader's attention from the narrator's central protagonist'.

108. Torgovnick, *Closure*, p. 14.

109. Sorensen, 'Beginning and Ending', p. 109.

110. *Ibid.*

111. C.H. Talbert, *Literary Patterns, Theological Themes and the Genre of Luke–Acts*, SBLMS, 20 (Missoula: Scholars Press, 1974).

112. *Ibid.*, p. 58.

113. The significance of these repetitive elements will be discussed in Chapter 6.

114. J.G. Davies, 'The Prefigurement of the Ascension in the Third Gospel', *JTS* 6 (1955), pp. 229-30.

115. Talbert, *Literary Patterns*, pp. 61-62.

116. The other high point of Jesus' life is the baptism which comes at the beginning of his public ministry (Luke 4.21-22). There God's confirmation comes in the form of a dove descending from the heavens and a *bath qol* affirming God's pleasure with Jesus.

117. Talbert, *Literary Patterns*, p. 64. Talbert cited Diodorus Siculus, 1.42; 2.1; 3.1; Josephus, *Ant.*, 8.1.1; 13.1.1; 14.1.1; 15.1.1; Polybius, 2.1; 3.1; 4.1; and Livy 31.1.2; 21; among others.

118. *Ibid.*

119. B. Uspensky, *A Poetics of Composition. The Structure of the Artistic Text and Typology of a Compositional Form*, trans. V. Zavarin and S. Wittig (Berkeley: University of California, 1973), p. 137. See also the discussion in Chapter 3 for more on literary theory and point of view.

120. *Ibid.*, p. 148.

121. *Ibid.*

122. For lists of inside views of Paul, Peter, the Jewish leaders, the Jews, and other characters, see Walworth, 'Narrator', pp. 51-53.

123. Uspensky, *Poetics*, p. 148.

124. See also Acts 2.12 'And they were all amazed and perplexed'.

125. While the point of view is external to the narrative, it will be noted below that the ascension is *told* by the narrator though *seen* from the point of view of the disciples.

126. Uspensky, *Poetics*, p. 149.

127. *Ibid.*, pp. 63-64. Uspensky employed the term 'bird's-eye view' because such a general point of view 'usually presupposes very broad horizons'.

128. *Ibid.*, p. 64.

129. See below, under 'Focalization'.

130. *Ibid.*, p. 64.

131. *Ibid.*

132. Uspensky, *Poetics*, p. 149. Uspensky continued:

> Subsequently, the narrator may shift to an internal position, adopting, for example, the point of view of a particular character and assuming his limited knowledge about what is to come—so that the reader forgets about the predetermined course of events in the story, despite allusions to it made previously.

Although the narrator of Acts does change from an external to an internal position in the story in the 'we' sections, those passages occur so late in the narrative that Uspensky's remarks do not seem applicable at this point. The 'we' sections are employed by the narrator of Acts for reasons other than that of framing the story or reader entry into the narrative world. For a discussion of the 'we' passages from a narrative perspective, see Walworth, 'Narrator', pp. 34-36, 40-41, 56-57; also S. Praeder, 'The Narrative Voyage: An Analysis and Interpretation of Acts 27-28' (Ph.D. dissertation, Graduate Theological Union, 1980), pp. 211-27; see also V.K. Robbins, 'By Land and By Sea: The We-Passages and Ancient Sea Voyages', *Perspectives on Luke–Acts*, ed. C.H. Talbert (Danville, Va.: ABPR, 1978), pp. 215-42.

133. In fact, Uspensky (*ibid.*, p. 149) maintained: 'Beginnings of this kind are common in narratives of different periods; as an example we may cite the Gospel of Luke, which begins from a retrospective position with a direct address to Theophilus'.

134. *Ibid.*, p. 150.

135. *Ibid.*, p. 74. Uspensky (p. 75) further noted: 'The imperfective form gives the effect of extended time; it invites us to place ourselves, as it were, in a synchronic relationship to the action, and to become witnesses to it'. While Uspensky was writing about the use of the imperfect in Russian, he did suggest (*ibid.*) that 'this verb form has the same meaning as the English continuous verb form. . . . The observer is thus placed in the center of the action, perceiving it from within'. The imperfect tense in Greek functions in a similar way—continuous action in past time. For a discussion of the imperfect periphrastic construction in Greek, see BDF, *Greek Grammar*, pp. 179-80.

136. *Ibid.*, p. 147. Here I distinguish between the 'I' of the preface and the famed 'we' passages which serve a different purpose. Contra Walworth, 'Narrator', p. 30, who seemed to suggest the passages functioned in similar fashion: 'when the narrator of Acts shifts to first-person narration, as he does in the prologue (1.1) and the famed "we" passages'.

137. Walworth, 'Narrator', p. 38. Still, Walworth's next statement is a bit overdrawn: 'There is no complementary exit from the story level to the reader's level, as we see in the Fourth Gospel'. There is a complementary exit from the story, however, it does not employ the same framing devices in closure as in entry.

138. An 'overt narratee' is one explicitly addressed and evoked by the narrator; see G. Prince, 'Notes Toward a Categorization of Fictional "Narratees"', *Poétique* 14 (1973), pp. 178-96.

139. C.J. Scalise, 'The "Hermeneutical Bridge" of the Gospel of Luke: Theophilus as Narratee and Implied Reader' (Unpublished Seminar Paper, The Southern Baptist Theological Seminary, 1985), p. 3; see Uspensky, *Poetics*, pp. 150-51.

140. H.J. Cadbury, *The Making of Luke–Acts* (New York: Macmillan, 1927), p. 198.

141. Cadbury and Lake, *Commentary on Acts*, p. 6. Interestingly, Cadbury is responsible for both evaluations!

142. The similarity of language in narrator and Jesus is a matter of phraseology as well as ideology; see Culpepper, *Anatomy*, pp. 41-42; Uspensky, *Poetics*, pp. 15-16.

143. Walworth, 'Narrator', pp. 37-38.

144. See the discussion below under 'Reader Response'.

145. C.H. Talbert, *Acts*, Knox Preaching Guides (Atlanta: John Knox Press, 1984), pp. 6-7.

146. *Ibid.*, p. 6, suggested that the purpose of the reference to the forty days was to indicate that the disciples were 'fully instructed'.

147. *Ibid.*, p. 7.

148. The fact that the angels addressed the disciples as 'Galileans' is significant. The narrative reveals that Galileans were witnesses at every major event in the ministry of Jesus; see C.H. Talbert, *Luke and the Gnostics* (Nashville: Abingdon, 1966).

149. Walworth, 'Narrator', p. 96.

150. *Ibid.*, p. 92.

151. S. Rimmon-Kenan, *Narrative Fiction: Contemporary Poetics* (London: Methuen, 1983), p. 120. See also the excellent article by Menakhem Perry, 'Literary Dynamics: How the Order of a Text Creates Its Meaning', *Poetics Today* 1 (1979), pp. 35-64, 311-61. Perry (p. 53) claimed the primacy effect manifests 'people's tendency to persist in the direction wherein they embarked on any activity'.

152. *Ibid.*

153. *Ibid.*

154. *Ibid.*, p. 76.

155. *Ibid.*

156. W. Iser, *The Implied Reader: Patterns of Communication in Prose Fiction from Bunyan to Beckett* (Baltimore: Johns Hopkins, 1978), p. 276.

157. *Ibid.*, p. 288.

158. W. Iser, *The Act of Reading: A Theory of Aesthetic Response* (Baltimore: Johns Hopkins, 1978), p. 229.

159. J.L. Resseguie, 'Reader-Response Criticism and the Synoptic Gospels', *JAAR* 52 (1984), pp. 307-24.

160. *Ibid.*, p. 309.

161. *Ibid.*

162. *Ibid.*, p. 312.

163. *Ibid.*, p. 313.

164. See especially the favorable references in the Lukan infancy narratives (1.32-33, 54-55, 68-69, 71, 74; 2.38 *et passim*) See Tannehill's discussion in 'Israel in Luke–Acts', pp. 71-76.

165. C.H. Talbert, 'The Redaction Critical Quest for Luke the Theologian', *Jesus and Man's Hope*, Vol. I, ed. D.G. Miller (Pittsburgh: Pittsburgh Theological Seminary, 1970), pp. 74-76.

166. Contra Maddox, *The Purpose of Luke–Acts*, p. 106, who argued 'the Kingdom has nothing to do with Israel, nor with Jerusalem'.

167. Tannehill, 'Israel in Luke–Acts', p. 81, correctly pointed out: 'If the author of Luke–Acts wished only to justify the Gentile mission and a Gentile church, that purpose was already accomplished with the story of Cornelius's conversion. . . . Nonetheless, Luke's fixation on unbelieving Jews is still only subsidiary to the main plot line'.

168. Resseguie, 'Reader-Response Criticism', p. 310.

169. S. Fish, *Self-Consuming Artifacts: The Experience of Seventeenth-Century Literature* (Berkeley: University of California Press, 1972).

170. M. Sternberg, *Expositional Modes and Temporal Ordering in Fiction* (Baltimore: Johns Hopkins University Press, 1978). Actually, Sternberg borrowed the term from the field of psychology where 'primacy' and 'recency' were used to describe the psychological process of human perception.

171. *Ibid.*, p. 96.

172. *Ibid.*

173. Rimmon-Kenan, *Narrative Fiction*, p. 74.

174. At least three second-century sources named the sequel to the Third Gospel 'The Acts of the Apostles': Irenaeus, *Against Heresies*, III. xiii. 3f., the anti-Marcionite prologue to Luke, and the Muratorian Canon (where the work is called 'The Acts of All the Apostles'); see F.F. Bruce, *Commentary on the Book of the Acts*, NICNT (Grand Rapids: Eerdmans, 1980), p. 17.

175. G. Krodel, *Acts*, Proclamation Commentaries, ed. Gerhard Krodel (Philadelphia: Fortress, 1981), p. 1.

176. Bruce, *Acts*, p. 17.

177. Talbert made a similar point in *What is a Gospel? The Genre of the Canonical Gospels* (Philadelphia: Fortress, 1977), p. 134.

178. Pope, 'Beginnings', pp. 749-50.

179. Resseguie, 'Reader-Response Criticism', p. 322.

180. Iser, *The Implied Reader*, p. 288.

181. G. Lohfink, *Die Himmelfahrt Jesu: Untersuchungen zu den Himmelfahrts- und Erhöhungstexten bei Lukas* (Munich: Kösel, 1971).

182. *Ibid.*, pp. 42-46; 72-74. See the discussion in Chapter 4.

183. C.H. Talbert, 'The Concept of Immortals in Mediterranean Antiquity', *JBL* 94 (1975), pp. 419-36; also 'The Myth of a Descending-Ascending Redeemer in Mediterranean Antiquity', *NTS* 22 (1976), pp. 418-39; *What is a Gospel?*, p. 41.

184. Maddox, *The Purpose of Luke–Acts*, p. 10.

185. This brief analysis of reader response could be greatly expanded by examining the response of real readers in the early church through sermons, commentaries, and meditations. In other words, in order to be comprehensive a phenomenological reader-response survey like the one above needs to be complemented by a history of reader responses.

186. Pope, 'Beginnings', p. 741.
187. *Ibid.*
188. Pope (*ibid.*, p. 736) commented: 'As listeners we want to be seduced, fascinated, entranced, snared, controlled, and a mere bloody nose won't do it ... unless it is a profound, visionary, a miraculous bloody nose: one that attempts . . . to lead us to some new discovery'. The redeeming value of these conspicuous strategies is that they do indeed lead to new, profound, visionary, even miraculous discoveries.
189. *Ibid.*, p. 745.

Notes to Chapter 6

1. Gerard Sloyan in the Foreword to *Sin, Salvation, and the Spirit*, ed. Daniel Durken (Collegeville: The Liturgical Press, 1979), p.ix.
2. Dante Gabriel Rossetti, 'St. Luke and Painter', *Poems* (New York: John W. Lovell, 1883), p. 157.
3. C.H. Talbert, *Literary Patterns, Theological Themes, and the Genre of Luke–Acts*, SBLMS, 20 (Missoula: Scholars Press, 1974), pp. 59-60, has summarized the various possible explanations of two accounts of the same event. This survey complements and expands Talbert's summary.
4. See G. Lohfink, *Die Himmelfahrt Jesu: Untersuchungen zu den Himmelfahrts- und Erhöhungstexten bei Lukas* (Munich: Kösel, 1971), pp. 26-27; also 167-202.
5. Still, as eminent a scholar as Fitzmyer has found the interpolation theory attractive. In his article, 'The Ascension of Christ and Pentecost', *TS* 45 (1984), p. 419, Fitzmyer suggested: 'many commentators ... consider it highly likely that these works existed at one time in an earlier form, to which Luke later added not only the infancy narrative and prologue, but even the secondary prologue of Acts 1.1-2 and the ending in Lk 24.50-53'. See also R. Pesch, 'Der Anfang der Apostelgeschichte: Apg 1, 1-11: Kommentarstudie', *EKKNT* 3 (1971), pp. 7-35.
6. See, e.g. G. Schille, 'Die Himmelfahrt', *ZNW* 57 (1966), p. 193, who argued that Acts 1.9-11 'wäre eine Kultätiologie für eine Versammlung der Jerusalemer Gemeinde auf dem Ölberg am 40. Tag nach dem Passa gewesen, bei welcher man der Himmelfahrt Christi gedachte'.
7. C.F.D. Moule, 'The Ascension', *ExpT* 68 (1957), p. 207.
8. J.G. Davies, *He Ascended into Heaven: A Study in the History of Doctrine* (New York: Association, 1958), p. 49; cited by Talbert, *Literary Patterns*, p. 64.
9. Lohfink, *Die Himmelfahrt Jesu*, p. 95.
10. See R.J. Dillon, *From Eye-Witnesses to Ministers of the Word: Tradition and Composition in Luke 24*, AnBib, 82 (Rome: Biblical Institute, 1978), pp. 173ff.

270 The Departure of Jesus in Luke–Acts

11. Talbert, *Literary Patterns*, p. 60.

12. Fitzmyer, 'The Ascension of Christ', p. 420.

13. Davies, *He Ascended into Heaven*, pp. 52-56; cited by Talbert, *Literary Patterns*, p. 59.

14. P.A. van Stempvoort, 'The Interpretation of the Ascension in Luke and Acts', *NTS* 5 (1959), p. 37. Actually, as van Stempvoort noted, E. Stauffer was the first to use the distinction of a 'doxological' interpretation.

15. *Ibid.*, p. 39.

16. One need only note the number of times van Stempvoort is quoted approvingly by authors of commentaries and journal articles.

17. S.G. Wilson, 'The Ascension: A Critique and an Interpretation', *ZNW* 59 (1968), pp. 277-81.

18. H. Flender, 'Heil und Geschichte in der Theologie des Lukas', *BEvT* 41 (1966), pp. 16-18. The study on focalization and point of view in Chapters 3 and 5 showed that both passages are from an earthly point of view, that of the disciples; see also Wilson, 'The Ascension', pp. 275-76.

19. Talbert, *Literary Patterns*, p. 60.

20. See the discussion on redundancy and information theory in Chapter 3.

21. R.A. Culpepper, 'Redundancy and the Implied Reader in Matthew: A Response to Janice Capel Anderson and Fred W. Burnett' (Unpublished seminar paper read at the annual meeting of the SBL, 1983), p. 4.

22. R. Tannehill, 'The Composition of Acts 3–5: Narrative Development and Echo Effect', *SBL Seminar Papers* (Chico: Scholars Press, 1984), pp. 238-40.

23. J.C. Anderson, 'The Implied Reader in Matthew' (Unpublished seminar paper submitted to the Literary Aspects of the Gospels and Acts, SBL Annual Meeting, 1983), p. 21.

24. Dillon, *Eye-Witnesses*, p. 171, is surely right when he claims: 'the context makes 24, 50-53 a *final departure* of the Lord from the disciples *whether or not* the variant at 24.51 be judged authentic'.

25. In both accounts, the disciples seem to include a larger group than just the apostles.

26. Luke has the insignificant variation of 'my Father'.

27. Tannehill, 'The Composition of Acts 3–5', pp. 239-40.

28. C.K. Barrett, *Luke the Historian in Recent Study*, FBBS, 24 (Philadelphia: Fortress, 1970), p. 57.

29. R. Maddox, *The Purpose of Luke–Acts*, FRLANT, 126 (Göttingen: Vandenhoeck & Ruprecht, 1982), p. 10.

30. Anderson, 'The Implied Reader in Matthew', p. 27.

31. Culpepper, 'Redundancy and the Implied Reader in Matthew: A Response to Janice Capel Anderson and Fred W. Burnett', p. 2.

32. E. Haenchen, *The Acts of the Apostles: A Commentary*, trans. Bernard Noble *et al.* (Philadelphia: Westminster, 1971), p. 146.

33. So among others, Fitzmyer, *Luke*, II, p. 1590; Marshall, *Luke*, p. 908.

34. Of Acts 1.6-11, vv. 6-8, and 11 either introduce or record conversation between the characters.

35. Culpepper, 'Response', p. 2.

36. Tannehill, 'The Composition of Acts 3–5', p. 239.

37. Anderson, 'The Implied Reader in Matthew', p. 27; Culpepper, 'A Response', p. 2.

38. M. Torgovnick, *Closure in the Novel* (Princeton: Princeton University Press, 1981), p. 15. Torgovnick contended: 'Readers, like characters, will—at least initially—lack the overview made possible by temporal distance'.

39. *Ibid.*, p. 11.

40. On the distinction between congruent and incongruent endings, see Torgovnick, *Closure*, pp. 17-18. Torgovnick (p. 17) maintained:

> When the author must more actively coax his reader into accepting an ending, we may describe the relationship between author and reader during closure as *incongruent*. Successful persuasion during closure results in the reader's acceptance of the ending, and converts an incongruent relationship into a congruent one.

41. In addition, the book of Acts functions much like an extended after-history, recording the later acts of Jesus' followers.

42. See Talbert, *Reading Luke*, pp. 3-6.

43. On primacy effect, see Menakhem Perry, 'Literary Dynamics: How the Order of a Text Creates its Meanings', *Poetics Today* 1 (1979), pp. 53-59.

44. C.H. Talbert, *Acts*, Knox Preaching Guide (Atlanta: John Knox, 1984), p. 6.

45. Schille, 'Die Himmelfahrt', pp. 184-85, was correct when he argued that Luke was not recording this period of instruction for the same reasons the Gnostics expanded the time-frame to 545 days in which Jesus gave 'secret instruction' to his followers. In Acts, the time period is relatively short, and the topic of discussion is no secret. Teaching about the kingdom of God was not confined to the post-resurrection appearances; it occupied a large part of Jesus' earlier teaching ministry. In addition, the disciples openly ask a question about the kingdom, confirming for the reader, not that they possess special, secret knowledge; but that they are being groomed to assume their role as ambassadors deputized to act in behalf of Christ.

46. Luke refers to 'forty days' elsewhere at Luke 4.2; and to the number 'forty' at Acts 4.22; 7.30, 36, 42; 13.21; 23.13, 21.

47. Wilson, 'The Ascension', p. 272, was able to comment: 'Thus it is not the 40 days which forces Luke to date the coming of the Spirit at Pentecost, but the date of Pentecost which forces him to use the 40 days'.

48. Much of the material presented here has already been presented in Chapter 3.

49. For Matt. (26.36) and Mark (14.32) the place is the Garden of Gethsemane; John (18.1) simply refers to a garden near the Kidron valley.

50. On the Lukan motif of Jesus' prayer on a mountain, see Fitzmyer, *Luke*, I, pp. 616, 798-99.

51. Here I disagree with Marshall's explanation that Luke has omitted the name 'Gethsemane' from the narrative 'due simply to a dislike of place-names in Aramaic which would be meaningless to Luke's readers'. See Marshall, *Luke*, p. 830.

52. On this prayer 'being exemplary behavior of those who are fully instructed', see Talbert, *Acts*, p. 7.

53. See my argument for this line of reasoning in Chapter 3.

54. Kirsopp Lake, *Beginnings of Christianity: The Acts of the Apostles*, Vol. IV, ed. F.J. Foakes Jackson and Kirsopp Lake (London: Macmillan), p. 10, suggested the two were identical.

55. The word also occurs at Acts 9.37, 39; 20.8.

56. See Chapter 3.

57. Haenchen, *Acts*, p. 146.

58. See Chapter 3. Lohfink, *Die Himmelfahrt*, p. 168, has shown the striking similarities between Luke 24.50-53 and Sir. 50.20-22.

59. Tannehill, 'The Composition of Acts 3-5', p. 240.

SELECTED BIBLIOGRAPHY

Books

Abrams, M.H., *A Glossary of Literary Terms*, New York: Holt, Reinhart and Winston, 1971.

Alsup, John E., *The Post-Resurrection Appearance Stories of the Gospel Tradition*, Calwer theologische Monographien, 5; Stuttgart: Calwer, 1975.

Alter, Robert, *The Art of Biblical Narrative*, New York: Basic Books, 1981.

Aristotle, *Poetics*, trans. S.H. Butcher; New York: Hill and Wang, 1968.

Bachmann, M., *Jerusalem und der Tempel: Die geographisch-theologischen Elemente in der lukanischen Sicht des jüdischen Kultzentrums*, Stuttgart: Kohlhammer, 1980.

Balmforth, H., *The Gospel according to Saint Luke*, Oxford: Clarendon, 1930.

Bann, V.S. and J.E. Bowlt, eds., *Russian Formalism: A Collection of Articles and Texts in Translation*, Edinburgh: Scottish Academic Press, 1973.

Bauer, Walter, *Greek-English Lexicon of the New Testament and Other Early Christian Literature*, trans. William F. Arndt and F. Wilbur Gingrich, ed. F. Danker; London: University of Chicago, 1979.

Barrett, C.K. *Luke the Historian in Recent Study*, Facet Books, Biblical Series, 24; Philadelphia: Fortress, 1970.

Black, Matthew, *An Aramaic Approach to the Gospels and Acts*, Oxford: Clarendon, 1946.

Blass, Frederick, *Acta apostolorum, sive Lucae ad Theophilum liber alter*, Göttingen: Vandenhoeck & Ruprecht, 1895.

Bode, Edward L. *The First Easter Morning*, Analecta Biblica, 45; Rome: Biblical Institute, 1970.

Book, C.L., et al., *Human Communication Principles, Contexts and Skills*, New York: St. Martin Press, 1980.

Booth, Wayne, *The Rhetoric of Fiction*, Chicago: University of Chicago Press, 1979.

Brown, Raymond E., *The Birth of the Messiah: A Commentary on the Infancy Narratives in Matthew and Luke*, Garden City: Doubleday, 1979.

Bruce, F.F., *Commentary on the Book of Acts*, The New International Commentary on the New Testament; Grand Rapids: Eerdmans, 1954.

Burchard, Christoph, *Der dreizehnte Zeuge*, Göttingen: Vandenhoeck & Ruprecht, 1970.

Cadbury, Henry J., *The Book of Acts in History*, London: A.&C. Black, 1955.

—*The Making of Luke-Acts*, 2nd edn; New York: SPCK, 1958.

Cassidy, Richard J. and Philip J. Scharper, eds., *Political Issues in Luke–Acts*, Maryknoll: Orbis, 1983.

Chase, Frederick Henry, *The Old Syriac Element in the Text of Codex Bezae*, London: Macmillan, 1893.

Chatman, Seymour, *Story and Discourse: Narrative Structure in Fiction and Film*, Ithaca: Cornell University, 1978.

Cherry, Colin, *On Human Communication*, Cambridge, Mass.: M.I.T. Press, 1957.

Childs, Brevard S. *Introduction to the Old Testament as Scripture*, Philadelphia: Fortress, 1979.

Clark, A.C., *The Acts of the Apostles*, Oxford: Clarendon, 1933.
—*The Primitive Text of the Gospels and Acts*, Oxford: Oxford University Press, 1914.
Colwell, E.C., *Studies in Methodology in Textual Criticism of the New Testament*, Grand Rapids: Eerdmans, 1969.
Conzelmann, Hans, *Die Apostelgeschichte*, Tübingen: J.C.B. Mohr, 1963.
—*The Theology of St. Luke*, trans. Geoffrey Buswell; New York: Harper, 1961.
Creed, John Martin, *The Gospel according to St. Luke: The Greek Text with Introduction, Notes, and Indices*, London: Macmillan, 1950.
Culpepper, R. Alan, *Anatomy of the Fourth Gospel: A Study in Literary Design*, Philadelphia: Fortress, 1983.
Danker, Frederick, *Jesus and the New Age According to St. Luke: A Commentary on the Third Gospel*, St. Louis: Clayton, 1972.
Daniels, Boyd L., and M. Jack Suggs, eds., *Studies in the History and Text of the New Testament in honor of Kenneth Willis Clark*, Salt Lake City: University of Utah Press, 1967.
Davies, J.G., *He Ascended into Heaven: A Study in the History of Doctrine*, London: Lutterworth, 1958.
Detweiler, Robert, ed., 'Reader Response Approaches to Biblical and Secular Texts', *Semeia 31* (1985).
Dillon, Richard J., *From Eye-Witnesses to Ministers of the Word: Tradition and Composition in Luke 24*, Analecta Biblica, 82; Rome: Biblical Institute, 1978.
Dibelius, Martin, *Studies in the Acts of the Apostles*, ed. Heinrich Greeven; trans. Mary Ling; London: SCM, 1956.
Dodd, C.H., *The Apostolic Preaching and its Development*, New York: Harper, 1944.
Drury, John, *Tradition and Design in Luke's Gospel*, Atlanta: John Knox Press, 1976.
Edwards, O.C. *Luke's Story of Jesus*, Philadelphia: Fortress, 1981.
Egelkraut, H.L. *Jesus' Mission to Jerusalem: A redaction critical study of the Travel Narrative in the Gospel of Luke, 9:51-19:48*, Frankfurt: Peter Lang, 1976.
Ellis, E. Earle, *The Gospel of Luke*, Grand Rapids: Eerdmans, 1981.
Epp, Eldon J., *The Theological Tendency of Codex Beze Cantabrigiensis in Acts*, Cambridge: Cambridge University Press, 1966.
Evans, C.F., *Resurrection and the New Testament*, London: SCM, 1970.
Farmer, William R., ed., *New Synoptic Studies: The Cambridge Gospel Conference and Beyond*, Macon, GA: Mercer University Press, 1983.
—*The Synoptic Problem: A Critical Analysis*, New York: Macmillan, 1964.
Flender, H., *St. Luke: Historian and Theologian*, Philadelphia: Fortress, 1967.
Fish, Stanley, *Is There a Text in This Class? The Authority of Interpretive Communities*, Cambridge, Mass.: Harvard University Press, 1980.
Fitzmyer, Joseph A. *The Gospel According to Luke: I-X*, The Anchor Bible; 2 vols.; Garden City: Doubleday, 1982.
Foakes-Jackson, F.J. and Kirsopp Lake, eds., *The Beginnings of Christianity*, 5 vols.; London: Macmillan, 1920-1933.
Forster, E.M., *Aspects of the Novel*, San Diego: Harcourt, Brace, and Jovanovich, 1927.
Franklin, Eric, *Christ the Lord: A Study in the Purpose and Theology of Luke-Acts*, Philadelphia: Westminster, 1975.
Friedman, Alan, *The Turn of the Novel*, New York: Oxford University Press, 1966.
Fuller, Reginald H., *The Formation of the Resurrection Narratives*, Philadelphia: Fortress, 1980.

Gasque, W. Ward, *A History of the Criticism of the Acts of the Apostles*, Grand Rapids: Eerdmans, 1975.

Geldenhuys, Norval, *Commentary on the Gospel of Luke*, Grand Rapids: Eerdmans, 1951.

Genette, Gerard, *Narrative Discourse: An Essay in Method*, trans. Jane E. Lewin Ithaca: Cornell University Press, 1980.

Gilmour, S.M., 'The Gospel according to St. Luke', *Interpreter's Bible*, Vol. VIII, Nashville: Abingdon, 1952.

Girard, Réné, *Deceit, Desire, and the Novel*, trans. Yvonne Freccero; Baltimore: Johns Hopkins, 1965.

Goulder, M.D., *Type and History in Acts*, London: SPCK, 1964.

Haenchen, Ernst, *The Acts of the Apostles: A Commentary*, trans. Bernard Noble; Philadelphia: Westminster, 1971.

Hanna, William, *The Forty Days After Our Lord's Resurrection*, New York: Robert Carter, 1866.

Harris, J. Rendal, *Codex Bezae: A Study of the So-Called Western Text of the New Testament*, Texts and Studies, 2; Cambridge: Cambridge University Press, 1891.

Harrison, James A., *The Complete Works of Edgar Allan Poe*, 17 vols.; New York: George D. Sproul, 1902.

Hendrickx, Herman, *The Resurrection Narratives of the Synoptic Gospels*, Studies in the Synoptic Gospels; London: Geoffrey Chapman, 1984.

Hengel, Martin, *Acts and the History of Earliest Christianity*, trans. John Bowden; Philadelphia: Fortress, 1980.

Hirsch, E.D., *Validity in Interpretation*, New Haven: Yale University Press, 1967.

Hultgren, Arland J., *Jesus and his Adversaries: The Form and Function of the Conflict Stories in the Synoptic Tradition*, Minneapolis: Augsburg, 1979.

Hurtado, Larry W., *Text-Critical Methodology and the Pre-Caesarean Text: Codex W in the Gospel of Mark*, Studies and Documents, 43; Grand Rapids: Eerdmans, 1981.

Iser, Wolfgang, *The Act of Reading*, Baltimore: Johns Hopkins, 1978.

—*The Implied Reader*, Baltimore: Johns Hopkins, 1974.

James, Henry, *The Art of the Novel*, ed. R.P. Blackmur; New York: Scribner, 1962.

Jeremias, Joachim, *The Eucharistic Words of Jesus*, trans. Norman Perrin; Philadelphia: Fortress, 1966.

Johnson, Luke T., *The Literary Function of Possessions in Luke–Acts*, SBL Dissertation Series; Missoula: Scholars Press, 1977.

Karris, Robert J., *Invitation to Luke*, Garden City: Image Books, 1977.

—*Luke: Artist and Theologian, Luke's Passion Account as Literature*, New York: Paulist Press, 1985.

—*What Are They Saying About Luke and Acts?*, New York: Paulist Press, 1979.

Keck, Leander and J. Louis Martyn, eds., *Studies in Luke–Acts: Essays Presented in Honor of Paul Schubert*, Nashville; Abingdon, 1966.

Keegan, Terence J., *Interpreting the Bible: A Popular Introduction to Biblical Hermeneutics*, New York: Paulist Press, 1985.

Kelly, J.N.D., *Early Christian Creeds*, London: Longman, 1972.

Kenyon, F.G., *The Western Text in the Gospels and Acts*, Proceedings of the British Academy, 24; London: n.p., 1939.

Kermode, Frank, *The Sense of an Ending: Studies in the Theory of Fiction*, New York: Oxford University Press, 1967.

Kingsbury, Jack Dean, *Matthew as Story*, Philadelphia: Fortress, 1986.

Klijn, A.F.J., *A Survey of the Researches into the Western Text of the Gospels and Acts*, Utrecht: Kemink, 1949.

—*A Survey of the Researches into the Western Text of the Gospels and Acts: Part Two, 1949-1969*, Leiden: Brill, 1969.

Koester, Helmut, *Introduction to the New Testament, Volume Two: History and Literature of Early Christianity*, Philadelphia: Fortress, 1982.

Ladd, George E., *I Believe in the Resurrection of Jesus*, Grand Rapids: Eerdmans, 1977.

Lake, Kirsopp, *Landmarks in the History of Early Christianity*, London: Macmillan, 1920.

Lanser, Susan, *The Narrative Act: Point of View in Prose Fiction*, Princeton: Princeton University Press, 1981.

Larrañaga, V., *L'Ascension de notre seigneur dans le nouveau testament*, Rome: Pontifical Biblical Institute, 1938.

Laurentin, R., *Jésus au Temple: Mystère de pâques et foi de Marie en Luc 2, 48-50*, Paris: Gabalda, 1966.

Leaney, A.R.C., *A Commentary on the Gospel According to St. Luke*, New York: Harper, 1958.

Lenski, R.C.H., *The Interpretation of St. Luke's Gospel*, Columbus: Wartburg, 1946.

Léon-Dufour, Xavier, *Resurrection and the Message of Easter*, trans. R.N. Wilson; New York: Holt, Rhinehart, and Winston, 1974.

Lewis, Jack R., *The English Bible/From KJV to NIV: A History and Evaluation*, Grand Rapids: Baker, 1981.

Lightfoot, J.B., *On a Fresh Revision of the English New Testament*, London: Macmillan, 1871.

Lohfink, Gerhard, *Die Himmelfahrt Jesu: Untersuchungen zu den Himmelfahrts- und Erhöhungstexten bei Lukas*, Munich: Kösel, 1971.

Löning, Karl, *Die Saulustradition in der Apostelgeschichte*, Münster: Aschendorff, 1973.

McKnight, Edgar V., *The Bible and the Reader: An Introduction to Literary Criticism*, Philadelphia: Fortress, 1985.

Maddox, Robert, *The Purpose of Luke–Acts*, FRLANT 126; Göttingen: Vandenhoeck & Ruprecht, 1982.

Mahoney, Robert, *Two Disciples at the Tomb: The Background and Message of John 20.1-10*, Frankfurt: Herbert Lang, 1974.

Malbon, Elizabeth Struthers, *Narrative Space and Mythic Meaning in Mark*, San Francisco: Harper & Row, 1986.

Manson, William, *The Gospel of Luke*. New York: Harper, 1930.

Marshall, I. Howard, *Commentary on Luke*, New International Greek Testament Commentary; Grand Rapids: Eerdmans, 1978.

—*Luke: Historian and Theologian*, Exeter: Paternoster, 1970.

Martin, Victor, and Rudolphe Kasser, eds., *Papyrus Bodmer XIV-XV: Évangiles de Luc et Jean*, Cologny-Genève: Bodmer, 1961.

Martini, Carlo M., *Il Problema della rescensionalità del codice B all luce del papiro Bodmer XIV*, Analecta Biblica, 26; Rome: Biblical Institute, 1966.

Marxsen, Willi, *Der Evangelist Markus: Studien zur Redaktionsgeschichte des Evangeliums*, Göttingen: Vandenhoeck & Ruprecht, 1956.

—*The Resurrection of Jesus of Nazareth*, trans. Margaret Kohl; Philadelphia: Fortress, 1970.

Metzger, Bruce M., *The Text of the New Testament: Its Transmission, Correction and Restoration*, 2nd edn; New York: Oxford, 1968.

—*A Textual Commentary on the Greek New Testament*, 3rd edn; London: United Bible Societies, 1975.

Miller, D.A., *Narrative and its Discontents: Problems of Closure in the Traditional Novel*, Princeton: Princeton University Press, 1981.

Miyoshi, M., *Der Angang des Reiseberichts: Lk 9,51–10,24*, Analecta Biblica, 60; Rome: Biblical Institute, 1974.

Morgenthaler, Robert, *Die lukanishe Geschichtsschreibung als Zeugnis*, 2 vols.; Zürich: Zwingli, 1949.

Munck, Johannes, *The Acts of the Apostles*, The Anchor Bible, 31; Garden City, N.Y.: Doubleday, 1967.

Neil, William, *The Acts of the Apostles*, New Century Bible; Greenwood, S.C.: Attic Press, 1973.

Neirynck, Frans, *Jean et les Synoptiques: examen critique de l'exégèse de M.-E. Boismard*, Leuven: Leuven University Press, 1979.

Nineham, D.E., ed., *Studies in the Gospels: Essays in Memory of R.H. Lightfoot*, Oxford: Blackwell, 1957.

O'Toole, Robert, *Acts 26: The Christological Climax of Paul's Defense*, Rome: Biblical Institute, 1978.

Pearce, J.P., *Symbols, Signals and Noise: The Nature and Process of Communication*, New York: Harper & Row, 1961.

Petersen, Norman R., *Literary Criticism for New Testament Critics*, Philadelphia: Fortress, 1978.

Plooij, Daniel, *The Ascension in the 'Western' Textual Tradition*, Amsterdam: Koninklijke, Akademie, 1929.

Plummer, Alfred, *A Critical and Exegetical Commentary on the Gospel According to St. Luke*, ICC, 27; New York: Scribner, 1896.

Rhoads, David and Donald Michie, *Mark as Story: An Introduction to the Narrative of a Gospel*, Philadelphia: Fortress, 1982.

Richard, Earl, *Acts 6:1–8:4: The Author's Method of Composition*, Ann Arbor: Scholars Press, 1978.

Richter, David H., *Fable's End: Completeness and Closure in Rhetorical Fiction*, Chicago: The University of Chicago Press, 1974.

Rimmon-Kenan, Shlomith, *Narrative Fiction: Contemporary Poetics*, London: Methuen, 1983.

Robinson, J., Armitage, *A Study of Codex Bezae*, Cambridge: Cambridge University Press, 1891.

—*The Story of the Bodmer Papyri*, Philadelphia: Fortress [forthcoming].

Robinson, W.C. Jr, 'The Way of the Lord', Dissertation, Basel, 1962.

Rohde, Joachim, *Rediscovering the Teaching of the Evangelists*, trans. Dorothea M. Barton; London: SCM, 1968.

Russell, D.A. and M. Winterbottom, eds., *Ancient Literary Criticism: The Principal Texts in New Translations*, Oxford: Clarendon, 1972.

Said, Edward W., *Beginnings: Intention and Method*, New York: Basic Books, 1975.

Salmon, George, *Some Thoughts on the Textual Criticism of the New Testament*, London: John Murray, 1897.

Schmidt, Karl L., *Der Rahmen der Geschichte Jesu*, Berlin: Trowitsch, 1919.

Scholes, Robert, ed., *Approaches to the Novel*, San Francisco: Chandler, 1961.

Schüssler-Fiorenza, Elizabeth, *In Memory of Her*, New York: Crossroad, 1983.

Schweizer, Eduard, *The Good News According to Luke*, Atlanta: John Knox Press, 1984.

Smith, Barbara Herrnstein, *Poetic Closure: A Study of How Poems End*, Chicago: University of Chicago Press, 1968.

Solages, Mgr de, *Jean et les Synoptiques*, Leiden: Brill, 1979.

Stagg, Frank, *The Book of Acts: The Early Struggle for an Unhindered Gospel*, Nashville: Broadman, 1955.

Stanley, David M., *Jesus in Gethsemane: The Early Church Reflects on the Suffering of Jesus*, New York: Paulist Press, 1980.

Sternberg, Meir, *Expositional Modes and Temporal Ordering in Fiction*, Baltimore and London: Johns Hopkins, 1978.

—*The Poetics of Biblical Literature: Ideological Literature and the Drama of Reading*, Bloomington: Indiana University Press, 1985.

Stevick, Philip, ed., *The Theory of the Novel*, New York: Free Press, 1964.

Streeter, B.H., *The Four Gospels*, London: Macmillan, 1924.

Swete, H.B., *The Ascended Christ: A Study in the Earliest Christian Teaching*, London: Macmillan, 1910.

Talbert, Charles H., *Acts*, Knox Preaching Guides: Atlanta: John Knox, 1984.

—*Literary Patterns, Theological Themes, and the Genre of Luke–Acts*, Missoula: Scholars Press, 1974.

—*Luke and the Gnostics*, Nashville: Abingdon, 1966.

— ed., *Luke–Acts: New Perspectives from the Society of Biblical Literature Seminar*, New York: Crossroad, 1984.

— ed., *Perspectives on Luke–Acts*, A.B.P.R. Special Studies, 5; Edinburgh: T. & T. Clark, 1978.

—*Reading Luke: a Literary and Theological Commentary on the Third Gospel*, New York: Crossroad, 1982.

—*What is a Gospel? The Genre of the Canonical Gospels*, Philadelphia: Fortress, 1977.

Tannehill, Robert C., *The Narrative Unity of Luke–Acts: A Literary Interpretation*, Philadelphia: Fortress, 1986.

Tiede, David L., *Prophecy and History in Luke–Acts*, Philadelphia: Fortress, 1980.

Torgovnick, Marianna, *Closure in the Novel*, Princeton, NJ: Princeton University Press, 1981.

Torrey, C.C., *Composition and Date of Acts*, Cambridge, Mass.: Harvard University Press, 1916.

—*Documents of the Primitive Church*, New York: Macmillan, 1941.

Uspensky, Boris, *A Poetics of Composition. The Structure of the Artistic Text and Typology of a Compositional Form*, trans. Valentina Zavarin and Susan Wittig; Berkeley: University of California Press, 1973.

Welsh, Alexander, ed., *Narrative Endings*, Berkeley: University of California Press, 1979.

Westcott, Arthur, *Life and Letters of Brooke Foss Westcott*, 2 vols.; London: Macmillan, 1903.

Westcott, Brooke Foss, and Fenton John Anthony Hort, *The New Testament in the Original Greek*, 2 vols., London: Macmillan, 1881.

Wilckens, Ulrich, *Resurrection. Biblical Testimony to the Resurrection: An Historical Examination and Explanation*, Edinburgh: Saint Andrews, 1977.

Wilcox, Max, *The Semitisms of Acts*, Oxford: Clarendon, 1965.

Williams, C.S.C., *The Acts of the Apostles*, Harper's New Testament Commentaries; 2nd edn; New York: Harper, 1964.

Wilson, J.M., *The Acts of the Apostles, translated from the Codex Bezae, with an Introduction on its Lucan Origin and Importance*, London: SPCK, 1923.

Wilson, R. McL., *The Gospel of Philip*, London: Mowbray, 1962.

Wilson, Stephen G., *The Gentiles and the Gentile Mission in Luke–Acts*, Cambridge: Cambridge University Press, 1973.

Wisse, Frederick, *The Profile Method for Classifying and Evaluating Manuscript Evidence*, Studies and Documents, 44; Grand Rapids: Eerdmans, 1982.

Yoder, James D., *Concordance to the Distinctive Greek Text of Codex Bezae*, Grand Rapids: Eerdmans, 1961.

Zahn, Theodor, *Introduction to the New Testament*, New York: Scribner, 1917.

Articles

Abrams, M.H., 'How to do Things with Texts', *Partisan Review* 46 (1979), pp. 566-88.

Aland, Kurt, 'Die Bedeutung des p^{75} für den Text des Neuen Testaments. Ein Beitrag zur Frage der "Western non-interpolations"', *Studien zur Überlieferung des Neuen Testaments und seines Textes*, Berlin: de Gruyter, 1967.

—'Neue Neutestamentliche Papyri II', *NTS* 9 (1962-63), pp. 303-16; 10 (1963-64), pp. 62-79; 11 (1964-65), pp. 1-21; 12 (1965-66), pp. 193-200.

—'The Significance of the Papyri for Progress in New Testament Research', *The Bible in Modern Scholarship*, ed. J. Philip Hyatt; Nashville: Abingdon, 1965.

Argyle, A.W., 'The Ascension', *ExpT* 66 (1954-55), pp. 240-42.

Baltzer, K., 'The Meaning of the Temple in the Lukan Writings', *HTR* 58 (1965), pp. 263-77.

Barrett, C.K. 'Is There a Theological Tendency in Codex Bezae?' *Text and Interpretation: Studies in the New Testament presented to Matthew Black*, ed. Ernest Best and R.McL. Wilson; London: Cambridge University Press, 1979.

Barton, G.A., 'Professor Torrey's Theory of the Aramaic Origin of the Gospels and the First Half of the Acts of the Apostles', *JTS* 36 (1935), pp. 357-73.

Black, Matthew, 'The Holy Spirit in the Western Text of Acts', *New Testament Textual Criticism: Its Significance for Exegesis*, ed. Eldon J. Epp and Gordon D. Fee, Oxford: Clarendon, 1981.

—'Notes on the Longer and Shorter Text of Acts', *On Language, Culture and Religion: In Honor of Eugene A. Nida*, ed. Matthew Black and W.A. Smalley; Paris: Mouton, 1974.

Blackman, E.C., 'The Hellenists of Acts 6.1', *ExpT* 48 (1936-37), pp. 524-25.

Brodie, T. 'A New Temple and a New Law: The Unity and Chronicler-based Nature of Luke 1.1–4.22a', *JSNT* 5 (1979), pp. 21-45.

Bulletin of the Bezan Club, I-XII (1925-37).

Burkitt, F.C., 'Professor C.C. Torrey on Acts', *JTS* 20 (1919), pp. 320-29.

Cadbury, Henry J., 'Luke—Translator or Author?', *American Journal of Theology* 24 (1920), pp. 436-55.

Clark, Kenneth Willis, 'The Text of the Gospel of John in Third-Century Egypt', *Novum Testamentum* 5 (1962), pp. 17-24.

—'The Theological Relevance of Textual Variation in Current Criticism of the Greek New Testament', *JBL* 85 (1966), pp. 1-16.

Coggins, R.J., 'The Samaritans and Acts', *NTS* 28 (1982), pp. 423-34.

Colwell, E.C., 'Biblical Criticism: Lower and Higher', *JBL* 67 (1948), pp. 1-12.

Cosgrove, Charles H., 'The Divine *DEI* in Luke–Acts: Investigations into the Understanding of God's Providence', *Novum Testamentum* 26 (1984), pp. 168-90.

Creed, John Martin, 'The Text and Interpretation of Acts i 1-2', *JTS* 35 (1934), pp. 176-82.

Crowe, Jerome, 'The *Laos* at the Cross: Luke's Crucifixion Scene', *The Language of the Cross*, ed. Aelred Lacomara; Chicago: Franciscan Herald (1977), pp. 77-101.

Culpepper, R. Alan, 'Story and History in the Gospels', *Review and Expositor* 81 (1984), pp. 467-77.

Curtis, K.P.G., 'Linguistic Support for Three Western Readings in Luke 24', *ExpT* 83 (1971-72), pp. 344-45.

—'Luke xxiv.12 and John xx.3-10', *JTS* 22 (1971), pp. 512-15.

Davies, J.G., 'The Prefiguration of the Ascension in the Third Gospel', *JTS* 6 (1955), pp. 229-33.

Davies, J.H., 'The Purpose of the Central Section of Luke's Gospel', *Studia Evangelia*, Berlin: Akademie, 1964.

Delling, G., 'Das letzte Wort der Apostelgeschichte', *Novum Testamentum* 15 (1973), pp. 193-204.

Dillon, Richard J., 'Previewing Luke's Project from his Prologue (Luke 1.1-4)', *CBQ* 43 (1981), pp. 205-21.

Duplacy, Jean, 'La préhistorie du texte in Luc 22.43-44', *New Testament Textual Criticism: Its Significance for Exegesis: Essays in Honor of Bruce M. Metzger*, ed. Eldon J. Epp and Gordon D. Fee; Oxford: Oxford University Press, 1981.

Dupont, Jacques, 'La portée christologique de l'évangélisation des nations d'après Luc 24,47', *Neues Testament und Kirche: Für Rudolf Schnackenburg*, ed. Joachim Gnilka; Freiburg: Herder (1974), pp. 125-43.

—'L'utilisation apologétique de l'ancien Testament dans les discours des Actes', *Ephemerides Theologicae Lovanienses* 29 (1954), pp. 289-327.

Egan, Kieran, 'What Is a Plot?', *New Literary History*, 9 (1978), pp. 455-73.

Ehrman, Bart D. and Mark A. Plunkett, 'The Angel and Agony: The Textual Problem of Luke 22.43-44', *CBQ* 24 (1983), pp. 401-16.

Enslin, Morton S., 'The Ascension Story', *JBL* 47 (1928), pp. 60-73.

—'Luke and the Samaritans', *HTR* 36 (1943), pp. 278-97.

Epp, Eldon J., 'Ascension in the Textual Tradition of Luke–Acts', *New Testament Textual Criticism: Its Significance for Exegesis*, ed. Eldon J. Epp and Gordon D. Fee, Oxford: Oxford University Press (1981), pp. 131-46.

—'A Continuing Interlude in New Testament Textual Criticism?', *HTR* 73 (1980), pp. 1-15.

—'Coptic Manuscript G67 and the Role of Codex Bezae as a Western Witness in Acts', *JBL* 85 (1966), pp. 197-212.

—'The Eclectic Method in New Testament Textual Criticism: Solution or Symptom?', *HTR* 69 (1976), pp. 211-57.

—'New Testament Textual Criticism in America: Requiem for a Discipline', *JBL* 98 (1979), pp. 94-98.

—'Toward the Clarification of the Term "Textual Variant"', *JBL* 94 (1975), pp. 153-73.

—'The Twentieth Century Interlude in New Testament Textual Criticism', *JBL* 93 (1974), pp. 386-414.

Falconer, J.W., 'The Aramaic Source of Acts I–XV and Paul's Conversion', *The Expositor* 19 (1920), pp. 271-85.

Farmer, William R., 'Modern Developments of Griesbach's Hypothesis', *NTS* 23 (1977), pp. 283-93.

—'A "Skeleton in the Closet" of Gospel Research', *Biblical Research* 9 (1961), pp. 18-42.

—'The Two-Document Hypothesis as a Methodological Criterion in Synoptic Research', *Anglican Theological Review* 48 (1966), pp. 1204-1206.

Fascher, Erich, 'Anastasis-Resurrectio-Auferstehung', *ZNW* 40 (1941), pp. 166-229.

—'Theologische Beobachtungen zu *dei*', *Neutestamentliche Studien für Rudolf Bultmann*, ed. W. Eltester; Berlin: Töpelmann, 1954.

Fee, Gordon D., 'p66, p75, and Origen: The Myth of Early Textual Recension in Alexandria', *New Dimensions in New Testament Study*, ed. Richard N. Longenecker and Merrill C. Tenney; Grand Rapids: Zondervan, 1974.

—'Rigorous or Reasoned Eclecticism—Which?', *Studies in New Testament Language and Text*, ed. J.K. Elliott; Leiden: Brill, 1976.

Fish, Stanley, 'Literature in the Reader: Affective Stylistics', *New Literary History* 2 (1970), pp. 123-62.

Fitzmyer, Joseph A. 'The Ascension of Christ and Pentecost', *Theological Studies* 45 (1984), pp. 409-40.

—'Matthew Black's *An Aramaic Approach to the Gospels and Acts* (Review)', *CBQ* 30 (1968), pp. 418-20.

—'Papyrus Bodmer XIV: Some Features of Our Oldest Text of Luke', *CBQ* 24 (1962), pp. 170-79.

—'The Priority of Mark and the "Q" Source in Luke', *Jesus and Man's Hope*, Vol. I, ed. D.G. Miller; Pittsburgh: Pittsburgh Theological Seminary, 1970.

Foakes-Jackson, F.J., 'Professor C.C. Torrey on the Acts', *HTR* 10 (1917), pp. 352-61.

Franklin, Eric, 'The Ascension and the Eschatology of Luke–Acts', *SJT* 23 (1970), pp. 191-200.

Friedrich, Gerhard, 'Lk 9,51 und die Entrückungschristologie des Lukas', *Orientierung an Jesus: Zur Theologie der Synoptiker*, Freiburg: Herder, 1973.

Gill, D., 'Observations on the Lukan Travel Narrative and Some Related Passages', *HTR* 63 (1970), pp. 199-221.

Goodspeed, E.J., 'The Origin of Acts', *JBL* 39 (1920), pp. 83-101.

Graefe, Ferdinand, 'Der Schluss des Lukasevangeliums und der Anfang der Apostelgeschichte', *Theologische Studien und Kritiken* 61 (1888), pp. 522-41.

Grant, Frederick C., 'Where Form Criticism and Text Criticism Overlap', *JBL* 59 (1940), pp. 11-21.

Grässer, Erich, 'Acta-Forschung seit 1960', *Theologische Rundschau* 41 (1976), pp. 141-94, 259-90; 42 (1977), pp. 1-68.

Grundmann, W., 'Fragen der Komposition des lukanischen Reiseberichts', *ZNW* 50 (1959), pp. 252-70.

Hahn, Ferdinand, '*Die Himmelfahrt Jesu*: Ein Gespräch mit Gerhard Lohfink', *Biblica* 55 (1974), pp. 418-26.

Hill, D., 'The Spirit and Church's Witness: Observations on Acts 1.6-8', *Irish Biblical Studies*, 6 (1984), pp. 16-26.

Holmes-Gore, V.A., 'The Ascension and the Apocalyptic Hope: The Significance of Acts 1.6-8', *Theology* 32 (1936), pp. 356-58.

Horbury, W. 'New Wine in Old Skins: IX-The Temple', *ExpT* 86 (1974), pp. 36-42.

Hume, Kathryn, 'Beginnings and Endings in the Icelandic Family Sagas', *Modern Language Review* 68 (1973), pp. 593-606.

Johnson, Luke T., 'On finding the Lukan Community: A Cautious Cautionary Essay', *SBL Seminar Papers*, Missoula: Scholars Press (1979), pp. 87-100.

Karris, Robert J., 'Windows and Mirrors: Literary Criticism and Luke's Sitz im Leben', *SBL Seminar Papers*, ed. Paul J. Achtemeier; Missoula: Scholars Press, 1979.

Keck, Leander E., 'Listening To and Listening For: From Text to Sermon (Acts 1.8)', *Interpretation*, 27 (1973), pp. 1184-1202.

—'Will the Historical-Critical Method Survive? Some Observations', *Orientation by Disorientation: Studies in Literary Criticism and Biblical Literary Criticism, Presented in Honor of William A. Beardslee*, ed. Richard A. Spencer, Pittsburg: Pickwick, 1980, pp. 115-27.

Kilpatrick, G.D., 'An Eclectic Study of the Text of Acts', *Biblical and Patristic Studies in Memory of Robert Pierce Casey*, ed. J.N. Birdsall and R.W. Thomson; Freiburg: Herder, 1963.

—'Western Text and Original Text in the Gospels and Acts', *JTS* 44 (1943), pp. 24-36.

King, Marchant, 'Notes on the Bodmer Manuscript of Luke', *Bibliotheca Sacra* 122 (1965), pp. 234-40.

Kodell, Jerome, 'Luke's Use of Laos, "People", especially in the Jerusalem Narrative (Lk 19, 28-24-53)', *CBQ* 31 (1969), pp. 327-43.

—'The Theology of Luke in Recent Study', *Biblical Theology Bulletin* 1 (1971), pp. 115-44.

Kreiswirth, Martin 'Centers, Openings, and Endings: Some Faulknerian Constants', *American Literature* 56 (1984), pp. 38-50.

Kurz, W.S., 'Hellenistic Rhetoric in the Christological Proof of Luke–Acts', *CBQ* 42 (1980), pp. 171-95.

—'Luke 22.14-38 and Greco-Roman and Biblical Farewell Addresses', *JBL* 104 (1985), pp. 251-68.

Lake, Kirsopp, 'The Practical Value of Textual Variation: Illustrated from the Book of Acts', *The Biblical World* 19 (1902), pp. 361-69.

Lay, Mary M., 'Temporal Ordering in the Fiction of Margaret Drabble', *Critique: Studies in Modern Fiction*, 21 (1980), pp. 73-84.

Leaney, A.R.C., 'The Resurrection Narratives in Luke (xxiv. 12-52)', *NTS* 2 (1955-56), pp. 110-14.

—'Why there were Forty Days between the Resurrection and Ascension in Acts 1,3', *Studia Evangelica* 4 (1968), pp. 417-19.

Lohfink, Gerhard, 'Die "Himmelfahrt Jesu" im lukanischen Geschichtswerk', *Bibel und Kirche* 20 (1965), pp. 43-48.

Lohse, Ernst, 'Lukas als Theologe der Heilsgeschichte', *Evangelische Theologie* 14 (1954), pp. 256-75.

MacRae, George, '"Whom Heaven Must Receive Until the Time": Reflections on the Christology of Acts', *Interpretation* 27 (1973), pp. 160-70.

Martini, Carlo, 'Problema recensionalitatis codicis in luce papyri Bodmer XIV (p^{75})', *Verba Domini* 44 (1967), pp. 192-96.

Menoud, Ph. H., 'Remarques sur les textes de l'ascension dans Luc-Actes', *Neutestamentliche Studien für Rudolf Bultmann*, ed. Walther Eltester; Berlin: Töpelmann, 1957, pp. 148-56.

—'The Western Text and the Theology of Acts', *Bulletin of the Studiorum NT Societas* 2 (1951), pp. 19-32.

Metzger, Bruce M., 'The Ascension of Jesus Christ', *Historical and Literary Studies: Pagan, Jewish and Christian*, Grand Rapids: Eerdmans, 1968.

—'The Bodmer Papyrus of Luke and John', *ExpT* 73 (1961-62), pp. 201-203.

Minear, Paul S., 'Jesus' Audiences According to Luke', *Novum Testamentum* 16 (1974), pp. 81-109.

Moessner, David P., 'Luke 9.1-50: Luke's Preview of the Journey of the Prophet like Moses of Deuteronomy', *JBL* 102 (1983), pp. 575-605.

Moule, C.F.D., 'The Ascension - Acts i.9', *ExpT* 68 (1957), pp. 205-209.

—'Once More, Who Were the Hellenists?', *ExpT* 70 (1959), pp. 100-102.

Mullenbrock, Heinz-Joachim, 'Modes of Opening in the Work of E.M. Forster: A Contribution to the Poetics of His Novels', *Modern Philology* 70 (1973), pp. 216-29.

Neirynck, Frans, 'ΑΠΗΛΘΕΝ ΠΡΟΣ ΕΑΥΤΟΝ Lc 24,12 et Jn 20,10', *Ephemerides Theologicae Lovanienses* 54 (1978), pp. 104-18.

—'The "Other Disciple" in Jn 18,15-16', *Ephemerides Theologicae Lovanienses* 51 (1975), pp. 113-41.

—'ΠΑΡΑΚΥΨΑΣ ΒΛΕΠΕΙ Lc 24,12 et Jn 20,5', *Ephemerides Theologicae Lovanienses* 53 (1977), pp. 113-52.

—'The Uncorrected Historic Present in Lk XXIV.12', *Ephemerides Theologicae Lovanienses* 48 (1972), pp. 548-53.

Nestle, Eberhard, 'Some Observations on the Codex Bezae', *The Expositor* 2 (1895), pp. 235-40.

Ogg, G., 'The Central Section of the Gospel according to St. Luke', *NTS* 18 (1971-72), pp. 39-53.

Oliver, Harold, H., '*Redaktionsgeschichte* for Textual Criticism of the New Testament', *JAAR* 36 (1968), pp. 41-45.

Osten-Sacken, P. von der, 'Zur Christologie des lukanischen Reiseberichts', *Evangelische Theologie* 33 (1973), pp. 476-96.

O'Toole, Robert F., 'Activity of the Risen Jesus in Luke-Acts', *Biblica* 62 (1981), pp. 471-98.

—'Christ's Resurrection in Acts 13, 13-52', *Biblica* 60 (1979), pp. 361-72.

—'Luke's Understanding of Jesus' Resurrection-Ascension-Exaltation', *Biblical Theology Bulletin* 91 (1979), pp. 106-14.

—'Why Did Luke Write Acts (Lk-Acts)?', *Biblical Theology Bulletin* 7 (1977), pp. 66-76.

Page, T.E., 'Review of Frederick Blass' *Acta apostolorum*', *Classical Review* 11 (1897), pp. 317-20.

Parvis, Merrill M., 'The Nature and Task of New Testament Textual Criticism: An Appraisal', *Journal of Religion* 32 (1952), pp. 165-74.

Pascal, Roy, 'Narrative Fictions and Reality', *Novel* 11 (1977), pp. 40-50.

Pease, Donald, 'False Starts and Wounded Allegories in the Abandoned House of Fiction of James Purdy', *Twentieth-Century Fiction* 28 (1982), pp. 335-49.

Perry, Menakhem, 'Literary Dynamics: How the Order of a Text Creates its Meaning', *Poetics Today* 1 (1979), pp. 35-64, 311-61.

Pesch, R., E. Gerhart, and F. Schilling, '"Hellenisten" und "Hebräer": Zu Apg 9,29 und 6,1', *Biblische Zeitschrift* 23 (1979), pp. 87-92.

Petersen, Norman, 'When is the End not the End? Literary Reflections on the Ending of Mark's Narrative', *Interpretation* 34 (1980), pp. 151-66.

Polhill, John, 'The Hellenistic Breakthrough: Acts 6-12', *Review and Expositor* 71 (1974), pp. 474-86.

Pope, Robert, 'Beginnings', *Georgia Review* 36 (1982), pp. 733-51.

Porter, Calvin L., 'Papyrus Bodmer XV (p[75]) and the Text of Codex Vaticanus', *JBL* 81 (1962), pp. 363-76.

Potterie, Ignace de la, 'Le titre kurios appliqué à Jésus dans l'évangile de Luc', *Mélanges bibliques en hommage au R.P. Béda Rigaux*, ed. A. Descamps and A. de Halleux; Gembloux: Duculot, 1979.

Praeder, Susan, 'Luke-Acts and the Ancient Novel', *SBL Seminar Papers*, Chico: Scholars Press (1981), pp. 269-92.

—'Jesus-Paul, Peter-Paul, and Jesus-Peter Parallelisms in Luke-Acts: A History of Reader Response', *SBL Seminar Papers*, Missoula: Scholars Press, (1984) pp. 23-39.

Prince, Gerald, 'Notes Toward a Categorization of Fictional "Narratees"', *Poétique* 14 (1973), pp. 178-96.

Ramsey, A.M., 'What was the Ascension?', *Studiorum NT Societas Bulletin* 2 (1951), pp. 43-50.

Reardon, B.P. 'Aspects of the Greek Novel', *Greece and Rome* 23 (1976), pp. 118-31.

Resseguie, James L., 'Interpretation of Luke's Central Section (Luke 9.51–19.44) since 1856', *Studia Biblica et Theologica* 5 (1975), pp. 3-36.

—'Reader-Response Criticism and the Synoptic Gospels', *JAAR* 52 (1984), pp. 307-24.

Rice, George E., 'The Anti-Judaic Bias of the Western Text in the Gospel of Luke', *Andrews University Seminary Studies* 18 (1980), pp. 51-57.

—'Is Codex Bezae a Homogeneous Text?', *Perspectives in Religious Studies* 11 (1984), pp. 39-54.

—'Luke 3.22-28 in Codex Bezae: The Messianic King', *Andrews University Seminary Bulletin* 17 (1979), pp. 203-208.

—'Some Further Examples of Anti-Judaic Bias in the Western Text of the Gospel of Luke', *Andrews University Seminary Studies* 18 (1980), pp. 149-56.

Richard, Earl, 'Luke - Writer, Theologian, Historian: Research and Orientation of the 1970's', *Biblical Theology Bulletin* 13 (1983), pp. 3-15.

—'The Polemical Character of the Joseph Episode in Acts 7', *JBL* 98 (1979), pp. 255-67.

Riddle, D.M., 'Textual Criticism as a Historical Discipline', *Anglican Theological Review* 18 (1936), pp. 220-33.

Ringe, Sharon H. 'Luke 9.28-36: The Beginning of an Exodus', *Semeia* 28 (1983), pp. 83-99.

Robinson, W.C., 'The Theological Context for Interpreting Luke's Travel Narrative (9.51ff.)', *JBL* 79 (1960), pp. 20-31.

Ropes, J.H., 'Three Papers on the Text of Acts', *HTR* 16 (1923), pp. 163-86.

Ryan, Rosalie, 'The Women from Galilee and Discipleship in Luke', *Biblical Theology Bulletin* 15 (1985), pp. 56-59.

Sandy, G.N., 'Recent Scholarship on the Prose Fiction of Classical Antiquity', *Classical World* 67 (1974), pp. 321-59.

Schneider, G., 'Zur Bedeutung von *kathexes* im lukanischen Doppelwerk', *ZNW* 68 (1977), pp. 128-31.

Schubert, Paul, 'The Structure and Significance of Luke 24', *Neutestamentliche Studien für Rudolf Bultmann*, ed. Walther Eltester; Berlin: Töpelmann, 1957.

Schulz, S., 'Gottes Vorsehung bei Lukas' *ZNW* 54 (1963), pp. 104-16.

Scott, C.A., 'An Aramaic Source for Acts i–xv', *ExpT* 31 (1919-20), pp. 220-23.

Silberman, Lou, '"Habent Sua Fata Libelli": The Role of Wandering Themes in Some Hellenistic and Rabbinic Literature', *The Relationship Among the Gospels*, ed. W.O. Walker; San Antonio: Trinity University, 1978.

Smith, Robert H., 'The Theology of Acts', *Concordia Theological Monthly* 42 (1971), pp. 527-35.

Snodgrass, Klyne, 'Western Non-Interpolations', *JBL* 91 (1972), pp. 369-79.

Sorensen, Gerald, C., 'Beginning and Ending: *The Virginians* as a Sequel', *Studies in the Novel* 13 (1981), pp. 109-21.

Sparks, H.F.D., 'The Semitisms of Acts', *JTS* 1 (1950), pp. 16-28.

Stagg, Frank, 'The Journey Toward Jerusalem in Luke's Gospel', *Review and Expositor* 64 (1967), pp. 499-512.

—'Textual Criticism for Luke–Acts', *Perspectives in Religious Studies* 3 (1978), pp. 152-65.

—'The Unhindered Gospel', *Review and Expositor* 71 (1974), pp. 451-62.

Stempvoort, P.A. van, 'The Interpretation of the Ascension in Luke and Acts', *NTS* 5 (1959), pp. 30-42.

Streeter, B.H., 'Codices 157, 1071 and the Caesarean Text', *Studies Presented to Kirsopp Lake*, London: n.p., 1937.

Suleiman, Susan Rubin, 'Redundancy and the "Readable" Text', *Poetics Today* 1 (1980), pp. 119-43.

Talbert, Charles H., 'An Anti-Gnostic Tendency in Lucan Christology', *NTS* 14 (1967-68), pp. 259-71.

—'Prophecies of Future Greatness: The Contribution of Greco-Roman Biographies to an Understanding of Luke 1.5-4.15', *The Divine Helmsman*, ed. J.L. Crenshaw and Samuel Sandmel; New York: KTAV, 1980.

—'The Redactional Critical Quest for Luke the Theologian', *Jesus and Man's Hope*, Vol. I, ed. D.G. Miller; Pittsburgh: Pittsburgh Theological Seminary, 1970.

—'Shifting Sands: The Recent Study of the Gospel of Luke', *Interpretation* 30 (1976), pp. 381-95.

—and Edgar V. McKnight, 'Can the Griesbach Hypothesis Be Falsified?', *JBL* 91 (1972), pp. 338-68.

Tannehill, Robert C., 'The Composition of Acts 3-5: Narrative Development and Echo Effect', *SBL Seminar Papers*, Chico: Scholars Press (1984), pp. 217-40.

—'Israel in Luke-Acts: A Tragic Story', *JBL* 104 (1985), pp. 69-85.

Thiering, Barbara, 'Opening and Closing Narratives in the Gospels and Acts', *Abr-Nahrain* 4 (1963-64), pp. 50-55.

Tiede, David L., 'Acts 1.6-8 and the Theo-Political Claims of Christian Witness', *Word and World* 1 (1981), pp. 41-51.

Toon, Peter, 'Resurrected and Ascended: The Exalted Jesus', *Bibliotheca Sacra* 140 (1983), pp. 195-205.

—'The Meaning of the Ascension for Christ', *Bibliotheca Sacra* 140 (1983), pp. 291-301.

—'The Significance of the Ascension for Believers', *Bibliotheca Sacra* 141 (1984), pp. 16-27.

—'The Exalted Jesus and God's Revelation', *Bibliotheca Sacra* 141 (1984), pp. 112-19.

Torrey, C.C., 'The Translation Made from the Original Aramaic Gospels', *Studies in the History of Religions, Presented to Crawford Howell Toy*, ed. D.G. Lyon and G.F. Moore; New York: n.p., 1912.

Trompf, G.W. 'La section médiane de l'évangile de Luc: l'organisation des documents', *Revue d'histoire et de philosophie religieuses* 53 (1973), pp. 141-54.

Tyson, Joseph B., 'Conflict as a Literary Theme in the Gospel of Luke', *New Synoptic Studies: The Cambridge Gospel Conference and Beyond*, ed. William R. Farmer; Macon, GA: Mercer University Press, 1983.

—'The Jewish Public in Luke-Acts', *NTS* 30 (1984), pp. 574-83.

—'The Opposition to Jesus in the Gospel of Luke', *Perspectives in Religious Studies* 5 (1978), pp. 144-50.

van Unnik, W.C. 'Luke's Second Book and the Rules of Hellenistic Historiography', *Les Actes des Apôtres: Traditions, rédaction, théologie*, ed. J. Kremer; Gembloux: Leuven University Press (1979), pp. 37-60.

—'Éléments artistiques dans l'évangile de Luc', *L'Évangile de Luc: Problèmes littéraires et théologiques*, ed. Frans Neirynck; Gembloux: Leuven University Press, 1973.

Van der Waal, C., 'The Temple in the Gospel according to Luke', *Neotestamentica* 7 (1973), pp. 44-59.

Vazakas, A.A. 'Is Acts i- xv.35 a Literal Translation from an Aramaic Original?', *JBL* 37 (1918), pp. 105-10.
Vööbus, Arthur, 'A New Approach to the Problem of the Shorter and Longer Text in Luke', *NTS* 15 (1968-69), pp. 457-63.
Völkel, M., 'Exegetische Erwägungen zum Verständnis des Begriffs *kathedzes* im lukanischen Prolog', *NTS* 20 (1973-74), pp. 289-99.
Voste, F.J.M., 'Torrey, C.C., *The Composition and Date of Acts* (Review)', *Revue Biblique* 14 (1917), pp. 300-303.
Wainwright, Arthur, 'Luke and the Restoration of the Kingdom to Israel', *ExpT* 89 (1977), pp. 76-79.
Watson, George, 'The Sense of a Beginning', *Sewanee Review* 86 (1978), pp. 539-48.
Weinart, Francis D., 'The Meaning of the Temple in Luke–Acts', *Biblical Theology Bulletin* 11 (1981), pp. 85-89.
Weiss, K., 'ἀναφερω', *TDNT*, Vol. IX, ed. Gerhard Kittel; trans. G.W. Bromiley; Grand Rapids: Eerdmans (1964), *s.v.*
Wenham, J.W., 'Synoptic Independence and the Origin of Luke's Travel Narrative', *NTS* 27 (1980-81), pp. 507-15.
Wensick, A.J. 'The Semitisms of Codex Bezae and their Relation to the Non-Western Text of the Gospel of St. Luke', *Bulletin of the Bezan Club* 12 (1937), pp. 11-48.
Wilder, Amos N., '*Semeia, An Experimental Journal for Biblical Criticism*: An Introduction', *Semeia* 1 (1974), pp. 1-16.
—'Variant Traditions of the Resurrection in Acts', *JBL* 62 (1943), pp. 307-18.
Willink, M.D.R., 'A Cloud Received Him (Acts I,9)', *Theology* 14 (1927), pp. 297-99.
Wilson, S.G., 'The Ascension: A Critique and an Interpretation', *ZNW* 59 (1968), pp. 269-81.
Wilson, W.J. 'Some Observations on the Aramaic Acts', *HTR* 11 (1918), pp. 74-79.
Witherington, Ben, 'On the Road with Mary Magdalene, Joanna, Susanna and Other Disciples', *ZNW* 70 (1979), pp. 243-48.
Wittig, Susan, 'Formulaic Style and the Problem of Redundancy', *Centrum* 1 (1973), pp. 123-36.
Wyatt, David M., 'Hemingway's Uncanny Beginnings', *Georgia Review* 31 (1977), pp. 476-501.
Yoder, James D., 'The Language of the Greek Variants of Codex Bezae', *Novum Testamentum* 3 (1959), pp. 241-48.
—'Semitisms in Codex Bezae', *JBL* 78 (1959), pp. 317-21.
Ziesler, J.A., 'The Name of Jesus in the Acts of the Apostles', *JSNT* 4 (1979), pp. 28-41.

Unpublished Materials

Anderson, Janice Capel, 'The Implied Reader in Matthew', Seminar Paper, SBL Literary Aspects of the Gospels and Acts, 1983.
Culpepper, R. Alan, 'Redundancy and the Implied Reader in Matthew: A Response to Janice Capel Anderson and Fred W. Burnett', Seminar Response Paper, SBL Literary Aspects of the Gospels and Acts, 1983.
Fee, Gordon D., 'The Significance of Papyrus Bodmer II and Papyrus Bodmer XIV–XV for Methodology in New Testament Textual Criticism', Ph.D. dissertation, University of Southern California, 1966.

Holmes, Michael W., 'Early Editorial Activity and the Text of Codex Bezae in Matthew', Ph.D. dissertation, Princeton University, 1984.

Keathley, Naymond, 'The Temple in Luke–Acts', Ph.D. dissertation, The Southern Baptist Theological Seminary, 1974.

Pervo, Richard I., 'The Literary Genre of the Acts of the Apostles', Th.D. dissertation, Harvard University, 1979.

Puskas, Charles B., Jr, 'The Conclusion of Luke–Acts: An Investigation of the Literary Function and Theological Function of Acts 28.16-31', Ph.D. dissertation, St. Louis University, 1980.

Rice, George E., 'The Alteration of Luke's Tradition by the Textual Variants in Codex Bezae', Ph.D. dissertation, Case Western Reserve University, 1974.

Scalise, Charles J., '"The Hermeneutical Bridge" of the Gospel of Luke: Theophilus as Narratee and Implied Reader', Seminar Paper, The Southern Baptist Theological Seminary, 1985.

Walworth, Allen J., 'The Narrator of Acts', Ph.D. dissertation, The Southern Baptist Theological Seminary, 1984.

INDEX

INDEX OF BIBLICAL REFERENCES

INDEX OF AUTHORS

JOURNAL FOR THE STUDY OF THE NEW TESTAMENT
Supplement Series